Lincoln's
Northern Nemesis

Lincoln's Northern Nemesis

The War Opposition and Exile of Ohio's Clement Vallandigham

MARTIN GOTTLIEB

McFarland & Company, Inc., Publishers
Jefferson, North Carolina

Library of Congress Cataloguing-in-Publication Data

Names: Gottlieb, Martin, 1946– author.
Title: Lincoln's Northern nemesis : the war opposition and exile of Ohio's Clement Vallandigham / Martin Gottlieb.
Other titles: War opposition and exile of Ohio's Clement Vallandigham
Description: Jefferson, North Carolina : McFarland & Company, Inc., Publishers, 2021. Includes bibliographical references and index.
Identifiers: LCCN 2021034534 | ISBN 9781476686295 (paperback : acid free paper) ∞ ISBN 9781476643717 (ebook)
Subjects: LCSH: Vallandigham, Clement L. (Clement Laird), 1820–1871. | Vallandigham, Clement L. (Clement Laird), 1820–1871—Exile. | Copperhead movement. | United States—History—Civil War, 1861–1865. | United States—Politics and government—1861–1865. | Ohio—Politics and government—1787–1865. | Lincoln, Abraham, 1809–1865—Adversaries. | Legislators—Ohio—Biography. | BISAC: HISTORY / United States / Civil War Period (1850–1877)
Classification: LCC E458.8 .G68 2021 | DDC 973.7/18—dc23
LC record available at https://lccn.loc.gov/2021034534

British Library cataloguing data are available
ISBN (print) 978-1-4766-8629-5
ISBN (ebook) 978-1-4766-4371-7

© 2021 Martin Gottlieb. All rights reserved

No part of this book may be reproduced or transmitted in any form or by any means, electronic or mechanical, including photocopying or recording, or by any information storage and retrieval system, without permission in writing from the publisher.

Front cover image: Vallandigham in his prime (Library of Congress)

Printed in the United States of America

*McFarland & Company, Inc., Publishers
Box 611, Jefferson, North Carolina 28640
www.mcfarlandpub.com*

Table of Contents

Preface   1

Introduction: Claims to Fame   5

1. The Making of a Pro-Slavery Northerner   9
2. Onto the National Stage   27
3. Seeing John Brown (In the Mirror)   31
4. The Westerner   37
5. Response to Sumter: Founding Fatherhood Denied   42
6. Defending Himself   50
7. Love Among the Polarized   55
8. The 1862 Fight for Freedom and Slavery   62
9. Tom Lowe, Vallandighammer   87
10. Let's Call the Whole Thing Off   94
11. Exiled, Welcomed and Removed   99
12. Lincoln vs. Vallandigham   138
13. The Campaign from Exile   149
14. Lincoln's Election Night and the Post-Election Spin   190
15. Literary Immortality   197
16. Canadian Winter   200
17. Vallandighammizing the Democrats   209
18. After the War   219
19. Wrong Gun in His Pocket   236
20. What Ever Happened To…?   242

Chapter Notes   251

Bibliography   263

Index   267

Preface

I spent 27 years as an editorial writer and columnist for the *Dayton Daily News* in Ohio, ending in retirement in 2011. During those years I would occasionally hear the name Clement Vallandigham; it might have happened four times. The references were brief, offering almost no information. All I knew was that he was a congressman from Dayton who opposed the Civil War and got in some sort of trouble for his views.

After a while I noticed that Vallandigham was the *only* historical congressman from Dayton I ever heard mentioned. I couldn't have named any others. So I decided that, if there was only one whose name lived on at all, I should know something about him. And I thought I might get a column out of the subject. I certainly was not thinking book.

But as I learned about Vallandigham, I was struck by the sheer color and size of his story. His story was fascinating, surprising, important and unknown. It seemed to me—as a lifelong political junkie of advanced years—that if one were to put together a book of the ten best political stories in American history, this could easily be in that book. I could easily imagine Vallandigham being as well known to Americans as, say, George Armstrong Custer, or, to pick a comparison that's fraught, Benedict Arnold.

The Vallandigham story is, to an almost eerie degree, about issues we are still struggling with: not only race and war, but civil liberties, loyalty versus treason, the size of government, nationalist fervor, hyper-partisanship and polarization (in the North, not just between North and South), partisan media, populism versus elitism, truth versus lies and the power of a party's "base." One sometimes hears that "history is a foreign country." But in this, my first deep dive into historical research, I found that mid–19th century American politics is a foreign country in roughly the degree to which urban Canada is foreign to Americans. I mean there's a *lot* that looks very familiar. Certainly, politics was practiced in much the same way then as in the most recent years, absent the technology. I eventually came to believe that if I were time-transported to the Ohio newspaper world during the war years or just before, I would not feel like a foreigner. I'd have a feel for the issues, the personalities, the political style and the journalistic style. The nature of politics in those days does not remind me greatly of the nature of American politics during most of my life and career; but it does remind me greatly of the nature of American politics as this is written, in 2020.

***

This telling is not precisely a biography of Vallandigham. It is primarily a story about the brief period, the war years—when he was at the center of compelling events crucial to the nation's turning point, though I do try to put those events in the context of his life. Nor is it a behind-the-scenes look at this story. It is about the scenes themselves; they are what I found compelling and what I thought readers would. By scenes, I mean news events: campaigns, conventions, arrests, trials, riots, journeys, speeches, shootings, deaths, congressional debates and the wars between the manically partisan newspapers that were at the center of politics. Near the top of my motivations is a desire to give readers a feel for what it was like to be a consumer of the news back then.

The public scenes don't leave one wondering much about what went on behind the scenes. Clement Vallandigham was not a terribly complex, tortured, subtle or mysterious character. Though his mind was fertile, and he was always thinking up new thrusts, one eulogist insightfully said he "never had a doubt. His mind seemed never poised in deliberation."[1] Nor was there any great mentor or other major shaper of his thoughts, nor any Vallandigham team. It was all him, and he was all there, in public.

There's another reason for focusing on the scenes themselves. In 1970, a professor at Marquette University, Frank J. Klement, the most prolific writer of his generation about Vallandigham's political faction, the Copperheads, published a biography of Vallandigham. A preface to a 1998 edition says that "a majority of Vallandigham's papers and other valuable records were destroyed in 1913 during a flood in Dayton." The flood came even as various Civil War events were being commemorated 50 years after their occurrence. The flood made history, and it apparently took some. As the preface's writer, Steven Rogstad, noted, "not a single substantive collection of (Vallandigham) material was available (to Klement) at any archive or library."[2]

The Klement book is the only one devoted to Vallandigham, except one by his brother James in 1872. To say I am deeply indebted to both those authors is an understatement. I do come to some different conclusions from Klement about important matters. This might be in part because I have the advantage of the digital age and of mountains of books about the Civil War era that he didn't have to work with fifty years ago. Brother James' biography—*A Life of Clement Vallandigham*—while lacking in skepticism—pulls together enormously valuable documents and various written materials. I am also grateful to Clement Vallandigham himself for bringing his speeches and some other writings together into two volumes.

Facilitating my approach, we have mountains of public records besides Vallandigham's speeches, his weapons of choice. We have newspaper archives, congressional archives, magazine articles, a trial transcript and legal filings, government records (including many letters), published memoirs, cartoons, diaries, letters and a little poetry.

***

I am indebted to the Dayton Metro Library, most specifically Nancy Horlacher and her staff in the local history department at the time of my research, especially Bill McIntire. They told me about crucial resources that I wasn't knowledgeable enough to even ask about. My research happened when the library system was in construction-caused turmoil, and materials were scattered all over town. Just keeping track of the stuff was difficult. Digging it out from under makeshift piles was all the more so. And, in the midst of all that, they put up with my physical presence for more than a year, always making me feel at home.

I am grateful to other libraries, too, mainly around Ohio, including those at the University of Dayton and Wright State University, but also to the Library of Congress, the U.S. National Archives (where Paul Harrison dug up some stuff I absolutely needed an expert to find) and the library at the New-York Historical Society. As a fan of libraries and librarians since childhood, I now know I didn't know the half of it.

Jim DeBrosse, formerly of the *Dayton Daily News*, then of Miami University, read a very early draft and provided useful notes. Lifelong friend, three-tour Marine veteran of Vietnam and retired law-enforcement officer Tom FitzGibbon tutored me on guns.

I am grateful, too, to the creators and some institutional exploiters of the internet. As a result of their work, massive amounts of material from the Civil War era and the rest of the 19th century—meaning books, academic journal archives, newspapers, and government records—are easily available to any researcher with a computer and hook-up. I had no idea of the enormity of this resource when I started. Its enormity has increased exponentially just since I started. I thank specifically the Library of Congress, Google Books, and archive.org, but there are certainly others making valuable material available. Despite being new to historical research, I'm confident in saying these people and organizations are making the writing of historical books easier than it has ever been. Often I'd come across in my reading a book (or something) that I thought I should have, only to find that I could find it online or order it in print (a scanned copy), though it had been out of print for a century. I hate to think how much time and effort would have gone into finding these resources otherwise.

***

A note about my endnotes or, as they used to be called, footnotes: I am worried about the potential for confusion. For one thing, as noted, Clement Vallandigham's only modern biographer was named Frank J. Klement. Beware the K and the C. For another, I frequently cite two Vallandighams. Beware the Clement and the James. For another, Clement put together two collections of his speeches and other writings, one in 1863, for a campaign, and a bigger one in 1864. For most purposes, the distinction makes no difference; indeed, many of his speeches are in both books. However, other researchers should be aware that *The Record of the Honorable C.L. Vallandigham on Abolition, the Union, and the Civil War* (1863) and *Speeches, Arguments, Addresses, and Letters of Clement L. Vallandigham* (1864) are two different books.

In the unlikely event that you are still with me, there's also this: The biography by Frank J. Klement—*The Limits of Dissent*—has had more than one edition. I quote above from a preface in a 1998 edition. However, mainly I'm using the 1970 edition. This is relevant only for page-number purposes in the endnotes.

A note about language: The book quotes much from the writing of the era. Some writing customs were substantially different from those of today. I have generally tried to stick with the originals, but couldn't always. Typically, for example, the p wasn't capitalized in "Democratic party." I saw no reason to mess with that. However, the writers of the day also didn't observe our modern distinction between "small r republican" (non-monarchical governments and values, basically) and "big R Republican" (the party). In such situations, I used the case which would, I thought, best communicate with moderns. In general, how to communicate most clearly was my chief criterion.

In all cases, the emphases I note within quotations are there in the original.

Unfortunately, this history could not be written correctly without use of the ugly word "nigger."

Introduction:
Claims to Fame

Abraham Lincoln's leading antagonist in the North was the sometime congressman from Dayton, Ohio, Clement Vallandigham. He was a Copperhead or Peace Democrat, a member of the wing of the Democratic Party that flatly opposed any war with the South over slavery. The Copperheads had no formal hierarchy, but Vallandigham was, without question, their highest-profile, most newsworthy, colorful, uncompromising, loved and hated man. (A copperhead snake is silent but poisonous. It can strike when you don't know it's present. Republicans pinned the label on the Peace Democrats as a statement that, if the disloyalty of the Copperheads was not yet obvious, that was only because they hadn't struck yet. Eventually some Copperheads came to embrace the term. Think "Obamacare.")

Various historians have called Vallandigham "the chief of the Copperheads," the "nation's outstanding Peace Democrat," "the prince" of the Copperheads, and the "leading spirit" of the war's opponents.[1] The press routinely treated Vallandigham as the top Copperhead. Whitelaw Reid, a prominent journalist, referred to the Vallandigham as "the prime mover" of the "conspiracy" to foster "submission to … traitors," that is, the leader of the Copperheads.[2] A nationally distributed newspaper satirist—writing under the pen name of Petroleum V. Nasby, who spelled words as he heard them—had Copperheads literally worshipping at a church named "St. Valandygum" (a pretty good phonetic spelling; swallow the last syllable).[3]

Isn't it remarkable how few people today could tell you who Lincoln's main Northern nemesis was? Millions of Americans know so many other names from the Civil War era: generals on both sides, cabinet members, leading abolitionists, the leadership of the Confederacy. But they don't know about his flat-out political opponents in the North. The reason for that is certainly not that his opponents were unimportant. As innumerable Lincoln buffs know, in the late summer of 1864, Lincoln and just about everybody else thought Lincoln was on the verge of losing his re-election bid to a Democrat.[4] That party's convention had been dominated by Copperheads, led by Clement Vallandigham.

Vallandigham's identity as Lincoln's leading antagonist is only one of several claims to fame that have brought him no particular fame. Indeed, he might have set a record for unrequited claims. Establishing that he has the record would be challenging. It would require comparing him to other non-famous people, of whom the author presumably has not heard. So all I can do is ask the reader to contemplate the likelihood of somebody else having more claims and less fame.

Let us start by establishing Vallandigham's non-fame. In the embarrassing number of years I worked on this book, I tried to respond to questions about what I was doing in retirement with a question: Have you ever heard of Clement Vallandigham? This was in Dayton. I asked journalists, politicians, history buffs and other people I took to be most likely to know of him. The most common answer was simply "No." But some people did have one sentence to offer about him. It typically ended in a question mark: "Wasn't he the guy who…?" It might go in a couple of directions from there. I think I'm right in saying that *nobody* knew the story told in this book. I also found—in telling the story to individuals and groups around town—that they were often amazed and fascinated that they hadn't known it.

Vallandigham was far and away the most prominent Daytonian of the 19th century, the city's first century, the most famous before the Wright brothers. Though he died in 1871, if, in the mid-1880s, a Daytonian were traveling elsewhere in the country and mentioned his hometown, the first word on anybody's lips would have been "Vallandigham." That's what Dayton was in the national consciousness: the home of Vallandigham.

As a community today, Dayton is far from indifferent to local history. It celebrates the Wright brothers, Paul Laurence Dunbar (the nation's first major black poet) and John H. Patterson (the founder of National Cash Register) among others. But the man who first put Dayton on the map is forgotten. He is eclipsed even by an out-of-town contemporary, a certain fellow from Illinois who has a club in his name and a statue downtown. There was, at last notice, a picture of Vallandigham at the law firm he founded. And his name hasn't been effaced from his burial site in Dayton. But that's about it, unless you count a certain inn halfway down the 50-mile drive to Cincinnati, where he met a preposterous death.

Professional historians have not ignored Vallandigham. He and other Copperheads have been the subject of much debate about, for example, whether their anti-war activities went beyond speechmaking and seeking office to concrete acts of subversion. But these historians haven't found much of a readership beyond the academy. Nor do they seem to have sought one.

Of course, historians and local boosters are not the only ones who might bring a forgotten or ignored historical figure to light. Sometimes this is done by people with a political agenda. Calvin Coolidge, for example, has benefited. In recent years, some conservatives have decided that his traditionally low standing among historians has resulted from the liberal biases of historians.[5] No such visible effort has been made in Vallandigham's behalf. Suffice it for now to say that, in the privacy of their own reading rooms, some modern-day political warriors would, if they ever got a load of him, find a lot to admire and identify with.

Nevertheless, in noting Vallandigham's lack of fame, I am not arguing that he deserves acclaim. The word "infamy" might be substituted for "fame." I'm just talking about the lack of notoriety.

Here are the other claims to fame, after being Lincoln's chief antagonist:

Two: Vallandigham, then running for governor of Ohio, was arrested by the

U.S. Army for his views, put on trial by the army, convicted of disloyalty and ultimately banished by none other than Abraham Lincoln. One thinks of the famous Tom Hanks line in *A League of Their Own*: "There's no crying in baseball." Is there exile in democracy? Political exile at that: an active politician exiling a leading opponent?

In fact, exile has been used in American history, but rarely. Some people were exiled after World War I during the "Red Scare." The anarchist Emma Goldman was the best known name. Socialist leader Eugene V. Debs was not exiled but put in jail for his views, not by the president but by the courts, using a law Congress had enacted to deal with people of Debs' views. President Woodrow Wilson's role, besides signing the legislation, was only to refuse to pardon Debs.

By any reasonable standards, this is a remarkable and unique claim to fame for Vallandigham: being banished while leading the opposition to a president, not to mention that the president was the revered Lincoln.

Three: As a result of being banished to the South, Vallandigham was nominated by the Ohio Democrats for governor in 1863. After a cinematic sojourn through the South, he ended up running the race from exile in Windsor, Canada, across the river from Detroit. Again, we are in unprecedented, claim-to-fame territory: a major-party nominee for a major office running from exile, and, not only that, but in a pivotal election during a national crisis.

Lincoln was up to his very high thighs in that election. Republicans saw the possibility of Vallandigham's election as potentially catastrophic to the war effort. When Vallandigham lost, Lincoln is reported to have wired the Ohio Republicans "Glory to God in the highest. Ohio has saved the nation."

Four: At the Democratic National Convention in 1864, Vallandigham—just back in the country—led the successful effort to pass a Copperhead platform. The platform used the word "failure" about the war, saying the war should be stopped immediately in favor of negotiations. Just as the Democrats were passing that platform, General William Tecumseh Sherman was taking Atlanta—and the war was becoming a looming victory for the North.

Presidential nominee George McClellan was not a Copperhead, but was chosen because he was seen as the party's strongest candidate and because the Copperheads didn't really have a candidate. He rejected the platform. Never before or since has the nation seen the embarrassing and absurd spectacle of a major-party presidential nominee running away from the central plank—the point—of the platform of the convention that nominated him. McClellan could thank Vallandigham.

Five: Vallandigham inspired a short story that became an American classic, with a title everybody has heard. It has been made into a movie several times over—both silent and talky—an opera and a television movie, not to mention a stage production and a radio production over and over. It has been taught to generations of American students and is still being anthologized.

Six: Vallandigham's life ended in one of the great American death scenes. His death, all by itself, ought to make him a national figure in perpetuity.

At the very least, Vallandigham would seem to make for a good question on the venerable American television game show *Jeopardy*. A search of the *Jeopardy* archives online does reveal Vallandigham as a question, but only as the Copperhead from Ohio, not the exile or nominee, his more remarkable identities.

That Vallandigham is generally forgotten today—and likely to be reviled when he is remembered—is all the more remarkable because he played to posterity relentlessly. He was deeply concerned with its verdict on him, and he repeatedly expressed perfect certainty that the verdict would be passionately positive.

Vallandigham was born in the tiny town of New Lisbon, Ohio, at the other end of the state from Dayton. There he grew up and was first elected to the state legislature. At last look, he was not mentioned on the village's website. The fact that the drinking straw was invented there was mentioned, as were various local contributions to the Civil War effort. Vallandigham's house is still standing, but not as a historical site. History's nastiest cut: The house is on U.S. Route 30—the Lincoln Highway. The address is on Lincoln Way. Vallandigham would not enjoy the irony.

1

The Making of a Pro-Slavery Northerner

The backdrop: In the mid–19th century, the nation was increasingly divided over slavery, which kept four million black people in chains in southern states. Abraham Lincoln was elected president in 1860 as the nominee of a party that opposed extension of slavery into the new states being formed as Americans moved west of the Mississippi River. The party platform did not call for ending slavery in the South. Nevertheless, the southern states seceded after the election, seeing their future as bleak in any country that would elect a president who hated slavery, as Lincoln did. Lincoln was unwilling to see the country break up, and the cataclysmic Civil War ensued. Clement Vallandigham blamed the war on Lincoln and his allies.

Vallandigham was pro-slavery. One sometimes comes across the notion—at least if one is researching a book on him—that he was against slavery but for state rights, including the right of states to allow slavery. It is an impression left by a certain passage in his biography to be noted later. It appears on amateur sites online. It appears in books with titles like *American History for the...*. It is not true.

He might not have been pro-slavery at every moment of his life. But during the war—during his only time of national political importance in the slavery debate—he spoke on the floor of Congress in flat-out support. He explicitly rejected Abraham Lincoln's pre-war insistence that the country could not survive "part slave and part free." He insisted that, on the contrary, "a confederacy made up of slaveholding and non-slaveholding States is, in the nature of things, the strongest of all popular governments."[1]

Vallandigham did oppose bringing slavery to Ohio.[2] But that's meaningless. Nobody was proposing slavery for Ohio. It was illegal under the Northwest Ordinance of 1787. And no constituency for it existed. Ohio workers didn't want to compete with slaves for work. Businessmen believed that the North's economy worked better than the South's. The issue wasn't Ohio slavery. It was *southern* slavery and slavery in the new states.

Why would a thoughtful Ohioan favor southern slavery? Southern support for slavery is more explicable. Mid–19th century Southerners grew up with slavery. They inherited it from people they loved and respected. Many were dependent on it. And, when challenged by outsiders who, they felt, didn't understand, they were insulted and became defensive. But why a Northerner?

Certainly the explanation isn't that Vallandigham simply accepted the status quo without thinking about it. He thought about it a lot. Northerners were bombarded with the case against slavery for decades, starting in the 1830s, when the abolitionist movement started to take hold.

Moreover, Vallandigham had several characteristics one might expect to lead him toward enlightenment on race. For one thing, he was not generally one to embrace prejudice against minorities. On Jewish issues, he was not only enlightened but aggressive. He introduced a congressional resolution saying other countries—specifically, in this case, Switzerland—must accord American Jews the same rights they accord other Americans traveling abroad.[3] And he was the only one in Congress to speak up when, early in the Civil War, an act was being promulgated that included a provision saying that military chaplains would be Christians. A historian described the episode: "Apparently on his own initiative and without any Jewish prompting, he spoke out clearly in defense of Jewish rights.... He denounced the underlying implication of the bill that the United States is a Christian country, in the political sense."[4] Vallandigham lost this fight in Congress, but the provision was later overturned after prominent Jews lobbied Lincoln, who insisted the "Christian" phrasing had been an oversight.

Nor did Vallandigham engage in the Catholic-bashing and immigrant-bashing that was a central part of American politics in the 1850s. Indeed, Vallandigham's Democrats were emerging as the party of immigrants, often Catholic. Nor was Vallandigham politically beholden to the big slave owners—the slavocracy—who Republicans wanted to believe formed the heart of political support for slavery.

Perhaps it is also worth noting that Vallandigham was deeply literate. He wanted to be seen as learned. He put his learning on ostentatious display. In one speech, he dropped these names from British history in one paragraph: "the great Hampden," "the ... honest and fearless Croke," Lord Hale, "the bloody Jeffries," Algernon Sidney, Finch and "Lord Russell."[5]

More to the point, Vallandigham considered himself deeply focused on morality, on matters of right versus wrong. In his early twenties, he wrote a long list of rules for himself, for example, that he would always "pursue the dictates of my judgment and my conscience."[6]

The son and brother of ministers, he was deeply religious. He said his favorite book was the Bible. He worshipped at various stages at Presbyterian, Episcopal and Lutheran churches. In 1855, at 35, he reported ecstatically to his mother that he had just had a religious awakening—though he had always been religious. He said, "whereas I was blind, *now I see*—and I feel a peace and joy which the world *never* gave, and which I know and am ASSURED it *cannot* take away."[7] The occasion was a series of sermons in which, according to the pastor, "high Calvinistic ground was taken with regard to the absolute sovereignty of God's electing love and the utter depravity and helplessness of man." Vallandigham had been raised a Calvinist.[8]

Religious participation certainly did not drive Northerners toward pro-slavery views. Indeed, the reason Vallandigham eventually left the First Presbyterian Church of Dayton was that the very pastor who had so moved him, the Rev. James H. Brookes, D.D., turned out to be eager to push his own anti-slavery views from the pulpit.[9]

The connection between slavery and churches is a little complicated. In

Vallandigham's teens—he was born in 1820—the abolitionist movement was centered in churches. However, those churches were mainly in New England. Churches in Ohio were generally not so caught up in the slavery issue, one way or the other. Some clergymen thought the New England churches were losing their way, becoming caught up in earthly matters, as opposed to saving souls, and were Puritanical busy-bodies sticking their noses into other people's business. Vallandigham's father may have had such views.

Vallandigham at least once described himself as "wholly of southern ancestry, with a slight cross of Pennsylvania Scotch-Irish."[10] That might explain a lot about his politics. Certainly plenty of educated, religious Southerners had views like his. In fact, however, his background was more complicated. The self-description was partly spin, offered when he was decrying war between North and South.

His father's people had been in North America for about 130 years when Clement was born. They had come from Flanders, now in Belgium.[11] They were Huguenots, meaning Calvinist Protestants; many Huguenots fled French Catholic persecution for the American continent. The Vallandighams (under a different spelling) lived for a time in Virginia in areas now in metropolitan Washington or nearby Fredericksburg. By the time of the American Revolution, Clement's grandfather was principal of a school in Prince George's County, Maryland. He later moved farther north, and for the last couple decades of the century was practicing law in and near Pittsburgh, Pennsylvania.

Clement's father was born in the Pittsburgh area, went to what became Jefferson College (and then Washington and Jefferson College), near nearby Washington, Pennsylvania. After college, he was assigned as the Presbyterian minister in New Lisbon, Ohio, just across the state boundary. There he raised a family in a house in which he is said (by a real estate website) to have presided over the marriage of William McKinley's grandparents. Other Vallandighams left Virginia for parts north, but later returned to slave states.

On his mother's side—the Lairds—Clement's Scottish grandfather came over from Ireland in 1766. He settled in eastern Pennsylvania at first, then moved to Washington, Pennsylvania, in the west. Clement's mother, Rebecca, was born in the eastern part of the state and was educated there—in York County—and in Washington, D.C. She apparently met Clement's father in Washington, Pennsylvania. She did have relatives on the Eastern Shore of Maryland, which was slave country, and Clement did spend some time there, especially in his late teens.

But he certainly did not come from slave owners and did not grow up around slavery or Southerners. Nor does the explanation for his views seem to lie in the nature of his home county of Columbiana in far eastern Ohio. It wasn't an extension of the South. Many people there were, like the Vallandighams, from Pennsylvania or other parts east.[12] Many were Scotch-Irish. After New Lisbon was formed in 1803 (the second Ohio town), the first newspaper was actually printed in German. As late as 1880 a third of the population of the county was of German origin.[13] There were even significant numbers of Quakers, also not a conservative force on race.[14] One measure of the county's politics: In 1860, not having changed much demographically from Vallandigham's youth, it went for Lincoln.

Let's temporarily leave open the question about the origins of Vallandigham's pro-slavery views.

***

He seems to have arrived in the world wanting to be a politician. He started practicing speechmaking early. His schooling was done at home, by his father, who ran a school for boys. If one of the subjects taught was oratory or elocution—which was common—the likelihood is that Clement got some positive feedback for his natural talent, and that, like other children, he pursued what the grown-ups told him he was good at. Speechmaking was a major path to political success in those days, when going to hear the politicians speak was a form of entertainment.

Of Clement as a young man, a friend said, "I have never seen any speaker who could so long and so well hold an audience through an address. His manner of speaking on the 'stump' as well as elsewhere, was precise, calm, and dignified, speaking for hours without making a blunder, without violating a rule in grammar or rhetoric or logic."[15]

His oratorical skill was not the only characteristics that developed early. His brother James told the following story: On a certain occasion in his late teens, Clement was surrounded by a group of slightly older boys. They were trying to get him to take a drink. He wouldn't. He had taken up teetotaling, which he held to until he was 34.[16] The boys persisted, and Vallandigham persisted. When the boys persisted some more, he drew a gun. But he didn't

The house in New Lisbon, Ohio (now called Lisbon), in which Vallandigham grew up, on what is now called Lincoln Way. Real estate agents say it is the house in which Vallandigham's father, the town's Presbyterian minister, married the grandparents of future President William McKinley (photograph by Leanne Krupp).

threaten them. He said he would rather shoot himself than take a drink. They backed off.

The story almost certainly came from Clement himself. Clearly his brother believed the story. But his brother ranked Clement's truthfulness roughly where Parson Weems—of the cherry tree anecdote—ranked that of George Washington. Even if the story is not true, it tells us something about how Clement saw himself and wanted to be seen.

Following his father, Clement attended Jefferson College, then in Canonsburg, near Washington, Pennsylvania, near Pittsburgh. He entered as a junior at 17 and spent a year there before leaving to spend two years teaching on the Eastern Shore of Maryland among his mother's relatives (where the drinking/gun-pulling incident happened). Then he returned to college. He was a competitive debater at school, fiercely upholding the cause of state rights. In some sort of discussion with the school's hothead president, Vallandigham upheld a certain view on constitutional law. The president disagreed and was apparently irritated by Vallandigham's certitude and inflexibility. One thing led to another, and the president denied the student his degree. After Vallandigham had returned home, the school reconsidered and offered the degree. Vallandigham, apparently not wanting to let the president off the hook, turned it down. So he was never officially a college graduate.[17]

Taken with the drinking story, the debate/degree story offers a pretty good idea of what kind of young man we're dealing with here. The certitude and self-confidence were exceptional.

After college, Vallandigham returned to Lisbon to study law under his brother, who became a minister only later. At about 20, Clement started giving speeches around town. He simply volunteered to do that at public gatherings where others were doing it. He won attention and many plaudits.

As for the content of the speeches, Vallandigham was a Democrat from the beginning. At 20, he represented his township at a Democratic state convention. In 1844, he threw himself into the presidential campaign, working for Democrat James K. Polk against Whig Henry Clay. He was elected to the state legislature before 25, and then again the following year.

Being a Democrat in Ohio then meant being a Jacksonian Democrat. Andrew Jackson, first elected president in 1828, was associated with the populist self-assertion of inland states (and of poor and uneducated people) against the old, somewhat aristocratic

Young Clement Vallandigham, perhaps in his days in the Ohio state legislature (courtesy Dr. William Shultz collection).

Massachusetts/Virginia dominance of national affairs. It was associated with universal suffrage for white males (as opposed to property-owning requirements). The party was tolerant of slavery, in the name partly of sustaining a North-South Democratic coalition. It was associated with state rights (partly fostered by the slavery issue), with limited government and with a populist distrust of anything as big and powerful as a national bank. It favored expansion of the nation, with a hard line toward Indians.

When Vallandigham came of political age, the main alternative was a Whig Party that had been born in opposition to Jackson and had taken its name from a British party associated with the effort to limit royal power; the American Whigs wanted to limit Jacksonian presidential power. The party became an unwieldy, complex coalition; it would be dangerous to say what individual Whigs favored as to policy. But the most important Whig was Henry Clay of Kentucky. He was associated with his "American system," under which the federal government would move beyond obsession with state rights and undertake interstate projects such as roads, canals and bridges. The idea was to use the nation's size and diversity as a tool to foster economic development. Young Abe Lincoln was a big Henry Clay guy.

Edmund Burke has been said to be one of Vallandigham's major influences. He was the British parliamentarian and political philosopher who is often called the father of conservatism. Vallandigham biographer Frank L. Klement wrote that Burke and Vallandigham "favored social order, toleration and evolutionary change."[18] Vallandigham's contemporaries at college and in Dayton also testified to his study of Burke. Some observers saw the influence of Burke in his writing and speaking.[19]

Burke is complicated, textured, even inconsistent. He was no ideologue offering simple, rigid, predictable solutions. In the words of Thomas Paine, who was no fan, he was not a "cluster" thinker. Just about any fair-minded person is likely to find a lot to like about Burke. He was and is admired as much for his writing talent as for his views.

In the big picture, though, it is hard to see Vallandigham as very Burkean. For one thing, Jacksonian Democracy itself was hardly Burkean. Burke was skeptical of real democracy and did not favor expansion of the franchise. And nobody has ever called him a populist. Moreover, Burke was anti-slavery. It was a real issue in his time and place, and he took a strong position.[20]

Vallandigham liked to mention Burke, as well as other historical Brits. But these references might be characterized as light. He would cite Burke's way with words, such as his observation that "it is no more possible to tax and please than to love and to be wise." He cited Burke's strong belief in political parties, and his line "when bad men combine, good men must associate."[21] He would note Burke's support for the American Revolution. But he didn't often invoke Burke's name in support of a controversial Vallandigham position.

Biographer Klement's point about Vallandigham's preference for "evolutionary change" would look better if Vallandigham had favored a gradual end to slavery. But he did not favor any kind of end.

To some, Abraham Lincoln was a more Burkean figure than Vallandigham. Like Burke, Lincoln looked to the end of slavery, and, like Burke, he didn't look for a sudden end, at least until the Civil War. Burke's recent biographer, Jesse Norman, describes Lincoln as a Burkean type: "His political persona was modest and mild almost to a fault." That was decidedly not a Vallandigham trait. "He did not trade solely 'on his own stock of reason,' but famously reached out to build a 'team of rivals.'"[22] Also very not Vallandigham.

In 2019, scholar Greg Weiner wrote a book called *Old Whigs: Burke, Lincoln and the Politics of Prudence*.[23] "Prudence" is not a word that has been widely associated with Vallandigham.

Whatever Vallandigham may have thought of Burke, what Burke would have thought of Vallandigham is, as they say, a whole other question.

Vallandigham did embrace the word "conservative," as the Democrats in general did. Posters inviting people to Democratic conventions might address "Democrats and all conservative men." This was an effort to say the Republican Party, with a substantial "radical" element around the slavery issue, was no place for a conservative. Many Whigs had seen themselves as conservatives, using the word somewhat like the word "moderate" in modern times. When the Whig Party disappeared, the Democrats wanted their support.

One does see in Vallandigham conservatism of a quite modern type. Here he is in 1855 speaking about the problems of democratic parties in Europe:

> Forgetting the true province of a political party, the Democracy of France and Germany has always failed, and ever must fail. It aims at too much. It invokes *government* to regenerate man, and set him free from the taint and the evils of sin and suffering; it seeks to control the domestic, social individual, moral, and spiritual relations of man; it ignores or usurps the place of the fireside, the church, and the lyceum.[24]

He was always decidedly conservative on race, long before he was officially pro-slavery. Race was a legislative issue during his days in Columbus. In the first half of the century, Ohio laws relating to the rights of blacks—to vote, to hold property, to serve on juries and even to live in Ohio—were in flux, under what were known as the Black Codes. As the Civil War approached, Republican legislatures would go one way on the Codes—toward liberalization or elimination—then Democratic legislatures the other. Vallandigham was a leader of Democratic efforts. By his own documented account, he voted over and over against repeal of the codes in two sessions.[25] And he specifically voted to forbid blacks to move into Ohio. Those positions were not extreme as Democratic views went.

***

The notion that Vallandigham opposed slavery is not the only misconception about him that has had some life. There is also the misconception lurking in the term "Peace Democrat," as the Copperheads liked to be called. Vallandigham's advocates liked to refer to him as a "peacemaker," as in "blessed are the."[26] He referred to himself that way at least once in a letter, using that Biblical reference.[27] The characterization seems to live on, at least about Copperheads in general. Judging from reviews easily available online, the 2013 movie *The Copperhead* (a work of fiction) left a lot of people under the impression the Copperheads were pacifists. That is profoundly wrong about Copperheads in general and Vallandigham in particular.

Listen to him on the Mexican War of the late 1840s. That war was opposed by many Whigs, including Abraham Lincoln, who saw it as concocted by (Democratic) President Polk to take land from a weaker neighbor and to add slave states to the union. Former President John Quincy Adams said the war was a search for "bigger pens to cram slaves."[28]

Vallandigham didn't see the problem. He saw military glory in Mexico, and he saw it trumping everything:

> Palo Alto is ours. Resaca de la Palma is ours; Monterey is ours; the living glories which encircle the brow of a (Gen. Zachary) Taylor are ours.... Ours, too, is the bright history of this period. To us belong the admiration of other nations, the gratitude of the present generation, and the applause of posterity in coming time. We consent to share it with none of the revilers of this war. We claim it all, all for ourselves and our children. Sir, if you will howl over its calamities, then in the name of the living, by the blood of the slain, you shall have no part in its glories.[29]

The war was the subject of resolutions in state legislatures. Vallandigham said, "The laws of the federal government extend over us; we are bound by them; and must bear our part of the burdens thus imposed.... As a ... State-Rights man, I would be sorry to see the day when the individual States shall cease to feel the deepest solicitude in the acts of the Government of the Union."[30] The day would come when his enemies would direct the same points at him.

During the Civil War, Vallandigham, instead of talking about the "government," talked about the "administration," which he saw no obligation to support. He saw others as denying that crucial distinction. He was—as will be seen—utterly furious at the suggestion that he should support war policy just because it was policy.

The Mexican War debate was, of course, to resonate during the Civil War debate. Copperheads liked to point out that Ohio's Tom Corwin—a Whig senator during the Mexican War, later a Republican and Lincoln's ambassador to Mexico—said during the Mexican War, "If I were a Mexican, I would tell you ... 'If you come into (my country) we will greet you with bloody hands, and welcome you to hospitable graves.'"[31] The statement stood out for its intensity. The Copperheads enjoyed asking rhetorically if Corwin's statement made him a traitor, as they were accused of being on the basis of milder statements.[32]

In the 1850s—when the country had no great standing army—Vallandigham created a militia in Dayton, with an eye on "the next foreign war,"[33] whatever it might be about, apparently. He was frequently referred to publicly as "Gen. Vallandigham," especially before he was elected to Congress; every indication is he loved that label, especially for political reasons.

Just after the war, Don Piatt, a noted journalist and political player, a Republican and an ally of a special Vallandigham nemesis, told a story about Vallandigham's pre-war days:

> I happened to be in Dayton when the governor of Ohio came to inspect the militia.... (I)t was a big thing.... (I)t struck me that the style and name should have been Brigadier General Clement L. Vallandigtudendammer and staff.... He was on a tremendous charger, and had his breast stuffed out like a wet nurse, and his behind like a bunty-tailed rooster. His epaulets dazzled the eye, his fearful sword banged to and fro.

Then, of course, Piatt contrasted the alleged pre-war swagger with the war record.[34] The description is a shamelessly partisan swipe, not to be taken too seriously. But that there was some kind of gubernatorial inspection makes sense, as does Vallandigham—rising politico—relishing it. The episode seems to fit with Vallandigham's love of the "glory" of the Mexican War.

***

Despite making it to the legislature in his early 20s, Vallandigham apparently was not happy when he contemplated his future in New Lisbon, which was not growing. It was a place that a lot of bright young men left.[35] Vallandigham harbored a desire to go west. Through his career, his rhetoric and politics showed an identification with the West. He wanted to be seen as a westerner. Jacksonian Democracy celebrated the West. The West was the American antithesis of New England, of which, as will be seen, Vallandigham did not approve. Beyond that, the West was the future, opportunity, manhood, bravery and Americanness.

But the definition of "the West" was changing. Once upon a time, it was anyplace west of the Alleghenies, the mountain range sloping southwestward from north central Pennsylvania. Any place in Ohio qualified. But by the 1840s western Ohio had taken off, leaving Vallandigham's part of the state in the eastern dust. The great city in Ohio was Cincinnati, on the state's western edge. By 1840 it had 46,000 people. In the next decade, it was to double and a half in population. Even at the 1840 level, it was the 6th largest city in the country. All the top five were on the East Coast except New Orleans. No other Ohio city came close. Cleveland, Dayton and Columbus were clustered at about 6,000 inhabitants.

Historian Ted Widmer writes that Cincinnati was "northern, southern and western all at the same time." It was "dedicated to the new gods of banking, insurance and science." (Northern.) But "slavery was never far away, festering beneath the city's gleaming surfaces. Slave owners were always noticeable in restaurants and taverns." (Southern.) Widmer quotes an abolitionist: "Cincinnati is the outpost of the antislavery cause—and more beset by proslavery influence than any other spot in the free states." As to the economy, Widmer notes references to the city as "The Metropolis of Pork," "Porkopolis" and "Hamsterdam." The ten slaughterhouses fostered a distinctive stink, ruined many a walk and "fed all the hungry people heading west."[36]

Vallandigham got an offer from Dayton. The times were intensely political. The 1840 presidential election had generated passions and crowd sizes that people were still talked about during the Civil War. Journalism, too, was intensely political. Every self-respecting town had to have both a Whig and a Democratic newspaper. Commonly, men who considered themselves leading figures in town would make sure the town had a newspaper espousing the views of their party. It was not expensive. Typically it required little more than bringing in an editor, because the printing press existed.

So Dayton Democrats reached out to the notoriously articulate young Democrat from New Lisbon with a deal that would involve him making easy payments on his own schedule that would result in him owning the newspaper.[37] He was to be editor of *The Western Empire*, a weekly later to be known as the Dayton *Empire* and to be a daily. Meanwhile, he would practice law in the firm of the man selling him the paper. Sweet deal.

Dayton had a lot to offer Vallandigham. It was as far west as he could go without leaving the state. Leaving the state would mean giving up his politically useful name identification in the east and in the capital, Columbus, in the center of the state. Also, Dayton was about as far west as he could go without being too far from his mother and unmarried sister back in Lisbon, for whom he was starting to feel some responsibility. And it was the West without "Indians." The area was full of Native American names: Piqua, Wapakoneta, Miami—but no Native Americans anymore.

Politics was his passion always. He certainly saw the editorship as a stepping stone to a political office. Meanwhile, his notoriety as the editor would generate legal business, especially from Democrats.

Journalism was politics and politics was journalism. Harold Holzer, in his book on Lincoln and the press: "The development of America's two-party system brought with it the birth of the *one*-party newspaper." Parties openly funded and promoted newspapers. Publishers "drafted party resolutions and platforms ... offered printing services and copy editing for orators and openly advised candidates." The newspaper business was about opinion more than news. The idea, as Holzer quotes Elizabeth R. Varon, was to "make partisanship seem essential" to men's lives and identities.[38]

Editors expected and got plum patronage jobs. The editor of the Republican paper in Dayton, for example, became postmaster under Lincoln[39] and continued for a while to function in both jobs. Many politicians owned newspapers; Abe Lincoln bought himself a German language newspaper, because there were many German-speaking voters in Illinois.[40]

When Vallandigham went west in 1847, he had been married about a year to a girl from Cumberland, Maryland, Louisa McMahon, to whom he remained married the rest of his life. They lost their first child, Willie, in 1848 to disease. They later had another boy, Charlie, who grew to adulthood.

What was Dayton like? A lot of people approved. In the spring of 1862, a prominent clergyman named Dr. John Henry Augustus Bomberger visited Dayton. He was an abolitionist who went on to be a founder and the first president of Ursinus College near Philadelphia. After leaving Dayton, he wrote back to a local newspaper:

> I have seen the most important inland towns of (many states), but none of them equal your city in those features which most naturally attract and please the eye. It's broad, capacious streets, its ... handsome houses, the beautiful yards...; its stately court-house, showing the wealth of your vicinity in native marble, and the generous liberality of your citizens; its numerous churches, some of them displaying a degree of architectural elegance, of which any city might be proud.... I was still more gratified to notice the prevailing morality of the place. It seems to me I was never so long in a city (six days) without seeing a drunken person, or hearing a sadly greater amount of disgusting profanity. This speaks well for the citizens of Dayton, and gives promise of a happy future.[41]

Dayton had about 3,000 people in 1830, 11,000 by 1850 and twice that by 1860. Montgomery County—with Dayton as its core—had been at 24,000 people in 1830 and more than doubled that by 1860. So just about everybody was from someplace else. Water transportation mattered. The new thing was canals. Ohio built two connecting the Ohio River in the south with the Great Lakes. One went through Dayton: the Miami and Erie Canal from Cincinnati to Toledo. It was actually completed in 1845. But the section from Cincinnati to Dayton dated to 1829. A heavy cargo could get to or from Cincinnati in 24 hours, with a horse tied to a vessel, towing it along.

Meanwhile, there was the National Road (now known as U.S. 40), the first federal highway. Congress put up the first money for it in 1806.[42] It started in Cumberland, Maryland, and was made in stages. By 1840, it traversed Ohio, then eventually made it to St. Louis. It became the main migration route westward, going through territory north of Dayton that is now the airport area. That gave Dayton an advantage even over Cincinnati, though Cincinnati had the Ohio River.

So, for the young, ambitious Vallandigham, the setting was fine. However, after a couple of years in Dayton, Vallandigham had had it with newspapers. He sold the paper and settled into the practice of law and the pursuit of office. He continued for the rest of his life to be the eminence behind the Dayton *Empire*, through many different ownerships.

He was a successful lawyer. In 1855, at 35, in sending his mother some money, he wrote "I have been *most abundantly* prospered above any former period of my professional life, within the last five or six weeks." That seemed to be a turning point.[43]

But mainly he was a politician. He sought his party's nomination for secretary of state. He lost, failing to get the hoped-for boost from his bi-border identity. Before that, he ran for local judge and lost. He ran for Congress in 1852 and lost. In 1853, he was chairman of the state Democratic convention. Then again in 1854 he ran for Congress and lost. He ran again in 1856, and was declared the loser. But that last race was so close that he appealed the outcome. And he got his first national attention.

His opponent was Rep. Lewis Campbell, an anti-slavery Whig—before the Whigs collapsed—who had defeated him twice before. Campbell had led the unsuccessful fight in the House against the 1854 Kansas-Nebraska Act. That was the pivotal act that fostered the birth of the Republican Party and is credited with reviving the political ambitions of Abe Lincoln. It said that voters in new states could decide for themselves whether to allow slavery. Before that, the new northern states could not have slavery. The congressional fight over the bill entailed a high-profile 36-hour standoff that seemed to verge on physical violence.[44]

In 1856, with the Whigs gone, Campbell was running as a Republican but was also a new recruit to the Know-Nothings, a new anti-immigrant, anti–Catholic movement. To modern Americans, it might seem odd that a person who was relatively enlightened on race would be anti-immigrant and anti–Catholic. But, in fact, the Know-Nothings and Republicans worked closely together, even forming a "fusion" party for a time.[45] Some saw a certain logic to the combination: The Know-Nothings, also known as the American Party, were against old-world, undemocratic, foreign values—including slavery. Best to say, perhaps, simply that party labels, political affiliations and political alliances were in flux.

Recent years had seen an enormous increase in immigration resulting from the Irish potato famine and a cluster of failed democratic revolutions in Europe, after which many people had to flee Germany and elsewhere. Between 1847 and 1854, immigrants increased the nation's population by about 10 percent. In 1854 alone, the influx was more than 400,000, five times more than, say, in 1844.[46]

Democratic "bosses" in American cities—widely seen as corrupt—were organizing Catholic immigrants into voting blocs, fostering a predictable backlash against Catholic political power.[47]

By 1856, Campbell was worrying about the North-South division over slavery. He apparently hoped that the two regions could unite against foreigners. A noted speaker, he was seen by some regional newspapers and himself as presidential material.[48] He had been a major, though unsuccessful, candidate for speaker of the House, and he was chairman of the important Ways and Means Committee.

In the 1856 race against Vallandigham, he was originally declared the winner by 19 votes. The Democrats decided the margin had been provided by mixed-race voters, then called mulattoes. The Ohio Constitution said only whites could vote. The usual mechanism for stopping a would-be voter with dark skin was to challenge him when he showed up at the polling place. Then a judge would decide if the man was to be considered black. But that mechanism wasn't in the constitution, and Vallandigham hung his hat on the simple specification that only whites could vote.

In the wake of the election, things got ugly fast. The Dayton *Empire* wrote, "The nigger has crawled out of the wood pile and slipped into a place where, under the (Ohio) Constitution, he has no business."[49]

Then, as now, the final arbiter in disputed House elections was the House. There was a House investigation. Vallandigham diligently sought evidence that mulattoes had voted for Campbell. Ultimately, after a long process, Vallandigham was seated on a near–party line vote. However, the Democratic chair of the relevant committee, Thomas L. Harris of Illinois, said the evidence in Vallandigham's behalf was "circumstantial," and that everybody in the House was just voting party. Harris proposed that the House not make a decision at all, given that the term was just about over anyway.[50]

Most noteworthy about the process, for purposes of this book, was Vallandigham's ugly speech to the whole House in May of 1858: The constitution, he said, "means *white—pure white!*—and not any shade." He said, "the term 'white' ... is a word of exclusion against the whole negro race, in every degree. Whoever has a distinct and visible admixture of the blood of that race is not white; and it is an utter confusion of language to call him white."

Vallandigham warned the House members that if they allowed these people to vote, the next thing they knew such minorities might claim "they are eligible to membership of this House, and to sit upon this floor as your peers…. Are you prepared for that?"

He was just getting warmed up. "It is," he insisted,

> this same spurious and mongrel race who constitute your "free negroes," North and South. They will not be slaves, and they are not fit for freemen. … They are your petty thieves now; … they do fill up your penitentiaries, and they would fill up your hospitals and your alms-houses, *if you would let them. Then* they will be your highwaymen, your banditti; they will make up your mobs. With just enough intelligence, derived from a white ancestry, to know, and enough of brutishness, inherited from the old African stock, to avenge, in any form, the ignominy and

degradations of four thousand years; with fetish ideas of religion, and fanatic notions of politics, they are the *sans culotte* [a reference to violent extremists of the French Revolution] who, led on by the worst of white men, will make your revolutions, and overturn your governments.[51]

That's the only racist rant by Vallandigham that I've come across. Typically, he assumed racism in his audiences rather than fomented it. But he certainly played to it. He regularly lambasted the Republicans for being obsessed with black rights, as opposed to white interests. He insisted the country was for white people. He explicitly said the interests of blacks should not be taken into account in the making of policy. He said the black race was simply "cursed"—"a servile and degraded race almost from the beginning of time"—and that blacks were better off under slavery in the South than they were in Africa or with freedom in the North.[52]

Typical was his complaint in early 1863 about an order by the army officer in charge of the "Department of the Ohio." Col. Henry Carrington, concerned about Copperhead violence, had banned the sale of guns and ammunition. Vallandigham referred to "this attempt to disarm the white man, while public arms are being put into the hands of the negro."[53] That was a reference to the Union army's new use of black troops. Vallandigham didn't specify what terrible things would result from arming blacks. He preferred to just put the race issue out there and let nature take its course.

He was offended when Lincoln respectfully referred to slaves and other blacks as "Americans of African descent." He found that "unctuous."[54]

The reason he went over his usual top in the Campbell case may have simply been that he was playing to a substantially Southern audience. He needed the votes of racist legislators and was apparently eager for them to see him as an all-out racist. He succeeded. Rep. Alexander Stephens, future vice president of the Confederacy, "pronounced (the speech) the 'best effort' he had ever heard in the House," according to the Cincinnati *Enquirer*.[55]

It was Vallandigham's first big national speech. It garnered much attention, not because it became a rant, but because the fight over the seat had been become a national story. The fight had been going on for well over a year, and it involved issues at the core of the nation's ever-intensifying division over slavery. The dubious nature of his victory notwithstanding, the embarrassing view of the Democratic committee chairman notwithstanding, the ugliness of Vallandigham's message notwithstanding, he could hardly have hoped for a better, more conspicuous way to enter Congress.

***

Vallandigham's racism does not explain his views on slavery or the war. Racism was the norm and was found in people with all manner of views on slavery and the war. (To this day, after all, society has many racists who wouldn't support slavery.)

Vallandigham's paper trail suggests that he went through three phases in his thinking about slavery: opposition, neutrality and support, in that order. His "progression" looks like the opposite of the learning curve we like to think of as common in racial matters. He advanced backwards to benighted.

Despite these changes (to be elaborated upon below), he was consistent in some ways. He always argued that the country's great problem was not slavery, but the anti-slavery movement. That's the view that animated him, drove him, defined his outlook. Like many others, he saw the anti-slavery movement as the pitting of the values of one section of the nation against those of another. He saw the movement as poisonous sectionalism at work. In 1849, he wrote, in his valedictory as editor of the *Dayton Empire,* "all and every agitation in one section, necessarily generating counter-agitation in the other, ought" be rejected before it is too late.[56]

Republican politicians certainly did play on sectional jealousies. They were less likely to talk of the moral horrors of slavery than of alleged southern control of the nation's politics. They spoke of the "slave power," that is, wealthy slave owners. The Republicans told white people of the North that they were being manipulated by powerful, somewhat hidden forces when it came to, for example, setting the rules for new states.

Vallandigham, in a speech to Dayton Democrats in 1855, said the anti-slavery forces "teach men to hate" not only slavery but slaveholders, preparing northerners "to destroy, at every hazard, the object of their hatred." That, he said, was what brought on "this present and most perilous crisis."[57]

He called his speech "History of the Abolition Movement." Among the villains he cited were some big names: "Not a Northern poet, from Longfellow and Bryant, down to Lowell, but has sought inspiration from the black Helicon of Abolition." Then there was "the poison from a hundred thousand copies of false and canting libels, in the form of works of fiction," a reference to *Uncle Tom's Cabin*, published in 1852, a hugely popular anti-slavery novel.[58]

Vallandigham in 1863: "[I]t was abolition—the purpose to abolish or interfere with and hem in slavery—which caused disunion and war. Slavery is only the *subject,* but Abolition the *cause* of this civil war."[59] Note that he made no distinction between the hard-core abolitionists and the soft-core, anti-slavery Republicans who only opposed extension of slavery to the West, preferring the extension of their own states' customs. In that way, he was typical of Democratic polemicists: the Republicans were abolitionists, period.

His preferred—and predicted—solution to the nation's problems was always the same: the disappearance—not merely the defeat—of the anti-slavery movement.

"In my judgment," he said in 1862, "you will never suppress the armed Secession Rebellion till you have crushed under foot the pestilent Abolition Rebellion first."[60] He meant the Republicans, and he insisted that he was talking about crushing them in non-violent ways.

Vallandigham believed that the framers of the Constitution had wrestled with slavery and had resolved the issue, allowing it to exist. He certainly had grounds for saying that. After all, the framers even gave slave states a sort of extra-credit: In determination of their populations for purposes of allocating House seats, they would get credit for 60 percent of their slaves.

Moreover, Vallandigham insisted, the Founders' arrangement had brought the nation generations of peace, stability and growth. So, he asked, are the anti-slavery people of the mid–19th century somehow smarter, more moral and squarer with God than the Founders? He saw the anti-slavery people as implicitly making that claim.

In an 1863 speech, he proclaimed, "I … have opposed … Anti-Slavery sentiment

... from the beginning. In school, at college, at the bar, in public assemblies, in the Legislature, in Congress, boy and man.... It cost me 10 years' exclusion from office and honor, at that period of life when honors are sweetest."[61] He presented this analysis of his political failures unsupported by specifics. The case is dubious. As will be seen, his region offered opportunities for a politician of his views.

The notion that the anti-slavery people were the nation's great problem held much sway. Henry Clay is worth hearing. The legislative operator known as "The Great Compromiser" for his role in momentous slavery debates in the decades before the war was a slave owner, but not a true believer. He said he wished slavery had never been introduced. But he was frightened by the anti-slavery movement. In a Senate speech in the late 1830s, he pondered the possibility that the abolitionists might succeed in uniting the North against slavery. He said the South would become just as united. "A virtual dissolution of the Union will have taken place," he said, "while the forms of its existence remain.... The collision of opinion (would) be quickly followed by the clash of arms."[62]

In 1831, a Virginia slave named Nat Turner led a bloody, vengeful rebellion, the most potent uprising yet. Many in the South thought that event stemmed in some degree from anti-slavery agitation in the North. They noted that Turner was relatively well educated and could have been reached by some agitation. Historian H.W. Brands on what happened next: "The Virginia debate (on slavery) had been open and free, but before long the promotion of abolitionist ideas became effectively forbidden in the South."[63]

After the flowering of the abolition movement in the 1830s, South Carolina Sen. John C. Calhoun, Clay's contemporary, famously doubled down. He insisted that slavery, far from being a necessary evil or an unfortunate status quo that was difficult to change—as was widely argued in the South—was a positive good. He said it gave blacks a better life than they would otherwise have, while also benefiting whites. That was the direction that Southern advocates went later.

Calhoun said—more than 20 years before the Civil War—that if the abolition movement were allowed to exist, in a few years "reasonable men and women in the North ... will be succeeded by those who will have been taught to hate" the South. The result would be disunion.[64]

In the years just before the Civil War, the Democrats were the only national party. They were proud of that and were determined to maintain their trans-sectional coalition. They knew that the collapse of the Whig Party had happened largely because its regional wings couldn't be reconciled on slavery. Vallandigham and others saw a warning to northern Democrats.

But in those years, Vallandigham wasn't supporting slavery outright. Let's start here: Biographer Klement reported on a relevant letter Vallandigham wrote to friend in 1850. I haven't seen the full letter. Klement cites a collection at the University of North Carolina of the papers of the recipient, one Stanley Matthews. That collection no longer exists. UNC librarians told me they don't know what happened to it; but they did have a notation saying the letter from Vallandigham was to be kept private by Matthews. I tried another Matthews collection elsewhere with no luck. I quote Klement as to the letter's partial content.[65]

When Vallandigham wrote to him, Matthews was 25 and climbing from a newspaper editorship in Cincinnati toward a judgeship. He was eventually to be a Republican U.S. senator from Ohio and a U.S. Supreme Court justice. He was chair of the commission that resolved the chaotic presidential election of 1876 in favor of popular-vote loser Rutherford B. Hayes, the Republican.

Klement quoted the Vallandigham letter as defining slavery as "a moral, social & political evil" which Vallandigham said he "deplored." Vallandigham also called it "a local institution" which only a state could act against. Klement wrote: "(H)e hoped the electorate of each new state would follow the example of California and write into its constitution an 'emphatic edict' against the institution. Not only had he not put 'one solitary proslavery sentiment' on paper, he wrote in 1850, but he had never 'entertained one in his heart.'"

That passage reads as though Vallandigham was defending himself against a charge of pro-slavery views. If so, the charge is understandable. In 1848, he had been at a state Democratic convention which adopted a resolution committing individual members to work to "eradicate" slavery (even as the resolution acknowledged that the government had no right to do that). Vallandigham voted against the resolution. He tried to rescind it in later conventions, finally succeeding in 1856.[66] That story captures the increasing northern polarization over slavery. At a certain stage, a majority of Democrats thought it was okay for Democrats to denounce slavery. Then they didn't—or those who did had left the party.

A big polarizing event was the Kansas-Nebraska Act of 1854. Until the 1850s, under the Compromise of 1820, only states due west of the southern states were permitted to have slavery. The 1854 adoption of state option had a galvanizing effect on anti-slavery opinion in the North. After all, the people who moved west tended to move due west. The prospect that free northern white men might have to compete with slave labor was deeply unpopular.

In October 1855, Salmon P. Chase was elected the first Republican governor of Ohio. Shortly thereafter, Vallandigham addressed a gathering of Democrats in Dayton.[67] He embraced polarization. He said his party had lost because it was too weak in its denunciation of the anti-slavery movement. He said, "Let us have, then, no hollow compromise, no idle and mistimed homilies upon the sin and evil of slavery, ... no double-tongued ... responses." But even as he called for one-sided ground on abolition, he flatly refused to take a side on slavery itself. He was resolutely irresolute. Toward the end of the second hour of his speech, he said, "Hear me: I express no opinion in regard to" slavery. He insisted that northerners had no more legitimate involvement in the practices of the South than they had in those of foreign countries. "Slavery in the South is to (northerners) as polygamy in the Turkish Empire ... (or slavery) in Persia," he said.

He lumped abolition with temperance. An anti-liquor movement was gaining strength. In response, Vallandigham said government had no legitimate say in whether a person drank. The issue was between a man and his god and his conscience. Similarly, government had no legitimate say in whether a man held slaves; the issue was between a man and his god and his conscience.

Another way he would, on other occasions, come at slavery was to insist, as many others did, that slavery and freedom were just different "forms of labor."⁶⁸ The South had its system, and the North had its, and both were satisfied, and that was that. He presented different "forms of labor" as a preposterous thing to go to war about.

In the 1855 speech, however, after denying that he had a position on slavery itself, he added what looked to a lot of people like a position on slavery. He said, "I know, sir, that it is easy, very easy to denounce (his critique of abolitionism) as a defense of slavery itself. Be it so; be it so." Then, in one of his typical all-encompassing sentences, he offered what was to become a mantra:

> If to love my country; to cherish the Union; to revere the Constitution; if to abhor the madness and hate the treason [that is, abolitionism] which would lift up a sacrilegious hand against ... this land, which is of more value to us and the world for ages to come, than all the multiplied millions who have inhabited Africa from the creation to this day—if this is to be *pro-slavery*, then in every nerve, fiber vein, bone, tendon, joint, and ligament, from the top-most hair of the head to the last extremity of the foot, I am all over and altogether a PRO-SLAVERY man.

He was declaring that, in political disputes, he would always be on the side of the pro-slavery people. Moreover, he was saying that that was the important fact about him, more important than his views on slavery, which he claimed to be irrelevant.

In 1859, in a House speech, he again proclaimed his neutrality about slavery itself. He said that so long as the question wasn't about slavery in Ohio, his position was "serene indifference."⁶⁹

In making the case against the anti-slavery movement, he did not harp on the rights of states. He emphasized, instead, the threat of secession, the dangers in sectionalism, the Constitution's treatment of slavery, and the allegedly dubious motives of the Republicans. This may have been because the states' rights argument ran into several problems for Northern Democrats. For one thing, as secession loomed, the real, hardcore states' rights position was let-the-South-go. That's the ultimate state right, after all. Vallandigham did not take that position.

Another problem was that the states' rights argument cut both ways. In the 1850s, one of the hottest national controversies was over whether Northern states should be obliged to return escaped slaves to their Southern owners. On this one, the opponents of slavery had the states' rights argument: Let the states decide for themselves whether they want to do that.⁷⁰ The South wanted federal force.

Then there was the Kansas-Nebraska Act itself. Many Southerners did not like its states' rights quality. They wanted a national guarantee of the right of slaveholders to bring their "property" anyplace they wanted.⁷¹ State rights, schmate rights; this was about slavery (and, they would say, individual property rights).

Even before that, Northern opponents of slavery had long enjoyed tweaking the Southerners over their opportunistic deployment of the states' rights mantra. In 1841, slaves from Georgia were escaping to Florida and taking up life with Seminole tribes. Georgia called upon the feds to send a military force to Florida to put an end to that. Joshua Giddings, an early anti-slavery congressman from northeastern Ohio, rose in opposition. He said, in effect: You guys are always saying slavery is purely a state institution, subject only to state regulation. Yet now you call on taxpayers in other states—states that have banned slavery—to support your institution.

Send your own troops!⁷² That resulted in what Giddings called "a peaceful riot" in the House.

At any rate, by the late 1850s the states' rights cry just didn't seem to be working in the North. The Republican Party was coming on strong. Every indication was that a lot people of the North—whether they cared about Southern slavery or not, and whether they were racists or not—simply did not want slavery in the new Northern states. They didn't care about state rights.

When, in January 1863, Vallandigham finally fully and unambiguously embraced Southern slavery in a congressional speech, the not-unheard-of argument that inequality between races fostered equality among whites.

"In my deliberate judgment," he said, "a confederacy made up of slaveholding and non-slaveholding States, is, in the nature of things, the strongest of all popular governments. African slavery has been, and is, eminently conservative. It makes the absolute political equality of the white race everywhere practicable. It dispenses with the English order of nobility, and leaves every white man, North and South, owning slaves or owning none, the equal of every other white man. It has reconciled universal suffrage, throughout the free States, with the stability of government."⁷³

The argument might be murky, but the explanation for Vallandigham's journey on slavery is clear: Polarization. Vallandigham made his proclamation just as the Emancipation Proclamation was officially going into effect. For a political warrior like Vallandigham, the issuing of Lincoln's proclamation was as if Lincoln and the Republicans had stuck their tongues out at him. He had been saying, in effect, "too far, too far, too far," when suddenly they went farther. "Doubling down" would be too weak a cliché to cover the enormity of Emancipation. This was imposition of a revolution on the white South.

In Vallandigham's eyes, everything he had said about the Republicans was being borne out. First he thought they would ruin the country, then he thought they *were* ruining the country. And yet the Republicans just barreled ahead, as if everything was going according to plan. They had suffered an election setback in 1862. And yet they persisted, unconcerned with public opinion.

For Vallandigham, it was no longer enough to argue that slavery wasn't worth a war. He couldn't settle for explicitly rejecting Lincoln's notion that the country could not survive part slave and part free. He had to go to the extreme, insisting that the part slave/part free plan was "the fundamental idea of the Constitution." Slavery was not just good; it was the best thing in the Constitution.

As I've talked about the Vallandigham story around Dayton, I've found that the first thing people want to know about Vallandigham is whether he actually favored slavery. So I thought I'd explore his journey on that score early on. But it has required getting ahead of the story.

2

Onto the National Stage

At various stages of the Civil War, all three congressmen from southwestern Ohio—two from Cincinnati and one from Dayton—were Copperheads. This has led some people to the impression that the region was politically some sort of extension of the South. This impression competes with a contrary one. If you listen to some boosters talk about the local outposts of the Underground Railroad (a network for spiriting escaped slaves northward to freedom), you might get the impression Dayton was a hotbed of anti-slavery agitation and Lincoln support.

The truth is in middle—smack dab, in fact. Dayton had two vibrant, ideologically antagonistic parties, and elections were often close. In 1860, Montgomery County (Dayton) went for Lincoln by 264 votes out of almost 10,000. Almost every time Vallandigham ran for anything, the margin was paper-thin. In 1858, he was re-elected by 188 votes; in 1860 by 134.

In 1870, the Cincinnati *Enquirer* wrote, "No (congressional) district in the United States, perhaps, has been as thoroughly fought over for the last thirty years" as Vallandigham's Third District. (The paper also noted that all of the district's congressmen "may be said to have acquired national reputations.")[1]

The competitiveness was true of the region generally. By the end of the war, the Democrats had lost all three of those congressional districts. One of the three was Cincinnati's George Pendleton. He was the Democratic nominee for vice president in 1864, a future presidential prospect and the namesake of the first big Civil Service Act, the Pendleton Act of the 1880s. He was widely seen as a less divisive, less colorful, but equally brainy version of Vallandigham. He was called "Gentleman George" precisely because he wasn't Vallandigham.[2] He won re-election in 1860 even as Lincoln was carrying Hamilton County (Cincinnati) by about 2 percent.

The third Copperhead congressman was Alexander Long, who served only one term. He was a special case, being, in effect, to the right of Vallandigham and Pendleton. By 1864, he was arguing that the North should simply let the South go, as opposed to the Vallandigham view that the North should pursue reunification by accommodating the South. Long was censured by the House for his views, 80–69, and he lost his renomination bid that year. His replacement in office was the Republican Rutherford B. Hayes, a military hero.

At any rate, both parties held important elected positions in the region, and both had vibrant newspapers that fomented, presided over and largely directed political warfare. The *Enquirer* was the only Democratic paper in Cincinnati out of several.[3]

The proximity to Kentucky—figure 55 miles from Dayton to the Kentucky suburbs of Cincinnati—certainly did affect the political atmosphere. Some southern Ohioans were simply horrified by the very idea of war with their Southern brethren; some passionately shared the racial views of those brethren. Still, too much can be made of the proximity. True, a third of the people in the southern half of Ohio had southern roots, by some estimates.[4] But some southern migrants had consciously moved to a state in which slavery was illegal. And many had intermarried with Northerners. And, anyway, Kentucky was not a state where slavery was as central to life as in the Deep South.

Counties on the southern edge of Ohio—the Ohio River—were not necessarily Democratic. Some east of Cincinnati were quite staunchly Republican. The geographic distribution of Democrats and Republicans in Ohio was complicated once one got beyond the staunchly Republican northern tier, settled by New Englanders. The distribution was not a city-versus-farm thing. And it was not economic; though the Copperheads were associated by many with poor farmers, almost half of the strongest counties for a Copperhead candidate were above the state average in income.[5]

Much had to do with where the settlers had come from. Many people in western Ohio came from eastern Ohio or Pennsylvania, New Jersey or Delaware.[6] They had experienced westward expansion without slavery, and they tended to think that was the way it ought to be, which tended to make them Republicans. Political differences between counties resulted in some degree from the fact that people tended to settle were people they knew had settled. It wasn't random.

Blacks typically were about one percent of a county's population. However, Greene County, to the east of Montgomery, had an unusual concentration of black people. Some southern whites who had freed their slaves brought them there. Then, in 1856, the first black university in the states opened there, Wilberforce. In 1870, Greene was one of seven Ohio counties with more than 2,000 blacks, about 7 percent of population.[7]

Southwestern Ohio had a heavy concentration of German immigrants. In 1850, 27 percent of the people in Cincinnati had been born in what is now Germany. In Dayton, 28 percent of the population was foreign born, mainly German and Irish, with German being the larger category.[8] Dayton had a German-language newspaper during the war. Sometimes two political rallies would be going on just blocks from each other, one of them for German speakers. A satellite city to Dayton was named Germantown.

Politically, the German-American population was complex. Some of those who fled to North America after the collapse of the European democratic revolutions at mid-century were reform minded and drawn to the Republican cause. However, many German immigrants were Catholics and drawn to the Democrats because they associated Republicans with the anti–Catholic Know-Nothings. Also, many immigrants were against the temperance movement, which had been associated the Whigs. And many German immigrants had simply been in the country long enough to take on the political complexion of their communities. Some studies have found that rural voters of German extraction were more likely to be Democrats than Republicans.[9]

Many Irish immigrants had come to get work building the canals. The Irish-American vote was largely Democratic, also because of the Know-Nothings and the temperance movement. And, being at or near the bottom of the economic spectrum, Irish-Americans often feared competition from freed blacks.

The competitiveness that resulted from the diversity fostered a politics that was intense, insulting, racial and, eventually, never far from violent.

***

"He never told stories for the purpose of causing laughter. He was too full of mental resources for that. He might illustrate a point of his speech by an occasional anecdote, but this was very rare," said a political friend speaking about Vallandigham.[10]

If Vallandigham was the anti–Lincoln in outlook, so was he in political style. But people generally liked him. He put them at ease. In conversation, they found him pleasant, engaging, polite and interested in what they had to say. He doesn't seem to have had many detractors over anything other than politics. He lived his life without a hint of scandal (except for absurd partisan hints offered during campaigns). He was, near as anybody knows, a faithful family man. He was a diligent and caring correspondent with young relatives, judging from letters presented in his brother's biography of him.

Once in Washington, he wanted the national stage fast. He was driven by the confidence that made him a public speaker at 20 and a legislator in his early 20s, and that had kept him going when he lost election after election in Dayton: the sense that he was at least as good as any of these guys, no matter the outcome of an election here or there.

His speeches were prolix and long-winded, but also erudite and impressive, often praised by people who didn't agree. The same speeches wouldn't go over well today. But he spoke in the style of the day, complete with long diversions into history.

Not everybody found him consistently engaging. At the height of Vallandigham's notoriety, Noah Brooks—Washington correspondent of the Sacramento *Daily Union*, confidant of Lincoln (whom he had known in Illinois), and intense Republican partisan—reviewed Vallandigham's congressional contribution.[11] He wrote that he "is the leading spirit in the mischievous faction of peace Democrats in the House. As I write, I look down upon him…. The man is a study as he sits quietly there, smoothly smiling and leaning his pleasant, rosy face upon his hand as he softly strokes his face, and watching cat-like for a chance to spring. The smaller tactics"—that is, the mundane business of the House—"he leaves to the smaller fry…. But when the opportune moment arrives, he is on his feet instantly, makes his point, persists in its being considered, and then sits down, watchful, attentive, and smiling as a spring morning, for 'a man may smile and smile and be a villain,' as Vallandigham is." Brooks was quoting Hamlet, who wasn't certain his observation was true outside of Denmark. Brooks continued:

> He is of medium size, well formed, about forty years of age, with a small head, regular and small features, nose slightly Romanesque, and dark-haired but growing gray. His complexion is fresh and fair, though a nearer view shows innumerable wrinkles about his eyes and mouth.

> He dresses with great neatness and care, and as he sits at his desk turning over his *Globe* [the Congressional Record of its day] smiling ever at the petty discussions ... or small jokes, ... he is altogether a personable man. He is what is popularly called a pretty talker, smooth, plausible, and polished.
>
> But when he makes a set speech and becomes excited, the expression of his face is fearfully changed—his mouth becomes wide and his thin lips are drawn tightly over his teeth, while a vindictive, ghastly grin replaces the pleasant smile which is his wont. Then the real man speaks out, and as he waves his arms in the air, fluttering his open hands convulsively and constantly, his voice rising higher and higher as he shrieks—"Can you tax any more? Can you draft any more? Will the people bear it?"—then the devil within breaks through his fair disguise, and Vallandigham the disorganizer, the mischief-maker, the ally of Jeff Davis and the devil, speaks. His power over his comrades is omnipotent. A word from him or a wave of the hand will send them all into the lobbies and cloakrooms ... or bring them back when they are called for.

That last sentence might be misleading. Vallandigham did not lead the Democrats as a whole in doing the work of the House. He was a gadfly. He liked to spend time on the floor debating, hassling the majority, making his points, rather than shaping and lobbying for legislation. He loved to give major speeches. They were his pride and joy, his way of defining himself and his movement. As will be seen, they almost always got better reviews than the one from Brooks. Vallandigham drew crowds in both Washington and Ohio and gave the people what they came for, impressing them and burnishing his own reputation in the process. His practice in youth had paid off. Perhaps it is worth remembering, too, that more people read his speeches than heard them. Newspapers often printed speeches of their favored politicians.

3

Seeing John Brown (In the Mirror)

Harper's Ferry, Virginia. Mid-October 1859. John Brown was there, making his impact on American history. Robert E. Lee was there, leading the forces of the United States Army confronting Brown. And Clement Vallandigham was there, inserting himself into this turning point.

Brown must have seemed to Vallandigham like a political godsend. For anyone portraying the anti-slavery movement as the greatest threat to public safety and national survival, Brown had to be Exhibit A. He was a notoriously bloodthirsty abolitionist, having engaged in murderous events in "Bloody Kansas," the 1850s forerunner of the Civil War.

And now, as if it wasn't enough for Brown to be politically convenient for Vallandigham, he had made himself geographically convenient. He conducted his most famous raid—and shook the world—at a spot on the rail line between Dayton and Washington.

Brown's plan was to abet a slave rebellion by raiding a U.S. armory in slave country, taking the weapons and ammunition, and letting slaves know those resources were now available to them. Vallandigham, like everybody else, heard about the Harper's Ferry raid in the news. It was huge news. It was huge for the South, because it brought the double nightmare to life: not only the dread of slaves with weapons, but the suspicion that northern opponents of slavery wanted to foster that nightmare, to destroy them, to make the South run with blood.

Vallandigham saw the raid as discrediting the anti-slavery forces in general; it showed where the anti-slavery movement had always been going. He was, in effect, a lucky prosecutor who finds his case being strengthened by outside events happening during the trial.

By the time Vallandigham got off the train, the world knew that the raid had been a failure, that Brown himself was in the hands of Col. Lee, and that Brown was injured. Vallandigham wanted to talk to him. Lee was letting various people do that, including journalists from the Associated Press and nearby papers. Politicians from Virginia were there. Vallandigham was the only politician from outside Virginia.[1]

Brown was eager to talk, eager to answer questions. Lee was ready to shut down the conversations in the interest of Brown's health, but Brown didn't want him to.

The meeting between Brown and Vallandigham in a barn where Lee was present and Brown lay injured was like something out of fiction. A creative writer would love the idea of them meeting, preferably at that dramatic spot, not at some congressional hearing. The scene seems made up.

Here, after all, were the extremes and the talent. Brown had an undeniable messianic charisma that captured the imagination of supporters and led them to extremes. Vallandigham was to become a similar kind of hero and spokesman for the opposite end of northern opinion. Brown saw the promises of the Declaration of Independence trounced upon by the "war" that was slavery. Vallandigham saw only support from the Founders for his own war against the war against slavery. Brown was certain that God's will was being thwarted by slavery and enacted by anti-slavery violence. Vallandigham would have been happy to debate with him about the Bible's say on slavery. Brown was seen by some as the very symbol of evil and benightedness. Vallandigham was on his way to that status.

Vallandigham in his prime (Library of Congress).

If screenwriters would love the setting, they would not be satisfied with the dialogue. The conversation was not exactly transcendent. It had a flavor that modern Americans would recognize. It resembled a petty, early–21st-century cable television argument among professional partisans—though it was certainly more dignified.

Vallandigham had one big question in mind. It was not why was Brown so certain God was against slavery, or why didn't Brown understand that the slaves were better off than they had been in Africa, or what level of violence would be acceptable to him. It was not what gave this unaccomplished man, Brown—this subject of some 20 lawsuits by the time he was 42—the moral authority to sermonize about the behavior of other people.[2]

The question was where did Brown's money come from. Vallandigham—like many others—was certain that Republican money had funded this violence against the American military. He wanted to be the one to bring that news to the American people. Brown was known to have been raising money in New England for a couple of years. He was known to have won the praise of some abolitionists. He had met with Henry David Thoreau and Ralph Waldo Emerson. He knew Frederick Douglass well. He got financial support from other prominent people—a group known as the Secret Six, not famous by name today—but it's not known whether they thought they were supporting a raid.

Vallandigham had special justification for wondering about ties between Brown and Republicans in Ohio: Brown had lived in the state for 50 years. Vallandigham said later that some of Brown's men—black and white—came from Ohio. And he said he had heard that the Brown raid plan was concocted at the Ohio State Fair.[3]

According to journalistic reports on the Vallandigham-Brown conversation,[4] Vallandigham came at the question about Republican involvement in various ways, as a lawyer might. He had questions like, "Have you been in Ohio this summer?" and "Were you ever in Dayton?" (Answer: Maybe; a year or two ago.) He was trying to place Brown at places where Republicans were gathered for a convention or some other purpose.

He was particularly curious—and apparently suspicious—about the northern Ohioan who had become the leading anti-slavery force in the U.S. House after the death of John Quincy Adams.

John Brown (Library of Congress).

> VALLANDIGHAM: Did you see anything of Joshua R. Giddings (when you were last in Ohio)?
> BROWN: I did meet him.
> VALLANDIGHAM: Did you consult with him?
> BROWN: If I did, I would not tell you, of course, anything that would implicate Mr. Giddings, but I certainly saw him and had a conversation with him.
> VALLANDIGHAM: I don't mean about this affair of yours (the raid). I mean about that rescue case (a reference to an Ohio controversy).
> BROWN: Oh, yes, I did hear him express his opinion on it very freely and frankly.
> VALLANDIGHAM: Justifying it?
> (If Vallandigham could not actually tie Giddings and other Republicans to the raid, he would have apparently liked to at least demonstrate that they were of a mindset like Brown's.)
> BROWN: Yes, Sir; I do not compromise him by saying that.

After a break:

> VALLANDIGHAM: Will you answer this question? Did you talk with Giddings about your expedition here?
> BROWN: No, Sir, I won't answer that, because a denial of it I would not make, and to make an affirmation of it I should be a great dunce.
> VALLANDIGHAM: Have you had any correspondence with parties in the North on the subject of this movement?
> BROWN: I have had correspondence.

And so the conversation went: nowhere.

Perhaps giving up on finding Republican links to Brown besides conversations—which were no secret—Vallandigham went to motive:

VALLANDIGHAM: Did you expect a general rising of the slaves in case of success?
BROWN: No, Sir, nor did I wish it; I expected to gather strength from time to time, then I could set them free. (Note: In truth, Brown had written a constitution for the new state of Virginia that he hoped would arise from his raid.)[5]

Vallandigham returned to Dayton without his prize.

Brown engaged with others at Harper's Ferry in short exchanges about the merits of his acts—justifying them on moral grounds. But Vallandigham apparently had little interest in challenging Brown's views. His focus was on those not present.

He did come away with something. Vallandigham's brother later wrote, "This interview made a very deep impression upon Mr. V's mind; he often referred to it, and spoke of John Brown as one of the most remarkable men he ever met.... Although Brown had been a very bad man, ... yet the desperate sincerity of the man in his anti-slavery views could not but awaken a feeling akin to admiration in the bosom of one who, in the vindication of his own peculiar views, was willing at all times to stake fortune, popularity, and life itself."[6]

Clement Vallandigham himself wrote publicly about the Brown exchange. A long letter to the Democratic Cincinnati *Enquirer* was partly designed to refute suggestions in Republican papers that he had somehow badgered Brown or behaved in a way inappropriate to Brown's physical condition. Vallandigham said he had not disembarked from the train to examine Brown, but to see the site, and that he just took the opportunity to ask questions when it arose, and that Lee policed the situation, and that Brown had no complaint with Vallandigham's behavior, which was apparently true.

The bulk of Vallandigham's letter is devoted to the argument that Brown must not be seen in isolation. "The conspiracy was, unquestionably, far more extended than yet appears," he wrote, without offering evidence, "having ... as its counsellors and abettors, men of intelligence, position and wealth. Certainly it was one among the best-planned and executed conspiracies that ever failed."

He seemed to be afraid that people might see its failure as an indication that the violent aspect of the anti-slavery movement was too incompetent and weak to be worth worrying about. Vallandigham emphasized the "large quantities of arms" Brown had, and the sophistication of his campaign, which he said was "like Napoleon" in one respect. Vallandigham spun the numbers: "During this short insurrection eighteen men were killed and ten or more severely wounded—twice the number killed and wounded on the part of the American force at the Battle of New Orleans."

Vallandigham argued that Brown was not as contemptible as the non-violent Republicans. "Brown was sincere, earnest, practical. He proposed to add works to his faith, reckless of murder, treason, and every other crime. This was his madness and folly. He perishes justly and miserably"—he was to be executed—"an insurgent and a felon. But guiltier than he, and with his blood upon their heads, and the blood of all whom he caused to be slain, are the false and cowardly prophets and teachers of Abolition."[7]

Vallandigham simply gushed about Brown:

> Captain Brown is as brave and resolute a man as ever headed an insurrection. ... He has coolness, daring, persistency ... stoic faith and patience, and a firmness of will and purpose

unconquerable. He is tall, wiry, muscular, but with little flesh—with a cold gray eye, gray hair, beard and mustache, compressed lips and sharp aquiline nose, of castiron face and frame, and with powers of endurance equal to anything needed to be done or suffered in any cause.... (H)e is the farthest possible remove from the ordinary ruffian, fanatic or madman; but his powers are rather executory than inventive, and he never had the depth or breadth of mind to originate and contrive himself the plan of insurrection which he undertook to carry.[8]

This 1939 painting of John Brown by John Steuart Curry captures his public image. Oil on canvas, 69 × 45 in. (175.3 × 114.3 cm) (Arthur Hoppock Hearn Fund, 1950 [50.94.1], image copyright © The Metropolitan Museum of Art. Image source: Art Resource, NY).

That last part was exactly wrong. Brown was certainly the brains behind his plan. He had always been great on the "inventive" end, coming up with multiple and exciting plans for businesses in his personal life, long before he entered the slavery fight. It was precisely in the "executory" end that he collapsed again and again. Harper's Ferry was yet another example.

When Vallandigham used words like brave, resolute, cool, daring, stoic, firm and "unconquerable purpose" and "powers of endurance," he was not making minor concessions. He was talking about his own most cherished values, his measure of a man. He was using words he would want to be used about himself, perhaps in preference to all others.

***

The argument that Vallandigham made about the connection between Brown and the Republicans struck a nerve. Abraham Lincoln was to take it up in a speech at Cooper Union in New York the next spring, the speech that is widely credited with sparking his presidential campaign. Lincoln didn't mention Vallandigham. He might not even have been thinking of Vallandigham, for the same case had been made often by others. Indeed, Lincoln proceeded as if it came from Southerners. To them, Lincoln said:

> You charge that we stir up insurrections among your slaves. We deny it; and what is your proof? Harper's Ferry! John Brown!! John Brown was no Republican; and you have failed to implicate a single Republican in his Harper's Ferry enterprise.... Some of you admit that no Republican designedly aided or encouraged the Harper's Ferry affair, but still insist that our doctrines and declarations necessarily lead to such results. We do not believe it.... True, we do ... declare our belief that slavery is wrong; but the slaves do not hear us.... I believe they would not, in fact, generally know (the Republicans exists) but for your misrepresentations of us in their hearing.[9]

4

The Westerner

Vallandigham's first big congressional speech on matters other than his own election came when a new Congress convened in December of 1859, after he was re-elected in 1858. (That was a normal gap for the time.) In the speech, he said "I" 175 times, not to mention the "me's" and "my's." He saw himself already as an object of public interest.

He gave vent to wordiness that is difficult to capture without putting off modern readers. With apologies: "I am of and from the West; the great valley of the Mississippi; of the free States of that valley, seated in queenly majesty at the head of the basin of that mighty river; yet one by interest, and one by the bonds of nature, stronger than hooks of steel, with every other State in that valley, full as it is of...." On and on like that.

But there was substance. He titled his speech "There is a West."[1] With Southern secession in the air, he said the following. (The emphases are in a written version he presented later):

"I am not a Northern man, nor yet a Southern man; but I am a Western Man, by birth, in habit, by education; and, although still a United States man with United States principles ... am wholly devoted to Western interests.... In all this controversy"—between North and South—"*so far as it is sectional,* I occupy the position of ARMED NEUTRALITY.... I have little sympathy with the North, no very good feeling for" it. He said, "I am as good a Western fire-eater as the hottest salamander in this House." The fire-eaters were the fiercest Southern sectionalists, the people who fomented secession. (Salamander was a less common political term.)

Technically, he barely qualified as a westerner. The 1860 census would reveal Chillicothe, Ohio—in the south central part of the state—as the midpoint of the country's population. Ohio, which had 10 percent of nation's population, was partly west and partly not.[2]

In some measure he was trying to respond provocatively to the charge that he was a Northerner with Southern principles (a "doughface," though he didn't use the term). He took up that charge specifically: "When I emigrate to the South, ... then, and not till then, will I have a right, and will it be my duty, and no doubt my pleasure, to maintain and support Southern principles and Southern institutions." Not exactly a denial. He did not identify any circumstances in which he would "maintain and support" Northern principles and institutions.

He urged Southerners to "defend" their rights "within the Union, firmly, fearlessly, boldly, quietly—do it like men." He said if they did that, "there is no power on earth that can subdue or conquer you." He made explicit what rights he was talking about. They included the constitutional right to be over-represented in Congress, the right to require Northern states to assist in the return of escaped slaves, and the right to extend slavery into the new states.

His freshest, most striking point was this: If the union were to break up permanently—which he insisted he was against—he might prefer to have Ohio and its neighbors join with the South rather than North. He acknowledged that the West, lacking access to an ocean, could not go it alone. But he said that access to the Gulf of Mexico would do, and the West had access to it via the Mississippi River and the South.

Having always decried sectionalism as the poisonous contribution of the Republican Party, he was now saying that what *really* got his goat was that the wrong sections were being discussed.

He said that "when I came to this city, two years ago, I brought with me an intense nationality," meaning a commitment to the nation. "But I had been here only a little while till I learned that a man without a section to cling to was reckoned but as a mere cipher.... I learned that, while there was a North and a South, there was no West." He said the North and South had "respect" for each other, but "the Western man was held to be a sort of outside barbarian."

The point was lame for many reasons, some of which he tried to address. He tried to argue that two very prominent Ohio Republicans in the House then—John Sherman and Thomas Corwin—were, though he didn't use the word, tokens in an Eastern party. He laughed off as a "miserable infatuation" the hope that Ohio Gov. Salmon P. Chase would be the Republican nominee for president in 1860 (and, implicitly, the hope that somebody from even farther west would be). He spoke of New York's William Seward as the leader of the Republicans, and he implicitly predicted his nomination.

He acknowledged that two westerners had been elected president fairly recently (William Henry Harrison and Zachary Taylor), but he seemed to see some meaning in the point that they both died early in their terms. (Perhaps some attempt at humor is lost in the official record.) At any rate, he didn't even mention Andrew Jackson, the last president to be elected twice and the great standard bearer of the West.

One of Vallandigham's important points was solid: The connection of the West to the North, rather than the South, was taken for granted. But the reasons were obvious. Most of the people in the West came from the East. The West didn't have slavery. It did, like the East, have prominent anti-slavery figures. It had large anti-slavery populations, including northern Ohio.

Still, tensions between East and West were real. One big irritant was railroads, the great new technology of the day. Sometimes headquartered in the East, railroads were crucial to commerce. Farmers and other businessmen worried about their prices, schedules and routes. These Westerners felt utterly dependent on the railroads, yet sometimes utterly unheard by them. This phenomenon resulted in battalions of politicians in the West becoming railroad men: The railroad companies, desperate to convince the Westerners that they were being heard, put high-profile

4. The Westerner

Westerners front and center. The three governors of Ohio during the Civil War had all been railroad men as well as politicians before becoming governor.

Other kinds of corporations were becoming important, too, with the industrial revolution, and they tended to be headquartered in the East, too. They tended to seek high tariffs as protection against European competition. But high tariffs could be a problem for Western farmers who wanted to export their products. Meanwhile, some Westerners felt snootiness emanating from the East.

But the East-West relationship was far from all bad. The railroads fostered business relationships. Many Westerners had relatives back East and were just simply not hostile. Vallandigham was not speaking not for the West, but for a certain force in the West.

Vallandigham referred to a statement by a Republican legislator that the North had a far bigger population from which to draw troops than the South. Vallandigham said, "I tell him that, if he means to raise the black standard of internecine war upon the South, he must find his recruits nearer home" than the West.

He portrayed the anti-slavery movement as a mere a power grab by the North. "I will not consent that an honest and conscientious opposition to slavery forms any part of the motives of the leaders of the Republican Party," he said. John Brown, yes; Republican politicians, no. He granted that some people might have had that moral concern once upon a time. But the issue had evolved into a simple sectional power struggle. The North has realized, he said, that it is more powerful than the South and has set out on "a war for political domination."

But, he said, the North's power would collapse if the West broke away. Addressing the North, he asked, "Did you ever dream of a WESTERN CONFEDERACY? Did that horrid phantom never flit across you in visions of the night, when deep sleep falls upon men?

"Dissolve this Union, if you dare," he said. "Compel the South into a southern confederacy, force us of the West into a western confederacy, and then tell me what position would you assume among the powers of the earth? Where then would be your pride and arrogance?"

He urged western Republicans to "lay aside this pestilent fanaticism on the subject of slavery, which you borrow servilely from the clergy, lecturers and other demagogues of the North. ... Lay it aside and be Western sectionalists." Sectionalism was necessary to defeat sectionalism.

He heaped sarcasm on the notion that the western Republicans were fighting a moral cause in the slavery battle. "Are there no objects of charity in your own midst—no poor, no sick, no lame, no halt, no blind, no widows and orphans—to whose necessities you may administer and thus find vent for that abounding river of humanity which wells up and flows out from the fountain of your hearts? Pardon me, but I despise and contemn your vassalage to the North as much as you can contemn and despise any man's servility to the South."

This expression of contempt is particularly striking in the context of Vallandigham's introduction to his speech, which was a long paean to courtesy and a complaint that he had been denied it.

On the prospect of Southern secession, he looked into possible election-year events and said to the South: "Do you ask me whether election of an anti-slavery, sectional Republican president, upon a sectional platform, pledged to administer the Government for sectional purposes, would, *per se,* be a justifiable cause of disunion?"

His answer to his own question began with "I cannot tell you." But he said, "I (would) not wait for the overt act." He meant an act against slavery. He would not wait for the "natural and inevitable effects" of such an election.

In subsequent years, Vallandigham was very widely called a secessionist. He always took great umbrage, insisting that the sanctity of the union was his top priority. Squaring that claim with this speech would've been hard.

This 1859 speech was one in which he offered his solution to the nation's monumental problem: "the immediate, absolute, unconditional disbandment of this sectional, anti-slavery, Republican party of yours. If not, then upon your heads, and upon the heads of your children, be the blood of the Republic."

It's tempting to say that this vision of a Republican disappearance is so fantastical as to justify the charge that Vallandigham really offered no solution. However, he may have had in mind the Know-Nothing story. That party simply died, quickly. The Whig Party had also died. So had other, less-important ones. Parties did come and go.

But the anti-slavery movement had been around for thirty years and had only grown. Few people took seriously the idea of it disappearing. That was a big reason the South reacted to Lincoln's election by seceding: No matter what assurances the South might get about the future of slavery, the anti-slavery movement would always be around. Even deeply into the war, Vallandigham was saying that—now that the abolitionists had seen how much devastation they had caused—they would stop their agitation if peace and union were re-established by armistice. The South never bought it. Neither, loosely speaking, did anybody else.

Frank J. Klement wrote—in *The Copperheads of the Middle West*, a different book than his biography of Vallandigham—that "Vallandigham and Stephen A. Douglas condemned 'Southern Fire-eaters' and 'Northern fanatics' with equal vehemence."[3] That notion shows up often in brief treatments of Vallandigham online and elsewhere, presumably stemming from Klement.

It has two problems. One, when Vallandigham talked about the Northern equivalent of fire-eaters, he meant Republicans, not just John Brown supporters. Two, the "equal vehemence" simply was not present. Vallandigham dedicated the core of his professional life to the fight against the abolitionists. As for the fire-eaters, he just mentioned them. He never suggested they should dry up and blow away. He saw them as a natural reaction to the anti-slavery movement. (He denied that the anti-slavery movement was a natural outgrowth of slavery, insisting, on the contrary, that it was an unnatural, recent revival of a long-settled matter.)

Vallandigham's notion of the West joining the South got him some attention. It was intriguing to the political classes. It worried many Republicans. Books have been written suggesting that some sort of Western conspiracy with the South came reasonably close to succeeding during the war.[4] There was, indeed, some plotting, some dreaming and substantial governmental concern.[5] In the South, hopes existed that something might come of this movement.

But the cause never caught on big. The most important polarization really was between North (including the West) and South. Vallandigham was speaking before the war. Once Ohio men were fighting for the North, he pressed other points, not that one. Times had changed fast.

The 1859 speech got much attention and helped shape Vallandigham's reputation. It was remembered by friends and foes alike. But perhaps its greatest importance lay in the fact that it demonstrated the weakness of "The West" as a cause. It sparked nothing.

5

Response to Sumter
Founding Fatherhood Denied

"The Union as it was; the Constitution as it is." That was the rallying cry—occasionally attributed to Vallandigham—of the Democratic Party during much of the war. Sometimes the phrases were in reverse order. It was a call for reunification without a change in the status of slavery. It was a strange cry, given that the first response of the Democrats to the secession crisis of 1860–61 had been to try to change the Constitution in ways designed to conciliate the South. Those plans centered on pursuit of a compromise way to treat the slavery issue in the new states. The plans failed to get enacted or to appease the secessionists.

Vallandigham had his own proposal. He put it forth on February 20, after the Deep South states had seceded, but before others had. He didn't gather a committee together, as others were doing in search of a solution to the crisis. He didn't even seek co-sponsors, though that was done in his day. He just sat down and drafted something. The purpose of it would be to convince Southerners that nothing like the anti-slavery movement could ever rise again.

What he offered was a compromise not between North and South, not between Republicans and Democrats, but, really, between the Constitution and the Articles of Confederation. The Articles lacked a strong executive and strong central government.

For Vallandigham, the problem at hand was that a regional candidate had been elected president, and his party controlled Congress. That situation represented a flaw in the Constitution. Under it, a majority movement in the larger of the two sections could have too much power. He said, "the framers of the Constitution—and I speak it reverently—...mistook wholly the real dangers to the system."[1] Never mind that he had spent years touting their brilliance in handling the slavery issue, and would spend more years doing that. He now said they worried about big states dominating small ones, when the great threat turned out to be one section dominating another.

"In like manner, too," he continued, "they seem to have utterly under-estimated SLAVERY as a disturbing element in the system, possibly because it existed still in almost every State, but chiefly because the growth and manufacture of cotton had scarce yet been commenced in the United States." Because of that growth, the use of slave labor had burgeoned in the South.

The Founders also gave way too much power to the presidency, he said. Its resulting "patronage (and) influence (were) altogether under estimated." And he pointed to various other "inherent defects ... which no human sagacity could have foreseen ... which have led to evils, mischiefs and abuses."

Vallandigham proposed an amendment beginning, "The United States are divided into four sections, as follows"[2]: There would have been official North, South, West and Pacific sections. To be elected president, a candidate would have to win not only the majority of Electoral College votes, but a majority of those votes in every section. If nobody accomplished that, the election would go to the House of Representatives, where a candidate would have to win a majority of states in each section.

The proposal would also have changed the operation of the Senate in the same direction: Any piece of legislation would require the votes of a majority of senators from each section (if one-third of the senators in any section demanded that). These provisions would weaken the presidency and federal government as threats to slavery.

This was not amending the Constitution; this was re-writing it. But Vallandigham wasn't done. He offered two other amendments. One would specify how a state might secede (a subject the Constitution neglected): by getting the approval of all the other states in its section. Vallandigham argued that secession would have been deterred if a formal secession process had been in place, as opposed to states simply announcing a decision.

Vallandigham's third amendment would have established the right of all new states to have slavery.

Under his plan, there could be no President Lincoln, because the South would never vote for him. An entity like the Republican Party could still elect senators. Indeed, it could still hold a majority in the Senate (not to mention the House, which would not be touched by the Vallandigham amendments). But the majority could not do anything that was anti-slavery.

Vallandigham's proposals were as revolutionary as the actual postwar 13th, 14th and 15th Amendments turned out to be, though in the opposite direction. He made no small plans. In defense of the sweeping nature of his plan and of its inconsistency with various views he expressed, this must be said: These were revolutionary, unstable times. In the 1860s, a lot of people changed their minds about a lot. Lincoln himself said in 1862, "The dogmas of the quiet past are inadequate to the stormy present."[3] And he adopted emancipation, which he had long rejected.

Vallandigham's rewrite of the Constitution was bold, thoughtful and creative. He made an effort to get off the beaten political path and offer a course that others had never considered. It was an honest effort to avoid war, if at the cost of preserving slavery. And if it promised to make him a latter-day Founding Father, well, that was a price he was willing to pay.

But it was DOA. For one thing, of course, it was a bomb thrown at the majority party. That's not a promising way to begin the Constitutional amendment process, which requires enormous support to succeed. For another, it was just way too much. Such a redo of the hallowed document would require some serious contemplation. But there was no time. States were seceding. For another, he was elevating sectionalism, hardening it, making it official, fostering sectional thinking at the expense of national thinking. To the Republicans, the fact that such an idea came from somebody sympathetic to secession—that is, hostile to the Union—seemed to make perfect sense, whatever his past take on sectionalism.

The idea was never—or virtually never—taken up by anybody else, North or South, Democrat or Republican. Vallandigham was to complain that the problem was that his proposal was originally misreported over the wires as a call for "four distinct nationalities," meaning nations. He said that interpretation had taken hold.[4] There is truth to this. But the reason it had taken hold was that nobody corrected it; nobody fought for Vallandigham's plan.

Perhaps the clearest measure of the lead-balloon quality of the proposal was that Vallandigham was able throughout the war to claim that his strong commitment was to "the Union as it is; the Constitution as it was," as if he had never offered his constitutional rewrite. It had disappeared.

If politics is the art of the possible, Vallandigham was no artist. The impracticality present in his talk of Western secession showed up again here. It was a pattern. Like John Brown, he was big with the big ideas, not so much with follow through.

***

Before Confederate forces bombarded Fort Sumter on April 12, 1861, starting the war, Northern public opinion was scattered as to how to respond to secession. Party positions hadn't congealed. One widely heard suggestion in both parties was to simply "let them go." It's a free country, after all. How can we square the idea of freedom with coerced membership in it? Anyway, we're talking about too wide a swath of land and too many people. We couldn't possibly control all that, at least not without becoming some sort of military dictatorship.

Horace Greeley, editor of the New York *Daily Tribune*, which was distributed nationally and had the largest newspaper circulation in the nation, said to the South "Go in peace." He is often identified as an abolitionist. But he said, "We hope never to live in a republic whereof one section is pinned to the residue by bayonets."[5] Some have suggested that he saw himself as calling the South's bluff, but that is not known.

Sumter changed everything. Of course, the attack didn't come out of the blue. The build-up had been long. There were those who said Lincoln could have and should have given up the fort, rather than try, as he did, to re-supply it. Many, including Vallandigham called for a negotiated settlement.

But when Confederate forces attacked, that mooted debate about the merits of war. This *was* war. What kind of nation doesn't fight back when its troops are attacked? Those troops were sent originally to protect Charleston itself against foreign enemies. This was an outrage.

Here's Pulitzer Prize winning historian James McPherson on the post–Sumter atmosphere and Lincoln's call for troops: "The response from free states was overwhelming. War meetings in every city and village cheered the flag and vowed vengeance on traitors.... From Ohio and the West came 'one great Eagle-scream' for the flag."[6]

Rage at the South—far more than thoughts about slavery or about the survival of the last, best hope for democracy—brought Lincoln overwhelming bipartisan support. Particularly notable was Stephen A. Douglas. Lincoln's longtime foe—his main opponent in the 1860 election—was fine with the spread of slavery, but he was now more hawkish than Lincoln. On the day after Ft. Sumter was fired upon, Douglas met at the White House with Lincoln for two hours. He recommended that Lincoln raise 200,000 troops, not the 75,000 Lincoln was calling for. He suggested fortifying other federal sites the Confederates might attack. He said publicly, "There can be no neutrals in this war, only patriots or traitors."[7]

Douglas died on June 3 of natural causes, including a liver issue, at 48. He didn't live long enough for any great public estrangement between him and Vallandigham to surface. But Vallandigham utterly rejected Douglas's stance and the post–Sumter consensus.

Douglas had so much stature in party—especially in death—that Vallandigham pretended he was doing Douglas's work. Before Sumter, Douglas had been engaged in congressional efforts to find a compromise. In that period, he said, "War is disunion. War is final, eternal separation." Vallandigham and other Copperheads would emphasize his push for compromise in claiming to uphold his cause. They boldly ignored the post–Sumter Lincoln-Douglas détente.

Vallandigham rose to deliver a much-anticipated address in the House of Representatives on July 10, in an extra session of Congress. No major battles had happened. The July 8 edition of Greeley's *Tribune* gives a good idea of the state of public opinion. The edition had several pieces denouncing as traitors people who were so much as calling for compromise with the South. (One of those pieces was by Greeley, who had come a long way from "go in peace.") Those articles didn't mention who these traitors were. The writers couldn't have come up with many recognizable names besides Vallandigham.

He was mentioned in four other articles. Three of those offered different (though not conflicting) details about a Vallandigham episode: He had visited Ohio troops outside Washington the previous day, and had been greeted badly. There was reportedly a hanging in effigy, and there were stones thrown. He insisted to the troops that he was "as good a Union man as any of them," and he criticized their "mob spirit." He showed "nerve and courage" according to one report and apparently benefited from protection by a unit from Dayton.

The fourth piece mentioning Vallandigham said that he had been present at a caucus of House Democrats that same day and had "intimated that he preferred the preservation of the Union." The paper said he "received little sympathy," meaning that his colleagues weren't buying his claim that he had been misrepresented by the press when treated as anti–Union. The article reported that all the others present favored prosecution of the war.

One perspective on the atmosphere surrounding Vallandigham's speech was offered in a collection of his speeches that he put together for the 1863 campaign. The book's introduction to this speech is unsigned, but was written very much in Vallandigham's style and most likely by him. It most certainly had his approval.

It said: "No speech was ever delivered in the midst of greater personal danger—not even Cicero's defense of Milo. The galleries were filled with an excited soldiery and infuriated partisans threatening assassination. A leading Abolition newspaper in New York had, two days before, declared that, if an attempt was made to speak for peace, 'the aisles of the Hall would run with blood.'" (The archives of the *Tribune* and *The New York Times*—the two Republican papers in New York City that everybody thought you meant when you mentioned an abolition paper in New York—have no such words I could find on those days. But Greeley did write that any such speech would be political suicide. Another piece in the *Tribune* said "the spirit of the soldiers and the people will bear with no treason," meaning views like Vallandigham's.)

The introduction to the written version of Vallandigham's speech continued, "Almost without sympathy upon his own side of the House, and with a fierce, insolent, and overwhelming majority upon the other side, Mr. Vallandigham, calm and unawed, met every peril, and spoke as firmly, solemnly, and earnestly as under ordinary circumstances.... Some three hundred thousand copies of the speech, in various forms, were published and circulated in the United States. It was published, also, in England and on the Continent."[8]

In the speech itself, Vallandigham castigated *everything* about Lincoln's handling of the war. He used the word "every" himself. He said, "I assert here, today ... that every principal act of the administration since (Fort Sumter) has been a glaring usurpation of power, and a palpable and dangerous violation of" the Constitution.[9]

Vallandigham called his speech "Executive Usurpation," and he waxed on that theme. His first example of executive excess was the closing of Southern ports through a naval blockade. He said this couldn't be justified as an act of war, because Congress hadn't declared war. Apparently self-conscious about being a Jacksonian decrying executive power—given that Andrew Jackson was often accused of taking executive power to excess—Vallandigham took up the Nullification Crisis of 1832-'33. South Carolina had insisted on its right to ignore a federal tariff. Jackson considered blockading the port of Charleston, but didn't.

Said Vallandigham, "Jackson! Jackson, sir! The great Jackson! did not dare do it without authority of Congress. But our Jackson of today, the little Jackson at the other end of the avenue, and the mimic Jacksons around him, do." Of course, in the Jackson episode, South Carolina hadn't fired on American troops.[10]

In entertaining the following list of criticisms of Lincoln, it is not necessary to be familiar with all of Vallandigham's references. What may be necessary is a deep breath. He excoriated Lincoln for the fact that soldiers had, without the consent of owners, taken up housing in private homes; for federal interference in the governance of Maryland (which was contemplating secession); for censorship of the telegraph wires and for infringement on the right to bear arms. He asked, "if all these things ... have been done in the first two months ... what may we not expect to see in three years?"

He said the right of free speech had "repeatedly" been denied. (He was mainly referring to events in border states.) He predicted that the free press and the right to petition would fall next. He said, "Freedom of religion will yield, too," suggesting that clergymen would be obliged to support the war.

He predicted the coming of "gigantic and stupendous peculation (embezzlement), anarchy first, and a strong government afterward—no more State lines, no more State government, and a consolidated monarchy or vast centralized military despotism." Democracy would be dead. The states would be dead. The whole American thing would be pretty much over.

He spoke of the "folly and mismanagement of the war so far." He said later revelations might reveal that the war was being fought as the result of a "deliberate conspiracy (by Republicans) to overthrow the present form of ... government, and to establish a strong centralized Government in its stead." He talked, too, of a possible "daring (Republican) plot to foster and promote secession."

He continued, "(W)hatever their purposes now (in fighting the war), I rather think that, in the beginning they rushed heedlessly and headlong into the gulf, believing that ... the display of vigor in re-enforcing Sumter ... and in calling out seventy-five thousand militia, upon the firing of the first gun ... would not, on the one hand, precipitate a crisis, while, upon the other, it would satisfy (the administration's) own violent partisans, and thus revive and restore the falling fortunes of the Republican party."

There was something to that. Throughout the secession crisis, some Republicans had pressed upon Lincoln the need to appear resolute, lest he lose support in the North.[11]

Vallandigham wasn't done listing. He said Lincoln used the war for patronage purposes, appointing "a horde of forlorn, worn-out, and broken-down politicians of his own party ... (as officers) without any limit as to the numbers."

He said the "great" question of civil war had never been submitted to Congress. Lincoln had addressed this point a week earlier than Vallandigham, in his July 4 message to Congress. Congress had not been in session when he acted. Calling it into session would be no minor, quickly accomplished thing. He said, "These measures"—calling for troops, borrowing money—"whether strictly legal or not, were ventured upon, under what appeared to be a popular demand, and a public necessity, trusting, then as now, that Congress would readily ratify them."[12]

Another Vallandigham complaint deserves special attention, because, with time, it became central to his story. It was about Lincoln's suspension of the writ of *habeas corpus*. That is the constitutional provision—inherited from British law—requiring that when a person is arrested, the arresting authorities must be willing to bring him or her to court and convince a judge that they have legitimate legal reasons for the arrest.

In the first weeks of the war, Maryland state legislator John Merryman was arrested by the army for attempting to hinder the movement of Union troops from Baltimore to Washington. With Merryman being held at Fort McHenry, his lawyer invoked his *habeas corpus* rights. But Lincoln decided to suspend those rights. Chief Justice Roger Taney ordered the prisoner released. Lincoln didn't release him and didn't respond to Taney. But in his July 4 message to Congress Lincoln defended his right to suspend the writ in an emergency. The power of the government to do that is, indeed, explicit in the Constitution, but it's in the article about Congress. Lincoln argued that it must be an executive power, because it is about an emergency, and Congress is frequently not in session.

Vallandigham was, judging from his words, utterly mortified. He argued that, first of all, Merryman—not being in the military—was not answerable to military authorities and could not be arrested by them.

"A private citizen ... is seized in his own house, in the dead hour of night ... by a band of armed soldiers, under the verbal orders of a military chief, and is ruthlessly torn from his wife and his children and hurried off to a fortress of the United States." To this point, his description is one that could have been applied to his own arrest two years later. But there was a special element in the Merryman arrest that no polemicist in Vallandigham's position could have resisted.

"And that fortress, as if in mockery, the very one over whose ramparts had floated that star-spangled banner immortalized in song by the patriot prisoner, who, 'By the dawn's early light,' saw its folds gleaming amid the wreck of battle, and invoked the blessings of heaven upon it, and prayed that it might long wave 'O'er the land of the free, and home of the brave.'"

Then Vallandigham offered a description of Taney, renowned then as the father of the now-notorious Dred Scott decision holding that black people (slave or free) had no rights that white people were obliged to honor. Vallandigham incorporated a quote from Daniel Webster about Founding Father John Jay.

"And, sir," Vallandigham said, "when the highest judicial officer of the land, the Chief Justice of the Supreme Court, upon whose shoulders, 'when the judicial ermine fell, it touched nothing not as spotless as itself,' the aged, the venerable, the gentle and pure-minded Taney, who...." Vallandigham's sentence had another 134 words extolling Taney and the writ. And it wasn't his last sentence on the subject.

When Vallandigham moved on to a critique of points Lincoln had made against secessionists, he said, "He forgets the still stronger case against the abolitionists and disunionists of the North and West. He omits to tell us that secession and disunion had a New England origin and began in Massachusetts, in 1804, at the time of the Louisiana purchase."

Some New Englanders did, indeed, oppose the Louisiana Purchase, fearing that the new states would identify with Virginia, not New England, and that the very nature of the country would be changed. Former Secretary of State Thomas Pickering proposed secession.[13] Later, as Vallandigham noted, the War of 1812 occasioned another secessionist movement in New England, partly because the war entailed an embargo on trade with England, which hit New England hard.

In truth, secession was never really a dirty word until after the Civil War. Various parties had flirted with it, including the Southern Democrats in the aforementioned South Carolina crisis over trade in the 1830s.

When Vallandigham and his political comrades looked at Republicans, they saw Federalists. The Federalists had been the dominant party in post–Revolutionary New England. They had promoted a strong central government and were opposed by the Jeffersonian, state-rights oriented forerunners of Vallandigham's Democrats. Many Jeffersonians suspected the Federalists of monarchical or dictatorial leanings. Under the last Federalist president, John Adams, the government had enacted the Alien and Seditions Acts to limit the freedoms of its critics. When some restrictions returned under Lincoln, Vallandigham portrayed the latter-day Federalists—not the war—as the reason.

Vallandigham had elsewhere insisted that the Federalists were the first ones to make a major fuss over slavery, when the issue was the admission of Missouri as a slave state in 1820.[14]

***

Uncompromising as Vallandigham's anti–Lincoln speech seems, it might entail one huge compromise: It did not call for letting the South go. In a letter about 10 days after Ft. Sumter, Vallandigham had written, "It is too late now for any thing except peaceable separation."[15] Afterward, Vallandigham bitterly insisted he did not hold that view and had never held it. In a letter to the Cincinnati *Enquirer* on August 20, 1861, he wrote and emphasized, "I NEVER, either in my place in the House of Representatives, or *anywhere else*, said any thing of the kind. It is a part of that mass of falsehood created and set afloat so persistently for the last few years."[16] Yet the "peaceable separation" letter—to the Rev. Sabin Hough, a pro-slavery writer—appears in James Vallandigham's worshipful biography of brother Clement.

Maybe the letter to Sabin captured only a passing mood. Or maybe by July Vallandigham had simply come to terms with post–Sumter public opinion. It looks like his willingness to buck the national tide knew its limits. There was simply no apparent constituency for letting the South go.

Obviously, Vallandigham did think in political terms. One clue about that comes from a young acolyte named Tom Lowe, into whose story we delve later. Lowe wrote to a friend in the South after Vallandigham's post–Sumter speech:

"I asked him what he expected his political future to be. He said he did not know and was not at all uneasy on the subject. If the Union *is* restored"—meaning through negotiation, with the survival of slavery—"he would have millions of friends South who would not forget him. If (the Union) is dissolved, the North will say he was not far wrong and that the war has been in vain, just as he said it would be."[17] Vallandigham apparently did not see any point in contemplating the possibility of a Union victory and reunification without slavery.

What Vallandigham said to Lowe was pretty explosive, should it have come to light, which it never did. Any public indication that Vallandigham cared during the war about being popular in the South would have been damaging. The Lowe letter raises the possibility that Vallandigham had thoughts about being president. There might have been other reasons for caring about his popularity in the South, but the presidency is the one that suggests itself.

6

Defending Himself

An ode to Vallandigham:

> *Vile traitor to the blood our fathers spilt for thee,*
> *And dark inheritor of Arnold's infamy;*
> *List to the hiss of moral serpents in thy breast,*
> *Lapping their forky tongues of treason from their nest,*
> *And spawning in thy heart's tartarian cell,*
> *New gems to make thee worthy of a hell.*

(The Tartars or Tatars were allies of Genghis Khan.)

This poetry is attributed to a Republican editor in San Francisco. It showed up in the Republican Dayton *Journal* on March 5, 1862. The above is the first half. The second part ends—hitting Vallandigham where he lived—*"Making thee hissed and hated through all coming time."*

Vallandigham was likened to Benedict Arnold as often as Trump to Nixon. The Ohioan became the favorite whipping boy of the national Republican press, which was deeply into whipping. Typically the charge was some form of treason, often with all sorts of ugly words surrounding that ugly word, as in the poem. But any other charge that might be made was made as well. One—spurious—was that he didn't support his widowed mother.[1]

It was an article of faith among Vallandigham's supporters that he was the most widely and unfairly abused man, not simply of his time, but of all time. The Cincinnati *Enquirer* typically said in 1862 that Vallandigham had faced "a storm of abuse, obloquy, slander and denunciation from every Abolition (meaning Republican) print and every Abolition orator from Maine to California, which in fury was probably never equaled."[2] The alleged unfairness of it all became a theme of Democratic newspapers.

Vallandigham, having gone out of his way to be the first, most visible and most provocative opponent of the war, claimed to revel in the abuse, playing the martyr. He said about himself in a speech in Columbus, "Had you believed reports of the Republican Press, you would, no doubt, have expected to see, probably, the most extraordinary compound of leprous and unsightly flesh and blood ever exhibited."[3] As will be seen, his private correspondence showed that he resented the abuse deeply.

The traducing of Vallandigham became a congressional issue. By early 1862, a paper called the Baltimore *South* had been shut down by the authorities for its political views, given Lincoln's great concern about the slave state of Maryland going

6. Defending Himself

Confederate. Then, on February 19, 1862, the rival Baltimore *Clipper* had this item about the *South,* mentioning various Democrats:

> DOCUMENTS FOUND: During yesterday a police force visited the office of the *South* newspaper and took possession of a number of letters, written by Senators BAYARD and SAULSBURY, of Delaware and the notorious VALLANDIGHAM, of Ohio. The documents contain touching sentiments"—that's sarcasm—"of poor bleeding Dixie, and various suggestions how the Yankee might be defeated."

That was it. The blurb was universally interpreted to say that some or all of the three men named had referred to "bleeding Dixie" (a term interpreted as suggesting Southern sympathies) and had suggested ways the South might win the war.

On the day the article appeared, Vallandigham went to the floor of the House to correct the record. But when he got there he found that he and the item were already the subject of discussion. Rep. John Hickman, of Pennsylvania, the chairman of the Judiciary Committee, had introduced the blurb to the House, with the recommendation that his committee undertake an investigation into Vallandigham's loyalty. The House could expel Vallandigham if he was found disloyal. It would take a two-thirds vote.

No sooner had Hickman broached the idea of an investigation when Vallandigham spoke up. He said, "I was just waiting for the opportunity to call the attention of the House to (the newspaper item) myself, having just received it from some unknown source a moment ago."[4] Apparently this ambiguous, undocumented newspaper blurb was part of the talk of Capitol Hill in this week when Gen. Ulysses Grant took Fort Donelson in Tennessee for the first big Northern win in the West and demanded "unconditional surrender," earning the nickname. (It was also the day before little Willie Lincoln died in the White House.)[5]

Vallandigham denied everything: never said "bleeding Dixie"; never discussed how the South might win. He said he had never written anything about politics to the Baltimore *South*. He also said he had never written anything to anybody in the Confederacy. "It is false, infamous, scandalous, and it is beyond endurance, too, that a man's reputation shall be at the mercy of every scavenger (and) a mere local editor of an irresponsible newspaper," he said. How could a congressional investigation be justified by something so wrong, so flimsy, so undocumented?

Hickman, a man known for having physically wrestled with two Virginia legislators as they rolled down the steps of the Capitol, responded by noting Vallandigham's reputation: "(T)he gentleman from Ohio ... knows that the suspicions which have existed against him—I do not say whether justly or unjustly—have been numerous, and in circulation for a long time past. It is the duty of the House to purge itself of unworthy members." He insisted the blurb seemed to be from a "responsible" source. He also cited a rule of the House that "common fame"—that is, the word on the street—"is a good ground" for an investigation.

Vallandigham took that as an opportunity to get beyond the charges of that blurb to others that had been swirling around him. He was loaded for bear, but he didn't want to bring up matters on the floor that others hadn't. So he baited Hickman. He asked him if he had ever heard of any "specific item on which any such suspicions (of his disloyalty) ever rested."

HICKMAN: Yes, sir.
VALLANDIGHAM: Well, let us have it.
HICKMAN: I have heard a thousand.
VALLANDIGHAM: Name a single one.
HICKMAN: I do not desire to do any injustice....

But Hickman also said, "I will reply to it directly," meaning Vallandigham's invitation. As the debate went along, he raised several charges against Vallandigham. The transcript in the *Congressional Globe* reads as if people were providing them to him as he spoke.

Hickman mentioned something called "the Breckinridge meeting" in Baltimore, which, he said, "gave rise to very many suspicions." And he brought up "a certain dinner in Kentucky" which he believed the newspapers said was in Vallandigham's honor. He also mentioned Vallandigham's anti–Lincoln speech of July 1861. Hickman said the speech "gave rise to a great many suspicions." (Later in this exchange he said that speech gave rise to thoughts of expelling Vallandigham back then.)

He continued: "And I appeal to every member of the House (as to) whether they have not heard suspicion upon suspicion against the loyalty (of Vallandigham).... I allege that it is a common rumor in the northern states.... (T)he gentlemen from Ohio is, at least, open to grave suspicions, if not direct imputation. That is my answer. Now I will hear the gentleman."

Vallandigham went to the specifics. He said that he hadn't been in Kentucky—a neutral border slave state with strong secessionist factions—since 1852, for Henry Clay's funeral. He said he had more recently been invited—by Union loyalists—but didn't go. As for a "Breckenridge meeting," he said he had never attended one in Baltimore or anywhere else. (John C. Breckenridge was the Southern Democratic candidate for president in 1860. He joined the Confederacy, serving as a general and then war secretary.[6])

Vallandigham apparently was worried that Hickman wouldn't mention one of the charges the Ohioan wanted to refute: He was reputed to have said that any Northern troops marching to the South through his district would have do it over his "dead body." Vallandigham brought up the charge himself, called it "absurd" and said "I denied it then, and I will not repeat the denial now" in what certainly sounded like a repetition of the denial.

The Dayton *Journal* had published the "dead body" story in December of 1860, saying the statement had been made at a bipartisan meeting of the Ohio congressional delegation designed to head off secession. The meeting had been called by Republican Tom Corwin, the senior member of the delegation. Vallandigham reportedly dissented from the very purpose of the meeting, saying secession was the South's business. And he went further, offering the "dead body" line and stormed out.[7]

The story was presumably given to the Republican paper by an unnamed Republican who was at the meeting. The "dead body" line doesn't quite ring true. It conflicts with Vallandigham's policy of hassling the authorities, not the troops (who he thought were mainly Democrats). It would have been ill-advised for a politician seeking enough mainstream acceptance to win elections. There is no other indication he was ready for civil disobedience (and jail) in opposition to the war. Of course, it's possible that he said something like that in the heat of an argument, then immediately regretted it. But he was pretty cool in debate.

In the Hickman confrontation, Vallandigham went on to deny another charge unmade by Hickman but widely made elsewhere: that he preferred peace to union, that is, that he would let the South go in peace. He said no evidence existed to sustain the charge; he wanted a negotiated re-union, not separation. As for Vallandigham's anti–Lincoln speech, Vallandigham dared Hickman to cite one disloyal sentiment in it. Also, he asserted that he would defend any vote he had cast.

Vallandigham expressed shock that charges of disloyalty could be made against "one who has bowed down and worshipped this holy emblem (the flag) of the Constitution and of the Old Union of these states (with) his heart's core." He went on in that vein. And he said "you will wait long" before you come across "something I have written, or something I have said that would indicate anything in my bosom" contrary to love of country. Inevitably, he counter-charged with the very charge against him. I "hurl it back defiantly," he said of the notion that he was the one undermining the nation. It was the anti-slavery agitators who had always done that. "Yet I am to be singled out now by these very men or their minions." He said his enemies had "wished, prayed that they might find some" unguarded remark or other mistake in his words.

Hickman started to say that he had found the anti–Lincoln speech disloyal. But before he got specific, somebody apparently offered him another piece of information. He said, "As the gentleman has called upon me (to provide specifics), I will answer further. Does he not know of a camp in Kentucky having been called by his name—that disloyal men there called the camp Camp Vallandigham? That would not indicate that in Kentucky, they regarded him as a man loyal to the Federal Union."

Vallandigham: "Is there not a town—and it may be a camp, too—in Kentucky by the name of Hickman?" A Camp Vallandigham had, indeed, been mentioned in newspapers (specifically in *The New York Times* in a piece by a Cincinnati newspaper man).[8] But the alleged camp faded from the news, as if, perhaps, it had never existed.

Finally, Hickman withdrew: "I have submitted this resolution"—calling for an investigation—"as a matter of justice to the gentleman from Ohio, and I am astonished that he had regarded it (as) a charge against him.... (W)hat better opportunity can be afforded to vindicate himself? ... But, as the gentleman from Ohio has expressed more loyal sentiment today than I have heard him express since the meeting of the present Congress, I am willing that he should go before the country.... Devotion to the Union is all I ask. I withdraw my resolution for the present."

Vallandigham was ecstatic. He wrote to his wife the next day: "You see by the papers this morning, I presume, that Hickman and I had a *bout* in the House yesterday. You will see it in full in the *Globe*, but cannot realise the scene.... I was never more gratified in my life with any result. In an instant *every* Democrat in the House took fire, resenting it"—that is, the attack on Vallandigham—"as an outrage upon himself. Corning was much excited, and old Governor Crittenden was deeply interested, and was just taking the floor for a speech in my behalf when Hickman surrendered and withdrew his resolution. I never spoke or bore myself better in my life—so all say, and so I believe too—though it was a sudden emergency. Many Republicans complimented me, and last night all the Democrats of the House, except a few who could not get out, called round and spent an hour or so in congratulation. It was a signal triumph; but the truth in regard to it will not find its way into the newspapers. Very probably it will be all misrepresented. But some day the country will understand it…. They will let me alone by-and-bye."[9]

Wrong. They never let him alone. Two months later, Ben Wade, Ohio's fire-breathing anti-slavery U.S. senator, characterized Vallandigham as "a man who never had any sympathy with this Republic, but whose every breath is devoted to its destruction just as a far as his heart dare permit him to go."[10]

Wade was a Radical Republican, finding Lincoln too restrained in his views about slavery, the South and the Democrats. He was chairman of a House-Senate military oversight committee that was giving Lincoln fits with criticisms of his generals. (The Stephen Spielberg movie *Lincoln* has a scene at a White House evening gathering in which Mary Lincoln says, "It's permissible to smile, Senator," and the senator responds, "I believe I am smiling, Madam." That's Wade.)

He was much like a modern liberal. Although the Republican Party of that day is the one that is most attractive to most modern liberals, it was also emerging as the party of business. However, Wade's biographer said "all his life he affirmed his belief that the aim of government was the protection of the weak from the strong. In keeping with this conviction, he championed the Negro, fought for the abolition of imprisonment for debt, interested himself in the protection of individual investors in corporations, advocated for free land for settlers, demanded a fair deal for the laboring man and supported woman suffrage."[11] On the last point, among others, he was way ahead of many Republicans, even some staunchly anti-slavery people.

Vallandigham responded to Wade furiously, calling him a "liar, a scoundrel and a coward."[12] That resulted in a debate in the House about whether Vallandigham should be censured for a too-personal attack on a legislator, but he wasn't.[13]

The exchange underlined a crucial characteristic of Ohio politics: When Vallandigham emerged to run statewide, he would not be doing so in Copperhead country. The philosophical spectrum from Wade to Vallandigham was pretty much the entire Northern spectrum. The fact that the left wing of the Republican Party and the right wing of the Democratic Party were both potent in Ohio was a statement about what was happening in the country and about how Ohio mirrored the country.

7

Love Among the Polarized

An editorial in the Dayton *Journal,* September 12, 1863:

> The stilt-mania has attracted our youngsters in full force. Everywhere we see the boys locomoting on stilts.... We cannot encourage their use. They are rather dangerous than otherwise. We have reliable information of boys falling with them; and in several instances these accidents have been attended with consequences so serious as broken arms, and badly bruised heads.... We recommend their discontinuance, and the substitution of marbles, ball, or almost any other play, in their stead. Some parents will act upon our kindly suggestion, while its full force will not, probably, be felt by others until they have a broken arm or leg or some other accident brought into the house.

In the North (not the South), life went on. It was different from the pre-war years, of course. Many young and not-so-young men were gone, though not nearly all. In Dayton as at other places, people went down to the newspaper offices regularly to check the battle casualty lists posted outside. Sometimes the latest dispatches were read out loud to those who came by.[1] Everybody knew somebody who was suffering. News and talk were about the war. Activities were often about the war, in the form, say, of charity drives for widows and orphaned children, or in the form of somehow pitching in to serve the troops as they passed through town and needed a good meal or something.

But people worked at civilian jobs, as before, at the hardware store or bank or law office. They worked farms, growing all manner of crops, including, around Dayton, tobacco. They socialized. They went to plays, lectures, circuses and concerts by such as the Christy Minstrels. Artemus Ward—something like a stand-up comic—would come through town. The occasional horse race was held—and covered by the newspapers.[2] There were "celebrated pugilists," sometimes appearing in the same venue (on different days) as plays or lectures.[3] In early February of 1863, as controversy was swirling about the just-enacted Emancipation Proclamation, *Uncle Tom's Cabin* was showing in Dayton. The *Journal* assured readers that this production was better than one that had shown in town earlier.[4] *Our American Cousin*, the play the Lincolns went to see at Ford's Theatre, played in Dayton the week before the assassination. It was performed by a different company, one out of Lexington, Kentucky, that put on about nine different plays over nine nights.[5]

Newspapers were full of ads for clothing stores—announcing that the latest fashions from New York had arrived—and for patent medicines, foods, legal services and printing services (offered by the newspaper itself). Bookstores would list the specific new books they had for sale; Victor Hugo's *Les Miserables* was big during the war.

In September of 1861, as the war was heating up, a state fair was held in Dayton. One day saw 25,000 tickets sold, though the "exhibition itself" was not nearly as good as the previous year, according to one critic. Meanwhile, 700 men were taking military training at a Camp Corwin, just outside of town to the east. And news arrived of a local man dying in a battle in what is now West Virginia.[6]

The economy took a major hit in Ohio at the beginning of the war as Southern markets were cut off. But it gradually improved as people adjusted, finding business partners to the east who had also lost Southern markets. Some people in Ohio even took to growing cotton.[7] And war contracts kicked in. Overall, the Northern economy actually grew in important measures during the war, dramatically unlike the South's.[8]

The Dayton *Journal* wrote on November 12, 1862: "We are assured"—by businessmen—"that ... the general trade of the city has been remarkably good, and some houses report a better demand for goods than they have enjoyed for some years past. The people buy freely for cash.... If customers cannot sate themselves in the numerous fine stores on Main and Third streets, it will be because they are at fault, not the stocks.... (T)he mass of the people are not in want." The piece went on to refer to a local wholesaler and a dry goods store as the "palatial establishments of Darst, Herschelrode & Co. and Perrine, Lytle & Shaw."[9] Of course, these various stores were the paper's advertisers. And, yes, the *Journal* was a Republican paper trying to minimize the negative impacts of the war. But its accounts jibe with reality.

The next month, the *Journal* ran an article saying new buildings were being erected, factories and machine were "all ready," jobs were plentiful and, while inflation was happening, wages were rising, too.[10]

The Cincinnati *Gazette* said that city had become a "great supply depot." Cannons, Gatling guns, gunboats, ambulances and more came out of Cincinnati.[11]

But the political situation was decidedly hot. That showed up in, for example, church life, which was vibrant in Dayton. Vallandigham complained bitterly about the churches as early as 1855. He said that "nineteen-twentieths of Northern pulpits resound every Sabbath, in sermon or prayer, with imprecation upon slaveholders."[12] It wasn't his imagination, by wartime, at least. In 1862, the Dayton *Journal* said the churches "as a unit" opposed slavery.[13] When the *Journal* acknowledged that there were exceptions, it denounced a pastor who declined to take a political position, seeing him as "like a spiritual eunuch, as he is devoid of a conscience or a spark of manly patriotism."[14]

In 1862, Vallandigham was paraphrased accurately as saying "the Churches had departed from the doctrines of Christ and him crucified, and taken up the negro and him glorified!" He said, "There will be no Union, no peace, no hope, no country, until you drive out those who have defiled the temple of the Savior of mankind, and restore the gospel in its purity."[15] He accused his opponents of being engaged in an "unholy and most unconstitutional crusade against the South."[16]

A convention of Democrats in Democratic Butler County (in Vallandigham's district) in 1863 held "that the (Northern) clergy of the present day are the devil's select and inspired representatives, preaching hate, envy, malice, vengeance, blood and murder."[17] One prominent Democratic politician called for a state convention "for the purpose of devising some plan for a new church organization in which Democrats may enjoy the privilege of ... the pure gospel ... unmixed with abolition and fanaticism, and without being insulted and denounced from the pulpit as disloyal."[18]

The war gradually became more intrusive. In April 1862 a battle at Shiloh, Tennessee, shocked the nation with its bloodiest two days ever: 24,000 casualties between the two sides. In August, the Antietam battle in Maryland saw almost that many casualties in just 12 hours. The North's biggest loss was the hope that the war might be short, a hope that had much life just before Shiloh because of a string of Northern successes.

In Dayton, at various negative turns in the war, local men would put out a call for volunteers; the *Journal* would encourage enlistment; the town would provide a place for encampments.

Meanwhile, political tensions rose to the point that both newspapers in Dayton worried about being physically attacked by partisans of the other party. Such assaults had happened elsewhere.

As the possibility of emancipation got more and more attention, a white mob was reported to have attacked black people in Madison Township, outside Dayton, as mobs had attacked blacks elsewhere.[19]

The worst news yet occurred in the fall of 1862, when the possibility arose of the Confederates invading Ohio through Cincinnati. (More on that below.)

However, among the activities that did not cease in Dayton was courtship. The story of one survives and offers insight into the nature of civilian life during the war. The man was Daniel Lucien Medlar, an impressively well-read hardware store clerk and avid student of current affairs. He had been born in Pennsylvania, but his family moved to Miamisburg, about 10 miles southwest Dayton. The Medlars owned land there. Lucien worked at J. Langdon and Brother Hardware Store as he tried to get started in his own business. The store was right in the middle of everything in Dayton, across from Courthouse Square—the site of many public political events. It was within a block of the newspaper offices and just about that close to the two main indoor venues for public events.[20]

When the war broke out, Lucien was about to turn 37 and was living alone at Phillips House, the main inn in town, which itself couldn't have been better located, being across from the south side of Courthouse Square, at the southwest corner of Third and Main. All manner of things happened there, including Abraham Lincoln's lunch on a day he visited Dayton.

Although Medlar belonged to a local militia group, it seldom trained, and he had developed a distaste for things military. He couldn't see himself in the military, and he never seems to have agonized over not enlisting, though many his age did fight.

We know about Lucien because he kept a journal. Most of its volumes have been lost. But one has had a remarkable life. Volume 4—covering the early part of the war years—was, according to a newspaper story from 1959, found in the mid–1950s in a "collection of scrap paper" in Franklin, Ohio, which is a few miles south of Miamisburg. It was rescued by the editor of the Franklin newspaper, Seymour B. Tibbals. When he died, his widow gave it to a fellow who worked for the *Dayton Daily News*, William L. Sanders. He donated it to the Dayton Public Library in 1960.

In 1970, Caroline Medlar happened to become a reference librarian there. Twenty years later, she was, of all things, the genealogy librarian. The genealogy people and the local history people worked closely together. One day the head of the local history department asked if Caroline was "related to the Medlar who wrote the Civil War era journal that was secured in the library safe." Caroline did not know about it, because it was uncatalogued.

Lucien turned out to be her husband's great, great, great uncle. She transcribed the diary, which is why a printed version of it sits on the shelves of the Dayton Metro Library (as it is now called), easily accessible to a researcher post–2010.

The information above is from Caroline Medlar's preface to the diary.[21] Other quotes from that book are scattered in this book, because Lucien was a pointed, informed, quotable observer of political and other public events and circumstances. He seemed to be in on much, just because he worked and lived at the center and was engaged. He'd come across an event happening at a public venue, and he'd pop in. He'd see a speech happening at the Courthouse and he'd stop to listen. He'd dine at the Phillips and take note of others there, including visitors passing through. Public and semi-public figures would shop at his store, and he'd strike up conversations. Or just hear things.

But what's most striking is his own story.

When the war broke out, Lucien was one of a group of Democrats who would get together in the evenings at the Dayton *Empire*. Vallandigham was often present, because Congress was often not in session. One thing Lucien liked about the *Empire* office was that it had newspapers from out of town, as part of exchange programs. He had his own subscriptions—*Harper's Weekly* (a popular national publication which evolved from Democratic to Republican with the war), a widely circulated Copperhead weekly out of Columbus and more. But he also liked to see other papers, both Democratic and Republican. He wasn't active in political affairs, just a political junkie.

He read well beyond politics. Being committed to self-improvement, he was trying to read a Shakespearean play a day and apparently often succeeding. He would spend hours a day reading at what he called his "sanctum," his room at the Phillips. Sometimes, too, he would attend two sermons a day and record his reviews.

Making political friends in Dayton in 1860–1862 meant making enemies. Lucien had heard of a Democrat or two who had lost jobs with Republican employers under circumstances that looked political. He found himself having to deny at work being a "secessionist." Lucien used extreme terms in denouncing others: "one-idead hair-brained, fanatic Republicans and abolitionists," for example. And he made clear that he was not talking about some divisive figure in the news, but about people who talked to him "every day."[22] He would refer matter-of-factly to "Black Republicans,"[23] the common partisan denunciation. He wrote that many Republican journals, including the New York *Tribune*, were "barbarous, heathenish, in their rage for blood."[24]

Meanwhile, though he took extreme umbrage at the other side's equally harsh words. "We are denounced by the Black Republicans hereabouts as a band of traitors, secessionists and rascals, and for no other reason than that we entertain, and openly and boldly express our strong and unqualified disapproval of Abraham Lincoln's war policy."[25] He called the people making these charges against him "eves-dropping slanderers" and wrote that he defied them to prove their charges.[26]

And yet, six weeks after Ft. Sumter, he wrote of the guys who gathered at the *Empire*, "We are for a peaceable separation ... if nothing else will do to preserve peace," that is, if negotiations toward reunification fail.[27] Well, nobody was negotiating. Lucien clearly regretted that secession had happened; that's apparently what he meant when he furiously denied being a secessionist. But he was saying that the government should accept secession. He wrote, "We are for war only as the very last resort." That apparently meant only if the South attacked the North. In truth, he was—at this stage—at least as close to being a secessionist as many of the people he called abolitionists were to being abolitionists.

Earlier—a week after Fort Sumter—he made this proposal to his journal: "And we Democrats say that we will not engage in this fratricidal strife. We mean to force all the fanatical Republicans to go and meet in deadly conflict the men of the South whom they have this quarrel with, and there settle matters as best they can. We have no quarrel with our brethren of the South.... In this conflict, we intend to stand as armed neutrals."[28]

Lucien's girlfriend was Clara Soule, an artist whose work to this day is in the Dayton Art Institute. She was the daughter of another artist who had lived in Dayton and, like her, had specialized in portraits. She was also the art teacher at the Cooper Seminary, a school for girls. She was nine or ten years younger than Lucien. They had been engaged since 1854, when she was 20. He might have been delaying marriage until a day when his finances would be in better order.

In the early war years, Clara's business suffered. She was head of a household of five, and she greatly feared she was going to have to break it up, sending people to live with others. She was getting no help—indeed, only trouble—from her father, an alcoholic. Lucien promised to help her through that crisis.

In truth, though, the only reason for the delay in marrying that shows up clearly in the record is that the relationship was decidedly rocky. Lucien often reports being depressed because of how things went at their last visit. He reports her treating him unkindly, coldly. He gives the impression she was moody and that maybe she had doubts about him, though he doesn't explicitly say either. Maybe he was moody, too.

And there was this: Clara was a Republican. Problem.

In Dayton, political division "coursed its virulent way into virtually every vein of community life," wrote the late Carl M. Becker, a Dayton native and head of the history department at Dayton's Wright State University, who wrote much about Dayton in that era. "It split church brethren into warring factions. It crystalized social patterns.... It helped differentiate goods in the marketplace, as loyal Republicans patronized only merchants of the faith, while Copperheads similarly judged men and their wares. It incited fighting in the public schools between students adorned with the Union League badge, an emblem of Republican virtues, and scholars displaying the Butternut charm, a token of Copperhead values."[29]

(The Butternut is a tree whose parts can, when boiled, produce a dye. "Butternut" ultimately became a term for Copperheads, in part because transplanted southerners in the North who were struggling farmers and were often seen as Southern sympathizers sometimes used the dye on their clothes. The term Butternut, when used by Republicans, had a snobbish quality.)

Inevitably, some of Clara's friends were Republicans, too. One whom she considered authoritative told her that the men who hung out at the *Empire* constituted a "Secession society." And Clara said to Lucien, "you were seen one evening so late as 11½ o'clock in conversation with Vallandigham in front of Langdons Store." This was serious.

It was at this point in his journal that Lucien made his denunciation of "evesdropping slanderers." He was clearly hurt by Clara's question on the subject. And he was hurt by what he saw happening in Dayton. "*Shame,*" he wrote, "on the man who will dodge around the corners, and in the dark alleys as a spy, ... like a dastardly villain ... skulking around, ... and then ... behind men's backs, utter his vile slanders."[30] Lucien didn't tell his journal what the undenied Vallandigham conversation was about, or why he thought the suggestion that he talked to Vallandigham in the dark was slanderous. He just expressed his horror that things had come to this.

Lucien and Clara discussed race. One conversation happened after Lincoln's election, before the inauguration. He wrote that "The artist"—for that was how he referred to Clara—"expressed herself horrified ... that I expressed my belief to be that the simple relation of master and slave was no sin, and that the negro was of an inferior race. I had to go back through a long line of history, and the ethnology of the races, to prove this portion of my argument.

"When I got through with my historical (recitation) I found that I had made quite a speech to my fair friend, and I have the vanity to believe that I pretty clearly convinced her that the African race was far inferior ... for she did (not) further argue the subject with me. My dear friend is not a student of history, and her arguments are hence governed more by her feelings and convictions of right and wrong, than by facts as recorded in history."[31]

Nothing in the diary suggests any origin of Lucien's views on race other than his readings. Like Vallandigham's, his defense of slavery sprang from no apparent southern influence in his life. He had no stake, no need to come up with a rationalization for somebody else's lifestyle. Perhaps he's even more interesting than Vallandigham, because anything a politician does will be interpreted as politically motivated. Lucien wasn't running for anything.

Proud as he was of his apparent success at "educating" the artist, his influence proved limited, at best. On July 4, 1861, lecturer became lecturee. Lucien's description of Clara's rebuttal lecture brings to real life the very arguments going on in the newspapers:

"I spent this evening most unpleasantly with the Artist," says the journal, continuing:

> She lectured me for nearly two hours, just as though I was a real out and out Secessionist ... and intimating in many of her remarks that I lacked a full and proper appreciation of the real subject.... When it is remembered that, but a short time since, and oft times, I declared myself in the most unqualified and unequivocal terms to her, my devotion to the *"Union, the Constitution, and the enforcement of the law"* ... (m)y astonishment at her uncalled for and unjust attack upon me, can be better imagined than I can describe it....

> The tone and temper, as well as much of the substance of her harangue, was ungenerous, intolerant and tyrannical. She avowed herself a *radical, unconditional abolitionist,* and said that she thought the slave justified in slaying his master to gain his freedom. She said she would do it, were she a slave and could not free herself in any other way. She said that she did not believe, she knew, in fact, that no slaveholder could be a Christian. I simply remarked, that it was not for me to judge this matter, that all men were accountable to God alone for their sins against him.
>
> The overshadowing thought, and the one which left the most profound impression upon my mind, and the one which most deeply wounded, and grieves my heart, is, that … (s)he has displayed much prejudice, bigotry, and, as a natural consequence, a great degree of intolerance.
>
> I have no respect for such characteristics in anybody, and the question presents itself to me now: How can I become reconciled to them in my friend, especially, when they seem to be one of her predominant characteristics.[32]

For modern people, it's difficult to understand how an apologist for slavery could, with a straight face, lament and agonize over "prejudice" and "bigotry" in somebody else, most *especially* in the context of a discussion of race. It seems like an event from satire, from *Through the Looking Glass*. But this sort of thing happened all the time, accompanied by no self-consciousness, no sense of contradiction, no sense of irony or humor, no awareness of a rebuttal. Lucien Medlar—this educated and morally serious man—really believed that he was the tolerant one in his relationship with a hater of slavery. And many would have agreed, certainly Vallandigham, for whom intolerance was a central characteristic of the "abolitionists."

When Clara brushed off Lucien's by-then formulaic insistence that he was for the Union, the Constitution and the law, she was behaving like the professional polemicists in the newspapers. She was saying that if Lucien was going to spend all his time denouncing the "abolitionists," denouncing Lincoln, talking up "peacable separation," hanging with the Copperheads and explaining the inferiority of black people, he couldn't expect her to forget all that just because he mouthed an inoffensive slogan.

The debate that took place in a home between an engaged couple and showed up in a diary could just as easily have appeared in the newspapers between sworn, contemptuous enemies. It is difficult to avoid the suspicion that the combatant lovers got their ammunition—including their characterizations of each other—directly or indirectly from media polemicists appearing in different outlets.

8

The 1862 Fight for Freedom and Slavery

The Republicans were—shall we say?—highly motivated to beat Vallandigham in 1862. No; not highly motivated. Obsessed. He was their top target. As the aborted House investigation indicated, the long knives were out. The Republicans were circulating and believing all manner of charges against him, and they were hearing his speeches. He wanted to be Republican Enemy No. 1, and he was. The effort to beat him emanated from the White House.

The Republicans did two major things to beat Vallandigham. First they redrew his district to make it better for a Republican candidate. Then they recruited the candidate of their dreams. Robert Schenck was an old friend of Lincoln who happened also to be highly credentialed and universally known. When the Republicans nominated him, he also happened to be in a hospital recovering from a war wound. Wounded warriors—and even non-wounded ones—made great candidates for years, during and after the war. So Vallandigham—who, after all, had never won big—was being hit with a heck of a one-two punch.

If Vallandigham was the most prominent Daytonian of the 19th century—as he surely was—Schenck has been called the most "distinguished."[1] The résumé was impressive. After being leader of the Whigs in the state Senate at 28, he went to Congress from Dayton, was an ambassador (to Brazil), became a battlefield Civil War general, suffered an injury, went back to Congress, had crucial chairmanships both during and after the war, and then became ambassador to Great Britain for the first half of the 1870s. He was very much a national figure.

In the early 1860s, Schenck and Vallandigham were neighbors. They lived downtown, as most lawyers did. They actually lived on the same block on the same side of the street, a short walk from the courthouse. (For locals: They were on First Street on the north side, between Ludlow and Wilkinson Streets. A city directory[2] listed their addresses as 319 [Schenck] and 323, but today's numbering system is different. Vallandigham lived toward the Wilkinson end, the west, on a piece of land that, as this is written, is a flat parking lot. Schenck lived toward the Ludlow end. His house, too, is long gone.) They had also been members of the same local club: a group of people who got together to read new plays, with everybody taking a different role.[3] The club was a natural activity for both men. They were orators and hams. They had roles in the same play at least once.

Schenck was from a prominent family. His father was a pioneer land surveyor who had come west from the Long Island/New Jersey area, where many Schencks had settled upon arrival from Holland. (The name is pronounced Skenk, not Shenk, the German version.) The father is considered the founder of New Carlisle, a town near Dayton. He was politically active in Cincinnati and knew Thomas Corwin, whom he preceded in the state legislature. The younger Schenck studied at Miami University, founded in 1809 in nearby Oxford, then taught French there for a couple of years. Then he studied law under Corwin in Lebanon—halfway between Cincinnati and Dayton—before moving to the booming city of Dayton. A natural speaker with a good name, he became fairly well known by riding the legal circuit around Dayton. He was slated for the legislature by the Whigs. He lost, then won. Perhaps because the

Robert Schenck, neighbor, vanquisher and enemy of Vallandigham; friend of Lincoln. (Library of Congress.)

Whigs were on a youth kick—trying to live down their reputation as an aging, waning party—he was chosen as the party leader in the Senate. Certain battles won him statewide attention. He moved on to the U.S. House of Representatives and spent most of the 1840s (his thirties) there.[4]

Abe Lincoln's single term in the House began in 1847, but really took place mainly in 1848. Lincoln and Schenck had a lot in common. They were the same age, born in 1809. They were Whigs from the West. They opposed the Mexican War. They opposed the extension of slavery. Both were on board with Whig leader Henry Clay's "American System" of "internal improvements."

So Lincoln and Schenck forged some sort of bond. This shouldn't be overstated. Biographies have been written about Lincoln without mentioning Schenck. But in 1849, Lincoln wrote to Schenck referring to a meeting they had had in Springfield, Illinois, and he asked for Schenck's help in landing a job with the federal "Land Office." The next year, Lincoln wrote a letter to President Zachary Taylor endorsing Schenck for ambassador to Brazil.[5] Later the two socialized occasionally before and after election 1860 presidential election.

By the end of the 1840s, Schenck wanted out of Congress. There was much to depress him. His wife had died of tuberculosis. The slavery issue was tearing the Whigs apart. The country was moving in a bad direction.

Corwin—a big Whig—recommended that President Zachary Taylor make Schenck an ambassador and requested a southern clime.[6] As ambassador to Brazil, Schenck reported to Secretary of State Daniel Webster, who had been a poker buddy, according to Schenck (who made the same claim about Henry Clay).[7] Schenck's job was largely about getting American access to various waterways. Before long—indeed, "shortly after his arrival in Rio in 1851"—he had had enough of South America and asked to be replaced.[8] That ambition had to await the Whigs' loss of the presidency in 1852.

Now Schenck wanted to make some money. He had three daughters (three other children having died in childhood), and he wanted to send them to private schools. He was practicing law with Corwin in Washington, but he also went into the railroad business, the hot new one. Unlike other politicians, though, Schenck did not simply take a job with the railroads. He went entrepreneurial, setting out to establish a new line. It would go from Fort Wayne, Indiana, westward to the Mississippi.[9] He spent some years traveling around to raise the capital. He thought he had the commitments, but the Panic of 1857 hit. It was much like a depression. It hit railroads particularly hard, and the plan died.[10]

Lincoln became a national figure in 1858, renowned for holding his own in campaign debates in his Senate race against Stephen A. Douglas. In 1859, Douglas went through Dayton on a campaign trip including Cincinnati and Columbus. The timing had to do with an Ohio election, but he was really running for president. Because of a throat issue, he apparently did not given a speech in Dayton. But he met a lot of people at the Phillips House and was generally shepherded around by Vallandigham.[11] Lincoln—invited by the Republicans—followed Douglas on the Columbus-Dayton-Cincinnati path, saying the idea was to correct the record.[12]

At this point, Schenck wasn't clearly a Republican. He found some of the Republicans too radically abolition-oriented for his tastes, feeling they could foster a war. And he didn't like the Republican candidate for president in 1856, John C. Frémont, the famed western explorer dubbed The Pathfinder. Schenck's brother, as a naval officer, had had dealings with Frémont in California and thought him a showboat and credit-grabber. Frémont liked to be seen as the reason California was in the union. William Schenck and others apparently thought they deserved some credit, too.[13]

But with Lincoln's emergence, Schenck was moving toward the Republicans, just as many former Whigs had. Corwin had been pushing him in that direction ever since Schenck came back from Brazil, presumably pointing out that there was simply no choice if Schenck had any remaining political ambitions.[14]

Meanwhile Schenck was Lincoln's best friend in Dayton. When Lincoln came through town, Schenck had lunch with him at Phillips House and sat near him as he spoke at Courthouse Square in the afternoon, from perhaps 2 p.m. to 3:30 p.m.[15] Then Lincoln left for Cincinnati. There is some confusion about exactly what happened next. But one widely repeated story holds that Schenck spoke at another gathering that evening outside the courthouse[16] and that he said something along the lines of, if we're looking for a presidential candidate next year, we could do a lot worse than the fellow who came through here today. That may have been the first time anybody outside Illinois had mentioned Lincoln for president publicly.[17] Lincoln reportedly said it was.[18] Speculation held that Lincoln appreciated that.

Soon Schenck declared as a Republican. The next year he went to work hard for Lincoln's election, making speeches in Illinois, New York and Ohio.[19]

Lincoln invited Schenck and others to tea on November 3, 1860, days before the election. The editors of Lincoln's papers say Schenck was being considered for the cabinet if Salmon P. Chase turned Lincoln down on being secretary of the treasury.[20] Lincoln told a friend he wanted to find something for Schenck. Meanwhile, Corwin had suggested Schenck for secretary of the navy. And an anonymous *New York Times* column had appeared promoting Schenck for the cabinet, which some people thought was a bit too forward and might have backfired on Schenck. When nothing materialized, Schenck wrote a letter to Lincoln insisting that what really hurt was that he never heard anything. He wrote of the "neglect and silence ... (a)fter all that had passed before." This apparently generated a response from Lincoln that assuaged Schenck.[21]

When, the next spring, Fort Sumter happened, Schenck told one of his daughters the following conversation happened.

"Lincoln sent for me and asked, 'Schenck, what can you do to help me?' He asked, 'Can you fight?' I answered, 'I could try.' Lincoln said, 'Well, I want to make a general of you.'

"I said, 'I don't know about that, Mr. President. You could appoint me as a general, but I might not prove to be one.' Then he did so and I went into the war."[22]

Lincoln did not have enough West Point generals to suffice. Appointing prominent figures to military officerships was nothing new in the days before major standing armies. Lincoln himself had been an officer in the Black Hawk War because he was a leader among the young men in his community. In the Civil War, picking such a high-profile person as Schenck was seen as a way of tying a community to the war effort, of giving it a rooting interest. Typically, these "political generals" did not emerge as the most important generals, and that was certainly true of Schenck. But the job was not just a matter of political patronage. Lincoln also appointed many Democrats as generals, to broaden the war's base of support.

Schenck's military career got mixed reviews. Very early in the war—when there was so little happening that everything that did happen got big press attention— Schenck had some troops on a train in the vicinity of Vienna, Virginia, now a suburb of Washington. He was dropping off troops to protect railroad bridges. The train got ambushed, and Schenck and others had to abandon some cars after decoupling. The Union side reported eight casualties; the South none. Schenck got criticized for not doing reconnaissance before the trip, especially because there had been indications of a Confederate presence.[23] It was one of the first skirmishes in the war with any loss of life. The poisonously partisan Democratic press loved the story. Even a prominent, non–Democratic journalist referred sarcastically to Schenck as the "hero of Vienna."[24]

The Vienna episode apparently caused Schenck some problems with the troops. Later that summer, reporting on First Bull Run, the Dayton *Empire* said in a headline "OHIO BOYS 'PROTEST' AGAINST BEING LED BY GEN. SCHENK."[25] The story didn't elaborate much, except to say the troops had been assuaged by Col. Alex McCook, a popular figure. Later, over time, there were some good reviews for Gen. Schenck.

A year after Bull Run, Schenck was at Second Bull Run. Like the first, it was a calamity for the North. But he was not blamed for either, being too low a general. This time he was injured. The 52-year-old man had been rallying his troops from his mount, with his arm above his head, holding a sword and moving it in a circle. He was shot at the juncture of his hand and wrist. He went to the makeshift hospital that was the Willard Hotel in Washington. It was a long, painful stay. Doctors were unable to save most of the use of his arm and hand.[26]

The injury happened on August 30, 1862. On September 9, he announced his candidacy for Congress. He later wrote about that for his personal papers: "When I was wounded and on my back, (Secretary of the Treasury Salmon) Chase and the others came to see me and said, 'You must run for Congress. You are the only man who can beat the traitor Vallandigham.' I protested, for I had determined never again to enter Congressional life. But President Lincoln came"—a claim that was to be verified, as will be seen—"and the demand was reinforced by others of our men in the lead of the administration. So I was again drawn into Congress."[27]

Anybody who believed that the idea of Schenck running against Vallandigham had materialized at the Willard had not been reading the Dayton *Journal*. That Republican operation had been promoting him all year. It wouldn't specifically mention the upcoming congressional race, but it covered, commented on, elaborated upon and found an excuse to report repeatedly on every move he made in the field. First, after a given event, there would be a letter from a soldier telling about what an outstanding job Schenck had done. Then there'd be a news story, then an editorial, and another. Then there'd be coverage of the official report Schenck submitted on the event, as generals regularly did after their engagements. That would be seized upon as an opportunity for another editorial. And so it went. A reader might get the impression that the George Washington of this war was Robert Schenck.

At one point, the paper had a piece about Schenck's involvement at McDowell, Virginia, near the border of what is now West Virginia. It was a rare case of Schenck—to his satisfaction—commanding an independent unit. His superior officer was Frémont, who seemed not to know about Schenck's 1856 view of him. The *Journal* piece said, "Fremont pronounces this one of the most brilliant and successful achievements of the war.... Schenck only needs the accidental accuracy of a rebel bullet to make him a Major-General, or immortal."[28]

No doubt, Schenck's effort—involving a long, fast march—had been impressive. But another view—perhaps more detached—of the battle in question emerges in the

Library of Congress Illustrated Timeline of the Civil War. It reads, "May 8, 1862: At the battle of McDowell, Virginia, Stonewall Jackson wins the first victory of his Shenandoah Valley Campaign ... repulsing an attack by Union troops commanded by General Robert Schenck."[29]

On August 6 came the inevitable in the *Journal.* It reported, "The Lebanon *Star* (in the county to the south of Dayton) suggests the name of Robt. C. Schenck for Congress in this district. He has a national reputation as a statesman, has proved a man of military talent, and possesses indomitable energy." This was before he was injured.

Though Lincoln valued his political generals, he was always clear that he needed them more in politics than in the army. When James A. Garfield, a young politician who had risen to general, went to Lincoln halfway through the war to ask whether he should stay in uniform or take a congressional seat to which he had been elected while serving, Lincoln was unequivocal: Congress.[30]

The Vallandigham seat was especially important to Lincoln. It was about "the fire in the rear." That was a phrase attributed to Lincoln by Massachusetts Sen. Charles Sumner. It meant the Copperheads. At a time when the military news was awful for the North, Lincoln told Sumner that he was less worried about the North's military chances against the South than about "the fire in the rear."[31] Well, Vallandigham was the great fanner of the flames, unless one prefers the metaphor of arsonist.

So we don't have to take Schenck's word for it that the president wanted him to run. If Lincoln was focused on "the fire"—and he was—he was focused on Vallandigham. And he knew Schenck and knew the district.

Would Schenck have run if not for the war wound? Leaving the war effort before it was completed would have been awkward. That was the concern that led Garfield to consult Lincoln. Leaving when things were going badly—as after Second Bull Run— would have been doubly awkward. But the pressure from Lincoln would have been there, and it could have served as a public rationale: that Schenck was serving the cause of the war in another way.

Obviously, the injury was yet another political asset for Schenck. Doubly so: It not only made voters more sympathetic to him, it explained his departure from the battlefield. Not that it shut up his opponents. After Schenck had been promoted to major general in his hospital bed, the *Empire*, which liked to portray Republicans as warmongers, said of the injured man, "Gen. Schenck don't want the war to stop.... He is making a good thing of it."[32]

Much younger men were still avoiding service. The only other Republican politician who had ever been mentioned as a possible candidate against Vallandigham— state Sen. Lewis B. Gunckel—was in his thirties and not serving. So Schenck was pretty close to the perfect candidate, sitting in a hospital with a painful and complicated injury.

In him, the Republicans had a man whose "hatred of Vallandigham and the principles for which he stood knew no bounds," according to Schenck's biographer.[33] A measure of that: In 1862, Schenck had received a letter from a daughter who mentioned Vallandigham. Schenck's three daughters, in their twenties, were living in the house in Dayton. The letter mentioned the local celebration of George Washington's birthday, on February 22. It was a pretty big holiday in those days, with patriotic speeches and "illuminations." Schenck's daughter knew that it was her father's favorite holiday, because he venerated Washington. She told him that the Vallandighams had celebrated the holiday big, illuminating their front windows with candles, in the style of the day. Her father wrote back saying that people were so phony about these things that "even Rebeldom had the impudence to select that day for the inauguration of Jeff Davis" as elected president of the Confederacy in 1862. And, he continued, "it had been in honor of <u>that</u>" inauguration—not Washington's birthday—"that the V's burned their candles."[34]

***

Then, as now, congressional districts were redrawn after every U.S. Census, and the Census was conducted in every year ending in zero. After the 1860 Census, Ohio was to lose two seats in Congress, because the size of districts had been increased to prevent the House from becoming unwieldy as the nation expanded.

Then, unlike now, district lines generally observed county lines. Since then, the U.S. Supreme Court has ruled that districts must be very, very close to each other in population size. That can't be achieved if county lines are observed.

The Republicans were in charge of the state government. They had to enlarge quite a few districts. They knew whose district they would start with. They had been gifted the chance to victimize Vallandigham. His Third District was three counties: Montgomery (Dayton), Preble (rural and to the west of Montgomery), and Butler (directly south of Preble, near Cincinnati).

In the 1860 election, Vallandigham had won by 134 votes out of more than 20,000, despite losing Montgomery and Preble. Lincoln lost the district by 115 votes, despite winning Montgomery and Preble.[35] Butler County was big for the Democrats, the base of Vallandigham's support, the reason he was in Congress.

In redistricting, the Republicans added Warren County to the district. It is directly south of Montgomery and east of Butler. So the resulting district was pretty much a square. Although Vallandigham never stopped charging gerrymandering, that certainly doesn't fit the traditional definition of a gerrymander, which entails squiggly lines drawn to bring in certain kinds of voters and avoid others. Non-partisan technicians might have drawn the same lines as the Republicans drew.[36]

And yet, the Republicans certainly knew what they were doing. Warren County did lean Republican. It had been Whig when it produced Tom Corwin. It had significant Quaker communities, to the point of being referred to in the press occasionally as "Quaker country."[37] The Quakers operated stops on the Underground Railroad in several towns, hiding escaped slaves temporarily in hidden compartments in their homes. Springboro, just outside Montgomery County, was one such community. Though some Ohio Quakers had come from Pennsylvania, others came from North Carolina and other parts south. Opposition to slavery was one of the reasons for these movements. Anti-slavery people voted Republican.

Adding Warren County to the old district produced a district which Lincoln had carried. Specifically, he got 52.3 percent of the two-party vote. The new district was

In Congress, Vallandigham represented Montgomery, Butler and Preble counties in Ohio. When Warren County was added to the district, he never won again.

hardly unwinnable for a Democrat, especially an incumbent. But it was a new problem for Vallandigham.

***

By the time of the 1862 elections, the state of the union had deteriorated horrifically on Abe Lincoln's watch. When he was elected, the country had been at peace, and had been much bigger. And now the South—a poorer, less mechanized, smaller foe—was proving terribly difficult to defeat, and was actually winning major battles.

After Lincoln's long, enervating efforts to get his top battlefield general, George McClellan, to fight aggressively, McClellan launched his effort to take Richmond at the end of June. After the Seven Days Battles, he turned back toward Washington, unsuccessful.

The newspapers were full of squabbles about whose incompetence on the Union side was responsible for which military disappointments. Republicans sometimes targeted Democratic generals, implicitly questioning whether their hearts were in the fight. The Republicans had political reason to worry about public opinion. Though the people of the North had largely bought into the war early on, the buy-in entailed the assumption that war would be run competently and would be won.

Another potential problem for the Republicans was Emancipation. Lincoln announced his historic proclamation just three weeks before the Ohio election of October 14. (The timing had to do with military matters, not the campaign.) The move made Lincoln a flip-flopper on the great issue. He had insisted that the war was about union, not emancipation, and he had said that he didn't have either the power or the inclination to free the slaves in the South. The proclamation fed the charge that the war was being fought for black people.

Meanwhile, infringements on free speech were giving the Democrats an issue. Then there was the ever-increasing need for more and more men to fight. Then there was violence between Republicans and Democrats in the North. The partisan rhetoric was warlike. In Bucyrus, Ohio—120 miles northeast of Dayton—the Democratic clerk of courts warned, not atypically, that "the day that sees one drop of Democratic blood shed or Democratic property destroyed, that day will see your town in ashes and your streets running with blood." After the election, a Democratic mob celebrated victory by firing shots into a Republican-owned store.[38]

One historian has written that "there was no more inauspicious time for an election, from the standpoint of the (Republican) party, than the fall of 1862. The Republicans were apathetic." The Democrats who supported the war were showing less enthusiasm than ever. And "The regular Democrats"—the Copperheads—"on the other hand, were thoroughly aroused."[39]

Still, the Republicans did have a clever gambit going for them. In 1861, to enhance their electoral chances, they had, in many states, dropped the name "Republican" in favor of "Union" Party or "National Union" Party. The idea wasn't simply to associate themselves with the Union army or the popular cause of maintaining the Union intact. It was to suggest that this was no time for normal partisan politics, and people had to *unite* under one leadership for the duration. The Republicans picked big-name War Democrats—supporters of the war as the realistic way to thwart secession—for high spots on their tickets.

Beyond all that, with the "Union" label, the Republicans were addressing the central charge that Vallandigham and others were making against them: that they were an obsessive single-issue party (slavery) with a narrow regional focus, with no concern for the nation as a whole.

The Union strategy had still one more impact that seemed promising in 1862: By removing some pro-war voices from the Democratic Party, it made that party more anti-war, moved it away from the political center. It gave greater strength within the party to people like Vallandigham. (In so doing, rather than uniting the country, it further polarized the two parties and perhaps the country.)

In 1861, Dayton diarist Medlar described the Union ticket in Ohio as three Republicans who could not be tainted with the charge of abolitionism, three good Democrats (including the candidate for governor, who won) and one fellow who had voted in 1860 for neither Lincoln nor Douglas but for a moderate, minor-party ticket.[40] But, crucially, all the candidates were pro-war.

The name "Union" infuriated the Vallandighammers (as they came to be called, sometimes with one "m," sometimes two). How dare the Republicans take that name, given that Republican agitation had caused the destruction of the Union! What business did a regional party have talking this way?

Perhaps with an eye on Republican efforts to win over Democrats, Vallandigham adopted a campaign strategy that might expand his own appeal. He would emphasize the civil liberties issue, or, as he referred to it, "arbitrary arrests," meaning those without *habeas corpus* at play. Maybe some Republicans would agree with his complaint.

How widespread were the infringements on democratic rights? Some numbers: Eleven political arrests of newspaper and political people happened in Ohio in 1862.[41] (Meanwhile, some 10 Democratic newspapers were mobbed, often by soldiers on leave and under the influence.) Most of the federal government's transgressions against peace-time civil liberties had taken place in the border slave states that had not seceded but had considered it: Maryland, Kentucky, Missouri and Delaware. In Maryland, the arrestees included about 30 allegedly disloyal members of the legislature, as well as a congressman and the mayor of Baltimore.[42] Elsewhere, some cases were pretty trivial. A Missourian found himself arrested after saying he "wouldn't wipe my ass with the stars and stripes." A man in Cincinnati was arrested using Confederate slogans on stationery he was selling.[43]

National Archive records show more than 100 people tried for treason by military courts during the war, most of those being civilians. The archives have another 65 soldiers and civilians tried in military courts on the lesser charge of "disloyalty," often in combination with other charges. Almost 80 percent of those cases dealt with something the defendant had said, not done.[44] Numerous other arrests occurred, some never getting to any court.

The impetus toward political arrests didn't spring full-blown in Washington. At the street level, people would take great offense at the (sometimes drunken) comments of neighbors and report them. Some people would just pass along gossip. Magazines would encourage people to inform.[45]

In the early 1880s, one John A. Marshall wrote a bitterly anti–Lincoln book called *American Bastille: A History of the Illegal Arrests and Imprisonment of American Citizens in the Northern and Border States on Account of Their Political Opinions during the Late Civil War*. The book has been much criticized by historians. One said that, contrary to it, "Prisoners were not brutally treated; and, though their prison terms were not pleasant, such hardships as they suffered were due to … general conditions of prison" in that day.[46] Whatever one thinks of *Bastille*, there's this: In a passionate, partisan search for alleged horror stories, with memories still fairly fresh, with cases still being talked about and with first-hand accounts available, the author came up with about 100 cases of allegedly unjust arrests and imprisonments he wanted to highlight, complete with names and (one-sided) case histories.[47]

What was Lincoln's role? Pulitzer Prize-winning historian Mark E. Neely, Jr., wrote that Lincoln never intended for his political opponents to be targeted. "All along, the policy had been aimed at dangerous Confederate sympathizers like John Merryman, at bridge-burners in Missouri, and at the legions of draft dodgers throughout the land. All along, the policy threatened freedom of speech and the press as well, but only incidentally."[48]

Harold Holzer had a different take. He wrote that in the summer of 1861, Lincoln turned toward "a new foe he judged to be nearly as dangerous as armed Rebels: anti-war, anti-administration, anti-recruitment newspaper editors."[49] Holzer wrote that "For the first year of the war, Lincoln left no trail of documents attesting to any personal conviction that dissenting newspapers ought to be muzzled. But neither did he say anything to control or contradict such efforts when they were undertaken."

Among Northern states, New York was a particular hotbed of Copperhead sentiment in the press. New York papers often got national distribution or got quoted by papers elsewhere, an administration worry. By the end of August in 1861, the New York *Post* was reporting that four papers "in this city and one in Brooklyn have been" banned from the mail.[50]

Two particular Ohio cases got much attention. On June 29, 1862, one John Kees, Copperhead editor of the Circleville *Watchman* (three counties east of Dayton) was arrested. He was a politician before he was a journalist.[51] The precise words that got him arrested do not seem to have been reported at the time. Newspapers settled for general terms about disloyalty and about discouraging enlistment and recruitment. Indeed, the Dayton *Journal* specifically said that the charges against Kees weren't known.[52]

But one quote has been provided by historian George Henry Porter. A Kees editorial referred to Union Gen. Benjamin Butler, who was ruling New Orleans and had become famous for threatening to treat women as prostitutes if they continued to heap abuse (sometimes in the form of the contents of chamber pots) on Union troops. Wrote Kees: "Why don't the men of New Orleans shoot the nefarious wretch (Butler) like they would a reptile or dog?"[53]

Court papers filed later have another specific quote. Kees wrote, "We advised all Democrats to stay at home, and let the authors and provokers of this war, the Abolition Republicans, fight out their own war themselves." A judge referred to "many kindred extracts."[54]

Kees is also known to have expressed the desire that the people he called abolitionists and "damned disunionists" be hung "till the flesh would rot off their bones and the winds of Heaven whistle yankee doodle through their loathsum skelitonz."[55]

The Republican Dayton *Journal* was not alarmed by this arrest of a fellow newspaperman, even without knowing the specific charge. It said, "If Kees is a traitor, he deserves to meet a traitor's fate."[56] Newspaper generally didn't stick together. The *Ohio State Journal* in Columbus—seen as the main Republican paper in the state—said "the (Cincinnati) *Enquirer* ought not be allowed to circulate anywhere."[57]

Kees gave up ownership of his newspaper upon his arrest, and the paper's name was changed. It spent only a week in suspension. He was released after two months. But the experience seems to have been a hard one; his mental health became a public issue.[58] He went to an insane asylum. A couple of years later he left the state, taking his family.[59]

A more consequential political arrest took place around the same time. Copperhead Edson Olds was a well-known political figure in central Ohio, a former congressman. He came up with a theory that Gov. David Tod was targeting Democrats for the draft. Tod was a former and faithful Democrat whom the Republicans had recruited to run under the Union Party banner in 1861.[60]

As governor, Tod was constantly burdened by the task of raising enough troops to meet the state's recruitment quota. He hoped that doing so would help avoid a national draft. In 1862, only 26 of Ohio's 88 counties met their quotas. Of those, 19 were in the south, where concerns about a Southern invasion were most intense. Many of those counties were highly Republican. But four of the 19 were among the most staunchly Copperhead in the state.[61]

Tod was targeting men everywhere. He made aggressive use of the "bounty" system—offering money to volunteers—then in wide use. The money had to come from someplace. On the basis of no evidence he provided, Olds concluded that Tod would not draft those who provided money for the fund, and that he would use the money to draft Democrats. Olds insisted that his "supposition is a natural one: that the Governor would like to send the Democrats to the war, so as to keep them away from the polls." Olds saw Tod's alleged behavior leading to violent resistance in the North. He said, "If the president wishes … to avoid bringing civil war and bloodshed into our peaceful cities and villages, let him make some proclamation by which we may know that this war is not prosecuted for the abolition of slavery, and this draft will become unnecessary."[62]

Tod had Olds arrested in the summer of 1862 the same way he had had Kees arrested: He asked Washington to do it. He said the arrest was necessary if troops were to be raised in the requisite number. As will be seen, Lincoln was deeply concerned about troop levels. Tod sent U.S. Secretary of State William Seward a copy of Olds' offensive statement. And he wrote, from his experience as a Democrat, that Olds is "a shrewd, cunning man, with a capacity for great mischief, and should at once be put out of the way … at least until I have succeeded in raising my regiments."[63]

Olds was arrested on August 12 and taken to Fort Lafayette, referred to by historian Holzer as "that notorious press dungeon,"[64] which was off Manhattan on the island that now has the watchtower of the Verrazano Narrows Bridge from Staten Island to Brooklyn. Olds, 60, later told a horror story about the conditions, involving dysentery.[65] As a clear result of his incarceration, while in prison, Olds was elected to the state senate upon the death of the incumbent, though Olds had not been a candidate before.

The three-and-a-half-month duration of Olds' imprisonment was about par, as was the fact that he wasn't charged and had no *habeas corpus* hearing. Charging and convicting him in a real court would have been difficult. And the authorities seemed to be satisfied to scare arrestees like him.

The Olds case had a very high profile. That facilitated candidate Vallandigham's desire to talk about other forms of political persecution. He referred, for example, to events in Indiana, where the Copperheads were a particularly potent force, more so than in Ohio.⁶⁶ Vallandigham seized upon a telegram sent to a Cincinnati newspaper saying the Indiana state militia might be called out to handle political tensions between Hoosiers. He characterized that as an attempt to silence Democrats, and he said "the same dastardly menaces have been proclaimed" in Ohio, though "that is a work which can not be done by ten or twenty or fifty thousand troops."⁶⁷

That set off the Dayton *Journal*. (This account of the campaign basically takes Vallandigham as speaking for himself and the *Journal* as speaking for the Republicans. At this stage, Robert Schenck had not been nominated and was still engaged in the war. Later he was in the hospital.) In a piece labeled "A Downright Lie," it said the troops in Indiana were to be raised to deal with people who refused to pay their taxes in protest of the war.

Meanwhile, the possibility of Vallandigham's own arrest was very much in the air.

His most important journalistic friend was Sam Medary, editor and owner of the Columbus weekly *The Crisis*. Then in his early sixties, Medary was known as the old warhorse of the Democratic Party. He had put out other newspapers, run for the Senate, chaired the 1856 Democratic National Convention and been appointed territorial governor of Minnesota, then Kansas.⁶⁸ When Lincoln won the 1860 election, Medary was put out of work in Kansas. He returned to Columbus and launched *The Crisis*. Utterly uncompromising in its partisanship, its eight pages were full of commentary from himself and pointed articles from other papers. It was a one-man operation. He was a lively writer who was assumed to know everything going on in his party. Everybody in politics read his paper.

On August 27, Medary wrote, "A report became current yesterday afternoon that Hon. C.L. Vallandigham and other of our

Sam Medary, Vallandigham's leading ally in the media, who opposed letting black people into Ohio (Ohio History Connection).

citizens were to be arrested and taken East in the midnight train last night. The report spread rapidly, and while no one placed much reliance in its truth, the Democrats believing that an 'ounce of preventative is worth a pound of cure' gathered in considerable numbers at various places waiting for the train, and determined that if Mr. V was to be arrested, it should be done strictly in accordance with the law, and not by kidnapping."

In other words, the Democrats believed the report and planned to thwart the arrest, but that was a little embarrassing now, because, "Midnight came and went without any movement looking to an arrest."

Also in the air was the possible shutdown of the Dayton *Empire*. The *Journal* was fine with that and tried to find a nonpartisan justification. It said, "When the *Empire* develops its malignity and treason boldly enough, it will be suppressed by the Democratic Secretary of War (Edwin Stanton), and its editors suffered to enjoy the felicities of the martyrdom they court."

Vallandigham, in the same speech in which he talked about Indiana—on July 4, to the Democratic state convention in Columbus—threatened reprisals for what might happen. "Men of the Republican party," he said, "it is your day now: tomorrow, it may be, it will be ours. Be warned in time. Stand by the Constitution—by law and order. Do nothing by usurpation or violence. (The country) must react. It will react, and there is no raging flood, no mountain torrent … like the madness of an oppressed and outraged people."[69]

He proposed open defiance of the authorities, if not of law. "Every civil officer knows what 'due process of law' is, and, when armed with such due process, it is the duty of every person to obey. But whoever comes with any other papers, or any pretense of authority … from the Secretary of War, Commander-in-chief, President, deserves to be met as a burglar." He meant that those federal officials didn't have the constitutional authority they claimed to have.

Thousands of people came to a later Vallandigham speech at Courthouse Square in Dayton. The Democrats said 7,000 attended.[70] The number was central in the lore of the speech that the Democrats tried to generate. They said that only because he was surrounded by so many friends was Vallandigham protected against the Republican "reign of terror." The introduction to the speech in Vallandigham's later campaign book made an amazing claim, given the risks being undertaken by thousands of Ohioans in uniform: "A bolder stroke was never made, nor a more fearless exhibition given, of high moral as well as physical courage" than when Vallandigham dared to give the speech.[71]

The *Journal* accused Vallandigham of pursuing martyrdom. No wonder. "I was born a freeman," he said, "I shall die a freeman,… and death never comes too soon to one in the discharge of his duty.… My opinions are immovable; fire can not melt them out of me. I scorn the mob. I defy arbitrary power.… Other patriots, in other ages, have suffered before me. I may die for the cause; be it so."

Notwithstanding these emotional highlights, the speech was mainly a disquisition on various liberties and the need for officeholders to recognize them, even in wartime. It was an erudite treatment of the history of liberty in England, the United States and Ohio, with lengthy quotations from all manner of documents.

Some people thought he had a good campaign issue. In December 1862, U.S. Sen. John Sherman, R–Ohio, said, "Of the few arrests made in Ohio, most ... resulted only in evil to the party that made the arrests." He mentioned the Olds case, characterizing Olds as "a man comparatively without influence" before his arrest, saying the speech that got him arrested "fell utterly harmless and impotent" at first, but then Olds had "been crowned a martyr" and elected overwhelmingly.[72]

Vallandigham went all out with the issue. He fought not only for *habeas corpus*, but for free expression, against warrantless searches, for civilian supremacy and more. He fought with great energy and ability, bringing more attention to the cause than anybody. He did his best—which wasn't bad—to make civil liberties a central issue in the 1862 campaign nationally. He fought the fight earlier in the war than others did. He fought it consistently and uncompromisingly. And he fought at the hardest of the times. After all, it's often easy to stand up for democratic practices in a democratic country. You want to find a hard time to do it? Try a cataclysmic civil war, when your constituents' offspring are being killed in appalling numbers and the people being denied their liberties are—or look like—apologists for their killers. At such a time, the authorities who are cracking down have the easiest of defenses. The public is likely to be more concerned with life-and-death issues than with imprisonment issues, especially if the imprisonments are not long.

Vallandigham's apologies for slavery were, of course, no deterrent to his support for civil liberties for white people. Confronted with his apparent inconsistency, he would have referred to Anglo-Saxon traditions, not universal values. Just as apologists for slavery could see themselves as forces against prejudice, they could see themselves as forces for individual rights: the right to own slaves, to make decisions about one's own life without the interference of a far-off government, to uphold one's own culture, traditions and economy.

Confederates often talked about the lack of rights as, yes, slavery. Famed diarist Mary Chestnut at war's end: "I shut my eyes and made a vow that if we were a crushed people, crushed by weight"—meaning the greater resources of the North—"I would never be a whimpering, pining slave."[73]

If Vallandigham's views about rights for black people need hardly be asked about, what about rights for Republicans? Suppose the Democrats were to come to power, and the South refused to rejoin the Union unless the anti-slavery movement was gone? Wouldn't he attempt to squelch the movement any way he could? He was, after all, so clear, so vehement in seeing the country's great problem as the movement itself. If it was the great existential threat to the nation, would he refuse to do what he saw as necessary?

Sometimes when Vallandigham attacked "arbitrary arrests," he talked in sweeping, ideological terms about the need to honor constitutional restraints on power. But sometimes his message was: How dare they do this to *us,* the real patriots, the ones who are actually sincere about wanting to preserve the Union and have always warned against their folly, the ones who did *not* talk secession over the Louisiana purchase or during the War of 1812, the ones representing those troops who are actually fighting the war, rather than dodging it (an eventually discredited claim about the Republicans).

We know this much for sure: Vallandigham saw a much better case for arresting abolitionists than Copperheads. Not even close. And, after all, the Republicans had been warned: When he had said "Men of the Republican party, it is your day now: tomorrow, it may be, it will be ours," he had quoted Lord Byron:

> *"For time at last sets all things even—*
> *And if we do but watch the hour,*
> *There never yet was human power*
> *Which could evade, if unforgiven,*
> *The patient search and vigil long*
> *Of him who treasures up a wrong."*[74]

***

"Arbitrary arrests" weren't the only Vallandigham issue in the 1862 campaign. He began his July 4 convention speech[75] by identifying the Democratic Party as "a party to which this country is indebted for all that is great and good and grand and glorious." This was a bit more than the usual rallying of a party. The point was: Now we have the first Republican president, and look what happened.

He emphasized his Democrats-as-the-real-Unionists theme, predicting, as he did in other speeches, that "in six months, in three months, in six weeks (perhaps), these very men"—running the government—"will be the advocates of the eternal dissolution of this Union, and denounce all who oppose it as enemies to the peace of the country."

He based this prediction on another prediction: Britain and France—the most important foreign countries to the U.S.—might recognize the Confederacy and side with it, because the South was doing so well in the war. That would cause the Republicans to give up—but not him. He said he would continue to oppose any kind of disunion.

Elsewhere in the speech, he reveled in the contempt of the Republican press, which contempt he insisted had been present since the disputed election of 1856. He said a Republican editor without Vallandigham "would be the most unhappy mortal in the world.... (N)o copy to be had."

Inevitably, he turned to race baiting. In that year, before Emancipation, Congress had been debating many racial issues raised by the war: whether Union generals should free the slaves in Southern territory they controlled; whether escaped slaves should be accepted by Union armies; whether blacks should serve in the Union army, and more. Vallandigham said the work of the current Congress "has been almost wholly for the 'Almighty African.' ... (F)rom the prayer (opening the session) to the motion to adjourn, it is negro in every shape and form."

He expressed outrage that a thousand fugitive slaves in Washington were getting medical care that was in short supply, and getting it at government expense, even as "Union armies ... marched barefooted ... without so much as a cracker.... (M)any a gallant young soldier of Ohio ... lies wan and sad on his pallet in the hospital, (while) your surgeons are forced to divide their time ... between (them and) ... slaves, who have been seduced or forced from the service of their masters."

Meanwhile, of course, the war itself raged on. Newspaper coverage during the campaign was often simply preposterous. The Dayton *Journal* criticized the *Empire* for highlighting every piece of bad news for the North.[76] But the *Journal* went to the other extreme shamelessly. If you were to judge by *Journal,* you would conclude that, great as Robert Schenck was as a military leader, that's how awful the now-legendary Confederate General Stonewall Jackson was. *Journal* headlines: "Jackson Falling Back." "RETREAT OF JACKSON." "FREMONT DRIVES JACKSON PRECIPITATELY BEFORE HIM." "Jackson and Ewell Defeated with Great Loss." "Jackson Retreating." "JACKSON SURROUNDED BY POPE." "JACKSON'S REAR IN DANGER." "JACKSON IN FULL RETREAT." "Jackson whipped in three battles."[77]

At the beginning of a major battle, the *Journal* would not settle for expressing optimism; it would report success. The coverage of McClellan's doomed march on Richmond reads like a long-pending, accumulating success. On May 9 at the top of the front page were two headlines on one story: "Onward to Richmond" and "Probable Capture of the Whole Rebel Army." The story, apparently from the New York *Herald,* read in part, "It is barely possible that we may have fighting yet, but the general opinion is that…. McClellan can advance upon Richmond without any formidable opposition."

On July 3: "CONFEDERATES DRIVEN FROM RICHMOND." Didn't happen.

Also on July 3, the *Journal* printed a proclamation from Ohio Gov. Tod. He said Union troops at Richmond were outnumbered (McClellan's false view) and that more troops were needed. Tod was implying that the North's capitol—not the South's—was the one in danger. He was paving the way for the call for more volunteers. So, while the *Journal* was calling the McClellan mission a success, the governor was, in effect, admitting it was a failure—in the same edition of the same paper.

One possible explanation for this contradiction: The Democrats were gathered in Columbus for their state convention and were portraying the nation's circumstances as darkly as possible. So the *Journal* was determined to spin things as positively as possible. Soon, though, the *Journal*—its need to foster recruitment trumping its need to win the election—felt obliged to amplify the governor: "The country is today in greater peril from open and secret foes than ever before."[78]

On another front, the *Journal* reported "Vicksburg Taken" a year before that happened.[79]

In July, Southern generals were eyeing neutral, deeply divided Kentucky. Many of the most prominent families there—the Clays, Crittendens and Breckinridges—had men in both armies.[80] Nobody knew which way the state would go. Lincoln was famously reported to have said that he hoped to have God on his side, but he must have Kentucky.[81] The Confederates nurtured the dream that a show of military strength in Kentucky would galvanize pro–Confederate people who had previously being quiescent.[82] Small, mobile Confederate cavalry units under Nathan Bedford Forrest and John Hunt Morgan had had some successes in southern Kentucky. Then, in July, Morgan and his 1,500 men on horseback were reported to be at Cynthiana, about 50 miles south of Cincinnati. That got headlines in Dayton, along with some follow up stories about whether it was really true.[83]

On July 18, the Cincinnati *Gazette* summarized the military situation it saw: "We shall not be surprised to hear, at any hour, of Morgan's cavalry being on the hills opposite Cincinnati."[84] Speculation had him crossing the Ohio at Maysville, about 60 miles up the Ohio River, east of Cincinnati. The mayor of Cincinnati alerted Secretary of War Edwin Stanton, but was not having any luck in getting troops, given Stanton's other concerns and given that Morgan didn't have a full army.[85]

Enter Confederate Gen. Braxton Bragg. Bragg is memorialized today in the name of the most populous military base in the world, in North Carolina. But he was not generally admired by his troops or peers. Historian James McPherson has called him a "bumbler."[86] Bragg was often denounced as nasty and vindictive. In 2016, a book was published called *Braxton Bragg: The Most Hated Man of the Confederacy*.[87] And that book is relatively defensive of him. But, whatever his abilities, Confederate President Jefferson Davis had a soft spot for him, and Bragg kept showing up in important roles.

Bragg saw the Forrest and Morgan efforts in Kentucky as building blocks.[88] By mid–August, he had thousands of men at Chattanooga, Tennessee, looking north across the border toward and beyond Kentucky. Referring to other units coming from elsewhere, he said, "I trust we may all unite in Ohio." He told another general, "My army has promised to make me military governor of Ohio in 90 days."[89] Beyond Cincinnati, all the territory up to Chicago was undefended. Moving into the North would have been consistent with Robert E. Lee's simultaneous move into Maryland. Jefferson Davis believed the war had to be brought to the North.

Confederate Gen. Kirby Smith, with an army separate from Bragg's, took Richmond, Kentucky, about 30 miles south of Lexington along what is now Interstate 75. Confronting hastily assembled Union troops there, Smith won one of the most lopsided battles of the war, capturing, killing or wounding most of the 6,500 Union forces, at the cost of about 500 casualties.[90]

That was on August 30, the day the Second Battle of Bull Run in Virginia culminated in a major Southern victory. Though Richmond, Kentucky, was not a major battle, combined with Bull Run, it spurred Jefferson Davis to proclaim a day of prayer and thanksgiving in belief that "God is for us."[91] Kirby Smith soon went on to take Lexington, about 80 miles south of Cincinnati. Meanwhile, Bragg was moving

Confederate Gen. Braxton Bragg, who has been called "the most hated man in the Confederacy," received the exiled Vallandigham, who had been called the "most unpopular man in the North" (Library of Congress).

north toward Louisville on a route parallel to Smith's when he issued this remarkable statement:

> Kentuckians, I have entered your State ... to restore to you the liberties of which you have been deprived by a cruel and relentless foe.... If you prefer Federal rule, show it by your frowns, and we shall return whence we came. If you choose rather to come within the folds of our brotherhood, then cheer us with the smiles of your women and lend your willing hands.[92]

Frown at us, and we'll go away? Yes, that's what the general said. (Given that the smiles he was talking about would be from women, "smiles" might have been a euphemism.) If his comrades sometimes found Bragg insufficiently resolute—and they did—one can see why.

When Union Gen. Lew Wallace (future author of *Ben Hur*) arrived in Cincinnati to take over the defense effort, he declared martial law in Cincinnati and two Kentucky towns on the river, Covington and Newport.[93] It was a given that the Confederates were heading for the Ohio.

At this point, the debate in Ohio about volunteering for military service changed. It had previously had something of an abstract quality. Vallandigham had been saying, if you believe that war can resolve the nation's problems, then volunteer; otherwise, you might do more good at home voting Democratic, thus participating in what he unmistakably considered the more important war, the one in the North against the abolitionists. He assured those who stayed home for that purpose that they were working for the Union, no matter what anybody else said.[94]

Now, however, what one believed about the war seemed beside the point. A hostile army was apparently on the edge of invasion. Who knew what that might portend? This was simply about defending the homeland. Now all manner of men who had not theretofore volunteered reconsidered when the governor implored able-bodied civilian men to report to Cincinnati.

On September 4, a committee that claimed to have been appointed by "the Citizens of Dayton," put this announcement in the *Journal*, with names of the members of the committee:

> The Enemy is at our Door
> MEN OF MONTGOMERY COUNTY:
> An audacious and desperate rebel army is rapidly concentrating on the Southern border of Ohio, which threatens even our immediate neighborhood.... It comes, not to attack a hostile army, for none such has existed here; but to rob and murder....
> Assemble with a rifle, or without it.... Prepare ammunition! Lose not an hour!

On the same day, on an inside page, without a huge headline, there appeared this:

> War! War! War!!!—There will be a meeting held this evening at Beckel's Hall (in downtown Dayton) for the purpose of laying before the citizens of Dayton the following:
> We, the manufacturers and mechanics (laborers) of the city of Dayton, after mature consideration, offer a suggestion as to the propriety of procuring three or more cannon for this city and State, if necessary, subject to the order of the government.
> It is hoped that every lover of his country will be there and ready to act.
> *Empire* please copy.

A Dayton letter writer told his brother in the army, "In our city, business has been almost entirely suspended on two or three days.... (T)he fire bells have been rung,

8. The 1862 Fight for Freedom and Slavery

and our citizens have hurried to and fro with what arms they could gather and, rapidly organizing into companies, rushed off to the threatened city"—Cincinnati. "Such excitement Dayton never saw before. Men of all parties, forgetting for the time to call each 'abolitionist' and 'secesh,' marched elbow to elbow with their trusty rifles over their shoulders."[95]

Eventually, Gen. Wallace announced that now more men were needed; not that the siege was over just that enough was enough. He had about 60,000 men.

During the siege, the Republican Cincinnati *Gazette* reported that the Confederates had released some prisoners in Kentucky, telling them to "go home and vote Democratic." The paper took this occasion to pursue its assaults on Vallandigham.[96]

Meanwhile, Vallandigham himself—42 years old, in good health and running for Congress—had to decide whether to fight. On September 4, addressing the local convention of Democrats that nominated him for re-election to Congress, he had supported a party resolution urging all to "rush to the rescue" of his state if it were attacked. He had said earlier that he would fight to defend his state. Now he said he would fight, but as a member of an organized militia unit.[97] He insisted that such units were the right and legal way to confront this threat. Without militia units, he said, the men would just be mobs sent to the slaughter. But Gov. Tod said there was no time to organize most of the militias. They existed only on paper, untrained, unorganized, with officers not even having been named. The men should just go; a show of force was necessary right now. Report to Wallace.

Vallandigham never did that. If he had, he'd be serving in the U.S. Army, in an effort he wouldn't vote to fund. In an 1860 campaign speech at New York's Cooper Institute, he said he would not vote "one dollar of money whereby one drop of American blood should be shed in a civil war."[98] He reiterated and emphasized the commitment elsewhere.[99] He didn't vote against war appropriations, but he ended up not voting at all on what he called "purely war measures" after July of 1861.[100] Some said that meant he was willing to let the South go. He responded that he didn't think the South could be kept in the union by war, only by negotiation.[101]

Most likely, the appropriations issue wasn't the only one on Vallandigham's mind as he contemplated Cincinnati. If he was in an Ohio militia unit, he would presumably be its top officer, as he had been in the pre-war years. That is, he'd be kind of like, oh, say, Schenck. If he just reported to Wallace, who knew how he might be assigned?

Whether and how he should serve in Cincinnati is not an issue that shows up in Vallandigham's collections of his writings or in his brother's biography of him. That suggests he really did not want to talk about it.

The *Journal* of September 5 was exceptionally newsy, reporting that 250 men had left for Cincinnati and that another group was to leave that day; that Vallandigham had been renominated for Congress by the Democrats, and that an aide to Schenck had sent a letter announcing his injury to a local relative. The letter read:

> Your Uncle was wounded about five o'clock Saturday afternoon. I was close to him at the moment. He had his sword in his hand waving it above his head, cheering on his men, who were under a tremendous fire of musketry and grape. I saw his sword fall from his hand and the next moment felt by the expression of his face that he was wounded. I said, "Are you wounded?"

and he replied, "My arm is broken." It was his right arm, and his horse began plunging.... (H)e was very faint....

We reached Willard's (in Washington) at half past seven or eight. At 10 o'clock, the (doctors) examined his arm. They say it can be saved, unless something unforeseen occurs, but that he will be two or three months getting well, and will lose in a great measure the use of his hand. The ball, a grape shot, entered just above his wrist, making an ugly hole, and breaking the head of the radius, and lacerating the tendons of the thumb and index finger. He suffers great pain of course. The only thing the doctors do is to keep the arm wet with ice water. All visitors are denied; but the President and Secretary Stanton, were here today. The President invited him to go to the Soldiers' Home and stay with him. (Lincoln and his family spent much of the summer at that site a few miles from the White House, finding it less hot and muggy.)

The siege in Cincinnati went on. The locals pitched in to feed and generally make life easier for the out-of-towners. One soldier developed a taxonomy of the local women from a troop's perspective: "The country lasses look after lads almost daily, but the Cincinnati belles abandon us to our pork and beans," he wrote to a newspaper.[102]

The volunteers—called squirrel hunters because many brought rifles they used for that purpose—built fortifications on both sides of the river. They were joined by local black men, who had been pressed into service by Wallace, as whites had been. The black men expressed concern about working in Kentucky, fearing they might be captured and pressed into slavery. A white commander searched for all the black Cincinnati men working in Kentucky and marched them back into Cincinnati, for which they expressed great gratitude.[103]

Through the fall, politics was happening in Cincinnati, too. Murat Halstead, perhaps the best known journalist in town, at the *Commercial* was still saying that the greatest danger to the North was not the Confederate Army, but the force Lincoln called "the fire in the rear." Halstead focused mainly on Vallandigham, but he was also fighting targets even closer to home. In Ohio's First District, the Democrats nominated incumbent Copperhead George Pendleton. Pendleton said that under the Republicans, "this Government (will) sink in the abyss of a military despotism, or licentious anarchy, so that neither you nor your children will live to see its resurrection."[104]

In the Second District, the Democrats nominated lawyer Alexander Long, the fellow who was to suggest letting the South go and was to live to regret it, politically speaking, anyway. In 1862, though, both Pendleton and Long won.

By the end of the siege, some small Confederate units did come very close to Cincinnati, causing some trouble in Florence, Kentucky, and elsewhere nearby. However, the military crisis largely dissipated after a battle October 8 (six days before the congressional election) near Perryville, Kentucky, 50 miles southeast of Lexington. It was called the bloodiest ever fought in Kentucky,[105] at 7,000 total casualties (4,000 for the North). Northern General Don Carlos Buell had brought a Union army up from parts south and met Bragg.[106] The battle was not a clear defeat for Bragg. But he retreated from Kentucky. He might have concluded that without Kentucky strongly behind him, moving into Ohio would have been unwise, especially given the size of the Northern force gathered at Cincinnati. But his decision caused much consternation among his peers and the Southern press, and it resulted in an interview with President Jefferson Davis, though that did not result in Bragg losing his job.[107]

While reports suggested that Bragg and his men did get the female smiles they were looking for, they did not get as many male recruits as they wanted.[108] On September 18 the mercurial Bragg wrote to his wife about having "made the most extraordinary campaign in military history." But he lamented, "We have so far received no (additions) to this army.... Enthusiasm runs high but exhausts itself in words.... The people here have too many fat cattle and are two well off to fight.... Unless a change occurs soon we must abandon the garden spot of Kentucky to its own cupidity."

Well before Perryville, the Dayton *Journal* was no longer paying much attention to events in Kentucky. The election was heating up, after all, and it had been a while since the Confederate generals had seemed to be drawing a bead on Cincinnati. And there was other news, including, in September, the Emancipation Proclamation. There was also the historic Battle of Antietam in mid–September, Robert E. Lee's first thrust into the North. It prompted one of the *Journal's* laughable predictions: "The whole rebel army in Maryland will be annihilated or captured this night,"[109] the wrongness of which was central to just about everything thereafter.

The *Journal* had the war pretty much over in mid–September. On the 18th, it insisted "The Skies are Bright.... (Stonewall) Jackson has no line of retreat which is safe for his cowed and dispirited forces.... Their finest army ... is whipped and crushed. Meantime, our gallant navy is doing its duty, and will soon subjugate the strongholds of rebeldom on the coast." Announcements of "glorious news," inevitable victory and inevitable Southern surrenders followed the next day.

Much of the paper's attention was focused on Corinth, Mississippi, where many Ohioans were fighting in the 23,000-man force of Gen. William Rosecrans to hold that crucial railroad hub. The effort culminated in success a few days before Perryville, though with big casualty figures. All this was, of course, political news.

Meanwhile, there was the report in September of Schenck's promotion to major general of volunteers (not the regular army), along with the news that he was not well enough to come to Dayton for the campaign, but would be well enough to serve in Congress.[110] Then, a week before Election Day, came testimonials to Schenck from three generals, including two who were German-born: Franz Sigel and Carl Schurz. Dayton had contributed a company to Sigel's German-American regiment, one of several such regiments from Ohio. Went one Schenck campaign cry "You Fight mit Sigel, You Vote for Me."[111]

The *Empire*, trying to minimize any political harm from the fact that Vallandigham hadn't voted for war appropriations, insisted that Schenck had "voted against supplies" for the Mexican War. The *Journal* denied this. Neither paper resorted to documentation, though the *Journal* headline was "Nail the Lie."[112]

In the last week of the campaign the *Journal* ran a headline saying "Vallandigham Responsible for the Draft."[113] The paper's argument was that, by encouraging Copperheads not to fight, he prevented the ranks from being filled by volunteers.

Meanwhile, what with Emancipation, the Democrats raised the prospect of a floodtide of blacks to Ohio. The *Journal* responded, "Where are the slaves to come from? Western Virginia has few slaves. In Kentucky the slaves ... are not freed by the

President's Proclamation." (It applied only to Confederate states.) Indeed, the *Journal* insisted that "the prospect of a decrease in the black population" was more likely, because plans were in the works for freed slaves to go to the Caribbean Islands. The paper said black people would prefer the weather in the Caribbean and would prefer not to have to compete with white laborers.

In that last week, too, Ohio Sen. John Sherman (brother of Gen. William Tecumseh Sherman) came to Dayton—to Beckel Hall, at the northwest corner of Third and Jefferson Streets—and "declared that Vallandigham ... did more even to bring on the war than any one in the country."[114] Presumably he meant that Vallandigham's very existence had led Southerners to believe that public opinion would prevent the North from fighting.

On October 11, to summarize for people who hadn't been engaged, the *Journal* said "The unparalleled efforts ... to carry this District and this county for Vallandigham show how important the contest is in the eyes of the traitors.... Frauds will be practiced, falsehoods will be scattered.... Bribery resorted to. It is a death-struggle for the case of armed treason. If the allies of Jeff. Davis are defeated in Ohio, it will shorten the war. It will unite the North. It will show that no considerable portion of the North demands peace at the sacrifice of national honor."

Vallandigham sounded optimistic. He said that Northern public opinion had turned against Lincoln and his tyranny. "Let the guilty tremble," he said. He argued—presenting no evidence for a view he was later to reject—that, "In the South the same reaction has begun," meaning a rejection of the war and its promoters.

Schenck won the election with 52.6 percent of the vote. But Vallandigham carried his old district with 51.6 percent, which was the biggest margin he had ever had. He carried Montgomery County for the first time, by 657 votes, with 51.9 percent. (Lincoln had won 51.4 percent.)

In those marginal margins lay the justifications, such as they were, for an epic spinfest. Typical was this from the Cincinnati *Times*: "The Hon. C.L. Vallandigham has obtained the greatest personal and political triumph ever won by any public man in the United States. In the face of a storm of abuse ... never equaled, Mr. Vallandigham has been endorsed by the constituents whom he represents in Congress ... by a majority of 800 votes, an increase of 700 since his last election in 1860.... The slanderers of Mr. V. ... had better, for shame's sake, cease their abuse. If they do not, there is no knowing to what position of prominence he may advance."[115]

That last point was about Vallandigham moving on to a statewide election. As political analysis, it was nonsense. Vallandigham's improvement in the old district reflected the fact that 1862 was the best Democratic year he had run in. There was a wave. The Democrats, having held only 8 of the state's 21 congressional seats before the election, now held 14 of 19. Vallandigham was the only Democrat to lose outside the very Republican northern part of the state. And most of the Democrats who won supported the war.

Although the new Vallandigham district was better for Republicans than the old, it wasn't better than the state as a whole. It was worse. Lincoln had carried it by much less that his 10-point statewide margin. So there was no rational way to make the case that Vallandigham's showing indicated that he'd be strong statewide.

Moreover, Vallandigham ran a few hundred votes behind the Democratic state ticket in 1862.[116] (There were statewide races for attorney general, secretary of state and "supreme judge."[117])

At this stage in the war, few soldiers were voting. Before the war, many soldiers couldn't have cared less whether they could vote. But the polarization of the Civil War era and the sheer numbers of troops changed things. At the start of the war, only Pennsylvania allowed troops to vote from outside the state, and that law was soon ruled in violation of the state constitution's insistence on residency, and on other grounds.[118] Early in the war, Democrats in Ohio and elsewhere called for letting the troops vote, believing the troops were overwhelmingly Democrats. But as time passed more people came to see the "soldier vote" as Republican; more Republican legislators came to support letting troops vote, and more Democrats to oppose. By late 1862, the public had clearly lined up for enfranchisement. That resolved the issue. But Ohio's enfranchisement, like that of many other states, didn't go into effect until the 1863 election.

Many of the Democratic victories in Ohio in 1862 were quite narrow—in the 52–48 range. So it does seem fair to speculate that some elections would have gone the other way if the soldiers had been voting. That was a widely held view attributed to, for example, Abe Lincoln.[119]

The one way for the Copperheads to really see hope in Vallandigham's numbers was to assume that the swing to the Democrats in general was ongoing, that the tide would only get stronger. Indeed, the Democrats had been seeing a tide all year. In Dayton, two local elections earlier in the year had gone their way and had been interpreted—by them—as referenda on Vallandigham.[120] Said the *Empire,* "Another year and there will not be left an abolition Governor to disgrace a single state in the Northwest. Mark the prediction!"[121]

In those days, elections were followed by "jollifications" or rallies by the winning party. The Cincinnati *Enquirer* reported that 10,000 people came to one for the Democrats in Newark, Ohio, population 5,000.[122] The most popular speaker at such events was the one big loser.[123] Vallandigham offered Democrats an irresistible opportunity to celebrate triumph and wallow in victimization (gerrymandering) at the same time. He spoke unselfconsciously across Ohio and Indiana. He portrayed himself as emblematic of the fact that the only way the Republicans could win an election was through political machinations.

He would speak for two or three hours and, at that, leave his audiences wanting more, some said. Critics would rate a Vallandigham speech as the best ever given in a given town. After one in Springfield, Ohio, a newspaper said, "We but quote the words of hundreds of others when we say that in beauty, simplicity, and strength, many of the passages of the speech were equal to the best periods of Webster."[124]

Vallandigham did not settle for declaring victory in the election. He declared victory for the cause he emphasized in the campaign.

"The people are once more masters," he announced at Centreville, Indiana, on October 20.[125] "*Habeas corpus* is here. Arbitrary arrests are at an end." Ironic seems an insufficient word to apply to his confidence in the end of "arbitrary arrests," given what was to happen to him. True, 1862 was probably the peak year for arrests and incarcerations on political grounds, but they continued throughout the war.[126]

Farther on, he said, "The people have spoken.... 'We will have the Union as it was, the Constitution as it is and the negroes where they are.... In the midst of a despotism worse than that of Austria, the people of these great States have risen in their might, and pulled down the temple of Abolitionism, never to rise again. Not a vestige of it will be left.'" He was on a predictive roll.

The efforts of Vallandigham and others to liken Lincoln to the worse tyrants seemed designed to imitate the charges of others about slavery. Joshua Giddings, for example, told Lincoln in 1860 that Washington was "at this time the most corrupt among all the Christian nations of this earth."[127]

Meanwhile, even setting aside slavery, the South during the war was confronted with the same kind of civil liberties issues as the North. Jefferson Davis suspended *habeas corpus* three times for a total of 17 months, though with the permission of his Congress. One of those occasions came just five days after Davis had chastised Lincoln for his "bastilles." At that point Davis declared martial law in several places, including Richmond. Several people were put in prison for disloyalty, including a former congressman who supported the Union. In east Tennessee several hundred Unionists were jailed. Like Lincoln, Davis was accused of "despotic" behavior. Some of his generals were more aggressive than he was.[128]

At any rate, some people ate up Vallandigham's post-election spin. "We do not hesitate to say that Mr. Vallandigham is, today, the most popular man in the State of Ohio; and, as a rebuke for the shameful manner in which he was gerrymandered out of his seat ... the people of Ohio would now be willing to bestow upon him any office within their gift," said the Hillsboro, Ohio, *Gazette*.[129] At Hillsboro—in southern Ohio, east of Cincinnati—at a public gathering, a resolution was adopted holding Vallandigham to be the best choice for governor in 1863.[130]

9

Tom Lowe, Vallandighammer

Tom Lowe—the young acolyte who reported asking Vallandigham how he thought opposing the war would affect him politically—survives in history only because he was an eager and able writer. Many of his letters to a brother in the army and to others are preserved at the Dayton Metro Library. They tell a remarkable story about the political times.

Lowe's political views raise a question about him already pondered here about Vallandigham: How did a very bright, morally serious, educated young man of the North come to join a movement known for sympathy to slavery? The question is all the more compelling in Tom's case, because his father was an anti-slavery Republican. Moreover, unlike less educated Copperheads, Tom Lowe had no reason to worry about economic competition from freed slaves.

The life of Tom's father is, itself, one for the history books. He was a first-generation Ohioan, having moved as a young man from New York state to Batavia, in the county east of Cincinnati. He became a lawyer. But he had an interest in things military, and he met another young southern Ohioan who did, too: Ulysses S. Grant. Grant recruited John Lowe for the Mexican War.[1] In Mexico, John saw much misery and illness but not much action. He regretted his decision to go, and he returned to wife and children in a year.[2] Prominent war correspondent (and future Republican vice presidential nominee) Whitelaw Reid wrote that John "returned from Mexico with a shattered constitution."[3]

John had married into a prominent family, and he became mayor of Batavia. But his law practice never flourished, and he moved to the bigger, growing city of Dayton in 1855 and, then, almost immediately to Xenia, 15 miles east of Dayton, apparently seeing a specific opportunity there. (Xenia was also the boyhood home of Whitelaw Reid.) When the Civil War broke out, John had hopes of being named a general by Lincoln, because of his military experience. Son Tom thought that dream was killed when Lincoln commissioned Schenck, because such an honor could only go to one Daytonian. John enlisted very early anyway and fought in what became West Virginia. He became a colonel. As with Schenck, his early action got public attention, because there was little war news, and the newspapers wanted all they could get.

John survived his first battle, but newspaper reports circulated that he had done so by hiding. The Lowe family was scandalized by the charge. Tom wrote in the

Dayton *Journal* that his father simply had a difference of opinion with some officers about the best tactics. That view eventually prevailed. Whitelaw Reid accepted it.[4]

But John was killed in the next battle. He was the first officer from Ohio to die in battle. A guess arose publicly that he had taken too big a risk, because he was trying to live down the rumor. Tom believed that. However, Whitelaw Reid told a different story. Or told the story differently:

> The Colonel's health was delicate, (but) he still felt that his place was at the head of his regiment. He looked forward to the battle in which he fell as the probable end of his military career; for, in a letter to his wife only four days before, he said: "I find myself hoping, and it is now about my only hope, that I will soon be at home, a wounded soldier, to receive your care for a little time, and then to lay me down to my long rest. Wait a little longer, dearest, a week, a day may relieve our suspense and bring my fate upon me. God rules over all things, and disposes of us as He thinks best."[5]

So maybe he did take an unnecessary risk. Maybe he knew he was going to. Maybe Reid didn't get it.

Tom Lowe's loss of his father—under circumstances that must have been infuriating to a son who knew his father as an eager volunteer, hardly a coward—was not what made him oppose the war. His viewpoint had older roots.

In his early teens in the early 1850s, the exceptionally bright student had attended Farmer's College near Cincinnati, a school also attended by future President Benjamin Harrison, distinguished journalist Murat Halstead and future leader in the Dayton business world Valentine Winters. Tom spent three years there, excelling academically and being proud of it. Two professors he particularly admired were anti-slavery. He devoted much energy to debate competitions. Historian Carl Becker felt that, combined with the "household legalism" Tom had grown up with, "these voluble exercises further developed in Tom an argumentative and clamorous approach to all human problems."[6] Argumentative Tom certainly was.

He left the school without a degree because of his family's financial situation. He did a stint at a bank in Cincinnati. Then, after briefly working with his father during the father's brief stay in Dayton, he left Ohio for another job. He was 17. The new job was in Nashville, again at a bank, where he was to be a clerk. Nothing in the historical record suggests that he specifically wanted to go south. But Nashville was a bustling city, the second biggest in the South, after New Orleans. And he had an offer.

On the trip down the Ohio River, a fellow passenger was traveling with about 15 of his slaves. Tom saw nothing awful in the way the slaves were being treated, and he sensed no great anger on their part about their lots in life. He wrote to his father that this experience expanded his views on slavery.[7] That fact alone doesn't seem enough to explain his eventual politics. It was a brief episode; later, he didn't refer to it often. What can be said for sure about the episode is that his background obviously did not do much to inoculate him against sympathy for slave owners.

In Tennessee, Lowe spent some time in Lebanon, about 30 miles east of Nashville, with a population of about 2,500, including 1,000 slaves.[8] He came to know sons of privilege who went to elite colleges, and he wrote that he preferred their values to those he saw prevailing in the North. Whereas the dollar was almighty in the North, he thought, the southern guys had a healthier attitude, seeing money as not necessarily more important than honor or tradition. Moreover, he came upon little that he recognized as antipathy toward the North, little taste for secession. He was mentored by prominent Whigs—not Democrats—who talked of compromise and seemed reasonable.[9]

An important mentor was William B. Campbell, the last Whig governor of Tennessee. Lowe wrote glowingly about Campbell.[10] "He is a noble American; I love him more & more every day. I listened to him for two hours one evening last week with most rapt attention." Campbell, who ended up opposing secession and even spent a short time as a Union general, rejected the Tennessee Democrats, seeing them as just as regionally focused as the northern Republicans. He asked them to contemplate one downside of secession: Suppose that the northern states were a foreign country. How much would slave "property" be worth if the neighbors to the north were not governed by the Fugitive Slave Act requiring cooperation in the return of slaves?

Lowe came to see slavery as necessary for the stability of the South. And he came to like Southern whites. He wrote in 1862 that "no one can appreciate the splendid parts of Southern character unless he sees a Southern Christian patriot's family. They are the noblest set of people on earth."[11] He mentioned a specific family and said its "views about slavery and Christianity" were very much like his own.

Lowe didn't become a Democrat in Tennessee. But he did rule out the Republicans. His new friends generally saw the Republicans as—yes—the nation's great problem, the reason there was sectional tension.

With the Whig Party pretty much gone, Tom saw something good in the American Party—the Know-Nothings—which was prospering in Tennessee. That party's anti-immigrant pitch didn't particularly resonate there; but the Know-Nothings were less hostile to the North than the Democrats.

Lowe did not take seriously the possibility of slavery spreading to the new territories. He thought it would be voted down there. That confidence obviated—for him—much of the expressed point of the Republican Party.[12] And it raised the possibility that the party's real agenda was the elimination of slavery everywhere.

While in Nashville, Tom was courting—via mail, mainly—a girl back in Dayton. She was Marsha, the daughter of Jonathan Harshman, of the banking firm of Harshman and Winters.[13] (Modern Daytonians know Harshman as the name of a road; he had owned property on it. And Winters was the name of a bank deep into the 20th century. Harshman's partner Valentine Winters was an ancestor of comedian Jonathan Winters.)

In piles of letters between Tom and Marsha, there is nothing about politics. Of course, unlike the Medlars, they were teens. Marsha wrote a lot about parties. Indeed, she was resistant to Tom's obsession with marriage, because she was having too good a time in the Dayton of the 1850s and felt she was too young. Against a relentless campaign, she held her position. He was constantly on her case about not writing him often enough or at great enough length, apparently not understanding that, while writing came easily to him, it doesn't to everybody. He also complained relentlessly that her letters didn't express the kind of unbounded love for him that his expressed for her.

When Tom returned to Dayton in 1857, he went to work for her father's bank. He was still not a Democrat. For president in 1860, he supported John Bell, a minor-party candidate from Tennessee who supported both slavery and union and carried Tennessee. But in Dayton the Democrats were the only alternative to the Republicans. Tom's attention turned to Vallandigham, the charismatic local leader, the soul of the Democratic Party. Tom admired him for ignoring "the daily persecution in Dayton, where one could not speak safely in his defense."[14] He felt that the personal strength that Vallandigham exuded actually protected him from "mobs," who were scared off.

When the war broke out, Tom's thinking was muddled. He wrote in a letter that victory was necessary. He felt if that the South won independence, it would be so full of itself that it wouldn't let the North live in peace.[15] But he kept saying he was for compromise, including recognition of the Southern government.[16] But how could that be a compromise? If the South got recognition, what would it *not* get? Recognition was the whole idea.

In moving toward an anti-war position, Tom had a family problem to confront: His younger brother Will had joined the army before the war, in his teens, and, still very young, was now an officer seeing combat and apparently thinking about a military career. He was at Shiloh, from which he wrote after the horrendous battle in 1862: "I feel quite lonely here…. All the officers of our two old companies are gone and I am the only one left."[17]

In his letters to Will, Tom often seemed to be trying to convince his brother that he was not the traitor Will saw Copperheads as. (We don't have Will's letters.) Tom insisted that he had some differences with Vallandigham. Nevertheless, the world came to see Tom as a Vallandigham guy. He was openly engaged in politics, writing articles for the newspapers and developing a high profile. He was with Vallandigham in his writing and he was there in his relations with the man.

In relations with Will, Tom would make such political concessions as sending him the Dayton *Journal*, not the *Empire*. Things remained cordial enough that when Will was on leave, he would stay at Tom's house. Tom's wife Marsha adored him.[18]

But Tom's hostility to the war eventually emerged clearly in the letters, as did his fury over Republican charges against Vallandigham and his supporters. Tom used the letters to vent, to organize his thoughts and to proselytize.

Tom's views were not simply anti-war; they were pretty close to anti-army. He said that if the North won the war, democracy would be dead. He said the army would be the most powerful force in the country. He said that was simply the way it was after civil wars, and he didn't want to live in a country like that. Tom eventually said the Republicans would never give up power, because they had committed so many crimes—infringements upon civil liberties, profiteering from war contracts—that they would worry about being prosecuted by the Democrats.[19]

In a campaign speech for Vallandigham in 1862, Tom Lowe said that letting the South go would be better than keeping it with "bayonets."[20] And, contrary to some of his letters, he insisted that there was no need to fear Southern aggression after a war, because the North was too strong. Like Vallandigham, he likened "abolitionists" to the Jacobins of the French Revolution, bloody fanatics. He said if anyone wrote to Washington reporting that he (Lowe) had talked treason, he would be taken away without trial. Lowe, like his hero, flaunted his book learning; he likened the Republicans to Charles I, Louis XVI and King Philip of Spain.[21]

Like Vallandigham, Lowe was deeply religious and utterly appalled by antislavery preachers. He tried to oust the leader of the First Presbyterian Church in Dayton, Dr. Thomas E. Thomas, for saying, according to Lowe, that he prayed that "this war may never cease until (slavery) is destroyed." Lowe said Thomas' view put him "as much in opposition to our Constitution as is the most ultra secessionist alive," because the Constitution was okay with slavery. Thomas, said Lowe, "would rather that the twenty four millions of whites in our country should destroy each other in this civil war than that it should end without liberating the 4,000,000 slaves."[22] He called the minister's position unpatriotic, though he was horrified when others made that charge against him.

Early in the war, Tom left the bank and opened a law practice. In 1862, he officially joined the Democratic Party and became active in it. He was quickly made an officer. He avoided military service by hiring a substitute. It was legal.

He said, "I hold any man excusable (from service) who has given his Father and only brother and (has) his Mother, sister, wife & child depending on him, as I have. But the majority of these cowardly Republican skunks have no better pretext than that their business will suffer if they leave it."[23]

He did not join the army. Like Vallandigham, he thought the important war was being fought in the North between Republicans and Democrats. He sounded like he was influenced by Vallandigham's public statements on whether to fight or stay home.

By the end of 1862, Lowe was expecting the party to put him up for the legislature in 1863, though he was still in his early twenties.[24] He was the kind of guy who was the youngest to have ever held any particular position he was holding. And he was known for being thick with the icon. At one stage, he was selected to present to Vallandigham an inscribed, gold-headed butternut cane that some female supporters had made for him. The relationship with Vallandigham included some socializing, and, when Dayton seemed threatened by Confederate guerrillas, the Lowes made sure Vallandigham's wife was spirited away.[25]

His political prospects notwithstanding, though, by end of 1862, Lowe was definitely not in a good mood.

***

Immediately after the 1862 election, political tensions in Dayton exploded into the assassination of a newspaper editor by a political opponent. Or that didn't happen. Or it kind of happened. What did happen for sure was a fatal shooting.

J.F. Bollmeyer was "co-editor" of the Dayton *Empire*. A big man in his early 30s, who had been born in Germany, he was an itinerant newspaperman and political appointee. The definitive account of what happened to him comes from Carl M. Becker, the Dayton-born historian, in a 1966 article *The Death of J.F. Bollmeyer: Murder Most Foul?*[26] This summary is taken largely from that.

Bollmeyer lived downtown. On the morning of November 1, he took a basket from home and went to the market on foot. On the way home, he was confronted by the hatter Henry M. Brown, a neighbor from across an alley who was walking toward the market. Brown's sons had had run-ins with Bollmeyer. Nothing political.

When the two men met on the street, a few people heard parts of the conversation. Brown seemed to believe that, as a result of the run-ins with his sons, Bollmeyer had said bad things about Brown, a charge Bollmeyer denied. Brown called him a liar. Bollmeyer put his basket down and was apparently stepping toward Brown. Brown, who was 52 and weighed only 120 pounds and was not in great health, pulled a gun. Bollmeyer said, "Don't shoot, Henry." Brown shot Bollmeyer in the head, killing him almost instantly. Brown was arrested later at his store.

The shooting sent the town into turmoil. Some assumed it was political. During the day, scores of Democratic men showed up at the jail wanting access to Brown; that night there were thousands of men. They found two "swivel" guns at the Dayton *Empire* and deployed them. Then the guns fell into the hands of workers at the jail. Then, 15 hours after the shooting, the army was on its way from Cincinnati. The crowd dispersed. There had been some violence, and people had been hurt. But there was not a conflagration.

Enter Tom Lowe. He wrote a piece for the *Empire* labeled "The Assassination of J.F. Bollmeyer." It embraced all the Democratic assumptions about the event without documenting them. He described what Brown allegedly said to Bollmeyer to start things: "I understand, sir, you have been complaining that my son killed your dog and that he with other boys annoys your family by ringing your doorbell." Lowe was, at best, confused about the facts. The dog had not been killed; the dog incident and the doorbell incident involved two different Brown sons.

Lowe continued: "Bollmeyer answered 'that is true, sir.'" Then, wrote Lowe, Brown accused Bollmeyer of bad-mouthing him. Bollmeyer denied it.

Brown responded, according to Lowe: "Well, you are a G—d d—d traitor and secessionist, and I am going to kill you."

Lowe wrote: "'Don't shoot, Brown—you are mistaken' answered Bollmeyer, in the kindest and most conciliatory voice and manner, but the assassin's hand was not stayed and in another moment he was dead."

Lowe insisted that Brown thought that shooting Bollmeyer "would be an act which the whole country would applaud," because Bollmeyer was a traitor. So, said Lowe, Brown "constituted himself the court, jury and executioner to punish him."

Lowe also said that Republican journals—like the Dayton *Journal*—had "advised" assassination of people like Vallandigham. (Not true, certainly not literally.)

Then, flipping out entirely, Lowe wrote: "Bollmeyer's blood seems the first dropping of a coming storm which will destroy every vestige of our freedom, 'bring anarchy upon us like night,' and a massacre that will 'seal our nation's eternal grave.'"

Tom's take on the Bollmeyer shooting caught on among Democrats. The Cincinnati *Enquirer* took up the cause and got into a spitting match with Murat Halstead's *Commercial*. The *Enquirer* said the *Commercial* was just the sort of Republican publication that fostered this sort of thing, and the *Commercial* said the *Enquirer's* effort to get political advantage out of a tragedy was typical of it.

Vallandigham said Bollmeyer's death was a "foul murder" resulting from not only the preaching of Republican newspapers, but from the preaching from the pulpit of a "Gospel of hate." He announced that Bollmeyer was killed "for no other reason than that he was an able and prominent Democrat." Vallandigham said Brown was a cousin of the notorious John Brown (which this author has not confirmed). Vallandigham was later to call Bollmeyer "the first martyr in the cause of constitutional liberty."[27] This was a backhanded acknowledgment that, his French Revolution comparisons notwithstanding, the Lincoln people hadn't actually put anybody to death for speaking out.

This episode dramatizes which "war" Vallandigham was focused on. With scores of thousands of men dying in the Civil War on both sides for what they saw as high causes, his idea of a "first martyr" was a Copperhead newspaperman in a peace zone.

The Brown trial didn't take place until the following September. It happened in the county north of Dayton—Miami County. It lasted nine days and had 90 witnesses: 51 for the prosecution and 39 for the defense. Some were actually witnesses, not to the shooting, but to the earlier incidents involving the sons. And people testified about such things as what Brown had said about Bollmeyer before the fateful day.

After four hours of deliberation, the jurors acquitted Brown, apparently finding that the smaller, older, less-healthy man had legitimate reason to fear that Bollmeyer was coming at him. Though the verdict inherently rejected the notion that Brown had been bent on political assassination, it did not get at whether his view of Bollmeyer was affected by what he had read in the newspapers.

The best bet is that Brown would not have confronted Bollmeyer if Brown hadn't been armed, but that his original intent was only to use the gun defensively if necessary.

The verdict didn't end the debate, of course. The Democrats—including Lowe—complained about Miami County being Republican territory. (It had gone for Lincoln by more than a thousand votes out of fewer than six thousand cast.) They also complained about the judge's practices.

By the time of the trial, the Bollmeyer shooting was no longer the big story, the big controversy about political violence in the city. It was looking only like a precursor.

10

Let's Call the Whole Thing Off

That Vallandigham favored peace-at-any-price was a charge long made against him. It was not true. He favored union at any price: Do whatever was necessary to get the South back in the Union. He was scandalized by the notion that he preferred peace to union. He thought of it as an ugly charge.

Then he proved it. In January of 1863, he insisted that no end of the war was in sight and said, if it wasn't stopped now, "I see nothing before us but universal political and social revolution, anarchy, and bloodshed, compared with which, the Reign of Terror in France was a merciful visitation." He said the Lincoln administration had once had the entire country on its side. "Five men and half a score of newspapers made up the Opposition." But, he said, "Defeat, debt, taxation, sepulchers, these are your trophies." How has the war gone? "Let the dead at Fredericksburg and Vicksburg answer."

He asked and immediately answered, "What then? Stop fighting. Make an armistice—no formal treaty. Withdraw your army from the seceded states. Reduce both armies to a fair and sufficient peace establishment."

That would have left the Confederate government in charge in the South. It would have required sacrifice only from the North, because the South had no armies on Northern land. Besides its armies in the South, the North had New Orleans, parts of old Virginia (West Virginia), parts of North Carolina, parts of Tennessee.

Oddly, the month before Vallandigham made his armistice proposal, he offered a House resolution saying that any employee of the federal government who proposed a peace that did not entail reunion of all the states would be "guilty of a high crime." (So much for his commitment to free speech.) At the time, he was fending off the notion that he would give up the South. And he had predicted the Republicans would. At any rate, there seems to be a contradiction here. Perhaps he would have argued that his proposal entailed reunification.

Vallandigham did insist that he didn't see his separation as a permanent solution. He said the regions would naturally move toward reunification if only the fighting stopped. He argued that they had so much in common—culturally, historically, ethnically, geographically (same rivers, for example), economically and in language and friendships and family ties, even politically, if you set aside slavery—that they couldn't remain apart. He expected reunification in about three years. He insisted it could happen because the anti-slavery movement would die as a result of an armistice, because its adherents would see how much harm it had done. And he said the

South would rejoin the Union when it saw that the North had learned its lesson. Possibly, the specific scenario he had in mind was the passage of constitutional amendments that would satisfy the South—if the anti-slavery movement ceased.

What he said was, "Declare absolute free trade between the North and South. Buy and Sell. Agree upon a (panel to handle trade issues). Recall your fleets. Break up your blockade. Reduce your navy. Restore travel. Open up railroads. Re-establish the telegraph" between the regions. "Reunite your express companies…. Visit the North and West. Visit the South. Exchange newspapers. Migrate. Intermarry" across geographic lines. "Let slavery alone…." That was the way back to unity.

Vallandigham acknowledged that he was suggesting recognition of the Confederacy: "informal, practical recognition." He said that already existed. "It is not formal recognition, to which I will not consent." His line in the sand.

Vallandigham's flip-flop might reasonably be seen as part of a pair with Lincoln's. Early in the war, Lincoln was accused of fighting a war about slavery, but insisted his only interest was in preserving the union. At a certain stage, though, the horrors of war and other factors led him to embrace the moment as a revolutionary one and to free the Southern slaves. Early in the war, Vallandigham was accused of having a secessionist agenda, but denied it. At a certain stage, though, the horrors of war and other factors led him to embrace the moment as a counter-revolutionary one and to let the South go (indefinitely).

He was in a counter-revolutionary mood. His proposal came in the same speech in which he finally and fully embraced Southern slavery.[1] The speech was his valedictory to Congress upon his 1862 defeat. He titled it "The Great Civil War in America." His first words were about his by-then famous election defeat: "Indorsed at the recent election, within the same district for which I still hold a seat on this floor, by a majority four times greater than ever before, I…."

He framed the war as a matter of northern sectionalism gone berserk. "Sectional jealousy and hate—these, sir, are the only elements of conflict between these states." Finally showing some recognition of the contradiction between his denunciation of sectionalism and his embrace of it, Vallandigham took back some words from his 1859 speech "There Is a West." He said, "Some years ago, in the midst of high sectional controversies, and speaking as a western man, I said some things harsh of the North, which now, in a more catholic spirit, as a United States man, and for the sake of reunion, I would recall." His presentation was tortured. "My prejudices, indeed, upon this subject, are as strong as any man's; but in this day of great national humiliation and calamity, let the voice of prejudice be hushed." So he admitted to being prejudiced against the North. *That* was his contribution to sectional reconciliation? As a demonstration of his new tolerance, he said he would not "exclude New England in any reconstruction." He allowed that New England had many people who were not like the "Yankees" and "Puritans" (he put the words in quotes) who had done so much to foment war. So he still didn't like Yankees and Puritans, but he was so large-minded that he would acknowledge there were other types in the section. Apology was not his best thing.

On slavery, he said the war "has annihilated, in twenty months, all the false and pernicious theories and teachings of Abolitionism for thirty years…. We have learned that the South is not weak, dependent, unenterprising, or corrupted by slavery, luxury, and idleness; but powerful, earnest, warlike, enduring, self-supporting, full of energy, and inexhaustible in resources.

"We have (learned) that African slavery, instead of being a source of weakness to the South, is one of her main elements of strength; and hence the 'military necessity,' we are told, of abolishing slavery in order to suppress the rebellion." Indeed, Lincoln had presented his Emancipation Proclamation as a military necessity. His hope was that it would bring black troops to the Union side, undermine the South's efforts to use slaves as non-combatants in the military, and complicate things on the Southern home front.

Vallandigham said: "Abolitionists have found out, to their infinite surprise and disgust, that the slave is not 'panting for freedom,' nor pining in silent, but revengeful grief over cruelty and oppression inflicted upon him, but happy, contented, attached deeply to his master, and unwilling—at least not eager—to accept the precious boon of freedom, which they have proffered him."

This talk of "happy, contented" slaves "attached deeply to (their) masters" was the rhetoric of the slaveholders themselves. Vallandigham insisted that "fewer slaves escaped, even from Virginia, in now nearly two years" than in six months during the Revolutionary War. (In truth, though, when Northern units took control in various Confederate territories, they were likely to be inundated with more escaped slaves than they knew what to do with. And about 200,000 black men ultimately joined Union lines. When you figure that there were 2 million male slaves of all ages, and when you figure the difficulty and dangers of escaping to Union-held territory and the danger that decision posed to loved ones left behind, a lot of men came over.)

Vallandigham—once so worried about John Brown fomenting a slave rebellion—said that "servile insurrection" turns out to "the least of the dangers to which (the South) is exposed. Hence, in my deliberate judgment, African slavery, as an institution, will come out of this conflict fifty-fold stronger than when the war began." He also insisted that people back home were coming around to his views on slavery.

And he made an interesting concession: "I deny that it was the 'slave power' that governed (the country before the war), and so wisely and well. It was the Democratic party, and its principles and policy, molded and controlled, indeed, largely by Southern statesmen."

Perhaps his overarching argument, and that of the Copperheads in general: He would not be "stopped by that … cry … about the sin and barbarism of African slavery. Sir, I see more of barbarism and sin, a thousand times, in the continuance of this war, the dissolution of the Union, the breaking up of this Government, and the enslavement of the white race by debt and taxes and arbitrary power."

A couple of negative responses to the speech came before Vallandigham left the floor of the House. One was from Rep. Hendrick Bradley Wright, of Wilkes-Barre, Pennsylvania, a Democrat who started by describing himself as "a peace man." He cited at length a series of quotations from Southern officials denying any possibility of compromise with the North, that is, of voluntary reunification.

In response, Vallandigham granted the impossibility of reconciliation with the existing Southern leadership. That was a major concession, since Vallandigham was universally and reasonably interpreted—both before and after the speech—as believing that the solution to the Civil War was to elect people like him to bring the South back into the Union. He did not enlarge on his new admission. But he insisted that "after some time, when passion has cooled and reason resumed its sway, I expect to see a return of union sentiment (in the South), and whosoever ... stands in the way shall be superseded by other men, just as (the war administration in Washington has) been superseded through the ballot box in the North and West" (a reference to the 1862 election).

The following two quotes constitute the entirety of the next portion of the debate as recorded in the official record.[2]

Wright: "I cannot conceive by what principle of reasoning the gentleman can satisfy himself that such a result could possibly, under any circumstances, be attained."

Vallandigham: "History and human nature."

Wright also said Vallandigham's point about future elections "surprised me more than anything (else) he said." And he lectured Vallandigham to the effect that if he thought the 1862 election outcome meant the public had turned against the war, he was deluding himself.

Overall, though, Vallandigham had to be thrilled with the response to his widely anticipated speech. (A reporter for the non–Democratic Boston *Herald* said it drew the biggest congressional crowd he had seen in a couple of years.[3]) It turned out to be Vallandigham's most celebrated speech, his most widely distributed. Many saw in it a historic effort. Democratic newspapers across the country—though especially in Ohio and the West—reprinted it, and some put it out in pamphlet form, including at least one paper in California.[4]

The Cincinnati *Enquirer* ran the speech "to the exclusion of our usual variety of reading matter," saying it "would add to the fame of a Clay or a Webster, or a Burke or a Chatham...."[5] Samuel Medary, the gatekeeper of Ohio Copperhead opinion, said in his *Crisis,* that "this is no ordinary speech—made by no ordinary man.... (W)ords of wisdom and burning eloquence ... run through every paragraph, sentence, and line.... (He is) the true representative of the whole people, of all the States, and the nation as it was" before the war.[6]

The "crowning effort of (Vallandigham's) public life." The "greatest effort of the age." "The master speech of his generation." "The coming man." These were some of the comments from around the country, compiled (credibly) by the *Empire* mainly. That paper also reported that the Paris, Illinois *Standard* said a hotel there had just been renamed the Vallandigham Hotel.[7]

There was even some Republican praise (along with abuse). Whitelaw Reid called the speech "remarkable" and said Vallandigham was "the fittest and most faithful exponent" of Copperhead views.[8] Said the Republican Cincinnati *Gazette*: "This man is the hero of our Northern rebels.... He waxes ... with an energy and force that (impresses) every hearer.... At a single step, the shunned and execrated Vallandigham has risen to the leadership of their" faction.[9]

Praise came from papers in New York, Boston and Philadelphia. The St. Louis *Republican* said the speech was "significant as the first occasion when (the Republicans) in Congress calmly listened to the semi-secession doctrine of Vallandigham or any other peace man." (It was certainly not the first time such sentiments were spoken in Congress, just, supposedly, the first time anybody listened.)

With the Southern reaction, there was a problem. The Confederate government expressed no interest in the armistice. Richmond was seeking victory in the form of permanent, universally recognized independence. And it was optimistic. The month before Vallandigham's speech had seen a Northern military debacle at Fredericksburg, Virginia, coming after others. The South had celebrated that and was still celebrating. For Richmond to leap at a peace proposal made by a Northern politician who was a member of the opposition and had just lost a congressional race would have been too much like suing for peace.

The Dayton *Journal* enjoyed reporting in February on what seemed like the official Confederate response to Vallandigham's speech: "The Richmond *Enquirer* ... says, 'We have no objection to Mr. Vallandigham and his Democrats dethroning the usurper (Lincoln). On the contrary, we encourage him in that enterprise; but he must expect no political alliance with us, and may as well drop the subject.' That's plain enough."[10]

The quote got Vallandigham coming and going. Yes, the enemy likes him and applauds his work. But, no, that work cannot achieve the goal.

The armistice proposal went nowhere, much like Vallandigham's proposal to divide the country into official regions, and like his flirtation with Western secession.

The widespread praise notwithstanding, the speech was semi-unhinged. Its defense of slavery (quoted in Chapter 4), insisting that a country being half slave and half free was the perfect arrangement, was weird and tortured. The call for an armistice undermined Vallandigham's definition of himself. His acknowledgment that reconciliation was impossible with the current Confederate leaders undercut the whole Copperhead posture. His embrace of ultimate reconciliation was arbitrary and unconvincing, especially to the degree it was dependent upon the anti-slavery movement drying up and blowing away. His simultaneous rejection and re-statement of his own sectional prejudice was incoherent. Intellectually, at least, he was all bollixed up.

11

Exiled, Welcomed and Removed

Vallandigham's candidacy for governor of Ohio in 1863 was in place before the armistice speech. He was, after all, an ambitious young politician—turning 43 in 1863—without an office, but with a passionate statewide and national following. The seat that was open was governor, being a two-year term contested in odd-numbered years.

The war made governors more important. States raised troops for the federal army. They put together their own militias. They could work hand-in-glove with the administration in silencing various anti-war voices. Governors made decisions about how to enforce the federal Fugitive Slave Law, that is, about whether to welcome escaped slaves. Conceivably, in a state—like Ohio—which might experience a Southern invasion, an anti-war governor might even send out peace feelers to the nearby states.

But the importance of the election went way beyond that. A victory by Vallandigham would have shaken the political earth nationally. It would have meant that the fire in the rear was now a conflagration.

Governors were the highest-ranking people short of the president who were elected by the public. A Vallandigham victory would be interpreted as an anti-war statement by voters. Ohio was the third biggest state and one that had been good to the Republicans. What would the troops do if they thought the voters were against the war? Desertion was already a big concern. It was easy; the troops weren't in Vietnam, after all.

Vallandigham's election would make him a contender for president. With the death of Stephen A. Douglas, no other Democratic civilian had so high a profile (though some Democratic generals were universally known). In the wake of the armistice speech on January 14, Vallandigham was being endorsed for president by various public meetings of Democrats, including one in Butler County, Ohio, and one in Lebanon, Pennsylvania. Both times it was unanimous.[1]

The race for the Democratic nomination for governor was hot. Vallandigham got many endorsements from newspapers and public gatherings even before he announced.[2] But many party leaders were afraid of nominating him. They saw the Republicans fighting hard for the political center, even to point of nominating former Democrats. They saw that War Democrats had generally done better against Republicans in 1862 than Peace Democrats had. And they doubted that Vallandigham had as much public support as his crowds might indicate. One historian: "Many who were opposed to his views were attracted to his speeches by the fascination of his oratory. It is probable that only a small minority within the party were willing to support his plan for securing peace."[3]

Hugh Jewett had been a wealthy railroad man, a former U.S. attorney and former state legislator when he was picked by the Democrats to run for governor in 1861. All those characteristics were common at the time for governors. He was a War Democrat. He was from the Zanesville area east of Columbus, neither a hotbed of abolition nor a particularly Southern-leaning place. Jewett only won 42 percent of the vote in 1861 against former Democrat David Tod, but some thought he would do better the second time around, which wouldn't have been unusual. The times and the issues had changed. To many Democrats, the best political bet seemed to be this: stand undeniably with the troops, but oppose emancipation, favoring a war only for union.

The convention delegates who would choose a nominee could reasonably be expected to see that Vallandigham's loss in 1862 was just a loss, not a moral victory, and to see that he was more toxic now, as a result of the armistice speech. Important papers in Cleveland, Cincinnati and Columbus jumped to Jewett's support. Vallandigham's campaign stalled. The recent defeat of a Copperhead candidate for governor of Connecticut hadn't helped.[4] Historian Eugene Roseboom put it flatly: "Ohio Democrats (were not) prepared to accept Vallandigham as their gubernatorial choice."[5]

Upon his return to Ohio, Vallandigham found himself in direct confrontation with another high-profile, recently defeated figure seeking redemption—besides Jewett. The other one was not a politician, but a general.

The story at the heart of this book involves one of the generals Lincoln went through on his way to Ulysses Grant, looking for a match for Robert E. Lee. Ambrose Burnside has been much abused in history. So certain things about his rise should be understood.

At the end of 1862, Lincoln had desperately needed a big military victory. He had just had a bad mid-term election, suggesting that voters were losing faith in the war and in him as a leader. He was worried that Britain and France might recognize the Confederacy if he was deemed unable to put down the rebellion. Republicans in Congress were complaining that Lincoln and his generals weren't nearly aggressive enough or successful enough. One moderately bright spot had been the Battle of Antietam in Maryland in September. The Union army had driven Lee back to Virginia after his only incursion into the North to that date. But it was only a defensive victory. Lincoln felt that a chance to actually destroy Lee's army had been missed by McClellan, who didn't give much chase when Lee retreated.

Burnside was a longtime friend and subordinate of McClellan. (He was also, somehow, the man after whom sideburns are named.) As a civilian in the late 1850s, McClellan had hired Burnside, his fellow West Pointer, for a railroad job, when Burnside had appealed to him after a business setback.[6] Burnside had also been McClellan's top general for a time during the war. His name popped up in the news regularly, including at First Bull Run and Antietam.

Early in the war, Burnside had made a name for himself by taking parts of the North Carolina coast in a partly amphibious campaign he had conceived, promoted, organized and executed.⁷ He was widely celebrated and honored. Oliver Wendell Holmes wrote an ode to him.⁸

The Dayton *Journal's* man in Washington—who used the byline Presto—stood with other commentators in saying, "Gen. Burnside has a reputation for activity in military operations, while McClellan, if there is activity about him, exhibits it in proclamations and orders."⁹

At least one knowledgeable observer wasn't so sure about Burnside: Burnside. When Lincoln asked him to replace McClellan, Burnside responded that "McClellan was the better general and only needed a fair chance."¹⁰ Biographer William Marvel presents Burnside as consistently believing and stating that he was not equipped to command armies, but only smaller units. It was a view that a great many people came to share. But

Ambrose Burnside, the general of blemished record who had Vallandigham arrested and wanted to put him in jail for the duration (Library of Congress).

Lincoln was desperate and liked him. Burnside finally took McClellan's job when he became convinced that McClellan was going to be fired anyway and that the job might go to Joseph Hooker, whom Burnside loathed.¹¹

Once in command, Burnside followed Lincoln's leadership in a way that McClelland didn't. He understood that his overriding order was to fight.

The belief circulated widely and nationally in December that Union forces had Robert E. Lee trapped at Fredericksburg, Virginia. Expectations—including those of the president—rose of a great victory. But there were delays, and by the time Burnside attacked, Lee was well fortified. The result was a Northern calamity. It included 12,600 Union casualties, to 5,400 for the Confederacy. Burnside quickly tried a second offensive, but it bogged down in mud. (One Union officer was said to have sent out a plea during that effort for "50 men, 25 feet high, to work in mud 18 feet deep.")¹²

As the South celebrated, the North recriminated. When Vallandigham called for an armistice on the grounds that the war policy just wasn't working, he was playing to very fresh anger and heartbreak in the North.

Burnside's role at Fredericksburg has been analyzed a lot. Historian Bruce Catton's take is not uncommon: When circumstances changed, "Burnside lacked the mental agility to change his plan."¹³ Jump ahead two years: There's another catastrophe involving Burnside, this one at the Battle of the Crater at Petersburg, Virginia, 1864. Catton ultimately made a similar evaluation of Burnside's role. At a certain stage, "the Union cause … would have been much better off if he had taken to his bed (and), pulled the covers over his handsome face."¹⁴

At that, Catton thought Burnside was likable and decent. He described him: "Physically, he was impressive: tall, just a little stout, wearing what was probably the most artistic and awe-inspiring set of whiskers in all that be-whiskered army. He customarily wore a high ... felt hat with the brim turned down and ... knee-length frock coat belted at the waist—a costume which unfortunately is apt to strike the modern eye as being very much like that of a beefy cop of the 1880s."[15]

Biographer Marvel came to a judgment of Burnside that overlapped with Catton's, but was more sympathetic. He insisted that one big reason Burnside "may be the most maligned figure of the war" is that he didn't fight for his reputation the way other generals did obsessively during and after the war. Burnside "sincerely believed ... that history would vindicate him. He was wrong ... and his silence has worked against him."[16] Marvel wrote that Burnside's "greatest flaw in ... public life" was "his trust in the essential goodness and honesty of men."[17]

After Fredericksburg, newspapers across the North were infuriated by what they saw as "bungling."[18] Nevertheless, Burnside's career was not destroyed. He had supporters in Congress. He was early among generals in supporting the Emancipation Proclamation. That, was particularly appreciated, because he was seen as a Democrat at the beginning of the war; it got him Republican support. If he had left his military career, he could have gone into politics. He was a hot prospect in Rhode Island, where he had lived before the war. The outgoing Republican governor wanted him to run for governor.[19]

But Lincoln did have to make a change at the top. Burnside knew that and welcomed it. When relieved, he was relieved. So Lincoln's search for a match for Robert E. Lee continued. And Burnside went to Ohio—as not the guy.

***

After winning election in October 1862, Schenck wouldn't have congressional duties for 14 months. Lincoln gave him a new job. He was to be in charge of "The Middle District," stretching from the outskirts of Washington up to New Jersey. It wasn't a battlefield position. But he had not been shunted to a desk job because of injury; Civil War battlefields saw plenty of one-armed officers. He had an assignment crucial to Lincoln: Keep Maryland in the Union and pacified. It was no easy task. Confederate sympathy was rampant. The state had given Lincoln only 2.5 percent of its votes in 1860, though Lincoln was on the ballot. Maryland had been won, not by Stephen A. Douglas, the mainstream Democrat, but by the farther-right Southern breakaway candidate John Breckenridge.

Schenck seemed perfect for the job: a Lincoln loyalist with both political and military experience. He was happy to have the promotion to major general and an independent command. But his biographer said that "he would soon yearn for the less hazardous duty" of combat.[20]

Upon his arrival, Schenck issued an order proclaiming that there was no "middle ground" in political affairs. He said that he would act against those he saw as expressing "sympathy" for the enemy as if they actually engaged in subversive acts. His friendly biographer described Schenck's approach thus: "Suspected contraband was seized on the slightest pretext. Citizens (suspected of disloyalty) were arrested on the flimsiest of charges and held without bail or trial. Slaves were induced to flee their masters. Newspapers were closed down. Suspected editors were sent southward."[21]

At one stage, Vallandigham himself was slated to speak in Baltimore. Vallandigham said the speech was to be about religion—specifically about the Bible as literature—not politics. Schenck said it wasn't going to happen, and it didn't.[22]

Early in Schenck's watch, the line between military and civilian authority was murky. But when Robert E. Lee moved into Pennsylvania in the summer, Schenck imposed martial law; there was no more murk. The new rules included a ban on guns in homes as well as controls on entry to the state.[23]

Lincoln had qualms about Schenck. He said he "loves fight for its own sake better than I do." But Lincoln basically supported him. He was uncomfortable when Schenck invited slaves to serve in the army, because Lincoln didn't want to drive slaveholders toward the Confederate side. But sometimes the slaves would just show up.[24] Slavery was breaking down in border states.[25] Lincoln didn't press the point.

One censorship incident was strange. Schenck suspended publication of a Democratic newspaper in Philadelphia known as the *Journal*. It had recounted a speech by Confederate President Jefferson Davis. Davis said the South was strong and not near surrender, that the people in the North who were talking about victory being near were fools, that the Emancipation Proclamation had backfired, that the slaves remained loyal, that Southern whites were now convinced the North is pure evil, and that one had to be deranged to think the country could still be re-united.

The Dayton *Journal* ran the Philadelphia paper's offending piece as part of its coverage of the Schenck story.[26] So here we had a Republican newspaper in Dayton running a piece that a Democratic paper had been punished for running. Clearly, the Dayton *Journal's* purpose was to showcase these Northern critics of the war (that is, the Philadelphia *Journal*) quoting Jefferson Davis approvingly. But one might reasonably wonder: If the sentiments in the speech were deemed so dangerous by a Republican authority, why would a Republican paper would reprint them? More important, one might wonder why a Republican paper could do that when a Democratic paper couldn't.

***

After his armistice speech, Vallandigham went on a speaking tour on the East Coast. (Perhaps his plans for that trip explains his effort to soften perception of his anti–East prejudice.) One speech was in Newark on February 14. He appeared with three Copperhead editors who had done prison time for their supposedly subversive writing. Vallandigham had apparently been invited because he was the leading spokesman for the arrestees' point of view and was, therefore, a potential arrestee. Martyrdom was on his mind. The *New York Times* paraphrased him, a practice common at the time[27]:

> There was no sensation, as he knew by experience, so awful as the fear of arrest.... He had passed sleepless nights and listened in terror to the rumble of a carriage, fearing that a minion of the Administration was about to tear him from his home and fireside, and incarcerate him in a loathsome bastille."

Vallandigham recited:

> *"Give us the nerve of steel,*
> *And the arm of fearless might,*
> *And the strength of will that is ready still*
> *To battle for the right.*
> *For the foemen are now abroad.*
> *And earth is filled with crimes.*
> *Let it, therefore, be our prayer to an Omnipotent God—*
> *'Oh give us the men for the times.'"*

When he said "foemen," he certainly did not mean the Confederates. And when he talked of "men for the time," he meant Valiant Val, as he was coming to be called by some.

At the end of February, a soldier from Dayton wrote home from Tennessee: "I think (General William Rosecrans) will soon have to send two or three regiments to Ohio to put down the traitors at home. Oh, how I should like to shoot some of those Northern rebels…. (W)hy don't you form yourselves into regiments and … gut the Dayton *Empire* and Cincinnati *Enquirer*?" The Dayton *Journal* printed the letter,[28] insisting it was from a strong Democrat. Local Copperheads saw it as a yet another threat to their safety, after the Bollmeyer case.

Then, on March 5, Sam Medary's Copperhead weekly in Columbus, *The Crisis*, was mobbed by, reportedly, about 150 men widely presumed to be soldiers. There was much damage.[29] The Dayton *Journal's* comment: "the wonder is that the loyal people of Columbus tolerated (*The Crisis*) as long as they have."[30] Striking words, given that the local *Empire* was an ideological twin of *The Crisis*. The words led to a conflagration of words between the *Journal* and various Democratic papers, including the *Empire*. The *Journal* stood accused of fomenting mob violence. It insisted it was against all mob violence. But it said, "*The Crisis* teemed with treason, from week to week, and gave all the aid possible to the rebels, but the Government, and not the people, should have taken it in hand."[31] It was for censorship of certain newspapers, but not by the mob.

The *Crisis* crisis was the occasion for Tom Lowe's completion of his input to brother Will about the army; in what has been reported here thus far, about the army becoming the dominant force in the country after the war, he had been holding back. The day after the assault, he wrote that

> The common people are alarmed—both Republicans & Democrats—and are arming with the avowed purpose of resisting any further Conscription. The mobbing of Gov. Medary's paper in Columbus has intensified these feelings, and you need not be surprised to hear of an outbreak and a general massacre at any moment. An immense majority of the whole people North are opposed to any further prosecution of the war…. God save the Republic! … I believe that the design of our rulers is to establish a monarchy, by the help of the Army…. The Army is sworn to obey the orders of the President. If you all construe that to mean all his orders, lawful or unlawful, then indeed are you as much the enemies of constitutional liberty as Jeff Davis himself, and there is no hope but in the strong right arms of the people…. I see that the (Will's brigade) has been in another fight. I hope you are still safe. Write soon. Lovingly, Brother Tom.[32]

Judging from his letter, Tom was surrounded by people who shared and, therefore, intensified his views.

After the Newark speech, Vallandigham spoke in New York to a group called the

Copperhead Association. The *Times* characterized him there as "threatening 'resistance' to the" national draft just instituted. Vallandigham complained about that characterization. In response, the *Times* put forth two quotations from him that, however incendiary, did not use the word "resistance" or urge it in other words. Nevertheless, the *Times* said "his language may excite others to such resistance."[33]

The *Times* was worried about local circumstances. Armed resistance was, indeed, what things were to come to New York, with the anti-draft riots of July 1863, the worst urban riots ever in the United States.

***

For Burnside, being sent to Ohio was not being sent to Siberia. True, he was put in charge of some states in which there was no war, somewhat like Schenck. His Department of the Ohio included Michigan, Indiana, Illinois and Ohio. But nobody was laughing at the possibility of the war spreading. And the Department also had Kentucky, always a passionate concern of Lincoln. Meanwhile, the possibility that Burnside himself would be called upon to lead troops again was very real. Indeed, fighting units that were associated with Burnside were transferred with him.[34]

For Burnside, Cincinnati, site of his headquarters, was almost a homecoming. He had been born and raised in eastern Indiana, in Liberty, 60 miles from Cincinnati and 45 from Dayton. The Burnsides had arrived in South Carolina from Scotland a half-century before the American Revolution; Ambrose's grandfather fought against the Revolution. Eventually, Ambrose's Quaker-influenced father, Edghill, turned against slavery and wanted to move to a place where it was outlawed. Much of his extended family made the move, too, but most found frontier Indiana too difficult and returned. Edghill stayed, ultimately becoming a judge and a state legislator. But, for a living, he was mainly a clerk of courts and always struggled to support a large family. Quaker influence notwithstanding, Edghill decided to take advantage of his political connections to get Ambrose into West Point for the free education. Forty-five state legislators recommended the boy.[35]

In the days before slavery was the great dividing line between the parties, the Burnsides were Democrats. Ambrose actually ran for Congress as a Democrat in Rhode Island (where his wife was from) in 1858. He had been head of the state militia as a result of his service in the Mexican War, though his war record didn't amount to much. He was recruited for elective office, also on the basis of his war service.[36]

His conversion from D to R during the war was not unusual for either officers or enlisted men.

When he arrived at his Cincinnati headquarters, he knew about Vallandigham, of course. Now he was told by Republican politicians, editors and others that the Copperheads of the West were dangerous. His subordinate in Indiana, Colonel Henry Carrington, reported that pro–South sentiment was prevalent there and growing, especially since the enactment of the national draft. Carrington said that a secretive pro–South organization called the Knights of the Golden Circle had 90,000 Hoosier members and plenty of arms and explosives provided from Kentucky. He said 200 armed men in a rural county had "declared for Jeff. Davis." And 200 armed men had turned back federal draft enforcers in Rush County, only one county removed from

Burnside's hometown. Lincoln and Secretary of War Stanton thought Carrington an alarmist.[37] There is not much evidence that Burnside was influenced by him.

But Burnside knew that Union officials—on up to Lincoln—were taking actions against dissidents. Burnside had Schenck, among others, as a role model. And there was this: Washington-based General Henry Halleck was the highest ranking military man. In a sort of orientation package, he sent Burnside a letter he had written to General William Rosecrans, then in charge of the Army of the Cumberland in the West. Halleck called for "more rigid treatment of disloyal persons." Unfortunately for Burnside, though, Halleck divided such persons into two categories: "neutral" and "avowedly hostile." The terms applied in border states, not Ohio, where few people were declaring neutrality or support for the South. Moreover, Halleck emphasized the need for generals to use their own judgment.[38] Even though the memo didn't apply clearly to his situation, Burnside must have seen meaning in the fact that Halleck sent it to him.

On April 13, having been in Ohio three weeks, Burnside took the step that set things in motion. He issued "General Orders No. 38." It did some obvious stuff: It forbade crossing into the South to aid the enemy or sending supplies or militarily useful information. But is also said, "The habit of declaring sympathies for the enemy will no longer be tolerated in the department. Persons committing such offences will be at once arrested, with a view to being tried … or sent beyond our lines into the lines of their friends. It must be understood that treason, expressed or implied, will not be tolerated in this department."[39]

"Implied" treason? It was not a concept Burnside invented. It was used by the military often, tracing back to British practices.[40] It referred to a speaker who communicates that he is for the other side without actually saying so.

The order might not have seemed particularly fateful to Burnside. He had issued a similar one in North Carolina, calling for the arrest of anyone who "uttered one word against the Government of the United States."[41] Clearly, looking at Washington, at Baltimore, at North Carolina and elsewhere, Burnside thought he was just following policy.

What was different about this situation was Vallandigham.

***

"Within Days" of the issuance of Order 38, federal authorities "were inundated with the most unlikely prisoners," wrote Burnside biographer Marvel.[42] Among them, weirdly enough, was none other than the courageously loyal Will Lowe, younger brother of Copperhead Tom. More weirdly yet, Will's problem had nothing to do with Tom. Tom went to his rescue.

Will had simply written a letter to an old schoolmate in the Confederate army. That was a problem. So was the fact that he expressed regrets Marvel called "nostalgic" for a peaceful time. So was the fact that the letter was found on the person of Jennie Moon, who regularly crossed the lines with such material.

As Marvel notes in a footnote, there are dramatically different understandings of Jennie Moon out there. She was the sister of Lottie Moon, a well-known woman remembered as a Confederate spy. In the category of small world, legend has it that

Lottie Moon had left young Ambrose Burnside himself at the altar when they lived near each other on opposite sides of the Ohio-Indiana border. Jennie, much younger, is also remembered as a spy and as staunchly and endlessly pro–Confederate. Both sisters lived long lives, Lottie as a journalist after the war and Jennie an actress even in silent films.

Ultimately, Burnside was convinced of Will's loyalty by an effort waged by Tom Lowe, his mother and several prominent citizens. One has to wonder if Burnside knew of Tom Lowe's politics. And whether he asked those who arrested Will about Lottie.

***

In the Vallandigham story, what happened next happened during a week of high national crisis. Lincoln's decision to send Burnside west had not solved his generals problem. Burnside was replaced by the Burnside-despised Joe Hooker. Hooker led the Union forces in the next great battle in the East, after Burnside's debacle at Fredericksburg. It was fought nearby, at Chancellorsville as part of another plan to take Richmond. Again, expectations rode high. Northern forces had Robert E. Lee seriously outnumbered. Again, however, the North lost the battle. War Secretary Stanton said the event was "the darkest day of the war" for the North.[43] Lincoln was utterly despondent. Multiple histories have quoted journalist Noah Brooks description of him just when he got the news:

"Never, as long as I knew him, did he seem to be so broken, so dispirited, and so ghostlike. Clasping his hands behind his back, he walked up and down the room, saying, 'My God! My God! What will the country say! What will the country say!' He seemed incapable of uttering any other words than these, and after a little time he hurriedly left the room."

For different reasons, the week of Chancellorsville was the most eventful, historic one of the century for Dayton, the most historic until a calamitous flood 50 years later to the season, in 1913. On May 1, 1863—during Chancellorsville—the Democrats held a big rally at Mount Vernon, Ohio, northeast of Columbus. It was the kind of event for which people from many miles around would pack a picnic basket and come and just listen to the politicians for hours. Samuel S. ("Sunset") Cox, a well-known congressman from the Columbus area would speak. So would candidates for various offices. But all eyes were on Vallandigham, and not just because he was the stem-winder speaker. Among the eyes on him were Burnside's, albeit by proxy. Given Vallandigham's reputation, Burnside sent two young officers to listen. They were in civilian clothes.[44]

No transcript exists—or existed even then—of what Vallandigham said. He spoke without notes. Much, however, is known. Vallandigham did his thing. He categorically rejected the war as "wicked, cruel and unnecessary," to quote one report. He said it was conducted for hidden purposes. If there were an actual mount at Mount Vernon, he would have castigated Lincoln up one side of it and down the other. He made clear that he was speaking as if Burnside were listening. And he made explicit that he wasn't going to modify his speeches at Burnside's order. (More on the content of his speech in the next chapter.)

It would be unfair to say simply that Vallandigham was courting martyrdom. He was standing up for what he believed in, including his free speech rights. But, yes, he did know that the arrest of Edson Olds resulted in Olds' election to the state senate. And he did know that political incarcerations were generally short, even if he could not assume that would always be the case. He decided to take a chance, not knowing how bad the downside of his actions might be, but seeing a huge possible upside—and no doubt honestly believing it was the right thing do.

As he spoke, one of Burnside's men took notes. The other listened and then went back to his room to write up some notes. When Burnside saw their reports—two days after the speech—he ordered Vallandigham arrested. Historian James G. Randall, in an exhaustive 1923 study of civil liberties issues in the Lincoln years, wrote that this was "the one conspicuous interference with freedom of speech," as opposed to freedom of the press, by military arrest.[45]

Knowing that Vallandigham was in Dayton, Burnside dispatched an officer and some troops late at night from his headquarters in Cincinnati. They arrived by train at the south end of downtown and marched north toward Vallandigham's house. At home besides Vallandigham were his wife and her sister, who was living with them, keeping Mrs. Vallandigham company during her husband's long absences. Vallandigham's son, whose ninth birthday would happen that year, doesn't figure into any of the descriptions of events. Perhaps he was locked away in a bedroom.

Vallandigham's war-years home on First Street, downtown Dayton, where he was arrested. (The Lloyd Ostendorf Collection.)

About 100 troops showed up between 2 a.m. and 3 a.m.[46] and took a position in the middle of First Street, facing the two-story house on the north side of the street. The troops announced their presence and demanded that Vallandigham come out and present himself for arrest. He came to a front window in his bed clothes and began a dialogue. He said he would not accede to this arrest, because he did not recognize the authority of the army to arrest him. He was a civilian, after all, and the civilian courts were still operating. So only the police could arrest him. And, anyway, all he had done was exercise his constitutional right to free speech.

At some point, he also noted that the leader of the troops had mispronounced his name. He had apparently accented the third syllable, not the second. "I don't care how you pronounce it," said Captain Charles Hutton, "that's the way you spell it. And you are my man."[47]

Some have speculated that Vallandigham was trying to draw a crowd, that he was speaking awfully loud, that he was trying to prolong the proceedings, that he even let out a strange whistle or something that seemed designed to wake people up. But no great crowd ever materialized.

After giving up on negotiations, Captain Hutton ordered his men to ram in Vallandigham's front door. They tried and failed. So they went around to the back door. This time they got in. The occupants were in a bedroom on the second floor. The troops came up the stairs. The adult residents—frightened for their physical safety, given the violence against property that had already taken place, given that it was in the middle of the night, given that they had never been through anything like this, and given that they didn't know what orders the troops might be under—made their way through a door leading to another bedroom. There they were cornered.

Vallandigham gave himself up, reiterating that he did not grant the legitimacy of this arrest, but was simply acceding to the military's greater power. The arrest scene was captured in a drawing in *Harper's Weekly*, sometimes cited as the most widely read publication in the country, on the front page of a popular national publication, *Frank Leslie's Illustrated Newspaper*, later in the month. Despite the nation's absorption in the news from Chancellorsville, everybody heard about Vallandigham, not necessarily the next day, but soon.

The troops took him to Cincinnati. Burnside was undecided about how to treat him. First he was put in a jail cell. But Burnside thought better of it, and brought him to the Burnet House, the place where the dignitaries stayed. Attorney Abe Lincoln had once stayed there while working on a trial. But then Burnside was warned that a Democratic mob might come down from Dayton looking for Vallandigham and try to free him. So it was back to the jail cell.

Indeed, when word spread about the arrest the next day, the streets of Dayton started to broil. A Democratic mob burned the *Journal* newspaper office and damaged buildings around it. That scene that has been captured in prominent paintings several times since.

Tom Lowe was in the thick, but not as a rioter. He had both an office and home (and family) in the endangered area. Facing a problem known to many polemicists, he later wrote to Will, "I hate (writing) narration, and my pen don't know where to begin. It is so much easier to handle ideas than facts, but the latter are, of course, the more interesting to you (Will) at this time, so I shall endeavor to tell about the riot as it appeared to me."[48] It turned out that Lowe had himself wrong: He was better with facts than with ideas.

"I did not hear, until I went to market in the morning, of the arrest of Vallandigham at the dead hour of the night. In common with every Democrat in the country, and they are a majority of the people, I felt it to be a great outrage…. But … it would surely make him Governor of Ohio.

"About eight o'clock in the evening, the excitement reached the boiling over point, and the mob consisting of 150 or 200 men and boys commenced firing guns and pistols at the *Journal* office from in front of the *Empire* office."

Vallandigham's arrest by the army as portrayed on the front page of the nationally circulated *Frank Leslie's Illustrated Newspaper*, May 23, 1863.

The two newspapers were on opposite sides of the same block on Main Street, but not exactly opposite each other. The *Journal* was one building south of Third Street, across which was the courthouse. Directly on the corner of Third and Main was the Phillips building. Lowe could see the scene on Main Street from his office.

He continued, writing as a Democrat who had once decided that mobs were a Republican thing. Of the current violent Democrats, he said, "It was a cowardly mob. In fact, every mob is a mean, bloodthirsty, but exceedingly cowardly animal—and you would have considered it a very small undertaking with your 20 men of the Co. A. 19th Regulars, to have scattered it to the four winds. I wish you had been here to do it."

He continued: "After firing some time"—at the *Journal*—"a turpentine ball was thrown in among the papers, and, in an incredibly short space of time, the flames burst from the roof.... I could not believe it possible (the rioters) were so hellish in their rage as to wish to bring destruction upon the innocent as well as those they deemed guilty—upon friend as well as foe."

Here Lowe told of turning his attention to his own home. It was set back from Main Street, across an alley from the business buildings. It caught fire. His family had to be evacuated: two small children, his mother-in-law and his pregnant wife, who was carried out in a chair with the help of neighbors. No one was hurt, but "everything war torn up."

"Martha and the babies stood all the excitement well," Tom reported. Martha had been "hysterical all afternoon"—before the fire—"but when the danger was actually upon us ... she became perfectly cool and collected and told us what valuables to move first.... I believe that delicate"—pregnant—"women bear excitement better and are cooler in the presence of danger than any others. Everybody was amazed at your sister"-in-law.

Lowe continued, referring to troops sent back to Dayton from Cincinnati by Burnside. "The (local fire) engines were ordered out"—deployed—"but it was not until after the soldiers arrived, about 11 p.m., and Capt. Christie ... had killed with his pistol one of the rioters, who was cutting the (fire) hose, that they were able to do anything. Everything from the Phillips House to the alley above our house, was burned. When the hose was turned upon my house the steam arose in clouds."

Then Lowe referred to a piece that had appeared in the *Empire* in March. It had said, "For every Democratic printing office destroyed by a mob, let an Abolition one be destroyed in turn. For every drop of blood spilled by Abolition mobites, let theirs flow in retaliation."[49] It was presumably written by William T. Logan, Bollmeyer's former co-editor, now the editor of the *Empire*.

Said Lowe, "The next day"—after the fire—"a great many arrests were made by the soldiers. Logan ... whose crazy article did more mischief than anything else, is in jail and will be tried for instigating the riot."

Then Lowe got back to his personal situation: "The most of the leaders of the (local Democratic) party"—he named four, including the mayor and John McMahon, Vallandigham's nephew—"went to Cincinnati in the morning to see Val, if possible. And therefore the rage of the Republicans fell heavy on me. They said cooler heads 'instigated' the mob, and as all these (other) men were away, they pounced upon me as their victim." Lowe said a federal official "says I narrowly escaped arrest. I was not at all alarmed, as I had done nothing & would not have felt at all disgraced if I had been" arrested.

He concluded his report: "Montgomery Co. is now under martial law, and the blue coats and bayonets on our streets are to me a reassuring if not a pleasant sight. My feeling is bayonets & despotism in preference to mobs and anarchy."

On the day after the burning of the *Journal*, Burnside's troops descended upon the *Empire*. They found a cache of hundreds of rifles and a pivoting cannon. This was said to have fed Burnside's suspicions that the Peace Democrats were a threat to the peace in the North. Probably, though, the weapons were for self-defense, given the attacks on other Democratic papers.

Burnside declared martial law to keep the peace. The *Empire* was shut down. The *Journal* was putting out the bare-bones of a paper using a church's press. The authority in town was the federal provost marshal. He was an army officer tasked—in most places—with running and enforcing the draft and handling issues of desertion and recruitment. It could be a dangerous job, the focus of anti-draft violence, especially in some rural areas. In most places, the provost marshal handled the nexus of military and civilian issues, including cases of alleged civilian cooperation with the Confederacy.⁵⁰ The very existence of a provost marshal—representing the newly elongated arm of the federal government—was a hot issue in some parts of the country. Before the war, the only local presence of the federal government in many communities was the post office. A lot of people preferred it that way.

However, no further violence erupted at Dayton. After the fire, the desire for local peace seemed to be strong in both parties. Among those cooperating was Postmaster W.F. Comly, the *Journal* editor whom Lincoln had made postmaster. He turned over to the army letters that were addressed to Vallandigham, as well as other letters.⁵¹

***

Burnside could have just put Vallandigham in jail and played the next step by ear. But, unlike most others making political arrests, he gave lip service to the innocent-until-proven-guilty standard. Also, he did not use long pre-trial confinements.⁵² The trial started on May 6 in Cincinnati, in front of a military court: nine officers appointed by Burnside. Such military commissions were not uncommon and use of them to try civilians was not unheard of.⁵³ (Some doubts have been raised about some of the commissioners, including one who had supposedly been convicted of keeping a "disreputable house." And Judge-Advocate James M. Cutts, who led the questioning for the army, was reportedly caught peeping at a woman through a transom at the hotel during the trial.⁵⁴)

Vallandigham rejected the authority of the court, repeating the arguments he had made at his arrest. He also said that he had been denied his *habeas corpus* right to have the legitimacy of his arrest ruled upon by a court. But he participated in the trial, defending himself, while his lawyers, led by former U.S. Sen. George E. Pugh, prepared a suit in federal civilian court on the *habeas corpus* issue. The hope was that whatever the military commission might do to Vallandigham, the civilian courts would overrule.

Newspapers large and small, in Ohio and elsewhere, ran transcripts of the ensuing trial, if not the day after testimony, soon.⁵⁵ From May 6 to the end of the month, the New York *Herald* ran at least one Vallandigham story or opinion piece on at least 16 days. On May 29, the Bedford, Pennsylvania *Gazette* ran five Vallandigham-related pieces. Southern papers, too, were following closely. On May 16, the Chattanooga *Daily Rebel* wrote, "The Republican (Abolition) papers of Ohio think that Vallandigham will be sentenced to death, but (that) the President will magnanimously pardon him on condition that he leave the country until the war is over.'"

The specific charges, under Order 38, were that Vallandigham

> *did publicly address a large meeting of citizens, and did utter sentiments in words, or in effect, as follows, declaring the present war "a wicked, cruel, and unnecessary war"; "a war not being waged for the preservation of the Union"; "a war for the purpose of crushing out liberty and erecting a despotism"; "a war for the freedom of the blacks and the enslavement of the whites"; stating "that if the Administration had so wished, the war could have been honorably terminated months ago"; that "peace might have been honorably obtained by listening to the proposed intermediation of France," that "propositions by which the Northern"*—presumably a typo—*"States could be won back, and the South guaranteed their rights under the Constitution, had been rejected the day before the late battle of Fredericksburg, by Lincoln and his minions," … charging "that*

11. Exiled, Welcomed and Removed

the Government of the United States was about to appoint military marshals in every district, to restrain the people of their liberties, to deprive them of their rights and privileges"; characterizing General Orders Nol. 38, from Head-quarters Department of the Ohio, as "a base usurpation of arbitrary authority," inviting his hearers to resist the same, by saying, "the sooner the people inform the minions of usurped power that they will not submit to such restrictions upon their liberties, the better"; declaring "that he was at all times, upon all occasions, resolved to do what he could to defeat the attempts now being made to build up a monarchy upon the ruins of our free government"; asserting "that he firmly believed, as he said six months ago, that the men in power are attempting to establish a despotism in this country, more cruel and more oppressive than ever existed before."

All of which opinions and sentiments he well knew did aid, comfort, and encourage those in arms against the Government, and could but induce in his hearers a distrust of their own Government, sympathy for those in arms against it, and a disposition to resist the laws of the land.[56]

Vallandigham was not charged with expressing actual sympathy for the enemy. He was not charged with calling upon troops to desert, or upon citizens not to enlist or to resist the draft. He was not charged with calling for any other illegal acts. Nor was he charged with breaking any law.

The ensuing trial revealed certain disputes about what Vallandigham had said and not said. But they weren't much about the list of charges. Vallandigham thought the young officers who had reported to Burnside had left some things out. He wanted it understood, for example, that he had made clear that he "always would refuse to agree to a separation of the States."[57] It was remarkable point to make, given his armistice speech. Now he was not only not repeating his recent proposal; he was pointing out that he was not repeating it.

Vallandigham got one of the witnesses—Captain H.R. Hill—to acknowledge that he (Hill) had left the following out of his report: that Vallandigham had said that the Richmond *Enquirer* called for the imprisonment of Vallandigham and a couple of others "because of our doing so much against Southern recognition and independence."[58]

Also, in response to a Vallandigham question, Capt. Hill, acknowledged that Vallandigham had referred to two people in Kentucky who, Vallandigham thought, had committed treason and should be hung, though a military court had imposed much lighter punishment. Vallandigham wanted everybody to know that he acknowledged that there was such a thing as treason, and that he was very much against it, even in this war. He noted that he also approved of the trying and conviction of a rebel spy by the military.

Vallandigham asked the witness, "Did I not expressly say, as Mr. Lincoln, in his proclamation, July 1, 1862, said, 'This *unnecessary* and injurious civil war?'" His point was that he couldn't be considered disloyal for saying what Lincoln said. The officer said he did not remember Vallandigham attributing the words to Lincoln.

Sensitive to the oft-made charge that he was fomenting violent resistance, Vallandigham asked the second of the officers, Captain John A. Means, this: "Did I not expressly counsel the people to obey the Constitution and all laws, and to pay proper respect to men in authority, but to maintain their political rights through the ballot-box, and to redress personal wrongs through the judicial tribunals of the country?"

The young officer responded as if addressing the judges, not Vallandigham: "He said, at the last of his speech, to come up united at the ballot-box and hurl the tyrant from his throne. I did not understand him to counsel the people to submit to the authorities at all times. I do not remember the language as stated, but part of it I remember."

Vallandigham and Captain Means agreed that Vallandigham had said he "spit upon" efforts to silence him, saying he took his orders from the Constitution: "General Orders No. 1." Vallandigham insisted that he had said he spit upon "arbitrary power generally," with a reference to an order promulgated in Indiana, not specifically 38. The officer said it was 38. Vallandigham apparently wanted it understood that what he said about 38 specifically was that he didn't take his orders from it, not that he spit upon it. It was a fine distinction the young officer might have missed.

The testimony of the officers took only parts of May 6 and 7. The prosecution asked for no further witnesses. No newspaper reports about the speech were offered in evidence. There was no corroborating testimony from witness who did *not* work for Burnside. No expert testimony was presented about when the military may arrest a civilian, about whether Vallandigham was protected by the First Amendment, about the case for having "judges" who report up a chain-of-command to the arresting authority, the general. There was no consideration of the meaning of "sympathy" for the enemy, though that was a key concept in 38. Nothing else.

Burnside was apparently intent on getting the trial over quickly. Some worried that if it dragged on too long, it could become a focus of Copperhead attention and action. Also, a long trial would undercut the urgency and impact of Order 38. It would also subject the army to the charge that it was devoting too much time to tasks other than fighting the war.

Vallandigham presented only one witness in his defense. He actually called three others—with no well-known names—but they didn't show. At that point, the court stipulated that it would assume that the other witnesses would have testified the same way as the one witness who did show.[59]

That was U.S. Rep. Samuel S. Cox, of the Columbus area, who had also spoken at Mount Vernon. Cox was a slightly more moderate Democrat. In March, the Dayton *Journal* had said of him that he "assumes to be the leader of the Democracy in the House."[60]

The first point Vallandigham wanted to make with Cox was that he—Vallandigham—had not metaphorically stuck out his tongue at Burnside specifically. The defendant asked, "Did you hear allusions to General Burnside, by name, and if so, what were they?" Cox said the only reference he could remember was when Vallandigham said he was not speaking by invitation of Lincoln, Burnside or Gov. Tod. "Was any epithet applied to (Burnside) during the speech?" No, said Cox, who noted that Burnside was an old friend, so he would have noticed such a thing.[61]

Then Vallandigham asked what Cox remembered him saying about 38. Cox said Vallandigham said only that he did not recognize it as "superior" to "Order No. 1, the Constitution, from George Washington commanding."

Question: "Were any insolent epithets, such as spitting upon, trampling under foot, or the like, used at any time in the speech, in reference to the Order 38; and if any criticism was made upon it, what was that criticism."

Cox responded that he didn't remember anything along those lines.

Cox said, "Mr. Vallandigham discussed these matters very briefly, taking up the larger portion of his speech with another proposition." That was a reference to Vallandigham's turn-the-tables argument that it was the Republicans, not the Democrats, who favored disunion.

"He charged," said Cox, "that men in power were willing to make peace by separation." Cox said Vallandigham said "there were private proofs yet to be disclosed, which time would disclose."

Vallandigham elicited the point that he had not mentioned the draft, much less counseled in favor of resisting it.

But Cox, too, was unable to confirm Vallandigham's insistence that he had quoted Lincoln about the war being "unnecessary and injurious."

Shortly thereafter: "Were any denunciations of the officers of the Army indulged in by (Vallandigham), or any offensive epithets applied to them?"

Cox: "He occasionally used the words 'the President and his minions,' but I did not understand him to use them in connection with the Army.... It was in connection with arbitrary arrests." But, of course, some such arrests had been conducted by the army, including the most relevant one.

A common charge about Democratic and Copperhead public gatherings was that somebody would always suggest a hurrah for Jefferson Davis, and the crowd would offer one, and no speaker would denounce that. So Vallandigham asked Cox, "Do you remember any rebuke … of men who hurrahed for 'Jeff Davis?'"

Answer: "Yes, I do. He denounced the applause of Davis."

Last question: "Was any thing said, in that speech, in reference to the war, except … as a policy which he insisted could not restore the Union, but must end, finally, in disunion?"

Answer: "I can only give my understanding. I do not know about inferences people might draw. I understood his condemnation of the war to be launched at its perversion from its original purpose." But, of course, Vallandigham had opposed the war from Day One, even when it was presented as being for union, not emancipation.

That was it. The prosecution did not cross-examine Cox. The trial ended at 4:30 p.m. on its second day. The commission issued its guilty verdict on May 16. It eliminated two charges: the one that said "Northern" where only "Southern" would have made sense; and the last one, about Vallandigham saying that Lincoln was "attempting to establish a despotism."[62]

It was an imitation of a trial. It had many of the elements, even up to disputes and sober deliberations over procedural questions. But the fix was in. The officers on the commission knew what Burnside wanted. For anybody on the commission to hold out for innocence would have required a remarkable act of courage. Moreover, the commission members saw their main job as winning the war. They were willing to let the lawyers argue later about how they had approached the goal. They were certain that Vallandigham and his political type undermined the war effort. And that was that.

Vallandigham's speech may have been an over-the-top denunciation of the Lincoln administration and its war policy, delivered with no concern for accuracy. But it was the work of a sophisticated politician/lawyer who had thought hard about where the line was between anti-administration and anti–Union rhetoric.

***

In sentencing Vallandigham, Burnside had two options before him on paper: exile and imprisonment. Exile of political figures was not an American tradition. After the Revolutionary era, political figures who had been loyal to the throne left the country, feeling unwelcome. But they weren't thrown out by the government. Under the Alien and Sedition Acts, there were political arrests, of course, including one of Vermont Congressman Matthew Lyon. He was indicted for accusing the John Adams administration of "ridiculous pomp, foolish adulation, and selfish avarice," among other things. He was sentenced to four months in prison, during which he was re-elected. He wasn't exiled. In the Civil War, the South exercised the exile option in 1862 in the case of William Gannaway "Parson" Brownlow, a Tennessee Unionist. First he was imprisoned, but when his health deteriorated, he was taken to the Kentucky border, whence he began a speaking tour of the North; after the war, he became governor of Tennessee.[63]

Exile was mentioned in Order 38 as an option, because the idea was in the air. It had a certain applause-line appeal: They like the South so much, huh? OK. Let's send them there.

Burnside chose the harsher option: prison at Fort Warren in Massachusetts for the duration of the war. That was one of the least unpleasant prisons, whereas Camp Chase in Ohio was one of the worst, with overcrowding and such.[64] However, Burnside was not doing Vallandigham any favors. The location was surely chosen to separate Vallandigham from his supporters in Ohio and discourage vigils outside the prison.

As Vallandigham's military trial was proceeding, so was his case in federal court. That case was heard in Cincinnati before district Judge H.H. Leavitt, an Andrew Jackson appointee.

That spring, before Vallandigham's arrest, Congress had granted Lincoln the right to rescind *habeas corpus* rights. (He had previously done so without congressional authorization.) But he had not yet acted upon his expanded authority, either specifically in Vallandigham's case or in any category into which Vallandigham's case fit. (Later that year, he did issue a general suspension in war-related political cases.) As Vallandigham events moved quickly in both courts, the Lincoln administration was watching closely. The case was all over the newspapers. At one point, Secretary of War Stanton drafted a specific suspension of the writ by Lincoln, just so any judge who might rule in favor of Vallandigham would understand that he would be seen as acting against the commander-in-chief.[65] But Lincoln decided not to suspend the writ. Treasury Secretary Salmon P. Chase, an Ohioan, knew the judges whom the case might come before and did not think either would rule for Vallandigham. He had seen a newspaper article saying they both had refused a legally similar application the previous year.[66]

Burnside sent the federal court a defense of his actions that takes four average-size book pages. It was delivered in the voice of a man who felt he has been called upon to explain the obvious. He did not take up the First Amendment, did not agonize and did not split hairs. He wrote that it was the duty of everybody in and out of the army to avoid saying anything to weaken the army "by preventing a single recruit from joining." He said he had no problem with political debate carried on "in a proper tone." He was not impressed by the alarms being raised about the loss of civil liberties. "There is," he said, "no fear of the people losing their liberties; we all know that to be the cry of demagogues."[67]

Vallandigham, in a letter to an ally, called Burnside's submission "execrable."[68] Judge Leavitt called it "manly and patriotic." By "manly" he presumably meant that Burnside took all responsibility upon himself.

In truth, it didn't matter what Burnside said, or what anybody said in legal briefs. Leavitt's mind was made up. He saw things just as Burnside did. And he had no interest in any constitutional analysis, any exploration of precedents, any lawyerly debate. He said as much.

Vallandigham's lawyer, former Sen. Pugh, wrote a 50-page brief making all manner of legal points, referring to, for example, precedents in British history. He wrote another 67 pages in his closing argument. (His opponents weren't, as a group, notably more succinct. One of them—not particularly verbose himself—was federal prosecutor Flamen Ball. He is mentioned here only because his name was Flamen Ball.) Some of Pugh's arguments were remarkably lame. In painstakingly going through Vallandigham's remarks at Mount Vernon, Pugh offered this: "Mr. Vallandigham said ... that it is 'a war not being waged for the preservation of the Union.' Observe those words carefully; they do not mean that 'the preservation of the Union' is not the avowed object, nor even that the Administration may not so intend, but only that the war is 'not being waged' in such a manner as to accomplish the object." Pugh was trying everything.

Leavitt, taking 12 pages, wrote: "If it were my desire to do so, I have not now the physical strength to notice or discuss at length the grounds on which the learned counsel has attempted to prove the illegality of General Burnside's (arrest) order."[69] Whether Leavitt really had strength issues is doubtful. He was 66 and served another eight years on the bench and was active even after that, attending a conference on prison reform in 1872 in London. He died in 1873. One possibility is that he was just telling Pugh that Pugh would test *anybody's* endurance.

Vallandigham's opponents got some fun out of noting that Leavitt was a Democrat. He had been a Jacksonian in Congress in the early 1830s, before getting his judgeship. In fact, though, he was elected to Congress and appointed to the court long before there was a Republican Party, and even before the Whigs were a force. His family was from Connecticut, and he had roots in northeastern Ohio, anti-slavery territory. (Leavittsburg, Ohio, is named for his family.) Those characteristics would say "Republican" to many familiar with Ohio politics in the Civil War era. And Leavitt wrote in a family memoir that he hated serving in Congress because, "In times of party division, it is impossible for anyone in Congress to preserve a conscience void of offense toward God and at the same time to bear true allegiance to the party."[70] Even then, he did not want his views taken for granted because of a party label.

The heart of his decision: "There is too much of the pestilential leaven of disloyalty in the community.... Men should know, and lay the truth to heart, that there is a course of conduct not involving overt treason, or any offense technically defined by statute ... which, nevertheless, implies moral guilt and a gross offense against their country.... If they cherish hatred and hostility to it, and desire its subversion, let them withdraw from its jurisdiction.... I have no fears that the recognition of this doctrine"—love-it-or-leave-it—"will lead to an arbitrary invasion of the ... personal liberty of the citizen.... But if there should be an occasional mistake, such an occurrence is not to be put in competition with the preservation of the life of the nation. And I confess I am but little moved by the eloquent appeals of those who, while they indignantly denounce violations of personal liberty, look with no horror upon a despotism as unmitigated as the world ever has witnessed." Slavery.[71]

Leavitt heaped praise upon Burnside with a shovel. "He had achieved, during his brief military career, a national reputation as a wise, discreet, patriotic and brave General. He not only enjoyed the confidence and respect of the President and Secretary of War, but of the whole country. He has nobly laid his party preferences" aside.

Leavitt may have identified with Burnside as a fellow former Democrat now horrified by much in the party. His kind of guy. Moreover, Leavitt just was not going to undertake oversight of a general in time of war. He said the arrest "was virtually the act of the executive department under the power vested in the President by the Constitution; and I am unable to perceive on what principle a judicial tribunal can be invoked to annul or reverse it." If power was being abused, the antidote was impeachment, not judicial review.

Before getting to the political part above, Leavitt did go purely judicial for a while. He pointed to a precedent set by the Circuit Court of which he was part in the case Chase had read about. The court had ruled that, in the case of an arrest by the military, the writ of *habeas corpus* could not be successfully invoked—and the arrest nullified—if the court thought the court would uphold the arrest upon hearing the case for it. Leavitt said he was bound by that decision.

On his last page, he made another point: that he was "morally certain" that any order he imposed on the military would not be obeyed. He said he did not relish confronting disobedience, given that he had no power of enforcement. But he said that factor alone would not have been enough for him to rule against Vallandigham.[72]

Vallandigham appealed to the U.S. Supreme Court, but on a tie vote it declined to take up his case, being as reluctant as Leavitt to mess with the military during a war. Chief Justice Roger Taney was ill and not present to vote.[73] After the war—in the landmark *Ex parte Milligan* case—the Court did rule that an army commission could not try a civilian if the civilian courts were operating.

***

If, in arresting, trying and sentencing Vallandigham, the Republicans had been looking for an issue to give the Democrats, they could hardly have done better. The subject lent itself to editorials, the main form in which the public was confronted with political debate. In the words of historian J.G. Randall, Vallandigham's arrest was the "*cause celebre* of the Lincoln administration."[74] To this day, editorial writers speak of editorials that "write themselves." And they love them. It's a day off. In this case, it was many days off. Democratic editors around the country pounced. They wallowed. They partied. They embraced life with a new vigor. When editorial writers in those days glommed onto a subject, they didn't let loose until they had said everything enough times to convince themselves that everybody got the message. They often did their thing on page one, but, even if not, they did it prominently in papers so small that a reader had to peruse the editorials to get his or her money's worth.

The devastating news about Chancellorsville was not competition for the Vallandigham story so much as fodder for Vallandigham's defenders. The Union generals and Lincoln were apparently helpless in confronting an enemy that was armed and could fight back, but they were proving their manhood by arresting a man armed only with words. After all, Burnside himself was the poster boy for supposedly ineffective generals; he was another godsend to the editorialists. And here was an administration claiming to fight to save the union while launching a war on the freedoms that made it worth saving. And here was an administration—in the wake of Emancipation—fighting for the rights of Negroes while denying the most basic political rights to a white man. This, for polemicists, was not a piece of cake; it was a banquet.

The North Branch *Democrat* in Tunkhannock, Pennsylvania, summarized nicely on May 13: "Mr. Vallandigham has been arrested without lawful authority and tried by a court without jurisdiction—without a jury—for an offense unknown to law." "We Have Despotic Military Government in Ohio," read a headline in the McArthur, Ohio *Democrat* on May 21. The editor said the news about Vallandigham "is the greatest dishonor that has been our lot to publish.... It is full of danger to our persons and our homes." The Bedford, Pennsylvania *Gazette* on May 22 insisted, "Let history record when Clement L. Vallandigham was put upon trial before Burnside's star-chamber court-martial, he demanded 'to be tried according the Constitution and laws of his country,' but was refused this sacred and inalienable privilege of an American citizen." Frank L. Klement in his Vallandigham book has a completely different and longer list of similar quotes. They were apparently innumerable.

And Democrats were not the only complainers. Republican papers generally paid less attention to the Vallandigham arrest than the Democrats, perhaps feeling some discomfort. But when they did write, the discomfort showed. The New York *Evening Post* was then edited by noted poet William Cullen Bryant, an anti-slavery man who had introduced Lincoln at Cooper Union. That paper said Burnside assumed way too much authority over civilians, treating them as if they were troops. The Democratic New York *Herald* monitored Republican voices and reported—fairly—on May 20 that the Vallandigham arrest had caught "the fire of the chief organs of the Republican party and a large proportion of the party itself."

Harper's Weekly editorialized at length. "(I)t is the unanimous hope of the loyal North that" Lincoln will undo the sentence, it said. Otherwise, the incident "would probably make (Vallandigham) governor of Ohio.... Vallandigham was fast talking himself into the deepest political grave every dug when Burnside resurrected him." The arrest was "superfluous." There was something to that. Vallandigham did not seem to be advancing toward the nomination for governor when he offended Burnside.

Anyway, the magazine said, "the spectacle of a man immured in a prison for opinion's or word's sake shocks our feelings and arouses our anger." But, the magazine continued, "if Vallandigham would go out of the country to the rebels or any where else, loyal people would heartily rejoice."[75]

Lincoln learned of Vallandigham's arrest from the newspapers. General-in-chief Henry Halleck—known in history as an inscrutable bureaucratic operator who tried to stay out of trouble[76]—claimed not to know about the arrest before the news broke. Lincoln wrote to Burnside and asked if the reports were true.

Some historians think Lincoln was not pleased.[77] Vallandigham was the most prominent person arrested on political charges during the war. He would instantly have a great many people coming to his defense. And, after all, he was not operating in a border state, where Lincoln was most open to taking extreme measures against opponents. However, Lincoln was later to say publicly he didn't know if he would have arrested Vallandigham.[78]

Lincoln did not like to overturn actions by his generals. He would only do that in a pinch.[79] And he knew that Burnside had had good reason for believing he was within administration policy. On May 8, Burnside had received a telegram from Stanton saying, "In your determination to support the authority of the Government and suppress treason in your department you may count on the firm support of the President."[80] That was shortly after the arrest, but still.

John Hay and John Nicolay, Lincoln's young aides, confidants and eventual ten-volume biographers, wrote this 50 years after Burnside's decision: "No act of the Government (in those years) has been so strongly criticized." That is one heck of a superlative. Not the Emancipation Proclamation. Not firing McClellan, a hero to millions, including thousands of his troops. Not rescinding *habeas corpus*. Not instituting the first national draft.

The authors had in mind the bipartisan nature of the criticism of Burnside. But they also said "the Democratic party (regarded) the incident as the most valuable bit of political capital which had fallen to them during the war."[81] Again, not Emancipation, the draft, Chancellorsville, Fredericksburg or either Bull Run. Not even Mary Todd Lincoln's spending habits.

The Vallandigham case was taken up by the cabinet. Historian Doris Kearns Goodwin wrote that "in a moment of rare accord, every member of the cabinet united in opposition to the Vallandigham arrest."[82] (However, two Stanton biographers have him supporting it; he might have been alone.[83]) Secretary of State William Seward could imagine the arrest and sentence precipitating a civil war in the North. Meanwhile, Republican Sen. Lyman Trumbull of Illinois saw the beginning of a military takeover.

Lincoln was ambiguous about his views when he wrote to Burnside, "All the Cabinet regretted the necessity of arresting for instance Vallandigham—some perhaps doubting that there was a real necessity for it, but being done all are for seeing you through with it."[84]

About the cabinet meeting, Secretary of Navy Gideon Welles wrote that "every one wished (Vallandigham) had been sent over the lines to the Rebels with whom he sympathizes."[85] That idea had been promoted by multiple editorials. Nevertheless, some people assumed it resulted from Lincoln's sense of humor. The Richmond *Daily Dispatch* said, "But this is the worst joke Mr. Lincoln has yet made."[86]

Hay and Nicolay wrote that Lincoln worried that undermining Burnside "could greatly encourage the active and dangerous" pro–South element in the West. But ultimately Lincoln decided that "the imprisonment of Vallandigham in the North would have been a constant source of irritation and political discussion." He adopted a course "the execution of which would excite far less sympathy with the prisoner, and, in fact, seriously damage his prestige and authority among his followers" by heightening his association with the South.[87]

Burnside complained, noting that the ship-him-south option had been fully considered in Cincinnati but rejected. Lincoln told him to do the shipment "without delay."[88] Many Republican papers approved, including the Dayton *Journal*, which said the decision would undercut the notion that Vallandigham was a martyr to free speech and would save the costs of his incarceration.[89] The paper's view is worth pausing over as a measure of the polarization of the time: a Dayton newspaper cheered the banishment of a Dayton politician who had the support of most voters in the county in the previous election.

Two weeks later, Burnside issued an order shutting down the Chicago *Times*, a Copperhead newspaper. This resulted in a big fuss along lines similar to the Vallandigham story. This time, Lincoln simply overrode Burnside, leaving the paper open. The episode demonstrates some distance between Lincoln and Burnside philosophically. But it also dramatizes that Lincoln could have simply overridden Burnside on Vallandigham, too, freeing him. The fact that a military court—not just a general—had ruled against Vallandigham made it politically harder. Lincoln may have seen his options as sharply limited. Still, Lincoln was the guy who decided that exile was the right treatment for Vallandigham under the circumstances. And he was to go out of his way to defend the decision at length, looking entirely sincere.

***

Nicolay and Hay wrote that the Vallandigham affair "occasioned general rejoicing in the South. The Government in Richmond saw in it a promise of counterrevolution in the North…. General (P.G.T.) Beauregard … suggested…. Lee should … send … 30,000 men to … 'march into Kentucky; raise 30,000 men more there and in Tennessee; then get into Ohio and call upon the friends of Vallandigham to rise for his defense and support; then call upon Indiana, Illinois, and Missouri to throw off the yoke of the accursed Yankee nation; then'—his plan growing more and more magnificent—call 'upon the whole Northwest to join in the movement, form a Confederacy of their own, and join us by a treaty of alliance.'"[90]

Southern and Northern newspapers developed something of a dialog about Vallandigham. In New York state—a site of major Copperhead pockets—the case engendered a protest rally. The Richmond *Dispatch* devoted a column-and-a-half on its front page of May 23 to a report on what the speakers said. It reprinted the letter that New York Democratic Gov. Horatio Seymour sent to the event. Then *The New York Times* reported and commented—at length—on what the Richmond paper had done.

Seymour made all the common criticisms of the Vallandigham arrest and said that "it is not merely a step toward revolution—it is revolution. It will not only lead to military despotism—it establishes military despotism." The rally adopted a series of resolutions against the arrest, describing those who perpetrated such things as "public enemies."

Much of the rhetoric from speakers was about standing up violently to the Lincoln threat. One speaker said the people would stand by Gov. Seymour "with guns and bayonets at all hazards." At least one speaker asked the crowd about its potential acquiescence to the new draft, receiving cries of "Never! Never!" One said, "there is a war here…. It is worse than the war that is now waging in the South." Southern editors made sure that Southern readers heard about all of that.

Not everybody in the North was impressed with the New York event. Said *Harper's Weekly*: "(N)ot one leading man, not a single man who commands general esteem, or who carries the least weight, ventured to be present, and the performance was, on the whole, the most wretched of all the wretched fizzles" ever in New York politics.[91] But the story of the rally wasn't over.

***

Before shipping Vallandigham southward, the authorities allowed him to write several letters. One went to his wife. One went to a newspaper editor whose support he appreciated and nurtured: Manton Marble of the New York *World*. He told Marble—with an eye on a wider audience—that "As to my fate, I am wholly unconcerned—prepared for any fortune—imprisonment, exile—death."[92] The return address he offered was "Bastile," providing the quote marks himself. Another letter was addressed to the Democratic Party, and another to the people of Ohio. In this last, he referred to himself as "Banished from my native State for no crime save Democratic opinions and free speech to you in" defense of those opinions. His message was that his message would not change. He said his "enemies little comprehend the true character of the man with whom they have to deal."

In another letter to Marble a few days later, he was self-conscious about his past criticism of the East. He said, referring to news about the New York rally, that he "rejoiced to know that the Democracy of the East & West are in perfect sympathy. We of the West must now depend upon you of New York & New Jersey who are free." He said, "Gov. Seymour ought to see to it that he is not kidnapped, too, some night. He has the force to prevent it."[93] So perhaps Vallandigham would've resisted if he could.

On May 22, the army put Vallandigham on a boat down the Ohio River to Louisville, a stretch which the North controlled. On the boat, the prisoner was treated more as a guest than a prisoner.[94] A newspaperman was present, along with military personnel ranging from a general to a "detail of soldiers" playing cards. Vallandigham took the opportunity to write to his wife. Newspaper reports had said she had, in Klement's words, "lapsed into insanity." But a later report had her doing better. Vallandigham assured her that he was "in fine spirits and enjoying excellent health."

From Louisville, it was quickly on to a train to Nashville, also in Union hands, 180 miles away. The trip went terribly slowly, because war-related trains took precedence. Next came another train ride, to Murfreesboro, Tennessee, south and east of Nashville. That was the headquarters of Gen. William Rosecrans' Army of the Cumberland (formerly the Army of the Ohio). It abutted Confederate territory. By now the journey had taken about 48 hours, and all were exhausted.

In Murfreesboro, after meeting a colonel he had known as a Democratic member of Congress (who had voted to seat Vallandigham), the prisoner was turned over to Rosecrans. The general's name was as well known in Dayton—and the country—as Vallandigham's. Many of the Dayton men and boys in the army were in his command. His name was often on the envelopes of letters Daytonians sent to their friends and loved ones in the field[95]; as armies moved, the postal authorities would always know where to find Rosecrans.

Rosecrans was born in Ohio and had lived in several parts of it, though not Dayton. During the war, however, his wife lived in Yellow Springs, near Dayton. A West Point grad, Rosecrans had come to national prominence by winning the battle at Corinth, Mississippi, a crucial transportation hub. He had emerged into the top rank of

Gen. William Rosecrans, as seen by the popular printmakers Currier and Ives, at Murfreesboro, Tennessee.

Union generals at the turn of 1862–63 as the leader at an exceptionally bloody battle known as Stone River (or Stones River or Stone's River). There the Union solidified its hold on central Tennessee (already having Nashville nearby) and extended it to include Murfreesboro, threatening Chattanooga. Lincoln had put Rosecrans in charge because he found Gen. Don Carlos Buell insufficiently aggressive. Rosecrans also took longer to act than Lincoln would have liked. And, in fact, the outcome under Rosecrans lent itself to more than one interpretation. But when Gen. Braxton Bragg (fairly fresh from Kentucky) finally retreated—further damaging his damaged reputation—Rosecrans rose. This was just after Burnside fell after Fredericksburg. Rosecrans and Stone River were the good news for the country.

Rosecrans rose so high that the erratic and powerful Horace Greeley floated his name for president in 1864 as a Republican. Greeley had concluded that Lincoln couldn't win. He said Rosecrans might be the "best and most available" (that is, electable) candidate. He said Rosecrans was "uniformly successful, a coming man," who could get the usually Democratic Irish vote by virtue of his Catholicism. Greeley claimed to have some of the most prominent Republicans with him, including Ohio Sen. Benjamin Wade. He was even expecting cabinet members William Seward and Salmon P. Chase to join him when the time came. He said to an associate whom he had asked to look into the Rosecrans option, "If you find Rosecrans the right man, I will go personally to Lincoln and force him to resign. Then (Vice President Hannibal) Hamlin will give Rosecrans command of the armies, and there'll be a chance of saving the country."[96] A coup.

About Rosecrans' temperament there was much dispute. Greeley's operative, one James Gilmore, "felt the instant warmth of Rosecrans at his best—his graciousness, wit, charm."[97] Gilmore said he was "magnetized with a sense of Rosecrans' genius," and he added that Ulysses Grant—another general with some successes to his name—had no such effect on strangers.

But biographer William Lamers, in a decidedly pro–Rosecrans book, offers some balance. "He was blessed with a brilliant, resourceful mind, and prodigious energy. No general, North or South, surpassed him in personal leadership, or in his courage in taking necessary risks on the battlefield. ... But in excess his virtues sometimes became faults. He made enemies unwisely and needlessly. A perfectionist, he was critical and impatient of slipshod performance in others, yet he had himself some difficulty in delegating responsibility. He was no compromiser.... His righteousness occasionally led to self-righteousness, and his bristling independence to impolitic speech and action." His "bitterest enemies" feared him, and "something in him would not let that fear subside." And "he was seldom out of trouble."[98]

In the spring before the Vallandigham arrest, Rosecrans got in some political trouble. He wrote an open letter to the Ohio legislature in response to a letter of thanks from it for his military success. He referred obliquely to Vallandigham's armistice plan and said, "He who entertains the sentiment is fit only to be a slave; he who utters it at this time is a traitor to his country." In reporting this, the *Hancock Jeffersonian* in Findlay, Ohio, said, "Rosecrans is a Democrat, but is nevertheless a patriot,"[99] an eye-catching concession. Rosecrans had, indeed, entered the war as a Democrat. But he was now aggressively denouncing slavery and calling for an end to it.

His letter got him denounced in the legislature as an "unpatriotic man and a traitor to his country." Twenty-two Democrats voted against "even printing his letter as part of the legislature's business."[100]

Meanwhile, Secretary of War Edwin Stanton, having apparently heard about the Greeley effort, saw Rosecrans as showboating for the Radical Republicans. He was not pleased.[101]

When Vallandigham met Rosecrans, the Rosecrans-Bragg portion of the Civil War was at a lull. Both armies were rebuilding. A reporter for the Cincinnati *Gazette*, R.S. Furay, provided the world with most of what it learned about Vallandigham's stop in Murfreesboro. Furay's account showed up in many newspapers, typically on the front page, both North and South, generally shortened, paraphrased and not attributed to him, with updates.[102]

Furay wrote that Vallandigham's likely arrival time at Rosecrans headquarters was a secret, so as to protect Vallandigham. So "there was no stir and no excitement.... (H)ad it been ... known ... that the notorious Copperhead ... had arrived ... it is the belief of those accustomed to reason most coolly that all sense of discipline and restraint would have at once been lost, and that a crowd of ten thousand men would have collected instantly round the Provost Marshal's," where Vallandigham and Rosecrans met. "What might have followed no human tongue can tell; but it is certain that each soldier in the army entertains for that man, Vallandigham, an intense and burning hatred, which can find expression only in curses." Foray went on and on like that. The troops' "especial detestation is reserved for the slimy reptiles of the North who...." It was partisan exaggeration, but there was some truth to his description of the troops' views.

Vallandigham's train arrived from Nashville at about 10 p.m. on a Sunday night. The orders from Burnside to Rosecrans were to take the prisoner to the farthest outpost of North-controlled territory, hold him there until morning, and then pass him to enemy control under a flag of truce.

Furay said, "General Rosecrans and others wished to converse awhile with the gentleman" before setting him off. No account of the resulting conversation comes from Furay, who apparently wasn't present. But what happened has been recorded in at least two different ways. One way seems to stem from Vallandigham himself. It is recorded in his brother's biography of him as well as the Klement biography. It goes like this: Midnight was approaching. Rosecrans wanted to talk politics. Vallandigham obliged. The conversation was cordial and gentlemanly, but at a certain stage Rosecrans told Vallandigham that if he turned Vallandigham over to his troops, they will "tear you to pieces in an instant." Vallandigham responded that the troops misunderstood him, and that he could win them over if he could talk to them, in which case "they will be more willing to tear Lincoln and yourself to pieces than they will Vallandigham." Though that looks pretty pugnacious on paper, this version of the story holds that Rosecrans did not take offense, but said he couldn't risk his prisoner's life by allowing him to test his theory. From there, the conversation reportedly became more congenial and personal. Wrote Klement: "Rosecrans regretted having to perform the duty of enforcing the penalty against his prisoner.... Laying hand on the prisoner's shoulder, Rosecrans turned toward a Col. Joseph C. McKibbin"—the former Democratic congressman who had known Vallandigham—and said, "He don't look a bit like a traitor, now does he, Joe?"[103]

Lamers' biography of Rosecrans has a different version of the scene, which it treats briefly. It says that, in response to Vallandigham's prediction that the troops might turn on Rosecrans after Vallandigham talked to them, Rosecrans shook his finger angrily. "Vallandigham, don't you ever come back here. If you do, I'll be God damned—and may God forgive me for the expression—I'll be God damned if I don't hang you."[104] The source of that quote is not clear; presumably it's Rosecrans or somebody he spoke to. Lamers has reporter Furay in the room. However, Furay's own account suggests that Furay didn't meet Vallandigham until afterwards.[105]

What's clear is that Vallandigham really did have great confidence in his ability to sway people. Also, he had an interest in people hearing that Rosecrans said he didn't seem like a traitor. Meanwhile, of course, Rosecrans was eager to be seen as having stood up to the monster.

The conversation was over by about 2 a.m. Then Vallandigham stepped into a wagon for a trip that, Furay said, "None of those who accompanied Mr. Vallandigham that night will ever forget it."

The Dayton *Journal* also claimed to have a "correspondent" at Murfreesboro when Vallandigham was there. Identified as "Cordova," he might have been Furay. Cordova wrote that Vallandigham "looked unusually pleasant" when he emerged from the Rosecrans meeting "and seemed to think a good deal, but said very little.... When all was ready, he very politely saluted us with a 'Good day, Gentleman,' entered his conveyance, which was a light spring wagon, drawn by two horses, and departed ... to where he belongs.... Thus ended the Northern career of Vallandigham." Cordova wrote, "The impression here is that he will immediately seek an interview with President Davis, ... and, unless he succeeds in making a favorable impression, will accept a commission and receive his recruits from the Northern States."[106] The *Journal* was selling the notion that Vallandigham was ready to fight for the South.

The two companies that usually accompanied Rosecrans when he traveled were assigned to accompany Vallandigham southward. Two wagons were at the front—with Vallandigham's first—and the troops behind. The "remarkable procession" proceeds down the "silent ... streets of Murfreesboro, through the quiet and slumbering camps, and down the Shelbyville turnpike toward rebellious Dixie," wrote Furay.

Along the way, Vallandigham lightly remarked to the other former congressman present, "Colonel, this is worse than Lecompton." The reference was to an inflammatory national controversy of the late 1850s in which President James Buchanan embarrassed fellow Democrats with the pretense that an obviously rigged plebiscite showed that Kansas voters supported slavery.

The temporary dividing line between North and South was between Murfreesboro and Shelbyville, which was 26 miles south. The retinue passed Northern "guard after guard, picket after picket, sentinel after sentinel, ... the magic countersign (signal) opening gates in the wall of living men.... The men on guard stood looking in silent wonder at the unwonted spectacle, little thinking that they were gazing at the great copperhead on his way through the lines."

Furay continued: "Just as the first faint streak of dawn appeared in the east, the party stopped at the house of a Mr. Butler, in order to wait for daylight; for we were now near our outposts," that is, the end of Northern territory.

The family stared about them in great surprise when they were wakened up, but made haste to provide whatever conveniences they could for enabling the party to take an hour's repose.

In May of 1863, the line between North and South was someplace between Murfreesboro and Shelbyville in Tennessee.

11. Exiled, Welcomed and Removed

For the first time, I was introduced to Mr. Vallandigham; and, as none of us felt like sleeping, we commenced what to me was an extremely interesting and profitable conversation. Mr. Vallandigham talked with entire freedom; told me with greatest apparent frankness his views of the policy of the Administration; discussed dispassionately the circumstance of his arrest and trial, and stated clearly what he supposed would be the ultimate results of his punishment. He manifested no bitterness of feeling whatever, seemed inclined to do full justice to the Government in reference to its dealings with himself, and spoke very respectfully of General Burnside.

"In spite of my fixed opinion of the bad and dangerous character of (Vallandigham)," Furay wrote, "I could not but entertain for him a sentiment of personal respect which had I never felt before." Furay meeting Vallandigham was something like Vallandigham meeting John Brown.

Furay continued: "After an hour passed in conversation, there was an effort made to obtain a little sleep, and Mr. Vallandigham himself had just fallen into a dose, which Col. McKibben," the former congressman, "waked him from, informing him that it was daylight, and time to move. Some poetical remark having been made about the morning, Mr. Vallandigham raised himself upon his elbow and (said), dramatically,

"'Night's candles are burnt out, and jocund day
Stands top-toe on the misty mountain top.'"

Furay continued: "He had evidently forgotten the remaining line of the quotation" from Romeo and Juliet, "but it seemed so applicable to his own case, in view of the wrathful feelings of the soldiers toward him, that I could not forbear adding aloud,

"'I must be gone and live or stay and die.'

"I indulge in no vanity when I say that the extreme appositeness of the quotation startled every one who heard it, including Mr. Vallandigham himself."

Hmmm. Are we to believe the lovely anecdote? Another poet, Edgar Allan Poe, might say, "Startled at the stillness broken by reply so aptly spoken…." Of course, in Poe's case, it was a raven talking, not a journalist. At any rate, literate people of that time really did know their poetry and their Shakespeare. So, OK, in the interest of poetry, let's give Furay the benefit of the doubt. No contradiction of his story seems to have entered history.

When the "cavalcade" reached the remotest Northern outposts, "Colonel McKibben and a Major Wiles now went forward with a flag of truce toward the enemy's videttes," meaning mounted sentries posted outside of Confederate territory, "who could be plainly seen stationed in the road, not more than a half mile off."

The rest of the retinue (except for the troops), said Furay, "took breakfast at the house of a Mr. Alexander, just on the boundary line between the United States and Dixie. After all were seated at the table (a colonel) informed Mrs. Alexander, who presided, that one of the gentlemen before her—pointing him out—was Mr. Vallandigham.

"Immediately the woman turned all sorts of colors, and exclaimed, 'Can it be possible? Mr. Vallandigham! Why I was reading only last night of your wonderful doings! I must introduce you to the old man, shurs!'

"The 'old man,'" wrote Furay, "is understood to be much more than half 'Secesh.'"

That is, a supporter of secession. "And he and a not remarkably handsome daughter united in giving the prisoner a warm welcome."

Furay finished his story by noting that he and Vallandigham then had "another long and interesting conversation," and that McKibbin and Wiles, having returned, had found an officer who had agreed to take Vallandigham.

That wasn't exactly true. The Confederate officer whom McKibbin and Wiles came upon had been taken by utter surprise, having heard nothing about Vallandigham's travel. He had said he wouldn't accept the prisoner until he heard back from his superiors. After two hours, with the Union officers waiting, he heard from a colonel, but that colonel passed the buck to General Bragg, whose headquarters was in Shelbyville, down the road.

McKibbin and Wiles, exhausted and knowing they couldn't fail to dispose of Vallandigham, concocted the plan of simply leaving Vallandigham in Confederate territory. They asked the Confederate colonel what would happen if they did that. The colonel acknowledged that if a lone man approached seeking protection, he would get it.

The Union officers sensed grave doubts about whether the South should take this guy, whether he was really a friend. The officers kept that to themselves as they went back to gather Vallandigham. Then, indeed, they dropped him off, not with an officer but a private. Various accounts can leave one with the impression that the private was caught by surprise by the event and hadn't a clue what was going on. Not exactly true. He knew something was up; he just didn't know what. The private left his own account, collected in an anthology in 1896.[107]

S.F. Nunnelee, identified as a captain in 1896, wrote: "One bright morning in May, I think it was, Colonel Webb"—with whom McKibbin and Wiles had dealt,

> sent for me and ordered me to go to the (edge of Confederate territory) and escort a flag of truce between the lines, and to put on my best "bib-and-tucker." I changed my wool hat for a new home-made gray jeans cap, or bonnet, which my wife had made, and proceeded, having a very indefinite idea as to the purpose of my mission.
>
> Arriving at the outpost [the edge]—I soon saw a wagon coming down the pike, two men being seated therein and driving like Jehu" [meaning fast and recklessly]. When they pulled up under a large oak on the side of the pike, I advanced and told the two officers, a colonel and a lieutenant [McKibbin and Wiles] that I had been ordered to protect their flag between the lines. One of them replied: "All right, come on!" Turning their wagon, they started back, and their trotter kept my horse in almost a full gallop to keep up. Coming in view of their outpost, the colonel asked me to remain there until his return. You may imagine what I thought. I was protecting his flag, which he tore away, leaving me without one, and I asked myself, Who is protecting me? Of course, I had no arms and didn't know the (Union) fellow who was posted a hundred yards ahead of me. In less than half an hour, I saw the flag returning over the ridge, and the wagon had an additional passenger.
>
> Returning at the same break-neck speed, we halted under the oak, and the third man was told to alight. As he stood up in the wagon, he said: "In the presence of this gentleman, [Private Nunnelee] I protest against being forcibly taken from the State and my family." The colonel (I think his name was Gibbons or McGibbons) said that they were simply obeying orders and that he must get out.

Actually, at this point, Col. McKibbin had been replaced by a Captain John C. Goodwin.[108] Thus, perhaps Nunnelee's confusion. At any rate, Vallandigham did climb down, Nunnelee said, "and I advanced and helped him lift his trunk out. As the colonel turned, the prisoner handed him some letters which he requested should be mailed to his family. Approaching, I gave him my hand, telling him who I was."

Oddly, it then turned out that Vallandigham and the private had communicated before the war, or at least the private had sent him "my paper." Vallandigham "at once remembered my name and, with some surprise, asked what I was doing there. I told him that I was playing soldier and was trying to keep Rosecrans and his men from running us over." Eventually, Vallandigham said, "They can never whip you."

Nunnelee continued, "He then gave me a brief account of his arrest, condemnation and expulsion from home." Through this whole process, Vallandigham was talkative and engaging, certainly not sulking or angry. "The day before he had asked General Rosecrans for the freedom of his camp but was denied, and intimated that if he could have addressed the troops, a large number of them would have mutinied; that many of them were opposed to the war and would not have fired a shot at us if they could help it."

Nunnelee left to pick up Col. Webb—the Confederate with whom the Northern officers had first spoken—and returned with him. At this point Vallandigham made a statement, according to Nunnelee: "I am Clement L. Vallandigham, a citizen of Ohio, in the United States, and for my political opinions have been arrested and without a fair trial for any offence have been forcibly driven from my state and family and am seeking an asylum in the Confederate States of America."

Actually, Vallandigham almost certainly did not say anything about asylum. That wasn't the plan. Later, he claimed that he said (and there is no reason to doubt it), "I am a citizen of Ohio, and of the United States. I am here within your lines by force and against my will. I therefore surrender myself to you as a prisoner of war."

The distinction is politically important. If he's seeking asylum, then he's seeming friendly toward the Confederates. For back-home political purposes, he must not. Of course, the idea of him being a prisoner of war was absurd. He could have just said he was there against his will, and that he would appreciate some help in getting to his next destination, but he did not want word to spread that he had asked for a favor. And he clearly did want the phrase "prisoner of war" to be circulated.

Nunnelee's account also differs from others as to sequence and such details as who was present at various points. But he clearly did some pretty close observing. He has Col. Webb responding to Vallandigham's little set piece with one of his own, equally carefully planned:

"As a citizen of Ohio, in the United States, you are my enemy, as are all your people who have combined against my people to destroy their homes and property. But as Clement L. Vallandigham, a citizen of Ohio, driven from his home and seeking an asylum in my country, I give you a true welcome and true southern hospitality until I learn what is in the mind of my superiors in office." Apparently the pursuit of asylum was an assumption on the Confederate side, with, perhaps, Col. Webb putting the idea in the Private Nunnelee's head.

Vallandigham, wrote Nunnelee, was then escorted by two companies on the six- or eight-mile ride to Bragg's headquarters.

Vallandigham's arrival became news quickly. A reporter for the Chattanooga

Rebel at Bragg's headquarters, 100 miles from his newspaper wrote, "Mr. Vallandigham is cheerful and seems to breathe freer on escaping from Lincoln's despotism. He very properly desires to avoid all public demonstrations, and only asks that he may find a quiet refuge in our midst, until such time as the people, relieved from the despotic influence, shall call him back again to their midst. He seems to fully realize the embarrassment of his position"—that is, his need of help—"and will, beyond doubt, be equal to its responsibilities. A dignified retirement and exclusion from all public matters will, to the minds of all proper persons, as doubtless his own, be the best course for him to pursue."[109]

The newspaper included these observations from its correspondent in an editorial that went on to disagree. That editorial is worth quoting at length. It illustrates much about the ensuing debate in the South about Vallandigham. It also shows insight into Vallandigham's state of mind.

"We cannot believe it is the wish of one of Mr. Vallandigham's sagacity and courage to settle down into a baleful obscurity among strangers.... Far, very far from it. The golden moment of all his life is the present moment." The piece suggests that Vallandigham's movement would die without him. Then:

> Our correspondent says that (Vallandigham) fully realizes the embarrassment of his position.... There should be no embarrassment.... The road ... is direct and gas-lighted all the way. It leads first out some Confederate port to Nassau, thence to Canada and finally into the Gubernatorial chair of Ohio. The return of Napoleon from Elba was the signal for general reaction in France. Thousands flocked to him.... Let Mr. Vallandigham's return be as speedy. Let the (passage) of a single month find him issuing an address to the people of his State from lower Canada proclaiming these things: "I am a loyal citizen of the Union ... thrown ... across the lines of the public enemy; whose refusal to receive or recognize me establishes ... my patriotism and my honor; I, Clement L. Vallandigham, persecuted, exiled, reviled and coerced by tyrants ... issue these words and declare myself a candidate for governor of Ohio." The effect would be magical.

The newspaper articulated what was to emerge as the Confederacy's policy on Vallandigham. It put forth Vallandigham's own position with far more insight than its correspondent who had met with him. It even described events that were yet to take place. Maybe the editor just knew something; he might have heard from Vallandigham. He was a very young Henry Watterson, later to become one of the best known commentators in American journalism, writing for the Louisville *Courier-Journal*. He was one of the early syndicated columnists, with a career spanning to World War I. (He once wrote to his fiancé, about Braxton Bragg: "Next to my love for you, the stoutest passion of my soul is an intense loathing for this infamous character.")[110]

The May 29 Richmond *Sentinel* also proposed Canada as the way to counter the "cunning and tyranny" of Lincoln and Seward.[111] That paper was new in 1863, and not the voice of the government, but certainly loyal to it; so it might have known what some in the government were thinking.

The authorities in Richmond treated Vallandigham as a forbidden love: They knew what they felt, but they knew they must not. Yes, he was their favorite Northerner, but he was against secession and permanent independence. So the romance just wasn't meant to be. Even Vallandigham's armistice proposal wasn't enough. He still *talked* union, at least for the long term. Indeed, he was back to saying "The Union as it was; the Constitution as it is."

The Confederates needed Vallandigham, but they needed him in the North. They loved to hear a Northern politician say the Republicans drove the South out of the country. They loved hearing a Northern politician call the anti-slavery movement phony philanthropy, indifferent to the suffering of white, urban workers in the North. They wanted and needed people in the North raising questions about the war from a Northern perspective and denouncing Lincoln furiously. In 1863, the politicians in the North who actually promoted letting the South go permanently were too few and too marginal to be of much value to the Confederates. Vallandigham, on the other hand, was a national figure. They wanted to nurture his career, because a better option wasn't available.

To Vallandigham's critics in the North, his occasionally-stated opposition to secession looked like the nearest thing to nothing, a merely ritualistic concession to political necessity. But to some in the South it seemed close to the heart of everything. Richmond was simply not looking for the kind of negotiated settlement Vallandigham talked about. Indeed, at this point, the people of the South hated the North more than ever.

Perhaps the best-known—and best—cartoon about Vallandigham, suggesting (fairly) that neither side wanted him, from *Frank Leslie's Illustrated Newspaper*, June 20, 1863.

Wrote the editor of the Richmond *Sentinel*, "So odious to us has the idea of reunion with the North become that we denounce the (faction) of which Vallandigham is chief" as thoroughly as the Lincoln administration.

Robert E. Lee thought that took things too far. In an anguished June 10 letter to Jefferson Davis, he said lumping the Yankees together is all wrong. We must, he said, "give all the encouragement we can, consistently with truth, to the rising peace (faction) of the North."[112] Let's not worry about the fact that they give lip service to the anti-secession view, he said. Their opposition to the war can be useful in bringing the North to the negotiating table. *Then* we can make clear that there will be no peace without secession and let them decide whether to give up on their dream of peace.[113]

***

Vallandigham was certainly not treated in the South as a POW. Arriving at Bragg's headquarters when the general wasn't there, he was put up in a comfortable private home.

Vallandigham might have been interested to know that the man he was dealing with was later to be called, because of his military record, "the Confederate Burnside."[114]

The Bragg-Vallandigham relationship—the meeting of the "Most Hated Man of the Confederacy" with a man called "the most unpopular man in the North" by a friend[115]—is not treated in one Bragg biography, and is passed over quickly by another.[116] Nevertheless, the arrival of Vallandigham had to be important to Bragg, because it was in the headlines. All the generals worried about the press. Bragg watched the papers closely.[117] He knew that his superiors in Richmond were concerned about Vallandigham, and he was quick to get in touch with Richmond. Furthermore, Bragg had to consider himself on relatively thin ice with Jefferson Davis, being under much fire from other Confederate generals after Kentucky and Stone River.

Official records show much Bragg involvement. When Vallandigham first met Bragg, he told him not only that he considered himself a prisoner, but that he did not want to remain in the South, that he would like to get to Canada. Pending that, he said, he'd like to travel a little in the South to see friends (a remarkable privilege for a POW). Bragg, obviously well-disposed toward Vallandigham and seeing no threat in him, signed a personal passport allowing Vallandigham to travel freely in Bragg's district.[118] Bragg said he had no authority outside his military district.

Bragg wrote a report to Richmond on May 27 saying, "On the 25th instant"—this month—"the Hon. C.L. Vallandigham of Ohio, United States, was brought by an armed guard of the enemy to the neutral ground between our pickets on the road from Murfreesboro to this place and was there abandoned by them." Not quite true; Vallandigham was never alone. But Bragg's retelling did become widely accepted. Perhaps Bragg didn't want Richmond to know that his army had actually accepted Vallandigham from Northern officers.

"I have admitted him within my lines and received him with courtesy due any unfortunate exile seeking a refuse from tyranny," Bragg continued. (Also, not a true characterization, of course.) "He desired to go the state of Georgia, and I have granted

11. Exiled, Welcomed and Removed

him permission for that purpose. Should the Government desire any other policy in similar cases, I shall be pleased to receive instructions."

Turned out the government desired another policy in this particular case. On May 30, Secretary of War James Seddon wrote to Bragg that he should find out exactly how Vallandigham saw his situation playing out. Seddon said, "If he claims to be a loyal citizen of the United States, he must be held in charge or on parole as an enemy alien." That is, he can't be out gallivanting. Seddon allowed that Vallandigham might be allowed to go to Wilmington, North Carolina, accompanied. That was the route through which people left the Confederacy by sea. Apparently the Canada option was on the minds of the Confederate officials from the start.[119]

Bragg rescinded Vallandigham's right to travel, and both Vallandigham and Bragg wrote to Richmond. Vallandigham made sure not to complain about the revocation. He reiterated that he wanted to be considered a prisoner of war, and he said all that he really asked was to be allowed to get to Canada.[120] The Confederate authorities certainly looked at the letter for any indication that he had abandoned his criticism of secession or his belief in reunification. They found none.

Bragg's letter to Richmond of June 1 elaborated on his original, inaccurate description of Vallandigham's arrival: "Fearing assassination by a licensed soldier," presumably of the North, "he made his way to my outposts and surrendered." Bragg ended by saying, "I suggest a conference with him personally or by a confidential agent."[121] In other words, don't just send him on his way; pick his brain first. Perhaps Bragg had found something pertinent there. Richmond embraced the idea.

Another visit to Bragg's HQ at Shelbyville coincided with Vallandigham's. Lt. Col. Arthur J.L. Fremantle, 28, was a Brit. He had taken leave from his colonial military duties to see the American Civil War out of professional curiosity. He claimed to have "the dislike which an Englishman naturally feels at the idea of slavery."[122] However, early in the war, watching from abroad, his sympathies came to lie with the South. He saw "gallantry" and "determination" there, compared to the North's "foolish bullying."

Not wanting to violate the North's blockade of Southern ports, he came into the South through Mexico. Starting from Texas, he went into Mississippi, then eastward, still in the South. He was treated cordially by Southern generals; they knew the Confederacy was trying to get Britain on its side. He interviewed several of them. Upon getting home, he published his diary. It was highly praised and has won much attention since.[123] He had a remarkable knack for showing up at newsy places, including Gettysburg.

In Shelbyville, Fremantle found Vallandigham in the company of two generals and "Bishop Elliott of Georgia." The Brit knew who Vallandigham was, and he talked with him, getting Vallandigham's view that if Grant failed to take Vicksburg—and control of the Mississippi—the North couldn't continue the war "on its present scale." This meeting is mentioned here because Fremantle returns in the story.[124]

Jefferson Davis decided that the appropriate Confederate official to interview Vallandigham was the mid-level one in charge of exchanging prisoners of war with the North. So the POW label had gained a little traction. The Confederates proved willing to declare a person a prisoner whom they hadn't captured and whom they were now trying to get rid of in precisely the way he wanted to be released. It was better than having Vallandigham meet with a higher-ranking person.

The next question was where to meet. Richmond? No. That would make Vallandigham too important. Lynchburg was settled upon. West of Richmond by 115 miles, north of Wilmington by 275, it was on appropriate train lines. Vallandigham would look somewhat as though he was simply taking a meeting while on his journey to Wilmington. His interviewer, Col. Robert Ould, would be sent to Lynchburg with instructions to also accompany Vallandigham to his final Southern destination, an appropriate task for someone of his rank.

Before leaving Shelbyville, Vallandigham was interviewed by a few journalists. The fellow from the Atlanta *Confederacy*—"W" by byline—was so blown away that he was moved to quote Gray's *Elegy* AND Milton's *Paradise Lost*. Vallandigham was more like

> *"'Hampden, that, with dauntless breast,*
> *The petty tyrant of his fields withstood,'*
> than Milton's fallen angel.
>
> *"'With Atlantean shoulders fit to bear*
> *The weight of mightiest monarchies.'"*

Descending to prose, the writer said, "This man will be triumphantly elected Governor of the great State of Ohio in October next.... What stupendous plans and purposes must now be passing through his mind!" Under certain circumstances, "it is not to be doubted by any one that the 'the gallant tribune of the people' ... will be the successful candidate for the Presidency in 1864."[125]

Within a week of arriving at Shelbyville, Vallandigham was on the road again, toward Wilmington circuitously. That city was the main port for "blockade-runners."[126] Geography there allowed Southern ships to rest unattacked and to get into action with effective protection. The train journey to Wilmington was slow and difficult, complicated by the priority given to military needs. The journey entailed first going slightly south to Chattanooga, then doubling back northeast to Lynchburg (via Knoxville), then going back southeast to Wilmington. The actual journey didn't get much press coverage, presumably because the authorities were not publicizing the travel details for fear of generating embarrassing crowds. Nevertheless, pro–Vallandigham Confederate soldiers did gather on the route to the Shelbyville train station, and other well-wishers were present in Chattanooga on June 2.[127]

What with a long delay at Knoxville, Vallandigham didn't get to Lynchburg until June 5. On the 300-mile ride from Knoxville to Lynchburg, Abingdon, Virginia, is almost halfway. If the train stopped there, the riders might have seen a somewhat belated report that appeared in the local paper, the *Virginian*, about the New York rally. They might have seen a passage about the speaker who asked the crowd if it would stand by Vallandigham and got the response, "Yes! Yes!"

As for the Lynchburg meeting, itself, thousands of Republicans would have loved to have a seat. Would the king of the Copperheads finally reveal himself to be the Southern operative they were certain he was? Would he offer military advice or even some sort of para-military help? Would he volunteer—or be asked—to bear a message back to Washington or some encouragement to Copperheads? Might he ask

11. Exiled, Welcomed and Removed

for prolonged Southern hospitality and just stay there? Could he become a formal advisor to Richmond, or a proposed go-between with Washington or with Northern Democrats? Might he propose a peace plan he hadn't unveiled? And would it—or anything else that took place—be secret or public?

Colonel Ould—his debriefer—had been a prominent figure in Washington before the war: the U.S. attorney. He had been the losing lawyer in a case of O.J. Simpson-type notoriety. Dan Sickles, a former New York congressman and future Northern general, had killed his wife's alleged lover (the son of Francis Scott Key). Sickle's lawyers were among the first to deploy the temporary-insanity defense. They won the case, with Edwin Stanton—future secretary of war—playing a lead role for them.

Ould had been a marginal Southerner. Born in Georgetown—in slave country—he went to college in Pennsylvania and Washington, then to law school at William and Mary in Northern Virginia.

Ould wrote a report about his meeting with Vallandigham, but it may not exist. What does exist is a summary of it written by a War Department clerk. The term clerk might be misleading. John Beauchamp Jones was a popular novelist with three books out. He had founded a publication called the *Southern Monitor* in Philadelphia a few years before the war and had decided that the Fort Sumter crisis was a compelling reason to leave the North. Indeed, his office was sacked shortly after his departure.[128] A Southerner by birth, he had taken a vehemently anti-abolition posture, skewering abolitionists as phony philanthropists in at least one novel, *The City Merchant*.

At 51, he thought he was too old to fight. He wanted a job that would yield a book. He ended up handling correspondence for the Confederate secretary of war, a position that did, indeed, yield *A Rebel War Clerk's Diary at the Confederate States Capital*, published in 1866, the year he died.

The Ould-Vallandigham conversation is not a major part of Jones book as to space. He was writing about many momentous events: battles, food shortages, soldier shortages. But he was very much aware of the Lynchburg meeting for all manner of reasons. Both he and Ould must have seen Vallandigham as a figure they had much in common with, given their own Northern connections and their politics. He was fighting the fight they would have been fighting if they had chosen life in the North during the war.

In his entry for June 17, 1863—a couple of weeks after the Lynchburg meeting—Jones wrote, "A sealed envelope came in to-day, addressed by the President to the Secretary of War, marked 'High important and confidential.'" Jones, who usually opened letters, passed it on unopened. "I can as yet only conjecture what it referred to," he wrote. "I care not what it is, if we hold Vicksburg." Grant's long, long effort there was the greatest pending war story in the wake of Chancellorsville. The next day in the diary: "I have good reason to suppose that the package marked 'important,' etc. … was the substance of a conversation which took place between Mr. Ould and Mr. Vallandigham."

The diary's next reference to Vallandigham came on June 22, by which time Southern troops had crossed into Maryland and Pennsylvania before the Battle of Gettysburg. Excitement was running high in the South. One newspaper said, "Not even the Chinese are less prepared by previous habits of life and education for martial resistance than the Yankees.... We can ... (exact) peace by blows leveled at (Yankee) vitals."[129]

The Jones diary:

> June 22d.—To-day I saw the memorandum of Mr. Ould of the conversation held with Mr. Vallandigham ... (who) says if we *can only hold out* this year that the peace party of the North would sweep the Lincoln dynasty out of political existence.... He seems to have thought that our cause was sinking, and feared we would submit, which, of course, would be ruinous to his party! But he advises strongly against any invasion of Pennsylvania, for that would unite all parties at the North, and so strengthen Lincoln's hands that he would be able to crush all opposition, and trample upon the constitutional rights of the people.

Jones continued: "Mr. V. said nothing to indicate that either he or the party"—the Copperheads—"has any other idea than that the Union would be reconstructed under Democratic rule. The President"—that is, Davis—wrote "with his own pen, on this document, that, in regard to invasion of the North, experience proved the contrary of what Mr. V. asserted." The diary entry concludes with this: "But Mr. V. is for restoring the Union, amicably, of course, and if it cannot be done, then possibly he is in favor of recognizing our independence. He says any reconstruction which is not voluntary on our part, would soon be followed by another separation, and a worse war than the present one."

There's a lot to unpack there. If, indeed, Vallandigham told the Confederates to just hold out until a Democratic president could be elected, that resolves the debate about whether he was a traitor. He was. Northern troops were dying by the tens of thousands toward the goal of getting the South to give up, and Vallandigham was saying, "Don't give up!"

Could he really have said that? The testimony is third hand. We don't have it from Vallandigham, Ould or any document. We have Jones' interpretation of a document. And he's not offering it under oath. And he's paraphrasing, not quoting.

Would Ould or Jones have any motive to distort? Hard to see it. Ould was just reporting to his superiors. Jones was not writing for war-time consumption.

We know that a Democratic victory in 1864 really was Vallandigham's hope for the future. But would he have been so indiscreet as to give it top priority in Lynchburg? One possibility is that he talked to Ould in a way that was designed to deliver the hang-in-there message while giving Vallandigham some deniability.

But set the hang-in-there advice aside. Even Vallandigham's advice not to go into Pennsylvania would have been explosive. Here we had a Northern politician offering military/political advice to the Confederacy, and doing so behind closed doors. One might argue that advising against an invasion of the North was acting in the North's interest. But he reportedly couched the advice in terms of Southern interests.

Vallandigham's warning that an invasion would unite the North around Lincoln was strained, given that Lee had invaded Maryland the previous summer at Antietam. There had been no great rallying-round Lincoln; indeed, the election shortly thereafter was bad for the Republicans. Perhaps this is what Davis was referring to in his note in the margin when he said that history contradicted Vallandigham's advice. Or he might have been talking about other wars.

Ironically, one big reason that Davis and Lee wanted to invade Pennsylvania was to help the Copperheads; their political judgment about the effects of an invasion was precisely the opposite of Vallandigham's. Lee specifically wrote to Davis about "the rising peace (faction) of the North," saying it offered a "means of dividing and weakening our enemies."[130] Lee and Davis both read the Northern newspapers and saw that Northern military setbacks such as Chancellorsville strengthened the Copperheads. For both of them, it stood to reason that a successful invasion of Pennsylvania would have the same effect.

Also worth pausing over is another point that Vallandigham reportedly made to Ould: That he wanted to see amicable reunion, but if it wasn't possible, maybe he'd agree to disunion. If revealed, this could have raised, among other things, a perjury issue. At his trial Vallandigham had quoted himself as saying at Mount Vernon that he "always would refuse to agree to a separation of the States."[131]

If he didn't say these various things to Ould, there was *a lot* of misinterpreting going on after that meeting. At any rate, the Ould meeting didn't figure into the political events of 1863 or later, its contents being unknown.

Vallandigham could have refused to meet with Ould, but that would have required him to restrain his most basic impulses. He always believed that people would benefit from hearing him.

After the conversation, Vallandigham and Ould were off to Wilmington. Only five weeks had elapsed since Vallandigham's speech at Mount Vernon—with his arrest, trial and sentencing, his re-sentencing, his journey down the Ohio to Louisville and ultimately to Murfreesboro, his delivery to the Confederates, and his stops in Shelbyville and Lynchburg intervening. The convention of the Ohio Democratic Party was slated to happen in a few days, June 11.

12

Lincoln vs. Vallandigham

Back home, the arrest had changed everything. Democrats all over the state were inflamed—and not just Copperheads. This was an unheard-of affront: to treat a serious contender for the gubernatorial nomination of a venerable political party like a criminal, just for expressing his views! The Republicans—for the arrest was seen by Democrats as political, not military—were the first American political party to do something like that since the Federalists. It looked to some like a turning point in American history. It certainly could be portrayed that way when combined with other political arrests. Meanwhile, the arrest had transformed a man notorious for extreme views into a symbol of democracy.

Dayton wasn't the only place to experience violence in the immediate aftermath of the arrest. In hugely Democratic Crawford County 60 miles north of Columbus, in Crestline, Vallandigham had been scheduled to speak on May 7. The Democrats got a substitute, but then found that the Republicans had rented all the available indoor space. Ultimately, the speaker told those assembled in a large stable that they needed to arm themselves against the possibility of more arrests. That speaker, one A.J. Douglas, was himself arrested the next night under Order 38. Democrats threatened to burn the village; peace was restored by federal troops, who had to be dispatched three more times to the same place.[1]

Ohio Democrats felt they were in the national spotlight. They noticed when the New York rally expressed the hope via resolution that Ohio would respond to the arrest by electing Vallandigham governor.[2]

Historian Eugene Roseboom wrote that spring elections in Cincinnati—before the arrest—had shown movement against Peace Democrats and toward Unionists. But "the public meetings and resolutions provoked by Vallandigham's arrest, many of them outside Ohio, swept away the ... opposition and insured his selection" as nominee for the governor. The scene where that selection happened was extraordinary.

Thousands descended on the state Democratic convention in Columbus. Roseboom said estimates varied from 25,000 to 100,000.[3] If 20,000 is the correct number, the same percentage of Ohioans today would be about 100,000. In those days, people often went to political conventions as observers and demonstrators without being delegates or journalists. But this convention was special by all accounts, in intensity perhaps even more than size. The Republican Cincinnati *Gazette* said "There has been no more enthusiastic convention (in Columbus) for years than this one now promises to be." The paper quoted an unidentified outdoor speaker calling for violence if the feds tried to interfere with Vallandigham's nomination; he got cheers.[4]

The politicians inside were eager to make clear that they had received the message of the people. On the first day of the convention, they voted 411–13 to nominate Vallandigham. Hugh Jewett had simply given up in the face of reality. The qualms of the political professionals about the electability—or soundness—of Vallandigham had simply been overridden. If the delegates had dared nominate Jewett, they would have tested the Peace Democrats' interest in peace in Ohio. Instead, they came to terms with the political truth: Ambrose Burnside had destroyed Hugh Jewett. Or, to put it another way, Vallandigham—the bolder, more inventive, more colorful and extreme candidate—had found a way to render his more conventional opponent irrelevant, a drive-by victim, dazed and with no response.

At a certain stage, Congressman Samuel Cox—the same who testified for Vallandigham in Cincinnati—tried to get George McClellan to seek the nomination for governor, to head off Vallandigham. Cox and friends were desperate for a name as big as Vallandigham's. McClellan had certain Ohio ties, having commanded the state's militia early in the war. Cox reportedly assured McClellan that his nomination and election were foregone conclusions if he said the word. It didn't happen. At this point, McClellan been removed by Lincoln. But that had been followed by the catastrophes at Fredericksburg and Chancellorsville. McClellan was hoping to be called back to his old job.[5] Then, too, he probably had no stomach for the political fight against a revered martyr. Cox's effort might have been worth a try, but his reported prediction of a McClellan nomination was dubious.

Some Southerners could not hide their glee over Vallandigham's nomination. One Virginia paper said, "The progress of discontent at the North … will … paralyze the energies of the Administration…. Vallandigham (is) now the most prominent, the most popular, and the ablest statesman of the North…. The agitations that are seen (in Ohio) … are the only signs that foreshadow the end of the war. Heaven speed them!"[6]

***

When the Democratic nominee for governor of Ohio learned of his nomination, he was in Wilmington, North Carolina, waiting for a ride: a vessel that would take him to Canadian exile. We don't know how he responded outwardly. But what a powerful, memorable moment it must have been: a banished sojourner, removed from everybody he knows, reduced to killing time in a remote outpost he never wanted to see, learns of the great honor of his life, the great redemption, the great moment for gloating, the news that his gamble had paid off big. But there was nobody to gloat at, nor, apparently, anybody to celebrate with.

It seems odd that nothing about the moment is recorded in the 570-page book Vallandigham's brother wrote about him. One might have expected Clement to share the emotions of the moment with this brother or with some of the other family members whose correspondence his brother collected for the book. Maybe there was something about the moment that Vallandigham didn't want to talk about.

We know that he and Ould had set out for Wilmington, population 10,000, shortly after their talk in Lynchburg (where Vallandigham had arrived on June 5), and that they couldn't go directly to Wilmington because of railroad issues. Therefore, they went out of their way to Petersburg, Virginia, first. They were apparently accompanied for at least the last part of the ride by a Major Norris, who also accompanied other visitors to Wilmington. When they did get to Wilmington, Ould immediate left, giving responsibility for the exile to the local general (not Major Norris).[7] We know that Vallandigham didn't get on a blockade runner until the June 17.

Word of Vallandigham's nomination reached the South by June 13, when the Alexandria, Virginia *Gazette,* for example, printed it. However, the local paper in Wilmington, the weekly *Journal*, never did print the news.

Vallandigham knew by June 15 at the latest. This information comes from our British soldier-visitor-diarist, Lt. Col. Fremantle. He happened to be in Wilmington on that day. He had put it on his list of places to see because of British interest in the American trade embargo. (He was struck by the presence of "eight large steamers … which ply their trade with the greatest regularity … which shows the absurdity of calling the blockade an efficient one."[8])

He was being escorted by the same Major Norris who had escorted Vallandigham on the train ride. Fremantle wrote in his June 16 entry, "Major Norris went to call upon Mr. Vallandigham," who was in bed at the time, but rose. "He told Major Norris that he intended to run the blockade this evening for Bermuda, from whence he should find his way to the Clifton Hotel, Canada"—in Niagara—"where he intended to publish a newspaper, and agitate Ohio across the frontier. Major Norris found him much elated by the news of his having been nominated for the governorship of Ohio; and he declared if he was duly elected, his State could dictate peace."[9]

Major Norris claimed to have talked a lot of politics with Vallandigham and claimed to have told him that reunification was "utterly impossible," to quote Fremantle quoting Norris. Fremantle wrote, "Vallandigham had replied, 'Well, all I can say is *I hope*, and at all events I know, that my scheme of a suspension of hostilities"— the armistice—"is the only one which has any prospect of ultimate success.'" Fremantle added in a footnote to his 1864 book, "I have often heard Southerners speak of this proposal of Vallandigham's as *most insidious* and dangerous; but the opinion now is that things have gone too far to permit reunion under any circumstances."[10]

When Vallandigham got the news of his nomination, he may not have been shocked. He had known when the convention would happen. He knew that his arrest could mean nomination. Since the arrest, he had been picking up inklings of the response: the violence of his supporters in Dayton and the news from New York, for example. He knew he was the dominant figure in Ohio news and that he had a lot of passionate support.

Still, the nomination was an explosion; he couldn't have known about it in advance, couldn't have known about the outpouring of people or the unstoppable oneness of the delegates. If, when he got the news, it was in bare-bones form—which would have been typical for the day—he must have been frantic to get more. He would have wondered what people had said at the convention. He would have wanted some indication of how his nomination was playing.

In Wilmington, Major Gen. William H.C. Whiting—first in his class at West

Point in 1845 and later to die as a prisoner of war in New York—was in charge of Vallandigham. But it was apparently Secretary of War James Seddon who got Vallandigham a spot on a specific vessel, the *Lady Davis*, which Seddon owned.

The blockade runners did not exist to run exiled Yankees to Canada. They existed to keep the South trading with the outside world. They were likely to be privately owned. The *Lady Davis* was not going to Canada. Its destination was Bermuda, about 700 miles east off the Carolina coast. The ship docked at St. George's Harbor, later to be a tourist destination.

Just as Vallandigham didn't know what was going on back home, the people there didn't know what was going on with him. The Southern authorities still weren't disclosing his itinerary. The Wilmington weekly wasn't equipped to report the Vallandigham story. A Yellow Fever epidemic had hit the town in 1862, perhaps brought in by somebody on one of the blockade runners.[11] The paper was weakened. It never took notice of Vallandigham's presence in town. It did report after he was gone that he had successfully run the blockade and had reached Nassau.[12] The mention of Nassau—about as far south from Wilmington as Bermuda is east—was a factual mistake.

The Dayton *Journal* reported on June 20 that Vallandigham had cleared the blockade. It also mentioned Nassau. It would continue to try to track his whereabouts. That wasn't easy.

Southern papers didn't follow him obsessively. One reason was that the view had prevailed that, admirable as he was relative to other Yankees, Southerners must keep their distance. Another was that these papers had limited resources and more pressing concerns. The edition of the Wilmington *Journal* that reported Vallandigham's voyage also reported that a Northern army was in position to attack Richmond.

Unattributed, brief newspaper items would surface saying Vallandigham had apparently left the South or an island, apparently heading for this place or that. Typical among papers North and South, the Chattanooga *Rebel* reported on June 19, "Vallandigham is doubtless safely out of the Confederated States at this time. He may possibly turn up among the Knickerbockers (New Yorkers) under the protection of Gov. Seymour. At any rate, his prospects for the Governorship of Ohio are good." In fact, though, neither Seymour nor New York figured into Vallandigham's flight.

How did the voyage go, given the dangers? Vallandigham told his brother a story about an adventure on the *Lady Davis*.[13] Supposedly the ship was stopped by the North's navy, and the captain was able to convince the Yankees that his ship was really British. Vallandigham's story was that, with the Northern vessel looming, the captain had consulted Vallandigham about what to do. Vallandigham knew that a number of British uniforms were on board, so he advised that the Southern sailors don the uniforms, thus confusing the Yankees into withdrawal.

In response to this story, biographer Klement pointed out that "it is unlikely that any Union warship was fast enough to catch or even approach the *Lady Davis* on the high seas," that vessel having found its calling precisely because of its speed. Klement also noted that the captain was unlikely to have consulted the landlubber, and that, anyway, the captain would have known about the uniforms, too, and would not have needed Vallandigham's advice.[14]

The event does not show up in the multi-volume, government-produced *Official*

Records of the Union and Confederate Navies in the War of the Rebellion, though many such events do show up. Nor does it seem to have been reported by others, with or without Vallandigham's claimed role. It didn't happen.

In Bermuda, Vallandigham had another unwanted respite. The British territory traded with British Canada, but ship departures for Canada were not an everyday event. He was there for a couple of weeks. Again, even as he was idle, he was stirring events. Indeed, he was stirring the president of the United States. Abraham Lincoln engaged in a prolonged, in-depth public discussion of the beached political whale. And the fall campaign began.

***

The big New York rally that was prompted by Vallandigham's arrest resulted in the adoption of resolutions that were sent to Lincoln, along with a public letter. The resolutions called the arrest, trial and sentencing of Vallandigham a "startling outrage upon the hitherto sacred rights of American citizenship." It made all the cases: Vallandigham was abducted without due process, only for "words spoken," that he was charged with no crime that exists in law, that he didn't get due process, that civilians are, under the Constitution, free to speak their minds, otherwise they're slaves; that Constitutional rights were being violated "persistently" in similar ways by people who should be considered "public enemies."[15]

As Lincoln was pondering a response, Burnside ordered his shutdown of the Chicago *Times*, a virulent Copperhead paper that had castigated Burnside for acting against Vallandigham. After turmoil in Chicago, Republicans split on whether Burnside was going too far. Though Lincoln overruled Burnside on Chicago, he was later to admit doubt about his decision.[16]

Meanwhile, Lincoln felt a need to explain himself publicly on Vallandigham. The Vallandigham arrest looked like an escalation, the most notorious, extreme case yet of suppression. Where was Lincoln going with this? The question was obviously being asked way beyond Ohio.

Meanwhile, there was the shocking nomination of Vallandigham and the shocking way it happened. Some saw it as a revolutionary event. The nomination for high office of a man convicted by the government of disloyalty was so boldly, dramatically, tauntingly in-your-face subversive. If history had gone a different way from that point, the uprising of the Democratic Party of Ohio might have come to be seen as the moment when the people themselves arose and said "Enough!" Vallandigham would soon be characterizing the moment that way. Others had already done so.

When a committee of Ohio Democrats planned to call upon Lincoln to complain about the arrest, Gov. Tod wired Lincoln, "Allow me to express the hope that you will treat the Vallandigham committee … with the contempt they richly merit. The Vallandigham faction will be annihilated at our coming election."[17]

"Contempt." We're talking about a committee including all but one of the Democratic congressmen from Gov. Tod's own state. These were people who, a couple of years earlier, Tod would have referred to as his "fellow Democrats." And they were mainly War Democrats at that.

(The one absent congressman was Cox. He didn't explain that in his 700-page memoir or his 500-page collection of his speeches; but one of those speeches—at least as it appeared in the book—made clear he agreed with the rest of the delegation.[18])

Lincoln chose simply to make his case. He wrote a letter back to New York.[19] Nobody doubted then or doubts now that he wrote it himself, though in length it's roughly the equivalent of five or six political columns in a newspaper. The letter was intended to be as public as the one he had received. It was printed in many newspapers, some of which also put it out in pamphlet form. It was a hit. The New York *Tribune* version alone sold 50,000 copies. One historian said, the letter "dominated the national conversation."[20] It has generally won rave reviews from historians. One called it "unanswerable."[21]

In the letter, Lincoln pointed to an episode in which Democratic icon Andrew Jackson rejected civil liberties norms in a military situation. He must have enjoyed doing that.

He went on to point to the provision of the Constitution that allows for suspension of *habeas corpus* "when in cases of Rebellion or Invasion, the public safety may require it." He said that the whole point of that provision is that sometimes "men may be arrested and held who can not be proved to be guilty of defined crimes." He said the federal government is obliged to ward off "sudden and extensive uprisings against the government," and sometimes "arrests are made, not so much for what has been done, as for what probably will be done." (That line was to come in for specific, repeated derision later by the Copperheads for its open-endedness.) Offering an example, Lincoln said the North would be better off now if, when it had the chance, it had arrested all the West Point grads who were now leading the Confederate military effort; he said everybody had known where their loyalties lay. He said, "I think the time not unlikely to come when I shall be blamed for having made too few arrests rather than too many."

He also insisted that sometimes civilian courts cannot act with the speed that's necessary in a military situation.

Lincoln wrote that Vallandigham was not arrested for criticizing the Administration. "His arrest was made because he was laboring, with some effect to prevent the raising of troops, to encourage desertions from the army, and to leave the rebellion without an adequate military force to suppress it," the president said. "(H)e was damaging the army, upon the existence and vigor of which the life of the nation depends.... If Mr. Vallandigham was not damaging the military power of the country, then his arrest was made on mistake of fact, which I would be glad to correct."

Indeed, army manpower was a real issue. Federal draft enforcers had to risk their lives in some communities; 38 people in the Provost Marshall operation were killed during the war.[22] Desertion was becoming more common. The most commonly used figure for total Northern desertions is about 200,000, about a tenth of the number who served. But that number had not been reached by mid–1863. Maybe half that.

In his most famous passage, Lincoln noted that desertion is—and must be—a capital offense. "Must I shoot a simple-minded soldier-boy who deserts," he asked, "while I must not touch a hair of a wily agitator who induces him to desert?" This struck a lot of people as a powerful argument. If Lincoln chose to deport (not execute) the wily agitator, rather than shoot the young soldier, whatever else this was, it didn't look much like despotism, certainly not if practiced only once and publicly defended in this way that was respectful of public opinion.

"Wily agitator" resonated. To some people, it seemed indisputably true, unlike a lot of the rampant name-calling of the day. Certainly, Vallandigham was being called far worse, and Vallandigham was calling Lincoln far worse, accusing him of despotism, not mere agitation. And the phrase drew a distinction between a man of Lincoln's responsibilities and a man of Vallandigham's: the statesman and the agitator. However impressive Vallandigham's rhetorical skills, he could have talked about Lincoln for an hour without laying upon him such a damaging blow as those two words. They were the words that historians have been most struck by.

But how true was Lincoln's charge?

The main response to Lincoln's letter to the New Yorkers came from Ohio. The Democratic convention that nominated Vallandigham for governor appointed a committee to follow up with Lincoln. This was the group Gov. Tod suggested Lincoln treat with contempt. Lincoln decided not to do that. However, Treasury Secretary Salmon Chase suggested that anything Lincoln might say to them should be in writing.[23] The former Ohio Democrat apparently thought he knew something about Ohio Democrats: Don't let them characterize your views, was his input. Lincoln—obviously comfortable with public letters—did meet with the Ohioans on June 25, but he suggested that they put their views in writing and let him respond.

The June 26 letter from the Ohioans[24] was better—more challenging intellectually—than anything that came from New York. The Ohioans certainly did not consider Lincoln's letter "unanswerable." They considered it grist. Their letter said the arrest had been an insult to the people of Ohio, who had been considering him for governor.

It pointed out that, Lincoln's protestations notwithstanding, the issues of military recruitment, the draft and desertion had not been mentioned at Vallandigham's trial. "No evidence … was offered with a view to support, or even tended to support, any such charge," it said. True enough. Unquestionably, those issues had been on the minds of Burnside and others; they were part of public debate. And Burnside referred to them in his filing in the *habeas corpus* case. But in the Mount Vernon speech, Vallandigham did not counsel resistance to military service. So the prosecutors apparently decided not to go there, but to stick with what he had said explicitly, judging that enough.

The Mount Vernon speech notwithstanding, Vallandigham did say in 1862, as noted earlier, that, for people who did not believe the union could be preserved through war, staying home and voting Democratic was a legitimate way to serve. That obviously did undermine efforts to raise troops, at least if anybody listened to Vallandigham (as Tom Lowe, at least, seemed to).

Lincoln would not have pored over the trial transcript. He was talking about Vallandigham's reputation.

Another issue the Ohioans raised was Mexico. They argued that if merely opposing a war is tantamount to encouraging desertion, then "every political opponent of the Mexican war might have been convicted and banished from the country." The point was clearly about Lincoln's stance on Mexico.

The Ohioans also argued that the charges Vallandigham faced "entitled him to a trial before the civil tribunals," rather than a military commission.

But the main focus of the Ohioans was on the Constitution. They argued that the Constitution did not allow for the abridgment of individual liberties in war-time. They acknowledged one exception: the provision that allowed for the possibility of Congress—not the president—suspending the writ of *habeas corpus*. Why have other rights been suspended, they asked: speedy trial by impartial jury; the provisions against "cruel and unusual punishments" and unreasonable searches and seizures; the guarantee of due process, and the right to an indictment by a grand jury?

The Democrats also insisted that the speed Lincoln was looking for could be achieved in civil courts. And they said that, anyway, once the government has rescinded *habeas corpus*, speed doesn't matter much, because the government has the defendant in custody. So a normal trial could be conducted.

Bottom line: "Does your Excellency," they asked, "wish to have it understood that you hold that the rights of every man throughout this vast country are subject to be annulled whenever you may say that you consider the public safety requires it in time of invasion or insurrection?" The letter said that Lincoln's talk of crimes not specified in the law suggested that a president or military commander could have a man "arrested without charge of crime, imprisoned and ... sentenced to any kind of punishment unknown to the laws of the land."

"Banishment is an unusual punishment," the Ohioans pointed out, "and unknown to our laws. If the President has the right to change the punishment prescribed by the court-martial, from imprisonment to banishment, why not from imprisonment to torture upon the rack, or execution upon the gibbet." They asked that the banishment be revoked.

Lincoln responded at length to them, too, on June 29.[25] He dealt with the constitutional issues the Ohioans had emphasized. But that was not really what was on his mind. As with his "wily agitator" letter, he wanted people to focus on what Vallandigham was actually doing. But he saved that for the end.

He began with a personal point on Mexico: "(Y)ou will find yourselves at fault should you ever seek for evidence to prove your assumption that I 'opposed in discussions before the people the policy of the Mexican War.'" The words he put in quotes didn't appear in the Ohioans' letter in precisely that way. And to deny that he opposed the war, he must have been choosing his own words very carefully. As a one-term congressman, he voted for a resolution saying the war had been "unnecessarily and unconstitutionally" started by President James K. Polk. Indeed, he made the big speech of his brief tenure on that very subject. Historian Doris Kearns Goodwin wrote of the "vehemence" of his opposition. However, the war was over by the time he came to Congress. Perhaps that was Lincoln's (strained) point.[26]

As for the constitutional points, Lincoln wrote that *habeas corpus* is "the great means through which the guarantees of personal liberty are conserved." And he implied that the Founders' willingness to suspend it in times of rebellion or invasion suggested that they saw a general need for a different approach to civil liberties then. He rested his case on the spirit of the *habeas corpus* provision. "If the liberty could be indulged of expunging that clause, letter and spirit, I really think the constitutional argument would be with you," he said.

As for the charge that he was claiming unlimited power, he said that if he abused his power he could be "dealt with by the modes (the people) have reserved to themselves in the Constitution," meaning elections, impeachment and whatever constraints Congress might come up with. (Of course, some Lincoln-bashers had anticipated that defense and had suggested that he was always on the path toward ending elections.)

He noted that his "modification" of Vallandigham's sentence to banishment had made it "less disagreeable," implying that it didn't raise a question about whether he could make it more so. As for insulting Ohio, he said he didn't know that Vallandigham was a candidate until late in the process. (But, of course, Burnside did know.)

Then Lincoln got to heart of the matter, as he saw it. Having made his defense, he now made his counter-attack. It was not aimed solely at Vallandigham.

"I certainly do not know," he said,

> that Mr. Vallandigham has specifically and by direct language advised against enlistments and in favor of desertion and resistance to drafting. We all know that (organized efforts), armed in some instances, to resist the arrest of deserters, began several months ago; that more recently the like has appeared in resistance to … a draft; and that quite a number of assassinations have occurred from the same animus. These had to be met by military force, and this again has led to bloodshed and death. And now, under a sense of responsibility more weighty and enduring than any which is mere official, I solemnly declare my belief that this hindrance of the military, including maiming and murder, is due to the course in which Mr. Vallandigham has been engaged in a greater degree than to any other cause, and is due to him personally in a greater degree than to any other one man.

Lincoln was not simply justifying his actions. He was campaigning. He was charging that the Democratic nominee for governor of Ohio was doing this great public harm. He continued,

> These things (the violent episodes) have been notorious, known to all, and of course known to Mr. Vallandigham. Perhaps I would not be wrong to say that they originated with his special friends and adherents…. And if it can be shown that, with these things staring him in the face, he has ever uttered a word of rebuke or counsel against them, it will be a fact greatly in his favor with me, and one of which, as yet, I am totally ignorant.
>
> When it is known that the whole burden of his speeches has been to stir up men against the prosecution of the war, and that, in the midst of resistance to it, he has not been known in any instance to counsel against such resistance, it is next to impossible to repel the inference that he has counseled directly in favor of it.

"With all this before their eyes," he said, "the convention you represent have nominated Mr. Vallandigham for Governor of Ohio."

Lincoln was, among other things, making it official that Vallandigham was *the* leading Copperhead nationally. Nobody would have argued. Perhaps recognizing what an extraordinary thing it was that so important a political adversary had been arrested and exiled, he made a proposal. Lincoln said that, unlike the letter from New York, the letter from Ohio did not even acknowledge that a rebellion was taking place and that an army was a legitimate means for dealing with it. Lincoln was trying to drive a wedge through the Ohio Democrats. He knew that most of the signers supported the war and that, in their letter, they had dodged the war issue as a way of maintaining a united front on the arrest. He wanted to make it as hard as possible for the War Democrats to stick with Vallandigham.

Pouring it on, he said, "Your own attitude (about Vallandigham), therefore, encourages desertion, resistance to the draft, and the like, because it teaches those who incline to desert and escape the draft to believe it is your purpose to protect them.... It is a substantial hope, and, by consequence, a real strength to the enemy."

Lincoln said he didn't really believe the Ohio Democrats wanted to sustain that hope. So he would helpfully offer them a way to make that clear. He asked them to accept three propositions by signing their names to the duplicate of his letter they each received, and returning it: (1) that there is an ongoing rebellion designed to destroy the union, and that military means for combatting it are constitutional; (2) that the signers wouldn't do anything that, in their judgment, would hinder the military; and (3) that they would help to ensure that the military people are paid, fed, clothed and otherwise provided for.

He said that if he received those signatures, he'd revoke Vallandigham's banishment, because for the "influential gentlemen of Ohio to so define their position (would) be of immense value to the army—thus more than compensating for the consequences of any mistake in allowing Mr. Vallandigham to return."

The Ohio Democrats, of course, responded at length. Their letter is letter dated July 1, at the beginning of the Battle of Gettysburg, while Vallandigham was sitting in Bermuda.[27] Much of their rebuttal was a rehashing of the constitutional points. When they moved on to Vallandigham's behavior, they said, "Permit us to say that your information is most grievously at fault.... (Vallandigham) has never made a speech before the people of Ohio in which he has not counselled submission and obedience to the laws and the Constitution." The Ohio Democrats said the charge that they "encourage desertions" etc., was just so much campaign nonsense: the norm of "political contests." They didn't address whether Vallandigham's rhetoric undercut efforts to man the army, nor did they address the point—unmentioned by Lincoln—that Vallandigham insisted that men who opposed the war could serve the nation by staying home and voting.

As for Lincoln's three propositions, they said that even if they might agree under other circumstances—and they said their views on the war were already well known—they couldn't sign. They saw the questions as an attack on their "dignity and self-respect" and their "sincerity and fidelity as citizens." And they said to sign would be to accept the legitimacy of Vallandigham's arrest and trial. They mocked Lincoln for willingness to revoke a supposedly legitimate punishment because of the opinions of a committee on three unrelated questions. They said Lincoln merely wanted to evade the questions they raised. The dialogue ended.

What does the exchange of letters say about Lincoln? Certainly, his letters undercut the notion that Burnside was way off the reservation. Lincoln wanted everybody to know that he, too, saw a need for unusual restrictions on civil liberties during this kind of war. He wanted to make the case for enhanced presidential authority (under, he insisted, the Constitution). And he was just as eager to deliver the message that this was *only* for wartime, notwithstanding the constant Copperhead refrain that it was a new approach to government by a new party.

The exchanges were dignified, generally intelligent, somewhat informed and almost thorough. The president and his critics seem guided—not by consultants telling them to stay "on message"—but by respect, if not for each other, then at least for the intelligence of others who might see their work. In a practice difficult for a modern political observer to get used to, they frequently addressed the points made by each other, rather than inventing easier targets or repeating semi-mindless "talking points."

Lincoln's use of public letters seems like a fairly obvious communication technique for a time when the written word was so crucial in politics; his desire to communicate directly with the public also seems unremarkable. In fact, however, the letters involved a transformation of the presidency, inadvertently fostered by Vallandigham. Most of Lincoln's recent predecessors had not been not gifted communicators; they didn't do this sort of thing. And his not-so-recent predecessors—the founding generation—played a different, less democratic form of politics.

The Vallandigham episode was the second time Lincoln had used public letters; the first was in response to Horace Greeley in 1862, when Lincoln said his top goal was saving the Union, whether that meant freeing all the slaves or none or some. (That was just before the Emancipation Proclamation.)

Harold Holzer wrote, in *Lincoln and the Power of the Press*: "Lincoln had come to realize that he could control 'public sentiment' best by bypassing the editors.... In so doing, he revolutionized the art of presidential communications." The editors might comment in print on his statements, but if his statements were present, the comments looked like "sidebars."[28]

As Lincoln's administration shut some newspapers, it mobilized others. In both ways, it embraced the idea that communication with the public was central.

13

The Campaign from Exile

When Lincoln made his conditional offer to re-admit Vallandigham, the Ohio Democrats could not check with Vallandigham to see what he thought. They didn't know where he was.

On Thursday, July 2—with the Lincoln exchanges just completed and percolating through the news—Vallandigham was able to board a vessel (the *Harriet Pinckney*)—that would take him and 600 bales of cotton from the Bermuda to Halifax, Nova Scotia, east of Maine.

He got a generally good reception in Canada. Canadians were divided over the Civil War, but not bitterly.[1] The slavery issue predisposed many to side with the North. But with Lincoln declaring early that the war was being fought to preserve the Union, not end slavery, sympathy for the South grew. Why should a region not be free to depart a country? Why shouldn't this be seen as a war for independence, like the revolution of (some) colonies against England? And why should Canada prefer to have a big, powerful country to its south, rather than two smaller ones?

Meanwhile, the widely read New York *Herald* was promoting a U.S. takeover of Canada, perhaps as consolation for potential loss of the South. That didn't help the North's cause in the farther north. Then, too, there were American tensions with England, Canada's parent country. Many in the North resented Britain's neutrality in the war and worried about England's possible recognition of the South. Early in the war, a classic international incident inflamed passions and had the Canadians worrying much about an American invasion, worrying even to the point of making military preparations. That was the "Trent Affair," in which an American vessel seized a British vessel that carried two Southerners on their way to seek the support of England for the South. Britain's reaction was furious.

And there were trade issues caused by the war. Canadians wanted to do business with the South, but the North was trying to prevent the South from doing business with anybody. In Halifax, blockade runners had become part of the local scene, and the North had captured a couple.

Vallandigham—whose arrival had not been expected but quickly became known—generated some controversy on editorial pages.[2] For most, though, the issue his presence presented was not whether the North or South was right in the war, but whether he had a right to speak his mind. His warm treatment was defended as a testament by democrats to democracy.

Vallandigham spent only one night in Halifax, before going to Quebec by ship and train. An unidentified Quebec paper quoted in an Ohio paper[3] said Vallandigham saw the sights in Quebec, met "a large number" of local people at his hotel, was entertained at a "select party" and was awarded a "special train ... at his disposal by the railway authorities" and went west to Niagara.

The Quebec *Morning Chronicle* took the occasion to editorialize about Lincoln's offer to re-admit Vallandigham. It called Lincoln's letter "one of the most puerile compositions we ever remember to have seen from such a source." This was apparently a reference both to Lincoln's proposal and to the idea of the Ohioans signing the letter and returning it.[4]

Vallandigham was importuned to stay a while in Quebec, but was intent on getting his campaign organized. He had notified friends and family that he would be staying in Niagara. When he arrived, his wife and son came. His running mate and other politicians came, some not from Ohio. The press came. He was interviewed by *The Times* of London. Nearby Buffalo sent a reporter, as did the Copperhead Chicago *Times*. His presence was a center of attention. In both Quebec and Niagara, consuls from Washington quickly learned that he was in town, as everybody else did. When the consuls reported the arrival to Washington, they received orders to keep an eye on him.[5]

The Vallandigham trek and the Lincoln exchanges were not exactly the biggest things in the news. Northern victories over the Fourth of July at Gettysburg and Vicksburg changed the military situation dramatically. The North now had control of the Mississippi, driving a wedge right through the Confederacy. Meanwhile, the legendary Robert E. Lee had been sent retreating from Pennsylvania, humiliated to the point of submitting his resignation (rejected). Before that, people had been wondering whether he could ever be beaten. In the South, the defeats resulted in some calls for peace, most notably in North Carolina, where five congressmen were elected favoring negotiations.

Vallandigham's hot streak was over. Ultimate victory in the war now seemed more likely and nearer, whereas Vallandigham had long claimed it wasn't possible.

He immediately set to campaigning, but he had some difficulty getting his message out of Canada. After interviewing him, a journalist from the Chicago *Times* crossed over into Buffalo and attempted to send a wire to Chicago with a Vallandigham letter to the public. The telegrapher simply turned down the request. The reporter tried again in Cleveland and was again rejected.

The Chicago *Times* wrote, "From the time that our reporter attempted to transmit the address by telegraph from Buffalo until he left Detroit for this city, he was dogged by a Government detective! Had he placed a copy of the address in the post office for transmission, no doubt the mails would have been refused by official authority!"[6]

The telegraph companies did, in fact, work hand-in-glove with the government on the war effort.[7] The government was putting a lot of money into extension and maintenance of the wires for military reasons. The various telegraph companies were going to benefit from that after the war. For that and other reasons, the wires were happy to join the war effort. It was the same way with railroads. When Burnside wanted to get troops to Dayton after midnight to arrest Vallandigham, he simply told the Cincinnati, Hamilton and Dayton Railroad to do it.

13. The Campaign from Exile

Even before his arrest, Vallandigham had complained about the wires being in partisan hands. The arrest made things worse for him. He was now a convicted traitor, or something like that. It's not hard to see why both telegraphers came to the same decision, given their orders to cooperate with the government.

The Vallandigham letter in question, dated July 15, ten weeks after his arrest, had been eagerly anticipated. Many saw this as history in the making. The circumstances were made for drama. Rumors and questions abounded about the exile. How was he being treated? Would he try to re-enter the country? What about his health and his wife's? Would he say that running for governor would be impractical? Would he line up with the Confederacy? Had he reached some sort of deal with the Brits and/or Canadians? Might he even call his people to arms in some degree? Might he renounce his American citizenship?

His message, when finally delivered, was read at Vallandigham campaign rallies, with a here's-what-they-didn't-want-you-to-hear sort of presentation. (More about those rallies shortly.)

He began with a dramatic first sentence designed to lock in his martyr identity. The subject of the sentence—"I"—was the 68th word. A description of his saga proceeded that word: "Arrested and confined for three weeks ... banished ... held ... given leave ... running the blockage at the hazard of being fired upon by ships ... of my own country, ... I...."

He said he was now under the protection of the British flag with "rights which usurpers insolently deny me at home." That got under the skin of a lot of Republicans.[8] How dare he suggest that the country the United States had broken from in pursuit of freedom—and that was withholding support in the current war—was the authentic practitioner of democracy! More than one writer noted that Benedict Arnold also breathed freely on British soil. At least one said that the reason Britain was free was that it had hung all its traitors.[9] That implied a suggestion about what should be done about Vallandigham.

Vallandigham felt a need to establish his lack of connection to the South. He said, "And I ... having refused ... even so much as to remain (with the Confederates), preferring rather exile in a foreign land...."

He referred to his "wearisome and most perilous journeyings for more than four thousand miles by land and upon the sea." But, after expressing thanks for the "unanimous" nomination for governor, he said, "I ask no personal sympathy." The important issue was "constitutional liberty and private rights," not his well-being (and, it's worth noting, not the war).

Of his nomination, he said, "It was an act of courage worthy of the heroic ages of the world." To the convention delegates, he said, "You are the RESTORERS AND DEFENDERS OF CONSTITUTIONAL LIBERTY, and by that proud title history will salute you." (Caps in his brother's bio.)[10]

After restating the civil-liberties issues, he said, "whoever gives his vote (to Unionists) ... would fairly forfeit his own right to liberty."

He said if "military necessity" is the pretext for suppression, "then, believe me, ... tyranny is perpetual. For, if this civil war is to terminate only by the subjugation or submission of the South to force of arms, the infant of today will not live to see the end of" the tyranny. Here he came to a passage that was to be much quoted: "Traveling a thousand miles and more through nearly one-half of the Confederate States.... I met not one man, woman or child who was not resolved to perish rather than yield to the pressure of arms. They are better prepared now ... to make good their inexorable purpose than at any period since the beginning of the struggle." This contradicted his insistence in his armistice speech that the Southerners were turning against the war, just as Northerners were.

His next claim—offered mainly in italics in the written version—was just a flat out lie: "Neither ... did I meet any one, whatever his opinions or his station, political or private, who did not declare his readiness *when the war shall have ceased and invading armies been withdrawn,* to consider and discuss the question of reunion." That was simply not the Southern state of mind.

The Richmond *Dispatch* called him on the point: "We do not know who were the persons with whom Mr. V. conversed. We are sure we have conversed with many more Southerners than he ever did, and we never heard the first one yet speak of reunion. He has certainly made a mistake somehow or other." The Dayton *Journal* was not going to miss the chance to report this shoot-down.[11]

***

As Vallandigham arrived in Niagara, war arrived in Ohio. This time it wasn't just an alarm. It also wasn't a full-scale invasion or a great clash of armies. But about 2,500 highly mobile Confederate cavalry troops crossed into Ohio to make as much trouble as they could in as much of the state as possible.

Their leader was one of the men feared the previous year, John Hunt Morgan. He was famed for this sort of thing: guerrilla-type raids of a sort that weren't taught at West Point—where he did not train, anyway. The idea was to scare civilians, to mess with the enemy's supply routes and infrastructure and to divert the enemy's troops from offensive missions. An aura surrounded Morgan of adventure and daring, of outside-the-box trouble-making. He was "the hero the western Confederacy desperately sought."[12] A certain kind of Southern young man signed up with him, one who would have been less attracted to the discipline and order of a regular military unit. "Morgan's men," as they liked to be known, worked on horseback, often without uniforms and with whatever weapons they deemed useful. Went one children's ditty:

> *I want to be a cavalryman*
> *And with John Hunt Morgan ride,*
> *A Colt revolver in my belt*
> *A sabre by me side.*
> *I want a pair of epaulets*
> *To match my suit of gray,*
> *The uniform my mother made*
> *And lettered C.S.A.*

That's Confederate States of America. Morgan was under the command of Gen. Bragg, to whom Morgan sold his diversionary tactics as a way to minimize the help that Gen. Ambrose Burnside, still in Cincinnati, might send Rosecrans. Apparently, however, Bragg did not want Morgan to go all the way into Ohio, because he might be needed closer to Shelbyville.[13] Nevertheless, after causing trouble in Kentucky, Morgan crossed the Ohio River, at first not into Ohio, but Indiana on July 9.

It was the first Confederate intrusion into a western state. Nobody had seen it coming, because there were no Confederate forces massed on the edge of Indiana. It came in a part of that state known for Copperhead sympathies. Rumors swirled. Was it a full-scale invasion? Some people heard that 12,000 troops had arrived, and that they were "bloodthirsty cutthroats."[14] Morgan's lieutenants sent out false telegrams designed to sow confusion about their numbers, whereabouts and plans. Gov. Oliver P. Morton called out the state militia. Burnside, among the shocked, ordered a defense of Indianapolis. But Burnside and others thought Morgan wouldn't stray that far into enemy territory.[15] They were right. And there was no Copperhead uprising, despite Gov. Morton's fears of one. Morgan turned back toward Kentucky and Ohio, successfully sending mixed signals about which he planned to enter, and where.

Morgan's journey almost never went well. It wasn't about swashbuckling adventurers out having a good time, scaring the locals and the authorities, then disappearing with cheers and laughter. It was exhausting, with troops having to ride in the saddle far longer than they could stay awake. They were constantly being chased, constantly losing men and horses. They were hugely outnumbered by Burnside's men and volunteers called up by Gov. Tod for the crisis; Tod reportedly got 100,000 respondents, more than he knew what to do with.[16] Morgan's men always had to forage for food, water and shelter. By the time they got to Ohio they were exhausted. They arrived at Harrison, northwest of Cincinnati and southwest of Dayton.

Nobody knew where they were going. In Dayton, alarm spread. Some people left. Some got armed and hunkered down. Martha Lowe, wife of Tom, picked up Vallandigham's wife Louisa and took her to ground deemed safer.

But Morgan headed east, cutting between Cincinnati and Dayton. He had thoughts of linking up with Lee in Pennsylvania. What followed was a long, bloody saga of a march across southern Ohio, with Morgan and his men—sometimes subdividing and pursuing various paths—looking for an escape back across the Ohio. There was a limit to their depredations. They didn't kill civilians except when provoked to an exceptional degree. They didn't burn down houses or willy-nilly destroy crops. But they stole horses they needed, getting themselves labeled as mere horse thieves by some, while ending up with Ohio farm horses that were utterly unsuited to the cavalry life. They stole other supplies, too. And they were not gentle. They took stuff they didn't need, apparently for the satisfaction of it, only to discard it on the trail. Stores got special attention. One of Morgan's officers wrote later that his men "pillaged like boys robbing an orchard. I would not have believed that such a passion could have been developed so ludicrously among any body of civilized men."[17]

At the east end of the state, Morgan turned north, still traveling along the Ohio, still looking for an escape across it. He was finally captured July 26 in Columbiana County, Vallandigham's home before Dayton, more than halfway up the state, with only 364 men left of his 2,500. About 500 had escaped back to the South.[18]

Little long-term damage was done to Northern infrastructure, such as railroad lines. The whole excursion may have backfired. One political effect relevant to the Copperhead cause: It showed Northerners something that Lee's thrust into

Pennsylvania also showed—or confirmed: that the Confederacy was decidedly not confined to defending its own territory; it was a threat. Wrote one soldier in Indiana, "I'm not sorry that something has occurred to wake up the people a little."[19]

Meanwhile, the Morgan Raid provided a test of the loyalty of the Copperheads. People had wondered: Confronted with the enemy, how would they respond? Would they sell out their neighbors and their country, or would they prove to be as loyal in the crunch as their spokesman insisted they were?

Testimony varies. Frank J. Klement, who tended to minimize disloyalty on the part of Copperheads, wrote that, "Several of Morgan's raiders later testified that the 'Copperhead' and 'Vallandighamers' fought (against them) harder than the others." Klement wrote that both Democrats and Republicans saw Morgan's men as "horse-thieves," "extortionists" and "blackmailers."[20] One of the raiders cited by Klement wrote that, before the raid, there were rumors of coordination between Copperheads and Confederates, but that this turned out to be nonsense.[21]

However, historian Jennifer L. Weber quotes different sources. Weber cites the letters of one Margaret Taylor, of Georgetown, east of Cincinnati (boyhood home of Ulysses S. Grant).[22] Wrote Weber, "In some neighborhoods, Morgan's actions were so specifically targeted that locals could only surmise that the Copperhead neighbors had briefed his men." Other sources elsewhere led Weber to similar conclusions.[23]

The end of Morgan's Raid was a subject in the first full-sized Dayton *Journal* after the fire destroyed that paper's building. The paper—caught up in a political campaign—saw Morgan's capture as a Vallandigham story. "'By the Blessing of Almighty God,'" it said, "Vallandigham has received a tremendous thump below the belt. John Morgan is captured."[24]

The *Journal* couldn't help noting on another page, "It is a curious fact that Morgan was captured within three miles of the birthplace of Vallandigham." What meaning the paper saw in that is not clear. Vallandigham took note, too, writing to a friend that if he was, as charged by some, Morgan's "pilot," he had piloted him to "a strong 'Vallandigham' township" for capture, after Burnside had proved incapable of capturing him anyplace else in Ohio.[25]

***

New York City was burning.

New York's port gave it a kind of link to the South that no other Northern city had. Before the war, Southern exports destined for Europe often went through New York, and European imports destined for the South did too. As a result, many monied Southerners spent a lot of time—and money—in New York. Southerners had accounts at stores around town, meaning that, at any moment, New York merchants were owed a lot of Southern money. And when the Southerners were in New York, they did the town. The economic ties fostered personal connections. The connections were so intense that when war loomed, the disreputable Copperhead Mayor Fernando Wood suggested that maybe New York should secede from both North and South and do business with both.

Another big force fostered Copperhead strength in New York: It was home to thousands of Irish refugees from the potato famine of the late 1840s. They had not come to the States to be drafted into a war in which they had no stake. The Democratic Party, in trying to organize them, pedaled the notion that abolition could be a threat, resulting in black competition for jobs. Lincoln lost New York City and Brooklyn (a separate city) by landslides twice.

With the coming of the first national draft in 1863, indeed, just as the names of draftees were being picked in New York, the city combusted. It was Monday, July 13. The rioting lasted through much of the week, taking well over 100 lives and becoming the worst civil uprising in American history, to this day. It was horrifically racist and lasted until troops who had fought at Gettysburg arrived to put it down.[26]

The events might as well have been designed to dramatize Lincoln's fire-in-the-rear comment of January: The North was, indeed, showing the ability to win the war with the South, but….

***

For Vallandigham, life as an international celebrity wasn't working out. Arriving in Niagara July 15, he was besieged by celebrity hunters, well-wishers and curiosity seekers. He was dominating the Clifton Hotel, something the proprietors didn't appreciate. He got all manner of invitations.

He attended rallies by invitation, as an observer of events having nothing to do with him. He also attended sessions of parliament as a special guest. There he saw himself become a subject of discussion, as his host lambasted Vallandigham's press critics.

(During the Trent affair, Vallandigham had gone after Lincoln, predicting the president would show weakness by backing off. Lincoln did back off, acknowledging that the U.S. had no business seizing the British vessel. He needed to avoid a distracting war with England. But Vallandigham had complained. "For the first time," he said, "the American eagle has been made to cower before the British lion." He had even supported a resolution praising the captain of the ship that had seized the Trent. George Brown, publisher of the Toronto *Globe* and an ally of the sitting pro–North government, interpreted this political potshot as evidence of an anti–British prejudice.[27] In fact, Vallandigham was closer to Anglophile than Anglophobe. He just couldn't resist taking every possible swipe at Lincoln.

The anti-slavery Brown stuck the needle in, saying that, of course, we in Canada should be hospitable to Vallandigham, just as we are to slaves who feel they have to flee the States.[28])

At a certain point, Vallandigham's Niagara hotel was planning to host U.S. Secretary of State William Seward. The hotel didn't want a volatile scene that would result from Vallandigham being there at the same time. Vallandigham moved to another hotel on the outskirts of town. But ultimately he decided he would be better off leaving Niagara entirely and going to Windsor, across the Detroit River from Detroit. Arriving there by train, he moved into the Hirons House on the river on August 24. It was prime land, looking directly across at Detroit, in the middle of the eventually bustling Windsor riverfront. He was in full sight of an American vessel separating him from his homeland, with a very visible, swiveling cannon, perhaps present in his honor.

For the Halloween edition in 1863, *Harper's Weekly* imagined Canadian farmers wondering what Vallandigham was doing there.

Windsor was a hamlet, so unknown that Vallandigham felt he must tell his correspondents where it was.[29] But it was a better spot for him than Niagara. Ohioans could visit him more easily, and there wasn't much other socializing to be done.

Vallandigham and his people planned his campaign under the watchful eye—from afar—of the Union military. In Detroit, the local provost marshal wired the top national provost marshal on August 27: "C.L. Vallandigham is at Windsor, opposite this place. There is an impression that he intends crossing into Michigan. If so, shall he be arrested; … if arrested where shall he be sent? Give instructions if he should go to Cleveland, Ohio. Please answer at once."

The order came back, "Get all the information you can about Vallandigham's movements and communicate it to General Burnside" in Cincinnati. Burnside personally wasn't in Cincinnati anymore. He had left to rejoin the actual fighting of the war, reinforcing Rosecrans. He took Knoxville, a rail center, without a fight. He took

13. The Campaign from Exile 157

The Hirons House in Windsor, Canada, where Vallandigham stayed during his 1863 campaign for governor of Ohio. It looked across the Detroit River to that city (courtesy of Museum Windsor, P5186).

that occasion to resign, but Lincoln rejected that, and Burnside said he'd stay as long as needed.[30]

Burnside's headquarters was still in Cincinnati, and a subordinate general in Indianapolis was in charge of Michigan. That general heard that Vallandigham would try to cross the river on or about September 15, a month before the Ohio election. He ordered that, if captured, Vallandigham should be sent to a POW camp in Lake Erie known as Johnson's Island. A general in Cincinnati said, "His friends threaten an uprising to meet him, but I doubt their nerve." However, Burnside still didn't want Vallandigham anyplace near Ohio, and the proposed prison was changed to Fort Warren in Massachusetts. Meanwhile, Burnside's office informed the governor of Ohio of Vallandigham's whereabouts.[31]

The rumors the provost marshal had heard about Vallandigham coming across did turn out to have some merit.

***

Oh, brothers, don't forget the time
When Burnside was our fate,
And laws were superseded
By order 38.
Then like a free-born western man,
Our Val spoke bold and true.
Oh, when he's chosen governor
What will poor Burnside do?

Won't he skedaddle,
As he's well used to do?[32]

Modern politicos might be skeptical of the predictive abilities of their 19th-century predecessors working without polls. Actually, though, the old politicos were not bad. Early in 1862, they had generally felt that it looked like a Democratic year. In 1864, the conventional wisdom was that Lincoln was going down—until Sherman took Atlanta, when the wisdom started to change. Now the conventional wisdom of the time is conventionally judged to have been right both times: Lincoln *was* going down until Sherman took Atlanta.

In mid-1863, the predicting politicos did not have a consensus about Ohio's race for governor. Many Democrats were confident about Vallandigham. All the passion was on his side. He had the great issue: freedom (for whites). Some Democrats thought that Republicans were playing right into their hands. The Democrats had just had a successful mid-term election after making democratic rights an issue. Now, with the Vallandigham arrest, the Republicans had strengthened their complaints. Amazing. For the Republicans to behave this way, even as they enacted the Emancipation Proclamation—making the war officially about black people, after all, not union—seemed to some Democrats almost too good to true.

Meanwhile, as spring turned to summer, the war was going badly for the North, another political boon to the Democrats. This was the third year in a row in which hopes for a quick end to the war had been raised and dashed. Indeed, now there was a national draft, for the first time ever.

Meanwhile, Vallandigham was unmistakably the more charismatic candidate, the genuine leader, the smarter guy. And, though the Democrats tried to portray his physical absence as a political handicap imposed upon them by the Republicans, many really saw it as an obvious advantage, dramatizing their complaints about the dictator Lincoln. They believed that exile added to the aura about Vallandigham.

Republicans were mixed in their expectations. Historian George Henry Porter wrote, "The Unionists began their campaign under considerable disadvantage and with much hesitation and doubt." Well-known Cincinnati journalist Murat Halstead, a relatively non-partisan Republican, could see the election going either way. He thought Vallandigham could be defeated by the newly established "soldier vote." But, writing to Treasury Secretary Chase, who was often critical of Lincoln, he said "we all know ... that if the vote were taken in Ohio between Vallandigham and the radical policy of the president—the foolish and hopelessly impracticable (Emancipation) proclamation—the election of Vallandigham would be the result."[33]

The Dayton *Journal* said in August that "the result of the campaign is very uncertain." It did not like to make such admissions.[34] Meanwhile, though, as noted early, Ohio's Unionist Gov. David Tod told Lincoln in June that the Vallandigham faction would be "annihilated" in October. He was speaking as a former Democrat about Democrats. He was promising that his people couldn't possibly support a Vallandigham. His prediction did speak for many. They saw Vallandigham as a peculiarly weak candidate before the arrest. Now they thought his reputation as a Southern sympathizer was locked in and was politically fatal.

13. The Campaign from Exile

If predictions were all over the place, it was because this was uncharted, volatile political territory. Does being exiled over a somewhat partisan dispute make a candidate a martyr or a pariah? There were no experts to turn to.

Certainly the Republicans knew that they were in a fight. A measure of that is that they were unwilling to go it alone, unwilling to put up a purely "Republican" ticket. A coalition with some War Democrats under the "Union" label wasn't magic, of course; the 1862 election had shown that. And many Republicans were against the idea, including Ohio Sen. John Sherman, no radical. They worried that Unionist state legislators wouldn't vote for Republicans for the U.S. Senate, that their party's message would be watered down and that Unionist officeholders would support a too-passive, McClellanesque military strategy, if not eventually McClellan himself. They also worried that dependence upon Unionist governors would make Lincoln and his military too timid and conciliatory in dealing with slaveholders. Still, when the Union Party met a week after Vallandigham was nominated, there was no question but that the Republicans were going to support another Democrat for governor.

However, the party dumped Gov. David Tod. Different people had different motivations. When a vacancy for the elective office of state auditor had appeared, Tod had appointed a Democrat. That was an irritant. Meanwhile, Tod had been slow to embrace Emancipation. And some thought Tod was vulnerable on the subject of political arrests, having participated in them and having been sued over the Olds arrest and brought to court. His public claim to have the "backbone" to arrest a certain editor led to some mockery, as did his alleged claim to the same editor that he—Tod—was the one who would decide what he could print.[35] All in all, the politicians didn't feel he had caught on. For parties to dump incumbents was more common in those days, not that big a deal. And the Republicans wanted to assert their authority: OK, we have to pick a Democrat, but we're not out of the game.

Along had come came another prospect. John Brough (pronounced bruff) was another version of Tod. He was a former War Democrat and a former railroad executive, having held elective office before cashing in. He had co-founded the Cincinnati *Enquirer* with his brother, then been a state legislator and state auditor. But he had not taken part in politics since 1848. A few days before the Unionist 1863 convention, perhaps sensing an opportunity, he gave a speech pledging total support for Lincoln in the war effort. Brough embraced military arrests and rejected the idea of a negotiated settlement of the war, saying the Confederates had shown themselves to be irreconcilable. Three newspapers endorsed him, and the radicals signed on. The whole sequence caught the public by surprise. Speculation flew about who really started the Brough boom. Democratic newspapers insisted the railroads were behind the whole thing—with some plan about railroad policy—but they didn't offer much reason to think so.[36]

Brough was more exciting than Tod. The clichéd description "big bear of a man" has applied to few any better than Brough. And he had a personality to match. Wrote historian Eugene Roseboom, "The Union party champion was a middle-aged, bearded corpulent, untidy-looking man, who chewed tobacco incessantly and was not overly temperate in other respects, in appearance and personal habits the antithesis of the handsome and puritanical Vallandigham. But he was a powerful speaker and every whit as courageous as his rival, while people admired his integrity, his honesty, and his flaming patriotism."³⁷ In an ordinary year, Brough might have been the more colorful candidate on the ballot.

His running mate was Charles Anderson, the brother of the North's commander at Fort Sumter, Robert Anderson. An old Whig, Charles had been a Dayton politician—prosecutor and state senator—before moving to Texas for health reasons. In Texas, he was appalled by secession, railed against it and was arrested by pro–Confederates. He escaped back to Dayton via Mexico and New York. That made national news. Lincoln then appointed him to a group touring England to make the Union case. Then Anderson went to war. He was injured at Stone River and returned to Dayton. By now he was a perfect candidate. As a measure of his national profile, he was chosen to speak at Gettysburg, where he immediately followed Lincoln to the podium.

John Brough, the second most colorful candidate for governor in 1863 (Ohio History Connection).

In the campaign, both sides were eager to draw clear lines. There was no ambiguity, complexity, uncertainty or middle ground. Let's do this.

***

The campaign was violent, racist, dishonest, extraordinarily exuberant, foreboding and utterly unique.

At Vallandigham rallies, his absence loomed over everything, heightening the specialness of the event and the sense of victimization that fosters a populist rebellion. His letters to voters surely got even more attention because they were read aloud than his speeches would have. His absence fostered a special degree of intensity in commitment to Valiant Val, the hero who was carrying on despite being separated from family and home. It fostered the view that coming out for him and voting for him was the least people could do.

Adding to the emotions of the day, a band might play a song with the lyrics, "Dearest love, do you remember when we last did meet?" or the title "Home Again."³⁸

When the absent speaker flattered his party for its courage and presented himself as an historic figure, when he spoke of his travails, his long journey in exile, when he made the issue democracy itself—and did it all with skills honed as if for such a moment—it was a heck of a spectacle.

Every day saw rallies.³⁹ Toward the end, there'd be more than one rally in or near any major city on any given day. The people who went to rallies were not—as later—small minorities with exceptional interest in politics. They were the people. This was a happening, a piece of history, an entertainment, a communal event to be talked about with neighbors for years after. The rallies were celebrations of Americanness, because the very idea of the people—including the poor ones, if not the black ones—electing those who would govern was central to the country's sense of itself, distinguishing it from just about any other. Meanwhile, even if the candidate wasn't present, other celebrities were, and this was a time when celebrities weren't always showing up electronically in living rooms. The town—or large parts of it on a parade path—would be decorated with patriotic colors or statements of political opinion. For a big rally, with big-name speakers, there would be an endless parade—the more endless the better—of horse-drawn vehicles, many decorated at least with a banner announcing geographic origin by township or ward, or sometimes a business name. The people who actually participated in the parades—not the spectators—may have been comparable in percentages of the population to today's rally-goers. The rallies would go on for hours, with speakers from far and near. In this campaign, many came from far: governors of nearby states; Cabinet members, including Salmon P. Chase.

A small rally might just have a speech, with no parade, hastily arranged because some semi-public figure—often with a military background—was in town for a candidate. Sometimes, in these cases, the venue would be a major one, like Courthouse Square in Dayton. Some venues would be out in the country; those events were "basket" (picnic) meetings. Congressman Cox spoke at Miamisburg in what is now metropolitan Dayton.

A *Times of London* correspondent described a Brough rally:

> The political meeting at Carthage reminded me of a Derby day at Epsom, only of a somewhat shabbier character, with a dash of an Italian masquerade and carnival frolic in it. The fair sex considerably outnumbered the lords of creation, and Young America mustered nearly as strong as the adult generation. There were huge triumphal cars, heavy boats and pontoons on wheels, drawn by four, five or even ten pairs of good well-fed horses, with an endless flutter of flaunting flags, ... a din of fife, trumpet and drum and the endless firing of light and heavy artillery. Pedestrians, horsemen, hack-carriages (meaning those driven by employed drivers) long teams of draught horses, wandered about the trackless turf in every direction, with no apparent purpose, save only the enjoyment of the open air and the jolly company. It was a fair, a picnic.... To eat, drink and be merry was the great business.... Here and there, indeed, in a corner under a canopy of some huge tree, Mr. Somebody from Indiana, or Mr. Nobody from Illinois, stumped away for very life, with a cluster of listless loafers around his extempore platform, pretending to listen, cheering occasionally, jeering more frequently; all this in a din of discordant music, the racking fire of great and small guns, and the shrill cries of apple women and vendors of firewater....
>
> Carloads of girls, as many as ninety in a single conveyance (aged from 10 to their teens), beamed upon the delighted male multitude.... (H)ere they were made to personify the 35 states.... The largest car, with the heaviest freight of young damsels, professed to bring to muster "soldiers' sweethearts." ... A huge piece of ordnance was paraded through the ground with the inscription "The Cannon our only Peacemaker." ... Poor Vallandigham was to be seen here and there suspended on huge gallows in effigy. One car exhibited (him as) ... a colossal man of straw with a mask said to be an excellent likeness ... at which some zealous Republicans ... kept hacking away with their sabres and poking with their bayonets.[40]

Even if some people were there with non-political motives, the rallies were the main tools for assessing how the campaigns were going. Politicos asked how many rallies were there, how many people attended and how enthusiastic were they. Especially attendance. There were certainly other measures of campaign vibrancy. The Democrats liked to point out that bookstores couldn't keep Vallandigham's collection of speeches in stock.[41] But the attendance-estimating game was played endlessly, aggressively and fraudulently. The main restraining force was a desire not to be laughed at by one's own partisans.

In this particular election, the attendance issue took on special importance, because the explosion of enthusiasm for Vallandigham upon his arrest had been breathtaking and unmistakable. It was the Democrats' great hope. Would it sustain? If so, was there the potential for a countervailing movement of sufficient energy to produce a greater number of voters? If you accepted that the passion for Vallandigham was extraordinary, and you held out hope for beating him anyway, you were hoping, in effect, that the North was terribly polarized.

Of the Democratic rallies, the *Crisis* in Columbus wrote: "(T)he 'Basket meetings' gotten up by the people themselves are the *most interesting* and *effective* of all. To those justice is seldom done in any newspaper reports. No account *can* do them justice. They are our political 'love feasts'—where a common devotion to a holy cause receives and imparts strength and direction." That last sentence might have come from a political scientist or a sociologist.

Crisis editor Sam Medary offered a lot of numbers about crowd sizes. He said Chillicothe in southern Ohio had seen a Vallandigham rally of 35,000 people, which, he said, was five times greater than the other side's rally a few days earlier. He said the Democratic parade was 15 miles long. Chillicothe is in Ross County, which had a population of 35,000. To believe Medary's number does not require believing that everyone went. People came to major rallies from other counties. For crowd sizes to be bigger than the local population was not unheard of. When Lincoln made his journey from Springfield to Washington after being elected, it was common.[42] Actually, though, you don't have to buy the number at all. Cut Medary's estimates by two thirds and you still have a remarkable chunk of the population. He made similar specific claims about rallies around the state.[43]

He said such meetings that "are now seen ... everywhere ... have never before been witnessed." Medary had seen everything. The standard for campaign enthusiasm had long been the presidential election of 1840, when the Whigs touched a nerve in American politics with a new kind of populist campaign, replete with slogans and symbols like log cabins, war heroism, cider, buttons and the 19th century equivalent of bumper stickers. But 1863 was not a presidential election. Yet its crowd sizes "were not even approached in" in 1840, said Medary.[44]

Exaggerating or not, Medary clearly had a point. Something remarkable was happening on the Democratic side. The Republican papers, of course, had a different tone, but certainly not the opposite one. There was some bragging, some arguing with the Democrats over just how big any particular crowd was, some rejoicing when a Copperhead rally bombed (typically in a small place and/or because of weather). But there was little along the lines of wow-this-is-unprecedented in coverage of Republican crowds.

13. The Campaign from Exile

The Dayton *Journal* actually fretted about crowd sizes. It said Republican statewide performance was spotty.[45] New, post-fire editor W.D. Bickham didn't see why Republican rallies in Dayton shouldn't be just as big as Vallandigham's, given the Democrat's difficulty in carrying Montgomery County in the past.

At the end of August, Bickham wrote, "Have we all gone to sleep again? The intermittent mode of conducting a campaign will not win." A week later, Bickham wrote, "The copperhead meeting last night was large and enthusiastic.... It was a humiliating spectacle to see so large a meeting of disloyalists at this time in Dayton." Bickham noted that the main speaker was Rep. Cox and said of the crowd, "It was about one-third larger than Hon. John Sherman's meeting."[46]

That had to hurt: The Copperheads had drawn more with a congressman than the Unionists with a U.S. senator, whose appearance the *Journal* had heavily promoted.[47] The admission was awkward, but Bickham felt he had to awaken the Republicans: Report for duty![48]

Meanwhile, he lampooned the Copperheads on the subject of crowd sizes. "We are assured on perfectly reliable authority—*Copperhead*—that there were fourteen million, nine hundred and eighty-seven thousand, three hundred and ever so many men, women, and children at the Copperhead meeting at Lewisburg, Preble County," next to Dayton, on the west.[49]

Despite his own focus on crowd size, he was not above minimizing its importance: "The Cincinnati *Enquirer* treats upon the 'size of Democratic meetings in Ohio' and says they are large. *Perhaps,* but we know the *sighs* of the party are very deep."[50] He was granting that his side was losing the crowd-size game.

***

An attendee at a Vallandigham rally in Mansfield, halfway between Columbus and Cleveland, insisted this happened: "(S)ome silly fools in breeches induced a woman to pounce on to a Democratic girl wearing a butternut breastpin ... to tear it off; but the Democratic girl was spunky, showed fight, and stripped her assailant almost naked. The last seen of the patriotic woman"—meaning the Republican, interesting as that usage is, coming from a Democrat with the word "patriotice" perhaps meant in sarcastic irony—"she was howling through the streets dressed in her stockings and crinoline—a costume more airy than elegant. Your correspondent heard of no more attempts to tear off butternuts during that day."[51]

Best, perhaps, to take that as a political/sexual fantasy and to see meaning, if any, only in the fact that it was written at all and then printed in a newspaper. When political and sexual fantasies come together, you know things are getting intense.

If crowd size was one measure of passion in the campaign, violence was another. By that measure, passion was everyplace. And the election would be tie. Newspapers on both sides reported all manner of incidents, generally in a way that reflected credit to their side and blame to the other. But they agreed violence was coming from both sides.

The Crisis itself was mobbed.[52] And a soldier in an encampment near Dayton died when some guys who had allegedly been at a Copperhead rally went to the base looking for trouble.[53] And a sergeant in the provost marshal operation in Dayton was shot at in neighboring Greene County,[54] perhaps a protest against martial law, perhaps an anti-draft thing. The mayor of Carlisle, near Dayton, asked for help from the military in keeping peace.[55]

Many reports of violence from around the state were too soft—too undocumented—and had too obvious a partisan purpose to be taken very seriously. The Dayton *Journal* vaguely excoriated local Copperheads for hassling respectable Republicans even to the point of going to their homes in groups and getting vulgar. If articles like that don't necessarily show actual violence, they do show the two sides to be eager to charge over-the-top behavior against the other, to convince voters that the other party was dangerous. It was.

On September 2, *The Crisis* had a story that captured the situation. It was labeled "Abolition Attack on a Democratic Procession—A Fight and Several Killed and Wounded." This was in Van Wert County, north along the Indiana border. The headline notwithstanding, Medary felt obliged to admit the violence was bipartisan, perhaps because that was universally known already. He wrote that, at a certain stage, armed Democrats suddenly came out of a store and started shooting at a crowd including women and children. Overall, there were two confirmed deaths and a "dozen" wounded badly. Medary felt obliged to comment about a story that seemed to contradict his insistence that the perpetrators of political violence were always the Republicans. He said, "Democrats interrupt no Republican meeting, disturb no Republican families, but there is a limit to forbearance as every man not insane must know." At least he ran the story.

When a train carrying former Sen. George Pugh, Vallandigham's running mate and his lawyer at Cincinnati, had a dangerous mishap, the Dayton *Journal's* first acknowledgment of the even read thus: "The Copperhead"—meaning Democratic—"press have invented a brilliant political dodge. Hon. George E. Pugh and Judge Thurman were going to a Copperhead meeting the other day, and the train almost ran off the track. The Copperhead press now complain that was an attempt to murder Pugh and Thurman. Brilliant, isn't it?"[56] That was the extent of the paper's analysis. In truth, though, either side would have had deep suspicions about such an event, depending only upon which side was endangered. Whether somebody had targeted Pugh was never established.

***

When the Dayton *Journal* published its first full-sized editions after the fire burned its building down, its new editor made clear in print on day one what his top mission was: to defeat Vallandigham in Montgomery County. His introductory statement had nothing about journalistic values, only political values. Nothing about following the truth wherever it might lead. Nothing about lacking fear or favor. Nothing about digging out stories that the authorities or others might not want to see printed. Nothing about promoting the interests of the community and shining a light on its needs. The investors in the paper's rebirth had not paid for a newspaper; they had paid for a Republican newspaper. And they didn't have to give the new editor any orders. He was already a soldier in their battle.

Civic and political pride prevented Dayton Republicans from accepting the

13. The Campaign from Exile

demise of the *Journal*. Efforts at revival began quickly. That involved a change in editors. Lewis Marot moved on. He had been one of the buyers of the paper when the previous editor-publisher became the local postmaster as a result of Lincoln's election.[57] He apparently ended up eventually at the Chicago *Inter-Ocean*,[58] though that paper didn't exist until a little later. The circumstances of his departure are not clear. He was furious at city officials for how they handled the perpetrators of the fire. And he may not have liked the idea of going into debt to rebuild. But it's also possible that some of the potential contributors to the rebirth wanted a say in the selection of an editor, and that they wanted somebody with special weight, special authority and color.

A leader of the rebirth effort was Lewis Gunckel, a 37-year-old state senator and future congressman. His project raised $6,000 from locals in $60 increments; that would be something like $1,200 each in 2020. With that as a lure, he recruited

W.D. Bickham, the long-time editor and publisher of the Dayton *Journal* after it was revived. His first self-assigned task was defeating Vallandigham in Montgomery County (Dayton Metro Library).

W.D. Bickham as editor and publisher, giving him the paper with an arrangement that would have Bickham paying off the investors from its profits over time.

Bickham was a 36-year-old native Cincinnatian who had been out to the Gold Rush without striking it rich. He had been an editor of several newspapers in California and the first librarian of the San Francisco Public Library. By the mid–1850s, he was city editor of the Cincinnati *Commercial*, under Murat Halstead. That paper came to have the highest circulation of any daily in the West, at 15,000 by 1860.[59] Bickham became a war correspondent and was nationally known because his work showed up in other newspapers and because he wrote a book about the war: *Rosecrans' Campaign with the Fourteenth Army Corps or the Army of the Cumberland: A Narrative of Personal Observations with an Appendix Consisting of the Official Reports of the Battle of Stone River!*[60]

Bickham said credibly that he could have taken a job with *The New York Times*, but that he wanted to find a young, growing city and grow with it.[61]

Even while a correspondent, Bickham had been on Rosecrans' staff. Having been with him at Stone River gave Bickham a special entrée with Daytonians. He played that card aggressively. In whipping up the Republican troops against Vallandigham, he wrote, "As Rosey said to his Generals at Stone River, 'You must fight, *fight,* FIGHT! or you will be whipped.'"[62] Rosecrans certainly had a way with words, didn't he?

Since the day after the fire, the *Journal* had been publishing a much reduced version, using the press of a church, the United Brethren House.[63] On July 28—with the election 10 weeks away—the paper put out its first full edition with its new facilities from an office up Main Street from the old space.

And Bickham jumped into the campaign. He was not subtle, not restrained. He liked to refer to Vallandigham rallies as "Copperhead celebration(s) of the anniversary of Benedict Arnold's treason"[64] or as "Aid and Comfort the Rebels" meetings.[65] That was Bickham.

So here's a guy who's new to town, who has this great megaphone, and who uses it immediately to call roughly half the people in his adopted community traitors. Seems like a strange way to break the ice. But it was clearly what the moment called for from him. There was no time for get-acquainted lunches.

Early in the campaign, Bickham kept going back to John Hunt Morgan and to New York. July 15: "Unless we prepare to enforce the laws, the New York riots will be repeated in the West." He was certainly reading *The Crisis.* He knew that Medary loved to insist that political violence in the North was a Republican thing, notwithstanding that May's events in Dayton. So Bickham wrote on July 17: "The demons of the Democratic party ... display a degree of ferocity that would have shocked the barbarians of the dark ages."

On the other hand, the *Journal* must not have enjoyed reporting this: "We learn that there was a company of Vallandighammers under arms at Hamilton (Ohio) to resist Morgan. They called their rendezvous 'Camp Vallandigham.'"[66] That had to make it a little harder to keep calling Morgan's Raid a Vallandigham thing.

There were attempts at humor. When Union forces took Charleston, South Carolina, Bickham wrote that the Copperheads were complaining that it was done in an unconstitutional way.[67] And, in noting Vallandigham's insistence that he "didn't see a (Southern) man woman or child who was not resolved to perish rather than yield," Bickham wrote, about the women yielding, "Well, perhaps they wouldn't, to Mr. Vallandigham."[68] And Bickham enjoyed noting Vallandigham's point about the political views of the children.

The *Journal* also reported humor from others. A rally sign: "The Constitution as it is; the Union as it was; and Vallandigham where he is."[69]

Though Bickham was relatively enlightened on race, he had his prejudices. He wrote about "Butternuts" in disparaging, snooty terms. He once described a Butternut vehicle in a Vallandigham parade as declaring itself to be from the "1th Ward."[70]

Bickham and the *Journal* paid little attention to their candidate, Brough, preferring, apparently, not to praise a Democrat too highly.

In keeping with the norms of the day, Bickham presented his Republican readers with comfort from other papers. The *Ohio State Journal* insisted that when Democrats were in Columbus to nominate Vallandigham, a group of them went to the local jail to ask the views of the prisoners and found that nearly all 600 were for Vallandigham. Bickham passed it on.[71]

13. The Campaign from Exile

The Republican papers were not afraid to be ludicrous in their partisanship. And their fellow Republican papers were not being critical when they passed the absurdity along. The Cleveland *Leader,* as reprinted in the *Journal:* "After the dispatch came announcing that John Brough was nominated, the city breathed free. Men looked happier—even Vallandighammers rather showed as though, after all, John B. would be a more presentable gentleman as governor than their own nominee."[72]

Republican papers regularly printed letters from troops calling Vallandigham a traitor and insisting that he was universally opposed by the unit in question.[73] The *Journal* had this one: "I saw in the Cincinnati *Enquirer* a letter said to have been written by one of the Forty-first Ohio saying that there was plenty of Vallandigham men in the regiment to which he belonged, and he wanted two hundred (Democratic ballots for them to cast)." (In those days, people could vote by showing up with a ballot or "ticket" that listed only the names of the candidates for whom the person wanted to vote.) The soldier's letter continued: "That is all a lie. The Forty-first is camped, near us, and they read it (the *Enquirer* letter) aloud on a stump, to a large crowd of them, and they said if there was a Vallandigham man among them, they would hang him. They said if someone would cut old Val. in two hundred pieces, they would agree to get two hundred men to eat him, thus get rid of the stinking carcass.'"[74] A future journalist, apparently.

As may be apparent by now, this book's accounting of political journalism in Ohio during the war focuses on three papers: the two English-language papers in Dayton and *The Crisis* in Columbus. Combined, especially with their reprints of pieces from other papers, they give a pretty good idea of what was going on statewide. The *Journal* represented the statewide Republicans well. The *Empire* needed help from *The Crisis* to represent the Democrats. And it was not publishing through much of the summer of 1863, having been shut down by the army. I focus more on *The Crisis* (until Sam Medary died in 1864).

But the rebirth edition of the *Empire* turned out to be one for the time capsules. It came on August 21, at the end of martial law. The *Empire* was, like many dailies, including the *Journal,* a 4-page paper. Big pages; small type; small headlines. Half the space was devoted to advertising. Some of the rest appeared every day, such as the full Democratic ticket and the editorial that ran on the day of the paper's return.

That editorial—printed always at the top left of the front page—was, like the *Journal's* introductory statement, not about journalism. "Friends of Constitutional Liberty," it began, "the Dayton *Empire* once more greets you…. It ardently expects at your hands a warm and friendly reception. An important campaign is before us, fraught with more of good or evil than any which has ever preceded it. The Life of the Nation and the Liberties of the people are at stake." The long editorial insisted that the Democratic Party "is unquestionably the true Union party," ignoring Vallandigham's armistice speech.

The very existence of the *Empire* suggests how limited was the success of the effort to repress dissent. True, some papers had been shut down. Even Burnside had success at that in one case. The editor of the Zanesville, Ohio *Citizens' Press* (east of Columbus) had written on May 7 that, since Republicans weren't volunteering to fight the war they supported, Democrats shouldn't either. That—given the military's sensitivities on the issue of recruitment—resulted in a warning that the editor had violated Order 38's ban on "disloyal statements" that would "weaken the government." The editor, already under pressure from local Republicans, closed up shop and left town.[75] This was just before Lincoln rejected Burnside's effort to close the Chicago *Times*. Maybe the Zanesville editor should have held on.

During martial law, the provost marshal had prohibited Copperhead papers from New York and Chicago from circulating in Dayton.[76] But the renewed *Empire* matched those papers in attitude (and even reprinted pieces from them). Meanwhile, the exile's words were everywhere, and his supporters more vociferous than ever.

In the *Empire*'s first edition was a derogatory story about the local provost marshal. The paper said, "We have just been handed the following letter addressed by the (provost marshal) to the ladies whose names appear:

> Mrs. Mary Oyler, Mrs. Sara Keith and Mrs. Kate Hall. Complaint has been made here that you have been known to make insulting Remarks to persons of Union Proclivities and to throw water upon good Loyal Union Citizens for singing Union Songs; I wish very Respectfully to inform you that such conduct is prejudicial to the Union cause and must be stopped forthwith; if any more complaints of like character are made to me I shall be forced to act against you in some way to prevent such proceedings in the future. Respectfully Lieut George L. Waterman, Commanding.

Earlier, a major had been in charge.[77] From here the paper editorialized, saying you've got to be kidding. If the ladies were doing anything illegal, it was a police matter. Page two was the heart of the *Empire*, the only page with little or no advertising. In the re-debut edition, it started with a little denunciation of Brough and a statement of optimism: "John Brough has proved to be the deadest weight the Abolition party of this State ever attempted to carry. It is reported that they are very anxious to have him withdraw from the canvass, in the hope of putting up somebody that could arouse a little enthusiasm in their despondent and dispirited ranks.... We can beat any man they can put up, but Brough a little easier than most of them."

Most striking on page two was an editorial reprinted from the Logan *Gazette*, 50 miles south of Columbus. The headline was "Questions for the People."

"What infernal influence is at work among the people, inciting hatred, strife, violence and personal feuds" the paper asked. "But a few months ago, ... men tolerated differences of opinion.... Democratic and Republican neighbors lived side by side, visited each other.... What a sad change the last few months have produced! The friendly visits have ceased, the kind act is withheld. Hatred has usurped the place of friendship."

The newspaper placed the blame for this situation squarely on the Republicans: "The Democrat all at once finds that old friends have become his deadly foes. The Democrat is taunted and insulted at every step, his wife and children are abused, his property and even his life are threatened.... Republican women so far forget their sex as to cry to the angry and brutal mob:—Go on! Kill them; burn their houses; if *you* don't *we* will."

The editorial went on to blame specific local political figures by name and specific organizations, but it mentioned no specific local events that had changed the atmosphere. It implored people not to join those organizations.

13. The Campaign from Exile

One interpretation of the editorial would hold that its heart is the beginning (the lament about troubled times), and that the end (the Republican bashing) is an effort to maintain the newspaper's standing with local Democrats.

At any rate, the question arises: What had changed in those few months? We're apparently talking about the arrest and nomination of Vallandigham.

***

The *Empire*, like many other papers, printed a lot of one-liners: statements of political or other principles strewn randomly into space that needed to be filled. On this day, one of the *Empire*'s one-liners was: "Freedom to the negro means slavery to the white man." In that same column was a list of quotes from Thomas Jefferson, followed by a list from Clement Vallandigham. The point is not subtle. (One of the latter's quotes: "Never with my consent shall peace be purchased at the price of disunion." Protesting too much.)

In the months after its return, the *Empire* had little news. Almost detached from immediate events, it ran editorials that rehashed old debates. It looked like it was struggling financially. And there were illnesses on the staff, mentioned in the paper in what seemed like an explanation for its poor performance.[78]

Medary, however, was at his best. He went all Vallandigham, all the time. One historian wrote, "By 1863, *The Crisis* had become the Peace Democrats' clearinghouse for pure antiwar, anti–Lincoln propaganda. Medary was paired with Vallandigham as leaders of the opposition (to Lincoln) in the Midwest."[79]

Medary wrote, "if any man is indifferent to the election of Vallandigham, he is unworthy of citizenship in the American Republic."[80] Nobody pretended this was to be a battle of ideas between people of good will. Said Medary, "Humbug, fraud and violence are the weapons of Abolitionism."[81] That was fundamental. If you didn't get the inherent, all-encompassing mendacity of the other side, you were not qualified for the fight.

Medary never portrayed the Confederates that way, of course. Like Vallandigham, when he said "enemy" he meant Republicans. And he insisted that the Republicans felt the same about Democrats. "On every side," he said, "the threats pour in upon us that the Democrats of the North are more offensive to the Administration party than the Southern '*traitors*.'" He said Democrats were "threatened to be put to the sword for political offenses, ... threatened with death and extermination.... This is just what (the Republicans) say themselves and is no fiction of ours."[82] In truth, one did come across admissions of daydreams about violence against Copperheads. But Medary would have been hard pressed to quote any recognizable names promoting such violence. If he could have, he would have.

Medary, though motivated primarily by his opposition to the war, would say things like, "The Great Issue in the Ohio election is the freedom of Speech and of the Press," along with *habeas corpus*, trial by jury and all other civil liberties. "It is the most momentous issue ever presented to a sovereign people. It is the last time that it may ever be presented!"[83]

***

In that same first edition upon the *Empire*'s return appeared a travelogue labeled "Our Foreign Correspondence." Dateline: Cork, Ireland, July 1863. The author was Tom Lowe. The piece was about the experience of traveling to Europe from the U.S., about the interesting people one met, the sights one saw, the transportation difficulties. As Vallandigham faced his crucial hour and Ohio faced the historic choice, the Vallandigham disciple—the up and coming politico in the Dayton Democratic Party, who saw the North at a great crossroads—was gone, his wife and two small children left behind. On May 30, with Vallandigham just banished, Tom had written a letter to his soldier brother Will beginning, "The uppermost thought in my mind to day is a trip to Europe." It is fun to picture Will's response. Did he have to read the letter twice? Did he check the envelope to see if it really was from his brother to him? Could it be literally true: With all that was going on in Will's life, in Tom's life and the nation's life, all Tom could think of was a trip to Europe?

The idea came out of the blue at Will. Nevertheless, to understand it, a look at Tom's previous letter to him is useful.[84] That letter was primarily a response to a political suggestion from Will. We don't have Will's suggestion, but Tom makes clear what its thrust was. "Suppose," wrote Tom, "I shd take your advice now and 'leave off' from the democratic party and 'set up' as a 'loyal' man."

It is clear that Will didn't often bring up politics; that was Tom's domain. When Will finally did go there, Tom responded at three times his normal length. He said he would love to do it—convert—because it would mean peace with "all my nearest and dearest relatives and friends." He offered many reasons he couldn't. He said the idea that "this war will restore the Union … seems to me insanity itself." And the great problem was the Republicans. He said they were actually trying to drive Democrats "into open rebellion."

He wrote, "You think it absurd to suppose the Army could be induced to be an engine of despotism. You are mistaken. If what you say be true as to their unanimous hatred of 'Vallandighamers,' they are ready now to rivet the chains upon a free people. For, deny it as men may, Vallandigham has a hold on the hearts of a majority of the northern people that no other man has…. If the authorities shd. say this fall that no 'Vallandighammer' shall be a candidate for any office," and the people should rise up, "you all wd. assist in putting them down."

Tom continued, "But you say, 'Submit to everything now until the war is over.'" He and his allies would do so gladly, said Tom, if they thought a democracy could be built "out of the ruins which would be left." But he said Lincoln would deploy the army against the Democrats, for fear of being prosecuted.

"I have written you at great length because you are my only brother. I love you. In these troublous times, I may lose my life at any time, and I wish you to comprehend my motives that you may be able to defend my memory. Preserve this letter for the future." Whether Will ever wrote to his brother about his fears for his own life, we don't know.

Besides being afraid of being killed and afraid for the future of American democracy, Tom was afraid of being arrested and of being drafted. He expressed this latter concern passionately to Tom at various stages, imploring his help in finding a substitute he could pay to serve in his stead.

So now he was gone. In the letter announcing the trip, he said that he considered taking his wife, children and other family members to "look for some pleasant place in the south of Germany, where we might all remain until our country became more settled, but the babies are too young," and his mother-in-law didn't want to go without her husband, the banker and businessman, who could not go.

"I at once gave up the (whole trip)," Tom wrote, "but it has been revived and I have about concluded after much deliberation to 'go it,' for the benefit of George's health and my own amusement and instruction." George was a Harshman relative whose health issues are not specified. Mainly, though—it's clear—he was a literary device. Tom got closest to the real reasons for the trip when he wrote that Martha "gives her consent from two motives—first to get me out of the country, out of politics and the danger of conscription, and second to have me become a fine German scholar and a travelled gentleman."

Also, he clearly relished having his travelogues printed in the *Empire* in great numbers and at great length. He loved to write. (Indeed, he probably missed his calling.) He was planning to hit Scotland and England, as well as Germany. In running the series, the *Empire* was promoting an up-and-coming Democrat whose name everybody knew, while adding a bit of variety to its pages. To hear about exotic places from somebody you knew was fun. And apparently the *Empire* didn't hold Lowe's absence against him. What Vallandigham felt about it isn't known.

If Lowe had timed his trip a bit differently—rather than trying to get out of town as quickly as possible after conceiving the idea—he and Vallandigham might actually have crossed paths in Canada. Lowe was at Niagara Falls a month before Vallandigham was. And, in the first installment, he wrote about being at Halifax on his way up the coast.

(Vallandigham may have come even closer to crossing paths with Will than with Tom. In one letter, Tom asked Will, "Did you see Vallandigham when he passed through Murfreesboro?"[85] There is no evidence that meeting happened. Tom had read the report of R.S. Furay about the Vallandigham-Rosecrans meeting. He wrote Will that "The Correspondent of the *Gazette* seems to have fallen quite in love with" Vallandigham.)

Certainly Tom wasn't leaving Martha alone. She had a strong support system and could live with her parents or invite Tom's mother to stay for the duration, which he expected to be six or eight months.

He claimed to be in emotional pain about leaving. "I do not trust myself to think much about your sister and the babies. Whenever I do, it seems impossible for me to leave them. If M were not so willing, I would not consider it at all." He said much the same in a June 14 letter, just before leaving. By then, his political mood had changed. "I leave … a little more hopeful as to (the country's) prospects than I have felt for some time. Mr. Lincoln's action in suppressing Burnside's outrageous order in relation to the Chicago *Times* etc. induces me to hope that the policy of 'crushing out' the opposition to the Administration will be abandoned and civil war in the North averted. The great Democratic party love the Union, but they love liberty more, and they are determined that the rebellion may succeed a thousand times before they will surrender their constitutional privileges." He wouldn't talk that way publicly about willingness to let the rebellion succeed. But he was expressing the Vallandigham view: The important battle is the one in the North.

Tom put at 50,000 the size of the convention that nominated Vallandigham, and he offered his analysis of the political situation. He said Vallandigham would carry the home vote, big. "The soldiers may defeat him, altho in my judgment the law allowing them to vote is unconstitutional, and their vote will probably be thrown out if it changes the result."

Tom concluded, "Take care of yourself my brother. You may be left the sole stay of the family one of these days." And he left.

Martha was miserable in his absence, judging from her letters. The kids were ill and/or misbehaving, and she missed Tom terribly. On September 8, she wrote Tom a sort of slap-in-the-face/get-a-grip letter.[86] We don't know what he had said that she was responding to. But we can pretty well guess that his political mood had changed back for the worse. And he might have raised the possibility of extending his trip. Martha wrote (with somewhat different punctuation):

> My Dear Husband, I commence this letter feeling as though I do not know what to say. For I am aware I do not express myself very clearly and you may feel hurt at some things I may say when God knows it is the last thing I would do. I received your letter last-evening.... I did not know what to do or think and had not a person in the world that I would go to for advice. I would not go to a democrat for—Alas!—none of them are God fearing people, and I have no use for them. (Why she felt that way becomes clearer lower down.) I would not go to a Republican and tell them how you felt toward your country for, of course, they would only laugh at your fears. And I must say I feel like doing it myself.... I think the democrats are having (things) pretty much as they want them.

She appeared to mean, not that the Democrats were winning the election, but that they were having a fine time campaigning. They were not being arrested; not having their newspapers shut down, not having their rallies banned or disrupted. They were able to exercise their democratic rights AND complain about not being able to.

She said, "So," not being able to talk to anybody, "I sat in my chair and cried and sang while (baby) Netti screamed and kicked. The more I thought, the worse I felt. I believe I felt worse because I had been working so hard putting up (a) front and thinking all the time (about) when you and the two darlings and myself would be living together again."

She wrote, "Tom, when you began the practice of the law, I felt no good would come of it." She apparently had wanted him to continue to work in her father's bank. "But you would not listen to me. When you began mixing in politics, I felt so again. But alas! It did no good. And I am sure you did no good by all you did...." Ouch. His wife continued, "except alienate your friends. To be sure you gained new ones, but alas! I don't admire them. They are all Spiritualists, Atheists, Infidels." Possibly some of the active Democrats were turning anti-church because of all the anti-slavery sermons. She continued: "Father hast admit that he has seen (Democratic) Mayor Gillespie drunk. And (Gillespie) is the only one that has pretended to be anything of a Christian. He is now turning almost heaven and earth to be elected, and I suspect he will."

"Now don't think, my darling, I have turned Republican," Martha continued. "Far from it. I abominate every thing connected with politics and can't help but feel if my darling husband had only been influenced a little by his wife, we might now feel very different. Especially when I look at my other friends living so quietly and happy.

"I know what your replies would be, but, Alas, I 'don't see it.' If you would only come home and be contented to live quietly 'as (illegible) preacher.' Anything under the Heavens but a politician. Never while I live will I be reconciled. You must wait until you get an ambitious wife like Marne. She thinks the young Democrats will have a fine chance when this war is over if they push boldly on." After some family news, Martha closed, as usual, "Your own Wifey."

Clearly, Martha saw Tom's political views as paranoid to the point of nutty. She dealt with that intelligently: not by lining up with others, but by trashing politics itself. She was saying they'd be happy if they just didn't have this subject to contend with: We share, for example, a deep interest in religion; let's go with that. Apparently Tom wasn't a bizarre or unreasonable person in most of life, as she found him in politics.

It was a case of the less educated person—the less cerebral, the one less impressed with her own intelligence—being the one with the stronger grip on political reality. Tom knew a good deal of history; knew, for example, how Napoleon had risen to power after a period of internal turmoil and violence. He was confident in his ability to see historical patterns, to assess things, to see around corners. Martha heard him out, but was more impressed with what her eyes and her common sense told her. As she kept cool when confronted with a house fire during her pregnancy, so did she when confronted by politics.

***

Central to the campaign discourse was Vallandigham's location. It was played both ways. Medary insisted that if Brough were a real man, he wouldn't take to the stump at all against Vallandigham, given the latter's inability to fight back.[87] But the Republican Cincinnati *Commercial* suggested that Vallandigham was choosing to stay in Canada as a political tactic.[88] *The Crisis* responded that the Republicans didn't know if they wanted Vallandigham to come home or not. If he stayed away, he got to play the martyr. But if he came back, they knew, "his eloquence reinspired, exalted, intensified by the outrages ... would so stir the hearts and souls of the people" etc.[89] But, in truth, the Democrats didn't know where they wanted Vallandigham either.

Beyond all that, Vallandigham's location raised a very specific issue: What would happen if he were elected? Ohio would have a governor who had been thrown out of the country. Presumably, a deeply, deeply humiliated Lincoln would let him back in, the people having spoken. After all, Lincoln had already made a conditional offer to let him back in. Indeed, there was much speculation that he would let the exile stay if he returned even during the campaign. The Hillsdale, Michigan, *Democrat* spoke for many when it said, "The President cannot be fool enough or bold enough to risk the consequences of ordering his re-arrest. Riots and mobs are never justifiable ... but the people may have no other remedy."[90]

The larger question was not whether Lincoln would let him back in, but whether

Vallandigham's opponents in Ohio would. Could the people who believed the Copperheads were traitors in a calamitous war say, "Well, the traitors have won," and leave it at that? Many of the most intense loathers of Vallandigham were armed soldiers, a category which had already made trouble for the Copperheads. Would they try to prevent him from campaigning or taking office? Would their fathers and brothers and other supporters? Everybody was talking about the possibility of major violence either before or after the election.

Enter George Pugh. Having been Vallandigham's lawyer, the still young (40) ex-senator had a grip on the hearts of delegates who nominated Vallandigham. He was a natural choice for lieutenant governor, being seen as a capable and respectable face of the campaign in Ohio. In the campaign, he decided to take on the location issue directly. At a rally in July at Fairfield, near Cincinnati, he said, as paraphrased by news reports, that if Vallandigham were elected, he—Pugh—would see to it that Vallandigham was duly inaugurated, even if it should require 50,000 men to escort him from Canada to Columbus.[91]

There was a prospect for voters to contemplate: An army in Ohio to fight off other Ohioans.

The Brough campaign decided that questions about whether Vallandigham could be inaugurated in peace helped Brough. On September 7, Brough said, "What will be the effects of electing Mr. Vallandigham Governor of Ohio? I will tell you: … It will bring civil war into your State, civil war to your own homes…. For I tell you there is a mighty mass of men in the State whose nerves are strung up like steel, who will never permit this dishonor to be consummated in their native State."[92]

Brough was saying Pugh was right: The Democrats would need an army to inaugurate Vallandigham. But Brough's statement sent the Democrats into tizzies. Medary said Brough was threatening civil war if he didn't win.[93] Vallandigham felt obliged to respond to Brough. He wrote a letter to be read at his rallies: "There will be no civil war in Ohio if I am elected Governor," he said, "unless Mr. Brough and his party inaugurate it; in which event we will crush out the rebellion in a very much shorter space of time then they have employed in putting down the 'slaveholders' rebellion.'"[94]

This was a candidate in a bad position: having to insist that his election wouldn't bring a nightmare. Inevitably, Vallandigham's critics focused on the "peace" candidate's fighting words about "crushing out" a "rebellion." The *Journal* said, "The traitor tells the people of Ohio that, if he gets into power, and the people resist … he will do what he refuses to do against the conspirators of the South."[95]

Of course, that argument was strained. "The people" resisting the inauguration of the election winner? No matter. The Republicans just wanted to keep people thinking about the possibility of an inauguration war.

***

At a certain stage in the campaign, Vallandigham's message was altered by the realization that Gettysburg and Vicksburg had changed the political atmosphere. All of a sudden, he was making no mention of the North's military failures as proof of his prophecy that the South couldn't be beaten.

Most strikingly, he discussed a potential postwar era in which the South had been forced back into the Union. He hadn't publicly contemplated that possibility before. Even privately, when he had told Tom Lowe of the possible outcomes he saw for the war, he hadn't listed that one. He now continued to insist that arms couldn't win a victory in the real sense, because the hearts of people couldn't be changed. And he privately told Manton Marble at the New York *World* that he didn't really believe military victory was coming. He referred to that hope as "that most unfortunate (recurring) delusion." But he told Marble the Democrats should make use of the hope. Specifically, he argued that the Democrats were better equipped than the Republicans to take advantage of military success. He said the Southern people would never want peace with Lincoln, but that if the Democrats were in power, the Southerners would turn against their warlike leaders. After all, the Democrats weren't the ones who pushed emancipation or a tough war policy.[96]

So Vallandigham, always having believed that military disaster should be political disaster for the administration, was now arguing that military success should be political disaster. Well, in his defense it must be acknowledged that he had to argue something. He couldn't just fold because the political tide had changed.

Meanwhile, Vallandigham's armistice proposal was playing even worse than when he had made it. Even Medary was struggling with it. The Brough-supporting *Ohio State Journal* of Columbus said Vallandigham "would to-day rather sacrifice the Union than the interest of the slaveholder." Medary printed that and responded, "The record has been too completely made … for such talk to make the slightest impression upon any minds fit for the outside of an idiot asylum."[97] But he simply did not address the Vallandigham proposal. Six weeks later, in mid–September, he was still struggling. The "assertion that Mr. Vallandigham was ever in favor of a division of these States … (is) so stamped with falsehood by all his acts speeches and political history that its use is a subject of scorn and contempt."[98] Of course, when Vallandigham made his proposal, Medary had praised "every paragraph, sentence, and line" of his speech.

***

Sen. John Sherman, who put Vallandigham in a category with Benedict Arnold, threw himself into the campaign for Brough. He traveled the state making a long, cover-all-the-bases case against Vallandigham that set the standard and got much attention. Sherman was a national figure, having almost been elected speaker of the House of Representatives. He was important in the Senate—central to the financing of the war—and would go on to have a Washington career extending almost to the next century. During the war, his brother's notoriety made him all the more a celebrity.

Having spoken against Vallandigham in Dayton just before the 1862 election, Sherman relished the prospect of being credited with helping to defeat him twice. He polished his speech as he went around the state. In Dayton, at Courthouse Square—at the event whose attendance embarrassed *Journal* editor Bickham—he began[99]:

"At the beginning of every contest you are assured by your public speakers that the contest is one of infinite importance. They generally exaggerate…. But (this election) is more important than any ordinary Presidential election." Among Sherman's points: Brough was a Democrat, and the Republicans were giving up a lot in that regard. Vallandigham had been convicted in a court "composed of members of his own party." (Republicans regularly said this without documenting it.) Judge Levitt was a Democrat and an "old man" who "owes nothing to Lincoln." It was "the wonder of wonders" that a party would nominate "such a man as Vallandigham." Even before the war, Jefferson Davis was Vallandigham's "most intimate friend and associate." Vallandigham's views derived from the fact that he owed his first seating in Congress to southerners, whom he hadn't bucked ever since. Vallandigham's election and Pugh's plan for 50,000 men would result in civil war. Vallandigham didn't vote for bills that paid the troops' salaries. As governor, Vallandigham wouldn't provide any Ohio regiments to fight the war. "Or he might commission Jeff Davis a colonel of the First Ohio Regiment." Vallandigham's proposed constitutional amendment of 1861 went farther than the rebels. "They wanted to split the country in two; he said four." Vallandigham, consumed "with hate, as he is, against the work of the Union army, … would be likely to do all he could to break it up.… Will you, men of Ohio, desert these soldiers, and place over them a man so infamous in their eyes, … their worst enemy?"

Somebody in the crowd said Sherman shouldn't be denouncing Vallandigham, because the latter was involuntarily absent. Sherman said the man would have a point if Vallandigham had been nominated before he was arrested. But, he implied, given that the Democrats had chosen to nominate somebody who had been banished, they had no cause for complaint that he was absent.

Sherman also took on Vallandigham's big issue: the political arrests. He saw nothing wrong with the suspension of *habeas corpus* in Vallandigham's case, because Vallandigham was arrested and tried in accord with military law, a very dubious argument. At any rate, Sherman said, it is ridiculous to decide a horse thief was unfairly convicted and then make him governor.

But he agreed that political arrests generally were a mistake. He said Olds' arrest got him elected, whereas before that he was "not fit game to capture." But, he said, "There are cases … in which the government must show its authority and power in putting down rebels at home, as well as abroad. And when that time comes, I want the government to take the head of the heap"—meaning Vallandigham—"and the small fry."

Sherman defended Burnside all the way. He said Vallandigham at Mount Vernon "said all he could say to prevent enlistments, and provoke desertions. He did it in a cunny way. He did not go at it as boldly and unhesitatingly as you would do, but he dodged and twisted around the matter to avoid any charge that might be made against him."

Sherman mocked the notion that Vallandigham had suffered as a result of his arrest. He said "All (Vallandigham's) subsequent treatment was of the most considerate kind. He was taken to the Burnet House, which I have always found to be the best tavern; and, after his conviction and sentence, was placed on board of the 'Lady Davis'"—Sherman must have said that name in a certain way, with an emphasis perhaps on "Lady"—"and transported to his friends. Now, I ask you if this is cruel and unusual punishment. I have no doubt Vallandigham rather liked it."

13. The Campaign from Exile

Sherman threw in a pitch to Irish voters, perhaps seen as particularly prevalent in Dayton. He said the hated British would benefit if the South won independence. At one point, judging from the written text, Sherman may have pronounced "Brough" with an Irish brogue, though, in fact, it was a British name.

Perhaps the most striking part of Sherman's speech today is his treatment of race. He said he would have preferred that the president not address the subject, but had simply let his generals free the slaves of rebels. He said, "I am willing to give to the negroes a portion of the southern States in which to live and prosper, and we will take the white people up here and let them live with us." He said he wouldn't let negroes vote or hold office, "but we can not deny their right to life and the pursuit of happiness." He said, "I tell you that as sure as there is an overruling Providence, the negro race of this country will not always remain slaves."

Very few years later, relatively conservative Republicans like Sherman did embrace black suffrage. During the war, they—including Lincoln—were in transition. During the 1863 campaign, the Republicans had no coherent, unified position on race. Certainly, they were on the defensive against the charge that Emancipation would bring a floodtide of blacks to the North. So they talked about ideas like Sherman's, or about sending freed slaves to the West or abroad. But they generally downplayed the subject. They knew that many in their base favored a degree of racial tolerance. But they also knew they needed a coalition.

Democrats were more united on race and quicker to take up the subject. Race was not a big part of Vallandigham's messages from Canada, but it was a big part of his campaign in every other way, including at rallies and in newspapers, where Medary led the way. One example is particularly striking in a time (now) when one party—the Republicans—has sometimes seemed defensive or embarrassed about the relative absence of black and brown faces at their conventions. Medary invited voters to look at pictures of Democratic and Republican gatherings, and said this: "The Democratic meetings are exclusively made up of *white people!* The Republican meetings are made up of *whites* and *blacks!* Choose ye between them!"[100] He headlined the article "The Difference" and he saw the choice as obvious: The Democratic Party was the party of white people and, therefore, should get the votes of white people. One imagines him adding "Duh!"

Search online and elsewhere today for references to Medary and you find few acknowledgments of his overt racism. Instead he is likely to be characterized as uncompromising, determined, a lively writer and impactful. (Columbus has an elementary school named after him.) This may be because he wrote mostly about matters other than race. But now the campaign was on; racism was the Democrats' go-to weapon. In the last days of the campaign, race wasn't just a subject for the newspaper; it was an obsession. Some examples from three editions[101]:

A headline read "'Father save us from negro Equality.'" The text said, "The above … appeal is the motto seen on one or more of the flags carried by the young Democratic ladies at nearly every Democratic (rally)." That was true. Wagonloads of young women were to be seen behind such signs. Said Medary, "Let every voter remember this appeal on the day of election."

A blurb: "If negroes are as good as white people, why did the Creator not make them alike?" Another blurb: "Truth Telling—An Abolitionist declaring that he is no better than a negro." And there was a bad poem titled "Rise ye who will not mate with slaves."

A Medary piece complained about how Republican newspapers were always running stories about how well black troops were performing in combat. It was sore spot for many Democratic editors. Medary insisted blacks couldn't fight—an extremely common refrain—and shouldn't be allowed to. Because of views like his, blacks were prohibited from enlisting in Ohio. An item in the Dayton *Journal* in 1863 described the local situation: "Several colored men of this (area) desire to volunteer, but there is no recruiting officer for that service in Dayton. Information touching such recruits may be obtained upon application to Mr. Jackson, barber, under the Phillips House."[102] Mr. Jackson would presumably connect the volunteers with opportunities elsewhere.

The *Crisis* piece didn't cite any articles saying black troops performed *better* than their white counterparts. Nevertheless, it said: "We thought it was only 'negro equality' that the Abolitionists were after, but it seems they will not stop at *equality,* but are determined to give the negro the pre-eminence in all things and subject the poor white race to a much lower condition than the negro."

Another piece asked—as many Republicans would, too—how the country could continue to deny citizenship to blacks after they have bled and died for their country. His solution: Stop using black troops now. Better, in other words, to let more white Northerners fight and die in this cause Medary didn't believe in than see blacks get citizenship. That piece included more than a column full of quotations from Lincoln, Salmon Chase and Horace Greeley designed to document the charge that they had always been for equality under the law.

There was a report on an event in Xenia, the town east of Dayton that had an unusually large number of blacks. "Abolition and Negro Outrage on Democratic men, women and children" said the headline of a story which likened the event to the French Revolution. The story said a "mob" of 500 black men and boys and some Republicans were treated well by the authorities after they "insulted" passing women.

Another piece complained about the Lincoln administration trading ambassadors with black nations in its obsessive quest for Negro equality. "All traditions of the past—all prosperity of the present—all philosophy of the future—have been ignored and buried by the tramp of the Negro to citizenship.... It is so written in the book of fate that all puny efforts of narrow minded men against the laws of God and nature ... must come to naught. We have lost all respect in the estimation of the world by the acts of the Lincoln Administration."

Toward the end of the campaign, Medary became self-consciously repetitive on race even as he put his appeal to racism in the most prominent space he had. He said he didn't now have anything new, but he went on for two-and-a-half columns, having obviously decided it was his job to hammer home the message. He was on the defensive about not having hit the race issue earlier and harder. "We took it for granted" he said, that everybody understood the horrors of black citizenship. Finally, he was reduced to capital letters: "EVERY VOTE FOR BROUGH IS A VOTE FOR NEGRO EQUALITY—FOR NEGRO CITIZENSHIP!"

Republican papers were largely content to make fun of the Democrats' fears. After a Brough parade, the Cincinnati *Commercial* wrote, "We observed that in the Union procession on Thursday, the ladies did not deem it necessary to advertise for any description of husbands. We have seen processions of the Vallandigham stripe when the ladies seemed so anxious for husbands that they were compelled to call on the fathers and brothers to prevent them from taking black ones."[103]

***

Vallandigham said the new draft demonstrated that the war was both unsuccessful and unpopular. (Never mind that the South had adopted the draft the previous year and that Vallandigham insisted Southerners were united behind their war effort.) Medary went farther. The editor said Democratic voters believe the enlargement of the army "is a mere excuse for the sending of troops into the State to deposit fraudulent votes into the ballot-box, or drive Democrats from the polls!" He thought maybe 25,000 or 35,000 troops. He continued, "Such is the contempt which this administration has established for itself in the minds of the people that they hesitate in attributing to it no extremes of dishonorable, dishonest motives."[104]

So here we have Vallandigham's great advocate coming up with an inflammatory theory, attributing it to "the people" and trashing Lincoln for its existence.

Medary said the draft's "enforcement (was) attempted for a war abhorrent to the feeling of nine-tenths of our people." And he opposed all drafts on principle: "(A) military conscription and a Republican Government are incompatible," he said.

"All wars of republics must be peoples' wars."

The Dayton *Journal* supported the draft explicitly and aggressively. It also supported using black troops and wanted Ohio to get credit for them in the quotas game, which would reduce the number of Ohioans drafted. Editor Bickham wrote that black troops might actually be superior to whites in some situations, because they were accustomed to the Southern heat.[105] The Morgan Raid made selling the draft a little easier, because of the threat to Ohio. Then, too, some people simply felt that a draft might spread the burden more equally than a volunteer system.

With the draft enacted but not yet fully enforced, new units were being formed for men who they thought they might get a better deal than if they waited to be drafted. One unit bought a *Journal* ad describing itself as the "easiest branch of the service."[106]

Gov. David Tod was prevailing on the feds to let him try to raise Ohio's quota through volunteers. He had succeeded at that in the past; and he was on the Republican team. So they had reason to let him try. They just wanted the bodies.

The Democrats were insisting that the Republicans were just delaying the draft until after the election. And by the end of August the *Journal* was wondering whether any delay might backfire politically. What if the effort succeeded right up until the election approached, then failed? "It would be far better to draft at once, and be done with the matter," said the paper.[107] However, on the day after that piece ran, the *Journal* reported that Ohio had met its quota (with 35,000 men signed up for three years) and would not have a draft. It snidely said "Rejoice, Copperheads, rejoice! You will not be...."[108] However, the reports of success turned out to be premature, and the debate continued.

The *Journal* blamed the very existence of the draft on Copperhead deserters. October 3: "It is officially announced that the number of deserters from the Federal armies exceeds 90,000 men." It said Ohio's share was about 10,000. And the pending Ohio quota was less than 8,000. "Don't you see that desertion is the cause of the draft?" But, of course, Copperheads were certainly not the only deserters.

With Ohio being near its volunteer quota, the draft issue faded somewhat. Democratic charges about what would come after the election were not borne out. But then Lincoln called for 300,000 more volunteers, and Ohio had a new quota to be filled without a draft.

***

On September 15, Lincoln leaned in. He declared the right of *habeas corpus* lifted for the duration of the war when the military conducted arrests relating to the war. He had already lifted the writ in more limited circumstances, and Congress had then authorized him to do what he had done. (Sen. Sherman voted against that.[109]) Now he was going farther.

This was a historic act; not as historic as Vallandigham pretended when he called it an imposition of martial law across the country. Life went on pretty much as before, just about everywhere. There was no great crackdown on civil liberties. Vallandigham remained on the ballot. Still, the new move did put another dent in Vallandigham's argument that his 1862 campaign had reformed the Lincoln administration.

In a statement from Windsor on September 17, Vallandigham said Lincoln's decision "appears in the midst of no riot, tumult or other popular convulsion (in the Northern states) and no preparation for any, and when even the odious 'conscription' is being executed quietly and without resistance wherever announced.... (The decision) can have but one object—the pending elections this fall, but especially the Presidential canvass of 1864."

"It is," he continued, "the full development of that which I have so often warned: ...the establishment of a 'formal and proclaimed despotism,' ... Oh, that the warning voice, feeble though it was"—he meant his own voice, and by "feeble" he meant isolated—"which two years ago ... cried aloud to the people that, one by one, their liberties were about to perish, and that ... no more State lines, no more State governments, but a consolidated monarch, or vast centralized military despotism, must all follow in the history of the future.... To-day (that voice) is lifted up again, and hereafter let no man tell you ... that there is no danger, no ground for alarm or apprehension. To-day your President is in form—as for two years and more he has been in fact—a Military Dictator.... Shall there be free State elections any longer, or another presidential election of any sort?"

He was just warming up.

"Next, after this declaration of martial law, will follow the armed seizure and occupation of your State by Federal troops, to intimidate or overpower you at the polls," he said. Shades of the Medary theory. "But this monstrous purpose will not and cannot be executed (unless) the people cringe or cower.... By the Constitution of

Ohio, no soldier or marine of the United States can ... become (a voter) of the State by being stationed within her limits. By the law of England ... all troops are required to be removed a prescribed distance—not less than one mile—from the place of holding an election; and this, too is the spirit at least of our own laws.... I counsel you ... in the name of the memory of your fathers ... the heroes of Greece and Rome, the spirit of Bruce and Tell, of Hampden and Sydney, of Henry, and Washington, and Jackson...."[110]

If Vallandigham and Medary had gone way over the top, perhaps it should be noted that the nonsense was thoroughly bipartisan. The charges against Vallandigham were as untethered as the charges against Lincoln. Eventually, Vallandigham was accused of everything the partisans could come up with[111]: proposing Lee's invasion of Pennsylvania in a personal meeting with Jefferson Davis (a "witness" came forth to this effect); helping to plan the New York anti-draft riots; taking a gubernatorial nomination that had been "arranged" by the rebels; conspiring with a secret, subversive organization to, for example, import 50,000 people from Kentucky to vote for Vallandigham; and, of course, failing to take care of his widowed mother.

Vallandigham was hung in effigy regularly. The following lines were perhaps the most widely repeated of the season, the biggest iambic hit in a year when many less impactful rhymes made the rounds:

> *Hurrah for Brough and Abraham*
> *And a rope to hang Vallandigham.*

Without question, references to the upsides of Vallandigham's potential death exceeded in number such references to Brough.

***

When James Vallandigham was writing a biography of his late brother, he received a letter from Dr. J.A. Walters, of Dayton, a friend of Clement. Walters said that he had visited Clement in Windsor in late September 1863 and found him making plans to cross over to Toledo secretly. His idea was to spend the last couple of weeks before the October 13 election stumping the state.

A little geography: Windsor is actually south of Detroit. The Detroit River runs between them, east and west. However, south of them the river heads south, to Toledo.

The doctor wrote that Clement said that on October 1 he would start by going "sixteen miles below Detroit, on the Detroit River, Canada side."[112] A "Mr. P. was to station horses for him every ten miles ... (Vallandigham) would cross the river in the night, and go through to Toledo in time for the train to Lima the same night." There was to be a rally in Lima, about 80 miles south of Toledo and a similar distance north of Dayton. Rep. Daniel Voorhees of Indiana, a Vallandigham fan, and others were to speak.

The doctor wrote that he had discouraged this idea with all the force he could muster. "I replied that so sure as he did cross into Ohio, he was a dead man; that the wild and almost demoniacal influence which always takes possession of a portion of the people in time of war has, by the action of the Administration press, been all turned against him; that under this influence I believed thousands stood ready to take his life, and would do it with a conscientious belief that they were doing God and their country service."

Vallandigham reportedly rejected this input. But ultimately the subject turned to weather for the crossing, and the doctor urged Vallandigham to take bad, danger-inducing weather as a sign. Vallandigham said he "believed very much in special providences." In the end, he did go to the appointed spot on the river, and the weather was bad, and he turned back.

The concerns the doctor expressed about his safety were bipartisan, shared, for example, by both of Ohio's Republican U.S. Senators. John Sherman wrote in his memoirs, "It was manifest that if Vallandigham entered the state … a quasi-civil war might have arisen. I heard men of character and influence say distinctly … they, if necessary, would kill him. Senator (Ben) Wade and I … had a conversation with Mr. Lincoln. We told him … of our confident belief that if his order of banishment was revoked, it would result in riots and violence in which Vallandigham would be the first victim."[113] Sherman was writing 33 years after the fact. Not an excitable man, he wrote, "It is difficult, now, to describe the intense excitement over the issue."

***

How did people see the campaign going as the campaign matured? A few perspectives:

A British correspondent said "'opposition to Lincoln and his war party is growing' every day."[114] On the other hand, the Richmond *Dispatch* told its readers not to be optimistic about Vallandigham. Six weeks before the election, in a bow to the requirements of Southern conventional wisdom, it said that if Lincoln didn't expect to win fairly, he'd cheat. But the main point was that "the time is not yet," and that the South must persevere, and "we may expect to profit by delay."[115]

The Richmond *Enquirer* wasn't quite as pessimistic. It said Vallandigham would win "with little difficulty" if the South succeeded in the biggest military situation at hand, at Chattanooga (about which more below). If Rosecrans were driven back, "The peace men in the United States would once more assert their manhood and speak out as they did before the late disasters (Gettysburg and Vicksburg) had choked their utterances."[116] The Augusta (Ga.) *Constitutionalist* said much the same.[117]

Meanwhile, Medary was seeing pessimism among distant Democrats. So, in his August 26 issue, he wrote, "We assure our friends out of the State … that every day adds confidence … and that Ohio will do her whole duty on the 13th day of next October. *Mark our prediction!*" He argued at one point that the military victories at Vicksburg and Gettysburg would *not* help the "abolitionist" ticket, because they made the Republicans smug. If the Republicans felt they didn't have to compete for votes, their true selves would emerge, and they would be rejected.

Medary continued to run pieces about the unheard-of size and enthusiasm of Democratic rallies, and to contrast them with their Republican counterparts. Apparently Sen. Sherman did as badly in attendance at Chillicothe as at Dayton.[118]

It's not hard to see why the Democrats were winning the enthusiasm battle, even

13. The Campaign from Exile

aside from their possession of the more charismatic candidate and the martyr. If they won, everything would change, or at least the political world would be upended. That's a great motivator. If, however, the Unionists won, the country would still be slogging through a godawful war whose outcome would still be in some degree of doubt. To get people to vote for that would be tough enough; to get them to love it, no.

The possibility that Vallandigham might carry the home (civilian) vote was taken very seriously, even by a lot of Republicans. A consensus held that he'd lose the soldier vote big. But the *Journal* was reporting that Vallandigham would challenge the soldier vote if it made the difference.[119] The paper pointed out that the secretary of state—the chief elections official—was a Democrat and would help. Some Copperhead papers were saying that if Vallandigham won the home vote, they'd consider him the governor.[120] By 1863, courts in three states had struck down the soldier vote on constitutional requirements that voting should take place at the place of residence.[121] What the Ohio constitution said was that voters must have been residents of the state for the previous year.[122]

In his September campaign letter that said there would be no civil war in Ohio if he won the election, Vallandigham he said that he would abide by the decision of "qualified electors." The *Journal* took umbrage. "Does he mean to insinuate that the *soldiers of Ohio,* who are fighting to preserve the nation are not 'qualified electors'? Why the introduction of that phrase?"[123] By October, Vallandigham was writing to New York newspaper editor Marble on the subject. "We will beat them—my friends all say—badly," perhaps even on the total vote, he said. And "the 'soldier vote' is clearly unconstitutional and will be forced & fraudulent besides. So it will be finally rejected."[124]

Under these circumstances, the Republicans were very highly motivated to win without the soldier vote, to avoid any post-election fuss.

***

In October, the military situation was not looking as good for the North as it had in July. In September, Rosecrans had moved southward from Murfreesboro to try to take Chattanooga on Tennessee's border with Georgia. Bragg moved out of that city, fearing he would be trapped in it. The armies met in northern Georgia in a battle that came to be named after Chickamauga Creek. It was the bloodiest battle ever fought away from the eastern seaboard, with 34,000 casualties on the two sides among the 120,000 troops. It was a defeat for the North and devastated Rosecrans' military career. The Confederates had been able to breach an opening that shouldn't have been there, and the Union troops had to retreat to Chattanooga. Lincoln famously said that afterward Rosecrans seemed dazed, like a duck who had been hit on the head with a mallet.[125] Rosecrans did end up with Chattanooga, but he was besieged there by Southern forces. Washington was alarmed. Secretary of War Stanton organized a then-unheard-of kind of reinforcement, getting troops to Chattanooga in 11 days via an improvised rail route, something many had thought impossible. The circuitous route took the 20,000 troops through Ohio just as the political campaign was reaching its climax. Some troops decorated their cars with "Death for Vallandighamers" and "No Peace Makers Among Us" signs. Some actually made political speeches at train stations.[126]

On Election Day, the Chattanooga siege was in place. Bickham at the *Journal* was on the defensive, because, in the constant battle among Northern generals for public reputation, he was known as Rosecrans' guy in the press. He insisted things were under control, because supply lines to Chattanooga were still open.[127] Tying the war and the campaign together, he wrote, "Independent of their general desire that the (North's) Army of the Cumberland may be defeated, the Copperheads have a particular desire that it may meet with disaster under the command of Rosecrans. They never will forgive him for his nobly patriotic letter … to … the Legislature of Ohio"—denouncing the Copperheads—"nor for his (actions on) Copperhead newspapers in his army." He had banned some. But, said Bickham, the Copperhead "never will have an opportunity to rejoice over disaster to him. We are altogether confident that he will triumph over the enemy."[128]

Ultimately, the siege at Chattanooga was broken by units of Generals Grant, Sherman, Hooker (the general sent by Stanton) and George Thomas. They made offensive thrusts into Bragg's territory.[129] By then, Grant had replaced Rosecrans with Thomas, who had been credited with having performed very well at Chickamauga.

Rosecrans, who did or did not give Vallandigham a piece of his mind. (Library of Congress, by E. Anthony, photographer firm.)

***

In the last month of the campaign, new issues emerged and others evolved. In mid-September, Vallandigham went to foreign policy. Napoleon III and friends were about to take Mexico. Vallandigham insisted that the Civil War weakened Lincoln's hand in such matters, reducing his options. Vallandigham and other Copperheads generally presented this as a reason for abandoning the war. The idea never caught on big.

Meanwhile, the Republican press was keeping track of the doings of the Southern press. Northern editors delighted in pointing to evidence that Southerners were rooting for Vallandigham. Vallandigham decided to lean in. He said he embraced his Southern support. He hoped that people would see it as ultimately useful in reuniting the nation. When Vallandigham had first been banished, an ultimately famous Thomas Nash cartoon in *Harper's Weekly* showed Lincoln and Davis playing badminton with Vallandigham as the shuttlecock, neither wanting him to land in their territory. Confronted with that, Vallandigham may have preferred the charge that the South did like him.

More common than cartoons as a campaign tool was poetry, defined here in the classical sense: lines that rhyme. Often set to well-known songs, often racist (from the Vallandigham side), these creations typically appeared in newspapers. One common theme was simply the horrors of war, with blame put on Lincoln. Another was sheer adulation of the hero:

> *Who was it that for insolence made*
> *Ohio's craven senator, Wade,*
> *Wear on his brow the brand "Afraid"?*
> *Vallandigham.*
>
> *Who is the man of iron mold,*
> *Braving the storm with bearing bold,*
> *As Clay and Jackson did of old?*
> *Vallandigham.*

And, to the tune of *Maryland, My Maryland*:

> *What name of glory do I hear?*
> *Vallandigham! Vallandigham!*
> *In accents ringing loud and clear—*
> *Vallandigham! Vallandigham! …*
>
> *A people by their birthright free—*
> *Vallandigham! Vallandigham!*
> *Were stricken down and fell with thee,*
> *Vallandigham! Vallandigham!*
> *But they will break the tyrant's chain,*
> *The galling fetters rend in twain,*
> *And smite the smitter back again!*
> *Vallandigham! Vallandigham!*

Many such examples showed up in book form, having been gathered by a publisher in Columbus from various newspapers around the state (without specific credits) in time for the end of the campaign.[130] The idea was that certain people would sing them in groups.

In the last weeks, nobody was taking anything for granted. Dayton had a Brough rally on October 1 of so great importance to Bickham that he didn't put out a paper that day. The governors of Illinois and Indiana spoke. Robert Schenck came in from Maryland. These speakers were making the rounds in Ohio, like Chase and Sherman.

The crowd on this day was cut by weather to some unspecified size, but by this time Bickham was finally saying "our people are now fully aroused."[131]

Meanwhile, divisions within the Democratic Party had been highlighted on September 22 by a gathering in Columbus of 200 War Democrats who denounced the nomination of Vallandigham and portrayed his election as a great danger to the country.[132] The 200 were well known enough to get considerable attention. That unusual event solidified some suspicions that the Vallandigham campaign was doomed.

More than that, as Bickham suggested, the very approach of the election was energizing the Brough camp. The Evansville, Indiana, *Daily Journal* on October 9: "Within the past two weeks, a great change has taken place among the people of the Buckeye State, and the Union party seems to increase in volume and enthusiasm with the most astonishing rapidity." The paper said the Unionists now wanted a landslide, not just a victory.

A few days before the election, the Dayton *Journal* reported that, "A Gentleman of this city desires to make a bet of from $100 to $500, that John Brough will beat Vallandigham on the home vote. Persons who wish to take such a venture, will call at this office."[133] In 2020 dollars, $500 would be about $10,000.

Very late in the campaign, attention turned hard to another new issue: cheating. In those days, the prospect of Election Day cheating arose frequently. But this time there was special vehemence, even obsession—on both sides. As early as August, Republican papers in Cincinnati were writing of Democratic plans to import paid Vallandigham voters from Indiana and elsewhere.[134] These charges were not documented or minimally convincing. They gave no indication of how the scheme might actually work. And, after all, Ohioans were not novices at administering and policing close elections.

Medary took offense at the allegations and wrote on September 12, "This is a cover for their own designs." He said, among other things, that the Democrats simply didn't have the money to pay people to vote, something he was in a position to know. Then he reiterated his own unsupported charges: "Will not the 30,000 soldiers to be transformed into compulsory voters for Brough be deemed enough?" And he added to them. "We have positive and reliable information that *voters* for Brough *from Indiana,* are already in the State! Did the *Vallandighammers* bring them?" He went on to claim also that the Republicans were determined to keep Democrats from voting. He vaguely cited an alleged orator who had said that if Democratic voters couldn't be convinced, they needed to be coerced.[135] Medary threatened, "If American citizens are to be kept from exercising the fundamental right of freemen by force, where will rest the blame for violence?"

For Medary, judging by his words, it was simply obvious that the Republicans would cheat. It was built into who they were. They had demonstrated their antipathy to democracy through their political arrests. "Men who will be guilty of such a crime upon Liberty will resort to all sorts of frauds and violence upon the ballot box.... *Frauds* without end will be attempted! *Coercion,* to the fullest extent! ... *Lying* such as would make old Lucifer blush! ... Every man is thoroughly posted: ... The last hope of our expiring nation hangs upon the success of the Democratic party!"[136]

On the Republican side, on October 5, the *Journal* made a reference to an anti-draft Irish street gang which had made news in the New York draft riots: "There is no time to be lost.... We have information from a reliable source stating that New York Dead Rabbits are now brought into Ohio. A corresponding class are coming from Indiana, Illinois and Michigan."

Surely one purpose of predicting cheating was to scare off potential cheaters by making them feel watched. The *Journal* was explicit about that. A week before the election, it reprinted the laws against fraud twice. "'(W)e think it well to let the instigators and their dupes' know the potential consequences," it said.[137] Another purpose had to do with political tactics: Don't let the other side be the only one to make a charge that anybody could make.

Finally, the *Journal* did offer its idea of specificity. On October 10: "Twelve Copperhead rascals, who were coming from Indiana to Ohio to vote, let the cat out of the bag at Richmond, Indiana, yesterday"—just across the Ohio border—"whereupon the citizens lodged them in jail and will keep them there until their opportunity for crime is passed." No such event is recorded that week in the Richmond *Palladium* newspaper or in any Indiana newspapers that show up in the Library of Congress newspaper archives.

"Besides these," the *Journal* continued, "a gang of twenty-three went to Cincinnati by another route, and on Saturday, some forty more were arrested beyond Richmond." Uh huh.

The Republicans thought the Confederates, too, were cheating. At the very end, Bickham saw—or said he saw—Jefferson Davis trying to engage the North's troops in combat, so they couldn't vote. "It is the game the rebels and Copperheads are playing together," he said. "We predict that Bragg attacked Rosecrans yesterday, or will do it to-day. Don't let that worry you, Union men. Ohio troops in each of our armies will be held in reserve" to vote.

Medary, in his last edition before the election,[138] was also focused on the troop vote. He insisted that "soldiers who will vote for Brough are furloughed; those who will not are kept on strict duty in the camps and without any polls being opened. Capt. Smith of the 'independent Cavalry,' from Cincinnati, now in Western Virginia, remarked to a citizen of Ohio that '*If a man in his company voted for Vallandigham he would shave his head and put him in the guard house.*'"

Smith!

Bickham and Medary were simply in say-anything mode. Medary: "John Brough, in a speech made in Hamilton, said, among other things, that 'It would be better that our armies in the field should be utterly annihilated and defeated than that the Union ticket in this State should fail at the election.'" Utter nonsense, of course.

Ultimately, you just have to laugh. Medary said of the Republicans (a decade-old party), "It has been a historical character of that party to charge all sorts of villainy upon others in the very shape designed by themselves."

***

In those last weeks, rallies were a daily thing near any given city. In Mad River Township, next to Dayton, "Over a Thousand Vehicles" and "Thousands of People" were reported in headlines about a four-mile parade. Said the *Journal*, "we notice(d) an effigy of Val., comprising principally a pair of battered unmentionables and a pair of boots to match 'em, an executioner pulling up and letting down the scarecrow in a very *suggestive* way."[139]

The day before the election, the Dayton *Empire* ran this: "It has been brought to the notice of gentlemen in charge of Democratic interests … that certain (Republican employers) are attempting to coerce … laborers … by threatening them unless they vote according to the sentiments of their employers." The *Empire* said that any worker who was thus threatened should "immediately report himself at this office … that we may publish" his information. It said that any such political discrimination would result in "an entire withdrawal of Democratic patronage (from the business), without which few (businesses) can subsist."[140]

The *Journal* responded in kind. It quoted the *Empire* correctly as saying that the Democrats could publish "all over the land" the names of offending employers "through means now in our power." Bickham wrote, "The 'means now in our power' … is the rebel institution known as the Knights of the Golden Circle," the secret, allegedly powerful, pro–South organization.[141] In the last couple of days of the campaign, the Knights played a role for Republican commentators much like the role black people played for Democrats: an alleged menace of which people needed to be reminded. The Knights got added to the stories of impending voter fraud. A headline: "Armed Copperhead Villains Sent to Ohio by Illinois Knights of the Golden Circle to Carry the Election by Force and Fraud."[142]

On the day before the election, the *Empire* ran a general summing-up editorial saying the great issue was not the war or loyalty, but "whether a man can be taken out of his bed by armed soldiers…" and treated as Vallandigham was. The paper said this was "the most significant contest yet known in the history of political parties," and "We look with confidence" to the outcome.

But three other editorials on the same page on the same day emphasized not the civil liberties issue, but race, as did another piece on the next page from a different newspaper. Said the *Empire*, "Let every vote count in favor of *white* men, and against the Abolition hordes." On Election Day appeared an *Empire* story with a headline by an editor who apparently got more outraged as he went along: "Horror! Horror!! Horror!!!" It turned out not to be about a colossal military massacre or about the canceling of an election or the arrest of all the Democrats in Congress. It began, "Can the mind conceive any greater deed of horror than the murder of two Rhode Island soldiers for refusing to be consolidated with a nigger regiment!"[143] Presumably fraudulent.

The *Journal* took up the racial issue after the Democrats held a local rally featuring those ubiquitous calls by young women for help in fending off black men. The rally had happened on the Saturday before the election. The *Empire* said it attracted the biggest crowd ever in Ohio.[144] (Among the floats was the door of Vallandigham's house which Burnside's troops had battered during what the *Empire* memorably referred to as "Burnside's only victory.") The *Journal* put the crowd size at, at most, 7,000 people, "half as large as ours."[145]

The *Journal*, clearly fearing that the race issue might be working for the Democrats, said,

> We do not hold these very young ladies responsible for the nervous apprehension of lurking evil evinced in the inscriptions on their wagons. They are too young to understand the importance of matrimony. They have never entertained a fear of receiving proposals, matrimonial or otherwise, from negroes. And they will never be in danger of any such association or alliance, while they do not themselves encourage them. When these young ladies arrive at an age to comprehend the subject ... they will have the conviction that it is a question of taste, and that respectable, well-bred ladies will have no difficulty in deciding the question for themselves. They will then learn that the declaration 'White husbands or none' is not only traitorous, but indelicate; and that it implies they are in danger of yielding to an inclination which is as monstrous as it is depraved.

That was relatively enlightened for the time (though, of course, many slaveholders never saw anything monstrous about interracial sex).

14

Lincoln's Election Night and the Post-Election Spin

For many Americans, the image of President Abraham Lincoln spending evenings near the telegraph machine at the War Department near the White House—in pursuit of news about the war—is sharply ingrained. But on the evening of October 13, 1863, he was at that same place with a different interest. He was looking for election returns. After all, in war against "the fire in the rear"—the force he saw as most threatening to his cause—this was by far the biggest battle yet. Lincoln himself had raised the already-high stakes when he jumped into the race, painstakingly laying out the case publicly that Vallandigham was a menace to the survival of the nation. So if the president was a bit hyper on Election Night, that's understandable. For Ohioans to embrace the man he had expelled would have been, among other things, a huge humiliation.

The scene at the War Department took on aspects of a political headquarters on Election Night, with people streaming in with bits of information or gossip or rumors or analysis they had heard. Doris Kearns Goodwin wrote that, "By midnight, everything indicated good results in both Ohio and Pennsylvania."[1] Ohio historian Daniel J. Ryan wrote, "All night long (Lincoln) was beside the telegraph in Washington, receiving information from Ohio. Brough was at his residence in Cleveland furnishing it."[2] There were exchanges between Washington and Cleveland. The Ohioans were reluctant to read too much into good early returns. They wanted to be sure not to mislead the president. But Lincoln knew Brough was ahead. "A little past midnight," according to Ryan, "Lincoln wired, 'What is your majority now?' and Brough's reply was, 'About 50,000.'" Lincoln knew enough Ohio politics to know that was big. His 43,000 vote victory in 1860 had given him a 10-percentage-points gap over Stephen A. Douglas. With only 443,000 votes having been cast in Ohio in 1860, it would have been hard to see in 1863 how a 50,000-vote gap could disappear. But, of course, Lincoln wanted not just a victory, but a big one. He wasn't celebrating yet. And he wasn't going to bed.

Vallandigham biographer Klement has Lincoln's correspondent on Election Night being Gov. Tod, not Brough, which fact Klement took from the papers of Lincoln's son Robert.[3] Ultimately, one is left with a picture of Lincoln fielding and perhaps sending telegrams left and right.

Treasury Secretary Salmon P. Chase was in Ohio campaigning for Brough (and unofficially for himself for president).[4] A note from Chase came in at about 1:20 a.m.

He predicted a margin of over 50,000 without the soldier vote.[5] At some stage, results from Pennsylvania resulted in a cheer from those gathered.[6] It entailed an incumbent Republican governor prevailing over a Copperhead challenge.

Wrote Ryan, "At five o'clock in the morning, in response to a final inquiry, Brough wired that his majority would be over 100,000, to which there came this answer, 'Glory to God in the Highest. Ohio has saved the Nation. A. Lincoln.'"[7]

That telegram appears in many historical accounts. Frank J. Klement wrote that nobody actually has the telegram.[8] Ryan, in a footnote, seems to attribute its existence to Navy Secretary Gideon Welles' diary, but it is not mentioned in the diary.[9] What's certain is that Lincoln would have sent some such congratulatory telegram. Whether he dictated those precise words or not, they clearly capture his response and mood. This is what Gideon Welles did write in his diary on the day after the election:

> I stopped in to see and congratulate the President, who is in good spirits and greatly relieved from the depression of yesterday. He told me he had more anxiety in regard to the election results of yesterday than he had in 1860 when he was chosen. He could not, he said, have believed four years ago, that one genuine American would, or could be induced to, vote for such a man as Vallandigham, yet he has been made the candidate of a large party, their representative man, and has received a vote that is a discredit to the country. The President showed a good deal of emotion as he dwelt on this subject."[10]

***

Vallandigham was simply annihilated. The margin was an unheard-of 101,000 votes out of 476,000 cast. In percentages 63–37. No such landslide was seen again in a race for governor of Ohio until 50 years later, when one of the candidates was a Socialist. The numbers are all the more remarkable—the rejection of Vallandigham all the more powerful—given that we're talking about a state which a year earlier had elected Democrats in 14 of the state's 19 congressional districts—districts that had been draw by the Republicans. The momentum toward a Democratic revolution that Vallandigham and others had seen in the 1862 election was brought to a screeching halt and reversed, all in just one year.

Brough's margin was 63,000 in the home vote and more than 39,000 in the soldier vote. In percentages, he got 57 and 95. But there was a stunning anomaly: Vallandigham won more votes than any Democrat had ever won for governor. Indeed, he won more votes—187,492—than any *victorious* candidate for governor had ever won except David Tod in '61.

How could he lose so big with so many votes? The answer, of course, is turnout. Turnout was extraordinary. Over 44 percent more people voted in 1863 than in 1861 (with the state having grown by perhaps 2.8 percent).[11] The 1861 election had set a record for turnout in races for governor.

But the comparison between '61 and '63 is less striking than this: More people voted in Ohio in 1863 than even in 1860 or 1864! And the 1860 election had seen the highest turnout in history to that point nationally, at 81.2 percent of eligible voters.[12] In Ohio, the percentage had been 83.[13]

Just as in later times, American politicos took for granted that turnout would drop substantially in a non-presidential election. They habitually compared non-presidential years only to other non-presidential years. Presidentials were a whole different matter; apples and oranges. If you didn't know that, you didn't know politics. Between 1860 and 1861, turnout dropped by about 26 percent. That was not unusual. (These were the turnouts in Ohio's major statewide elections—1860: 443,000; 1861: 359,000; 1863: 475,000; 1864: 471,000.)

Turnout figured into post-election spin. Staggering as the margin was, it did not put the outcome beyond the realm of spin. Nothing could do that. The spin of the Medary Democrats was this: (1) Vallandigham got the typical Democratic vote, and then some, despite the defection of Brough and his type from the Democrats. So now, *really!*, more than ever, the Republicans must stop calling Copperheads traitors. How many people can be traitors, after all? And (2) the Brough side got more votes than Vallandigham by cheating.

Medary pointed to the huge difference between Brough's votes and the typical Republican vote in gubernatorial elections and asked, "Where did those votes come from?" Obviously: Indiana, Michigan, West Virginia and even Illinois.

Medary noted the margin and asked, "Does anybody believe this is honest? Every man we have met since the election reports votes in his Ward or Township which were not honest, nor legal; yet they were received and counted, and as far as could be known, every one of them voted for Brough.... Total strangers without number were around many a (polling place), swearing in their votes without a blush of shame upon their cheeks. Some of these have been charged"—he didn't mean by authorities, but maybe by people he talked with—"with voting two or three times, going from one voting place to another.... We all know that for days before the election, long trains of cars came into the State from every quarter loaded with voters, hurrahing for Brough, some in soldier's clothes and some not. A Vermont regiment boasted that they voted along the road in Stark and Columbiana counties, and that they were going to New York to vote there in November. This they told a gentleman who rode with them on the cars."

He continued: "Many poor working men were *forced* to vote for Brough or be dismissed from employment.... A number who did not submit to this dictation were dismissed the next day. So bold were these Republicans that they gave their reasons for it as though it were a common business transaction. Suits will be commenced against several of these men under our election laws."[14]

It was all a crock. No major specific allegations of cheating in the home vote were reported in the Democratic newspapers; much less did such charges find their way into courts or other investigative bodies. All pre-election talk of organized fraud on both sides simply came to naught.

Ultimately, nobody paid attention to Medary. Vallandigham, who was quick to claim fraud when he lost narrowly in 1856, didn't tell Medary to back off—at least publicly. He settled for saying that his side had lost "by what means it is now idle to inquire."[15] That looks like an effort not to embarrass Medary and others wanting to hold to the delusion.

In a computer file containing my notes from *The Crisis* in the last half of 1863, the word "fraud" appears more than 50 times. The vast majority of uses came after the election. Eventually, though, the charge just faded away, like a song that ends with the repetition of a certain line getting softer and softer until it's inaudible. There was no explicit abandonment of the argument.

Medary went through the multiple stages of political grief: denial, rationalization, blame, threats, depression, claims of moral victory, and finally, inevitably, prediction: "Now we predict that it will not be a year before these same men"—the Unionists—"will be hunting for a Vallandigham man to put on their tickets … and nothing will be a greater feather in his cap than to have it said he voted for Vallandigham. Just mark our words."[16] Actually, he went through all the stages of grief in his very first edition after the election, writing endlessly.

In the edition after that, he led with and defended a hysterical piece from a Pennsylvania paper saying, "We cannot have any further hope in the ballot box; that has passed.… Standing armies are destructive of freedom, as we shall soon see.… Democrats, be not deceived, you will never again witness a free election.… Your civil rights are gone.… Your right arm must answer.… You should organize in every county … for defense."

In Medary's third edition after the election, he made an admission about the campaign: "Some of our stump orators, in their heated eloquence, had given an opportunity for this turn in the programme."[17] That is, mistakes were made. He was talking about Pugh and his proposed army to get Vallandigham to Columbus if elected. Medary is noting that Pugh raised the subject of post-election violence before Brough did. Medary was actually late to make the point; it was a common charge against Pugh. In truth, though, Pugh just happened to be the one who spoke up first. The issue was destined to arise in the campaign. It was in the air. Indeed, that was why Pugh raised it.

In those post-election editions, Medary was simply discombobulated. He would say the voters had voted for war, so be it. Then he'd say the election should not be seen as a vote for war, because the Republicans had said a vote for the Copperheads would bring war in Ohio; and they had promised peace faster than the Democrats could bring it. When he was in that mood, he would argue that the real peace side—his— would have won a referendum on peace. He'd say that what the Republicans might do now couldn't be predicted, then he'd predict it. He would say that the war would go on forever or until every slave was free; then he'd say the Republicans would give up on the war in 1864 and run as peace candidates in the presidential election.[18]

He had so much space to fill that he didn't have decide what to say; he could just say everything. No one would edit him. He was not unique; he was a type among editors. Anybody who gets immersed in mid–19th century American history comes upon quotations from Horace Greeley again and again—and again. At first, the impression one gets is that he was exceptionally insightful and quotable. Then one notices him contradicting himself. Eventually, one realizes that the phenomenon at work was simply that he wrote so much for so long that eventually he said everything.

***

If the election had been very close, the first place to look for fraud would have been the soldier vote. Anecdotal evidence offered cause for concern.

The official statistics about the soldier vote record the votes that were cast in camp. That is where most soldiers voted. However, some camps instead sent troops home to vote. Secretary of War Edwin Stanton was concerned that Ohio's soldier-vote law might not hold up in court. So he instructed the commander at Camp Chase near Columbus to send troops home to vote. Indeed, he told commanders to provide transportation. These actions might be interpreted as looking out for the troops' rights. But Stanton made his motivations clear to the governor: "If there be any other action of this Department that will contribute to the defeat of the public enemies let me know."[19] By "enemies," he obviously did not mean the Confederates. Meanwhile, Treasury Secretary Salmon P. Chase and other government executives tried to make sure that civilian federal employees from Ohio also got home.[20] Those numbers wouldn't have been large.

Historian Arnold Shankman pored over the troops' letters and diaries and over newspapers across the state. He concluded, "There was much truth to the charge of electoral irregularities"[21] in camps. Some of his horror stories were from the Democratic press, but he also had the likes of this:

> Thomas Galwey of the Eighth Ohio Infantry (wrote home): 'Not more than one-third of my regiment who voted were qualified, being under age, residents of other states, or unnaturalized foreigners. But so biased had we simple men become, by the misrepresentations of the so-called loyal and patriotic 'Union' man who had been sent out at public expense to canvass the soldiers to vote for the bloated English-man (Brough), that we excused any irregularity in the mode of conducting the election as being a military necessity.'"[22]

Galwey, wrote Shankman, "was elected a judge for the election although he was not yet 21, as the law required." A soldier from Tennessee wrote to his wife about the Ohio election, saying that he had himself counted votes from minors. He told his wife, "You need not say anything concerning this to anyone."[23] There were apparently also cases in which pressure to vote for Brough backfired: One lieutenant said "many" troops were voting for Vallandigham to spite their superiors.[24]

And yet, the evidence of real, overwhelming troop hostility to Vallandigham is overwhelming. One soldier wrote home to somebody who was sending Democratic ballots that, "It is useless to send more tickets. I stand nearly alone here, the defender of the patriot exile, Clement L. Vallandigham. There is a perfect furor of excitement against him; and others … have yielded to the damnable pressure." Another soldier wrote that his company had two Vallandigham voters. One received "a good whipping at Camp Dennison for hallowing for the traitor and then deserted." The other became "ashamed" and voted for the Union.[25]

In 2011, scholar Jonathan White wrote a book called *Emancipation, the Union Army and the Reelection of Abraham Lincoln*. A central purpose of White's book is to cast doubt upon the notion that an overwhelming majority of the troops became Republicans. Even he, however, acknowledges that the troops had a special loathing for Vallandigham.[26] It's worth remembering that if a young man had Copperhead leanings, he might not volunteer. Moreover, if a soldier *developed* Copperhead feelings, he could desert.

Soldier turnout wasn't as high as the home vote. Fewer than 30 percent of Ohio troops voted in camp.[27] How many voted at home and how many didn't have the opportunity to vote, or didn't take the opportunity to go home isn't clear. Historian

White wrote that 20 percent of the troops chose not to vote in 1864. He said that number was generally higher in other elections.[28]

The soldier vote flipped 15 of Ohio's 88 counties from Vallandigham to Brough. Montgomery County came close to being in that category. But editor Bickham managed to get his victory in the home vote by almost nothing: 66 votes out of 10,000. Montgomery County soldiers in camps officially went hugely against their homeboy: 933–25. That gave Brough a 55–45 victory in percentages in the county overall. The only county near Dayton to go for Vallandigham was hugely Democratic Butler.

If there were several factors fostering a big Brough vote among the troops, there was also one shrinking that vote (besides backlash among the troops). General Rosecrans had a message for an Ohio soldier going home to vote in October: "Tell them that this army would have given a stronger vote for Brough had not Vallandigham's friends over yonder killed two or three thousand Ohio voters the other day at Chickamauga."[29]

The year 1863 didn't see a lot of important elections, but those that happened generally came out well for the Republicans or Unionists, even if not as well as Ohio's. In Pennsylvania, the margin for the incumbent Republican governor was only 51.5 to 48.5 percent. In Connecticut, a state that was always deeply divided over the war, the Democrats put up Copperhead Thomas Seymour for governor. He won the home vote but lost the election on the soldier vote. One possibility is that the mere association with Vallandigham was enough to cost the Democrats one or both of those close elections. Meanwhile, Republicans did well in New York elections and won the governorship of Iowa big.

If Gettysburg and Vicksburg hadn't happened, the Democrats might have won a couple of those elections. But certainly not Ohio, the margin there being so big. Why was Vallandigham's defeat so overwhelming? Of course, his status as an exile convicted essentially of disloyalty recommends itself as the big reason. But the notion that a convicted "traitor" couldn't possibly win seems to be somewhat undermined by the fact that he got enough votes to win in a typical turnout. In that hyperpartisan era, the judgments of the army and government about his loyalty didn't resolve the issue for many voters.

One temptation for analysts is to assume that Vallandigham's vote represented the usual Democratic mid-term showing, and that he lost because a lot of people who typically skipped non-presidential elections came out to vote against him. That's probably too facile. The best bet is that division in Democratic ranks—and Brough's identity as a Democratic—did cost Vallandigham some Democratic voters. But the election engaged just about everybody, and that fact increased the vote of both candidates.

The issues that brought people out were issues that sent them mainly to Brough: the fear of something like civil war in Ohio; the fear that Vallandigham might obstruct the war effort in concrete ways, not just talk; his out-of-the-mainstream call for an armistice, and the related fear of an armed enemy in perpetuity not far south of Ohio. Fear. Vallandigham and his side played to fears, too, of course: fear of dictatorship and repression, fear of black people, fear of prolonged war. But he had the wrong fears for that moment.

***

Tom Lowe didn't engage in any Medary-like post-election spinning, rationalizing, floundering or lying. He wrote after the election that the outcome had resolved the debate about the nation's future: "The people have voted in favor of the war and the way it is at present conducted," he said, "and it has to go on, of course."[30] How devastating an admission! This was the man who was certain that the majority of people were Copperheads, that people were more intent on winning the war against repression than the one against secession, and that Vallandigham was the most popular figure in the North. But Lowe felt he had to come to terms with what seemed to be as conclusive an outcome as democracy ever offers.

And yet, in long retrospect, what's most striking about the election is that 43 percent of the home vote went to a man who, if he could have, would have changed the course of American history. In the middle of a war that was about the survival of the nation as people knew it, these voters wanted a flat-out opponent of the war, no matter what any military court or president said about loyalty.

Most striking is that this was not just national division. The Civil War was division. This was subdivision. And the minority provided a good base for the next fight.

15

Literary Immortality

Clement Vallandigham inspired a classic of American fiction. The title "The Man without a Country"—if not the plot—has been known to millions of Americans in every generation since the war. It has been taught to high school students well into the modern era. Early in the 20th century, Harvard put out its shelf of "Harvard Classics." One volume was dedicated to American short story writers. Six writers were featured. Five were among the names one might expect: Twain, Hawthorne, Poe, Irving and Harte. The sixth was a less-known writer who was represented by this one story. The story was eventually adapted to film more than once in the silent film era. A talkie was made in 1937, the same year as an opera by Walter Damrosch. A television movie was made with Cliff Robertson, Beau Bridges and Peter Strauss. The story has been produced on stage innumerable times. It was big in the era of radio drama. As this is written, one can find on YouTube a radio version introduced by Bing Crosby after World War II, as well as other versions. The story has been anthologized again and again, including quite recently.[1] It has been in cheap paperbacks and presented more than once as an encased gift book, standing alone, despite its brevity.

The author was Edward Everett Hale, not to be confused with anybody with some of those names. Edward Everett was the orator/statesman/educator who spoke for two hours at Gettysburg, where Lincoln spoke for the two minutes; the *other* Gettysburg Address. Edward Everett Hale was his nephew. Nathan Hale was the young soldier/spy in the American Revolution who, it is said, regretted that he had but one life to give for his country. The author in question here was his grandnephew. (And Edward Everett Horton was an actor.)

Author Hale, in explaining the origin of his story decades later, said this:

> In ... 1863, an important election was pending in Ohio. A man named Vallandigham, (now) long since forgotten except from his connection with this matter, was the candidate of the party which opposed the National Government. This Mr. Vallandigham had said that he did not want to belong to a nation which would compel by arms the loyalty of any of its citizens; he did not want to belong to the United States. General Burnside ... sent Mr. Vallandigham, with his compliments, to the rebel commander on the other side of the Ohio. He said that if Mr. Vallandigham did not want to live in the United States, the United States did not want to have him there, and presented him, with his best respects, to the commanding general of the enemy.

Facts were not Hale's best thing. His explanation is almost as fictional as his story. But he was certainly honest when he said his motive in 1863 was to defeat Vallandigham. "By an accident," he said, the story wasn't published until after the election, when "Mr. Vallandigham had been completely forgotten."[2]

In the 21st century, entertainment-savvy people might refer to the story as a "high concept" one: It lends itself to an intriguing summary. The plot is the reason the story has lived so long. It is set during the trial of Aaron Burr, very early in the 19th century. Its connection with real events is designed to make it seem true to the reader. The narrator seems to have been present for events he describes. Many readers thought it was true. In truth, Burr, after killing Alexander Hamilton in a duel and after being vice president, went south and west, to the area of Texas and Louisiana (and spent time in Ohio). In 1807 he was arrested and put on trial in Richmond for treason, charged with planning to set up his own country or something on American-owned land. He was acquitted. In the story, a fictional young follower—Lieutenant Philip Nolan, the character inspired by Vallandigham—is also tried. A judge asks if he has anything to say that would demonstrate his loyalty to the United States. He responds, "Damn the United States! I wish I may never hear of the United States again!"

That stopped things. The judges recessed and came back with the sentence: Nolan would spend the rest of his life on U.S. Navy ships at sea, and he would never be told anything about the United States; he would never even hear the name of his country again. That's the high concept. The story is primarily about his life at sea and how he handles not knowing anything about his country. It's about the lesson he learns.

How remarkable it is that this story inspired by Vallandigham has been so widely known for so long, yet has brought him no fame. That said, there is no injustice here. If the story were linked to him, *that* would be an injustice. Edward Everett Hale gets him profoundly wrong. The story is based upon a misunderstanding fostered by partisan passions.

Hale wrote the explanation quoted above in 1898 for an introduction to his story as reprinted in *Outlook* magazine. The occasion was the Spanish-American war, which Hale supported. He thought God gave the United States "certain duties in defense of the civilization of the world." And he thought opponents of this new war needed to contemplate the experiences of Vallandigham and Nolan lest they go similarly astray.[3]

But, of course, Vallandigham never said that he did not want to belong to the United States. And he never would have said it. It just wasn't him. He wanted to be in his country's senate and probably entertained thoughts about being its president. Nolan was fine with being sent away; Vallandigham was outraged to his bones. Maybe Hale thought he spotted some Tom Lowe–like instincts in Vallandigham, some hidden thoughts about leaving. But Hale made no claim to be plumbing the depths of Vallandigham's soul. He claimed to be responding to what Vallandigham actually, explicitly said.

Hale was a minister and writer in New England, where people generally loathed Vallandigham as enthusiastically as he loathed them. The story appeared first in the *Atlantic Monthly*—out of Boston—in the December 1863 issue. (The issue came out the week that Lincoln—and Uncle Edward—spoke at Gettysburg.)[4] Hale was dealing with the Vallandigham portrayed in Republican newspapers and magazines. Whether some print outlet actually quoted Vallandigham saying he didn't want to live in the country, or paraphrased him to that effect or somehow just left the impression, Hale got a notion in his head. He had long been fascinated by the connection between a person and his country.[5] So this notion in his head connected with a subject he had long wanted to write about. Hale's literary and political passions combined to create his own Vallandigham.

"The Man without a Country" has long been taught as a parable about patriotism. The story about the story is another parable: about the mind-bending effects of political passions. Nobody in Hale's life was likely to correct his misimpressions about Vallandigham. Whether we are talking about Massachusetts as a whole—which went for Lincoln with 72.2 percent in 1864—or about his church world or about the literary world around *The Atlantic*, the preponderant predispositions were Hale's own. That probably means they strengthened his own. He was misled—right into literary history.

16

Canadian Winter

Perhaps the harshest blow to Vallandigham as a result of the 1863 election debacle was that the Petroleum V. Nasby changed the name of his church. It was no longer the St. Valandygum. Nasby delivered this message to President Lincoln personally, saying that he was one "who hez repoodiated Vallandigum." (He was not rigid in his spelling.) He did so in the course of hitting Lincoln up for a postmaster job. He made clear that he still held all the views associated with Vallandigham. He apparently didn't see that as a political problem, so long as he rejected the man himself.[1]

Now, Nasby was a fictional character. He was created by Republican newspaper editor David Ross Locke of Findlay, Ohio, and later Toledo. Locke wrote as Nasby. Locke/Nasby was a favorite of Lincoln, who was known to read him to his cabinet.[2] Fictional or not, the abandonment by big fan Nasby had to hurt the already humiliated politician Vallandigham, who was now as isolated politically as geographically. Nasby was saying that the problem was not the Copperheads' views, but their leadership. The unkindest cut.

After the election, Vallandigham continued to live in Windsor. He tried to look on the bright side, at least publicly and with friends. In an October 28 letter, he said he was "happier than Lincoln." He said that the Democratic Party had achieved great unity in the election. He insisted that "the greatest boast in the future will be I was a (Democratic) warrior in '63." And he predicted a Democratic "sweep" in the 1864 election.[3] And yet ten days before the 1863 election, Vallandigham had written, "Remember one thing: if we fail this fall we shall have no presidential election next year."[4] He meant that the Republicans would be emboldened in their fight against democracy. Three weeks after that—failure having intervened—that alarm was gone, and all was, somehow, looking up.

Political friends were raising money for Vallandigham's wife and son in Dayton, as they had been for months. He was out of a job, after all. Democratic newspapers openly solicited contributions to defray his expenses. They would ask that the money be sent to the paper, and they would report on contributions. They raised plenty. Meanwhile, Vallandigham claimed to be happy to spend most of his time reading. But he wasn't only reading. He was thinking.

In February 1864 he was visited by members of a secretive organization called the Order of the Sons of Liberty, generally seen as not simply anti-war but anti-North. It was thought of as the same group—or the same kind of group—as the

Knights of the Golden Circle and the Order of American Knights, names known to Americans. You needed a scorecard to keep track of the names of the secret, subversive groups. The Knights of the Golden Circle had pre-war Southern roots, having been associated with the effort to expand the country to the south for the purpose of adding slave states. Now the Sons of Liberty were about the war.

The Sons who visited Vallandigham were distressed. They saw the organization as under siege by Republican authorities and maligned unfairly. They thought they needed a fresh start. New name. New leader. New image. They turned to Vallandigham for his national standing.[5]

At least three takes exist on these secretive groups:

One: They were hugely potent and dangerously subversive organizations of scores of thousands of men in several western states, guys who were armed for and planning various major public uprisings, including one in Chicago during the 1864 Democratic convention. They were bent on Western secession and/or they were bent on the release of thousands of Confederate prisoners from Northern prisons. This was the general view of them promoted by the Republican governors of Indiana and Illinois (Oliver Morton and Richard Yates); each state had experienced a "Copperhead legislature" after the 1862 election. Both governors frantically tried to alert Washington to this potential conflagration in the rear.

Sharing the governors' views was Joseph Holt, the U.S. judge advocate general, the highest legal official in the War Department. He compiled a very high-profile report on the alleged activities and plans of the secretive groups.[6] Holt's views were widespread in the army and in Republican circles. Those views resulted in a trial—often referred to as a "show trial"—of various alleged conspirators in Indianapolis in the run-up to the 1864 election. That trial was substantially about the threat of secession in the West or something like secession. There was another, similar trial in Cincinnati in 1865, more focused on the plot to release prisoners.

Views similar to Holt's exist today. Stephen E. Towne, a university archivist in Indiana, copiously researched government investigations into subversive activities during the war. He wrote that investigators "amassed significant evidence" of violent and illegal plans.[7] Similarly, journalist-turned-scholar Jennifer Weber wrote, speaking of letters about dangerous and traitorous activities, "these kinds of letters exist from too many different parts of the country and too many disparate sources (to be dismissed).... Much of (the correspondence) was private letters sent between friends and family members. There would be no reason for people to fabricate … for that kind of audience. Finally, it is clear that not every writer had strong political predilections."[8]

Two: These groups were, collectively and individually, the nearest thing to nothing. This was the view of Frank J. Klement, a fair portion of whose career was dedicated to arguing that the Copperheads were not any sort of threat, other than as a legitimate political bloc. He made this argument not primarily in his biography of Vallandigham, but in two other books.[9] He believed the Copperheads were all sound and fury; that some very concrete plans fizzled when the Copperheads chickened out; that the government reports were partisan and hysterical.

In truth, few important subversive Copperhead plots ever came to fruition. Confederate prisoners were not freed. Northern railroad tracks were not destroyed. But part of the explanation for that might be that some plots were thwarted. Towne writes, for example, that in Butler County, as the draft approached in 1863, local authorities were so concerned about resistance that they sought troops from Dayton. Those troops solved the problem, with help from "armed groups of Union supporters."[10]

Three: Whether the secretive organization were massive or small, they were—at least at a certain stage—peaceful and loyal. They were Democrats dedicated to counterbalancing Republican political organizations called the Loyal League(s) or Union League(s), which also operated with some secrecy. This was the view—or at least the presented position—of Vallandigham.

The people Vallandigham met with in Canada asked him to be head—"Supreme Grand Commander," specifically—of the organization. He accepted. For many Republicans who were certain these groups were Confederate fronts, his acceptance made perfect sense, telling you all you needed to know about him.

Eventually, in 1865, as the war was coming to an end, he was to testify at length about his involvement. He was a witness, not charged with anything, though the government would certainly have loved to do that; he would have been the top prize. He insisted that he had only agreed to participate with the Sons if their efforts were legal and peaceful and not pro-Southern, but pro-Democratic. He said he told the Sons that he had never liked the idea of secret organizations, but perhaps the time had come, because the Republicans had theirs. He testified that the Sons said they were going to newly specify that they had no Southern connection and that they recognized the legitimacy of the government in Washington.[11]

One author later wrote that Vallandigham was attracted to the group's stance within the Democratic Party, that is, to its antipathy to George McClellan, the War Democrat who was seeking the Democratic presidential nomination.[12] But Vallandigham himself later insisted his overriding interest in 1864 was in the party's platform not the nomination.[13]

At any rate, his involvement was anything but secret. By the time of the trial, he had publicly defended the organization at every opportunity. He called the Sons "a militant Democratic group" within "the great national (Democratic) party," dedicated to civil liberties and traditional Democratic values (state rights, mainly). He likened the organization to one of the same name during the American Revolution.[14]

His testimony did establish that he knew that some members of his organization were prone to illegal activities. But he presented himself as the enforcer of the straight and narrow, at least for the organization (as opposed to the behavior of individual members). He said he didn't know about Confederate financial help for any of the accused, or about plans to free Southern prisoners in the North, or about plans to sack and burn Chicago during the convention, or about plans for a Northwest confederacy. He presented his involvement with the organization as very limited.

The prosecution made no great effort to break down his story, though other witnesses cast doubt upon it. At Indianapolis in 1864, various witnesses had tied him to subversive activities. They said, for example, that a day had been set for a "rising" by the group, and that Vallandigham was supposed to give the signal, though they never said that day actually came.[15] They said a Confederate who was to organize a prison-escape scheme at Johnson's Island on Lake Erie (which failed) reported to Vallandigham.[16] But the testimony came from the likes of a government spy of discredited credibility[17] or defendants who really *had* cooperated with Confederates and had their own credibility issues. The testimony was often second and third hand, reporting what the witnesses claim to have understood or heard, rather than what they knew.

Besides meeting with the Sons in Canada, Vallandigham met with Confederate operatives stationed there. The Richmond government had invested $5 million for Canadian operations to subsidize anti-war newspapers and candidates in the North and more. Confederates crossed the border to rob banks in Vermont; they burned some steamboats, planned to free some Southern prisoners and planned to infiltrate the 1864 Democratic convention in Chicago.[18]

Vallandigham met with an operative named Jacob Thompson. Vallandigham testified that their conversation was one between two men seeking peace. But he said they came to loggerheads as to how peace would come about: Vallandigham wanted reunification, and Thompson did not. Thompson was later to claim that Vallandigham had initiated him into Sons and told him its size (300,000 members total, with more in Illinois and Indiana than Ohio's alleged 40,000). Vallandigham denied giving any such information or inducting Thompson.

Biographer Klement insisted that Vallandigham simply had more credibility than Thompson, that "he had a reputation for veracity, even with his enemies. Thompson, on the other hand, had his reputation tarnished by charges of corruption while holding public office."[19] However, in a 1994 book, scholar David E. Long concluded that the Ohioan colluded with the South. He specifically took on Klement, insisting that Thompson had no motive to fabricate charges against Vallandigham and that Vallandigham had a great deal to lose by testifying honestly if Thompson's charges were true. Long concluded that Vallandigham and the Sons participated in plans to attack Northern POW prisons, kidnap the governor of Indiana and more, all toward the goal of the Northwest ultimately joining with the South.[20]

But Thompson really did have a motive to make stuff up: to inflate himself. He had been sent to Canada to further the Confederate cause somehow, and had been funded from Richmond. He had reason to want people to believe he had done major good for the cause, though that's not obvious from events. Getting Vallandigham on board would have been big.

It is not credible that Vallandigham would have taken the political risk of conspiring with the Confederates in acts of sabotage. He still saw himself as a viable politician in the North; he had all manner of political endeavors ahead. Perhaps his calculus would have been different if the possibility existed of a successful Northwest secession. But how could somebody who had just suffered his monumental defeat possibly believe that Ohio was going to secede?

Moreover, the notion that he saw the Sons as merely an answer to the Republican Union Leagues is entirely credible. Defeating the Republicans was—had always been—his greatest passion. Here was a politician without office, and here—presented to him in Canada—was an office in a political organization dedicated to his top goal. Here was a way to be a national player.

Still, getting involved with the Sons was a very bad idea. It was the act of a desperate or semi-desperate man. It meant associating with an element that could only hurt him. His number-two guy—and the real driving force behind the organization—was Harrison H. Dobbs, its leader in Indiana. Dobbs took financial help from the Confederates. He did, indeed, have a plan that included an uprising, release of Confederates in prison and seizure of government supplies. According to Klement, it horrified his fellow Copperheads.[21]

Open as Vallandigham was about the organization, membership in it was confidential, making it still a "secret" society. Copperhead spokesmen had been at pains for years to pooh-pooh the idea of secret Copperhead societies. Sam Medary was perhaps the pooh-pooher-in-chief. He insisted that, having been at the center of Democratic politics for decades, he had never seen any such groups. Indeed, he said, it was only Republicans who dealt in secrecy.[22]

So Vallandigham and Medary eventually had a difference of opinion about whether a secretive organization was necessary. Maybe Medary would have changed his mind, too, if somebody had offered him the top job in such an organization at time when he was out of work and stranded in a foreign country.

***

If the Sons of Liberty successfully stroked Vallandigham's ego in Canada, when he needed it, another organization found another way: It invited him to give a speech. That speech is irresistible as a window to his soul, a way to see him as he saw himself in his metaphorical and literal winter in Canada. The main listeners were approximately 35 pro–Vallandigham students from the University of Michigan.[23] They had come up from Ann Arbor. The date was November 14, 1863, a month after the Ohio election. This was a period in which he had written to his wife, "*posterity will vote for me*, and there will be neither chance nor motive for violence or fraud."[24] And, anyway, "Two years ago, few dared name me kindly; now millions praise—I will not say revere—me. And yet I am but just entering upon the full vigor of mature manhood," at 43. One has to wonder if the first draft did say "revere."

He began his speech by saying he was content to be judged by posterity. "Without further personal allusion, therefore, ... allow me to pass to another subject."[25] He then changed the subject from Clement Vallandigham to Clement Vallandigham:

"At forty, ... (y)ou will feel that there is a lifetime yet before you; and if you are of strong will and brave spirit, ... your past failures and defeats you will regard then as but probation and discipline, and indeed, as so many assurances of final triumph. Press on! But not in haste." He recommended the "motto… 'I bide my time.'" "Read history," he suggested, "and learn that the patriot, the hero, the statesman, the orator, whom you reverence or admire in the pages of Plutarch and Livy, or of Hume, Gibbon, and Macaulay, was reviled and persecuted in his own day, and suffered death, it may have been, at the hands of the men of his own generation. Ponder, too, the wisdom of Moses, who, before the pleasures and honors of the king's court, preferred rather that Red Sea and forty years in the wilderness, and death and an unknown grave, that he might become a great lawgiver, and the founder of a new religion and of a powerful people."

He didn't confine himself to this dissertation on himself. He promoted study of the classics. He passingly encouraged future clergymen to stick to "legitimate duties," a category that didn't include politics. But in addressing the future lawyers and the "many" prospective politicians he said he saw before him, he came back to his story repeatedly. In his ending, he spoke of the need for a political combatant to have "faith in his vindication." He said without such faith, no man ever achieved greatness. And without that faith, one should not even think about trying to "endure that cruel and crushing weight" that comes with being "the patriot-statesman."

One might get the impression that, when he was reading all that history as a boy and young man—even before his reading as a political exile—he identified with the scorned and defeated, the metaphorically exiled. But the relentless pursuit of elective office seems an unlikely course for somebody like that. Time would show clearly that he wanted a long career at the center of things.

The speech suggested that when he returned, he would certainly not be chastened and apologetic because of his defeat. It would take a lot more than an election defeat to change Clement Vallandigham. But a lot more was coming.

***

By the spring of 1864, still in Canada, he needed an exit-and-re-entry strategy. He came up with a doozy, one that would rock the political world. Again, he made no small plan. But that would only become clear with time.

On top of the usual and obvious reasons for wanting to go home, he was starting to look ridiculous, pathetic. Some of his partisans were calling upon him to come back and fight the fight, including the Copperhead Chicago *Times*. Waiting until the end of the war—whose timing no one could predict—would have been embarrassing. And, as biographer Klement suggested, Vallandigham's unfortunate involvement with the Sons of Liberty provided an extra spur to get out of Canada, a need to change the subject.[26]

More people than ever thought Lincoln would not arrest him again. By the summer of 1864, not many more politicians or partisan journalists had been arrested on political charges. Military commanders had noticed that the Vallandigham affair had not been a boon to the career of General Burnside. Meanwhile, after the landslide, Republicans didn't have much political reason to worry about Vallandigham. Many thought of him as a bigger problem for the Democrats than themselves. Moreover, they really were not much worried about Vallandigham's effect on the draft, desertion or recruitment. Lincoln's conditional offer to let him return symbolized that.

Given the election outcome, Vallandigham could no longer dream of a triumphal return to his home state on the shoulders of Democratic activists. But he knew he would be a hero to many as the still unbowed martyr. Moreover, a specific role might be open to him at the Democratic National Convention in Chicago that summer: shaping the platform. Although he would have preferred some candidate other than McClellan, there really wasn't anybody who could challenge the general. Nevertheless, the chances of getting a Copperhead platform were good, because the delegates would include a lot of Copperheads. If Vallandigham could engineer a platform to their liking, he would be back at the center of national politics. And he might shape McClellan's presidency—and get a role in it, a role that might be utterly historic in shaping the country's future. Meanwhile, at the very least, in Chicago he'd be one of the biggest shows in town.

The war was going badly again for the North. By mid–1864, Grant was trudging through Virginia, taking enormous losses and seeming to get nowhere. This was of monumental importance politically. The Republicans flatly needed the war to be going well. Now the conventional political wisdom became that Lincoln could not be re-elected. Not only were the Republicans weakened; so were the War Democrats. The Copperheads rose again within the party, Vallandigham's humiliation of 1863 notwithstanding.

In Ohio, the Brough victory had not calmed things down. The 1864 political season was as violent as 1862 and 1863. At least five Democratic newspapers were mobbed. Another, in Columbus, that was threatened—or saw itself as threatened—issued a threat through an editorial that it would make abolitionists pay if it were mobbed. It was not attacked.

Among those attacked was the Dayton *Empire*. About 15 soldiers entered and shot it up. Then a crowd gathered. Tempers flared after a spectator shouted something about the army and the government wanting to protect "niggers." Maybe a dozen shots were fired. An uninvolved spectator was killed. A couple of soldiers were hurt. An army captain took responsibility for the attack in an apparently drunken speech at Courthouse Square. These facts appeared in a wire report that seemed to be an amalgam of the Republican and Democratic takes on events.[27] (The drunken captain was transferred and promoted.[28])

Although two Republican speakers had reportedly tried to calm things, the *Empire* insisted that the vast majority of Republicans present were of no help whatsoever and even contributed to the problem.[29] When the *Journal* offered the *Empire* help in recovering from the attack, the *Empire* publicly and angrily rejected the offer. But publication of the *Empire* was not interrupted.

The *Empire* was under new ownership. It had been sold in late 1863 to brothers knows as the Hubbards, who had previously owned a paper in Logan, Ohio, 120 miles east of Dayton. Different owners; same deity: Vallandigham. The Hubbards hit particularly hard on race. Their ultimate charge—like that of many Copperhead papers—was that the Republicans favored inter-racial marriage, or "miscegenation," as they called it, mistakenly saying Republicans had invented the term and embraced the concept.[30] (In truth, Democratic operatives had invented the word and falsely put it in Republican mouths.)

The racial issue that got most attention from the *Empire* was the notion that black troops performed well in combat. "The Abolition papers have been in ecstacies over the foolish stories told about the bravery of the negroes at Port Hudson. Of course, the story was all false, for it is simply nonsense to talk of negro bravery. In any fair fight, one thousand white men would easily whip ten or twenty thousand negroes, perhaps more."[31] Later, a Cincinnati paper sent an *Empire* writer into repetitive tizzies (not captured here), the like of which occurred on no other subject: "(T)he Cincinnati *Gazette* says, 'The safety of 1600 men who reached Colliersville … is ascribed to the gallantry of the negro convoy of 200 men.' … Two hundred niggers protect sixteen hundred white men, and the latter owe their safety to the bravery of the former! … (That) is the most direct and outspoken slander of the white soldier that we have yet seen."[32] Despite it all, white troops attacked the *Empire,* not the *Gazette.*

When Vallandigham in Canada saw the wire report about the *Empire* being attacked, he flipped out. He issued an explicit call to violent reprisals, one that was not aimed at the actual perpetrators. On March 7, he wrote a much-noted letter to the *Empire* that also appeared in its entirety in, for example, in the *National Republican* in Washington, whose name captured its mission:

> I read, several days ago, the telegraphic announcement of the "riddling" of the Empire office by "furloughed soldiers." ... I ... express to you my profound regret that you were not prepared to inflict on the spot ... the complete punishment which the assailants deserved. But I am gratified to learn that some of them did soon after receive their deserts. But these cowardly acts ... do not primarily come from the "soldiers." There is, therefore, but one remedy for past and preventive of future injuries, and that is instant, summary, and ample reprisals upon the persons and property of the men at home, who, by language and conduct, are always inciting to these outrages.

He was talking about the Dayton *Journal*. Just as Lincoln thought the important wrong-doers in the desertion issue weren't the troops, but those who agitated them, Vallandigham thought the important wrong-doers in the *Empire* attack weren't the troops but their agitators. Moreover, Vallandigham, like Lincoln, was uninterested in the precise words of the alleged agitators (which he never quoted), but in their general attitude. He saw no importance in the fact that they never actually said "Destroy the *Empire*!" Indeed, the similarities between his charge against the *Journal* and his enemies' main charges against him couldn't be more striking. After all, he never actually said "Desert!" One has to wonder whether, in the process of formulating his charge against the *Journal*, Vallandigham had an epiphany about the frame of mind of his critics: "Oh, THAT's what they're talking about!"

A resulting Chicago *Tribune* headline said "Vallandigham Urging War in the North."[33] The Xenia *Sentinel* went in the same direction: "C.L.V. always declared that he was in favor of 'enforcing the laws.' Now ... the banished Coriolanus advises his political friends to fight, to inaugurate civil war in Ohio. Whoever heard of a man by principle and constitutionally in favor of peace, advising war?"[34]

The *Journal* was more than a thorn in Vallandigham's side. It was the greatest force of opposition locally by far, certainly far more important than any politician. Here was a man—Vallandigham—who was a demigod in his own party locally and a national figure. But he was hounded by this little newspaper with a young, aggressive, respected editor who had publicly made it his top goal to defeat Vallandigham at home—and had succeeded.

The *Empire* also blamed Bickham for the violent attack on it. It relentlessly excoriated him for behavior that "incites the mob."[35] Strikingly, the *Empire* made this criticism two days *before* the attack. It warned of "the bloody time (the *Journal*) is laboring so assiduously to inaugurate." It complained of the *Journal's* portrayal of "all who differ with them in opinions as 'traitors,' 'Copperheads,' 'sympathizers with secession,' 'enemies in the rear,' &c, &c."[36]

Somehow these labels were deemed by the *Empire* to be more threatening to the social peace than the *Empire's* charges that the Republicans were bloodthirsty, war-mongering, corrupt, self-serving despots who were bent on destroying democracy, were themselves unwilling to fight their war and were—the ultimate charge—more interested in the welfare of blacks than whites.

Bickham's offer to help the *Empire* after the violent attack and his denunciation of the attack just seemed to make the *Empire* editors angrier. They saw only hypocrisy. That debate raged. In the course of it, the *Empire* denied that Vallandigham had promoted violence. "No he don't," the paper said, "and you know it, and everybody who has read his letter knows it. He only advises honest men to defend their lives and property against just such pusillanimous poodles as you."[37]

In an effort to justify reprisals against people who hadn't actually committed an act, the *Empire* presented a half dozen cases in which Union officials had undertaken such reprisals themselves. One case was local: when a provost marshal soldier was shot at in neighboring Greene County, six innocent people—apparently Democrats—were arrested in the hope that they would know the culprit and give him up. Another involved Schenck in Maryland. According to the *Empire*, "When the barns and houses of some of Schenck's 'loyal' pets ... were burned to the ground by persons unknown, his Majesty, Schenck, assessed the damages upon the 'disloyal' citizens within a certain number of miles and compelled them to pay it."[38] The *Empire* was apparently unimpressed by the distinction that these actions were taken by authorities, not vigilantes.

The *Empire* was struggling to find the right message. In complaining about the "mob," it felt itself constantly on the edge of complaining about the troops, which it definitely did not want to do. The paper insisted it had never done that. It noted that, while the attackers had unmistakably been soldiers, they were a small minority of the soldiers downtown at the time; about 150 didn't join in. Still, the politically dangerous edge was there. This was certainly one reason the paper and Vallandigham harped on the *Journal*: politically safer.

Recriminations over the *Empire* episode were still in the air when the Ohio Democrats began their state convention in Columbus on March 23. Going in, Vallandigham was understood to be the candidate of five county delegations for president of the United States. Montgomery and Butler Counties were among them[39]; another was Franklin (Columbus), Medary country. But Vallandigham was up for something somewhat smaller: delegate to the national convention in Chicago. He needed that desperately for his plan to work.

The state convention was the first since the one that had nominated Vallandigham for governor in a frenzy. Some delegates in 1864 were not eager to be seen as ignoring the ultimate reaction of the voters in 1863. On the first ballot for four delegates to Chicago, three candidates won the necessary majority vote: a former senator, a former chief justice and Congressman Pendleton of Cincinnati. The next three finishers, in order, were Rufus Ranney (the party's nominee for governor in 1859), Vallandigham and Medary. Medary pulled out in favor of Vallandigham. But Ranney won the run-off by five votes out of more than 400. The Vallandigham supporters raised a major fuss on the floor of the convention, but a recount didn't change things.

Vallandigham's problem in Columbus was not that the convention was dominated by War Democrats. Two of the four chosen delegates were Copperheads. The majority of delegates just didn't want Vallandigham himself, even for this low position. They didn't want to be represented by him, associated with him. Things had changed profoundly from the crazed moment a year earlier.

But Vallandigham, still in Canada, had another card to play: Dayton.

17

Vallandighammizing the Democrats

In the dark on June 14, Vallandigham got on a ferry back to the United States. He was disguised in a cape and beard and surrounded by four friends.[1] They were not obstructed as they headed for Detroit. Once there, they walked to the train station and got on a sleeping car going south. The train rattled south on a path that is now roughly Interstate 75. It passed Dayton—and the famous passenger's wife—on its way to Hamilton in Butler County, where it would stop before proceeding to Cincinnati. In Hamilton—named for a man Vallandigham insisted the hated Republicans stemmed from—the Democrats of Vallandigham's 3rd District were meeting in preparation for the party's national convention, to which they would send two delegates.

When Lincoln heard that Vallandigham was back, he took no action. He said, "I don't believe that Vallandigham has returned," meaning, apparently, returned to his old ways. "I never can believe it, and I never shall believe it until he forces himself offensively upon the public attention and upon my attention; then we shall have to deal with him. So long as he behaves himself decently, he is as effectually in disguise as a slovenly man who went to a masquerade party with a clean face."[2]

That quotation was provided by Noah Brooks, the journalist and Lincoln confidant. It came in the course of Brooks' description of a conversation between Lincoln and Fernando Wood, the former New York mayor who became the most prominent Copperhead in the House of Representatives when Vallandigham left. Wood had some sort of relationship with Lincoln. On this occasion he was telling Lincoln that Democrats would not rise again politically until peace arrived, so Lincoln shouldn't worry about them. But the point of the conversation may have been to advise Lincoln not to arrest Vallandigham again. Said Wood, "He has had more notoriety already than he deserves." There was clearly some competition between the two Copperheads, at least from Wood's perspective. And Vallandigham notoriety did not help Wood.

Vallandigham was to, indeed, force himself on public and presidential attention, but in a way that the president apparently didn't mind.

In Hamilton was gathered the Vallandigham's base. Here he remained a hero, venerated. Here he did not have to worry about competition from statewide figures. This convention was—once the hero arrived—American politics at its most ecstatic, its most celebratory. Vallandigham didn't storm the convention immediately upon reaching town, but was taken to a farm house a couple of miles outside of town. From there he messaged his nephew John McMahon (of his wife's family), who had studied law under Vallandigham and practiced with him and was now a Democratic activist (and future congressman). The message said Vallandigham would speak at 3 p.m. that day, the 15th. The mere reading aloud of that note at the convention, was noted as follows by the next day's *Empire*: "Such a scene we never witnessed before. It was an imposing sight. The whole crowd joined in one prolonged, furious and overwhelming yell that lasted several minutes."[3]

Vallandigham was immediately made a delegate to Chicago, even before his appearance. When he made his entrance, his greeting caused the *Empire* to forget the preceding election. The paper said, "The hold that Mr. Vallandigham has upon the popular heart is a very striking and wonderful fact. It was never better demonstrated than yesterday."

It wasn't just the *Empire*. The Republican Cincinnati *Commercial* reported the moment "when suddenly Vallandigham appeared and was escorted to the platform. Men rubbed their eyes to be assured they were not dreaming and then broke out into one universal yell, indefinitely prolonged. There he was indeed, and in truth, with the old sardonic grin and the glistening teeth, but fatter and heartier than ever, and looking as though martyrdom agreed with him."[4]

Vallandigham did not deliver one of his stem-winders, but spoke for about twenty minutes about himself primarily, and his story. The war was not present in his speech, except as backdrop. The election of 1863 was certainly not present. The issue was his arrest and his behavior before and after. He didn't precisely explain the timing of his return, just said he was back because he hadn't done anything wrong, that he was willing to face any civilian court, that Order 38 was discredited and defunct, and that he had a constitutional right to be back. He said that no "public man" (politician) had been arrested since his arrest and no newspaper in a loyal state had been shut down. He said "hundreds" of other critics of the administration had gone much farther than he had in denunciation of Lincoln and the war, even to the point of supporting "Southern independence." And he said he was unwilling to be the only one punished.

So he had come a long way from speaking of a "reign of terror" to saying "Why single me out?" His portrayal of the civil liberties situation represented a complete rejection of his campaign letter from Canada in which he had said that Lincoln's newly sweeping suspension of *habeas corpus* was proof that dictatorship had arrived.

Vallandigham rehashed the debate about his alleged encouragement of desertion, non-volunteering and resistance to the draft. He re-embraced every word of the speech that got him arrested. He emphasized his commitment to peaceful, ballot-box means of political combat. He attempted to muddy up his call for reprisals, saying violence should never be initiated by Democrats, but only used in self-defense. He also made his pitch on secret or "oath-bound" political societies: The times were special and "when bad men combine, good men must associate," a quotation from Burke so widely known he didn't have to credit it.[5]

Vallandigham then left quickly for Dayton. The *Commercial* described his arrival there in a long piece that, like its piece from Hamilton, showed up in the Chicago *Tribune*[6] and elsewhere. The piece described first a mob scene at the train station in

Hamilton. And it described the surrounding of Vallandigham's house by curious and insistent spectators (also alluded to in the *Empire*). The *Commercial* said that, as the news of Vallandigham's return spread, "men came running from all quarters of the village" of Dayton.

The piece was notable mainly for its many insults of Irish-Americans. Republican partisans often presented them as Copperheads and, indeed, as typical of the Copperheads. From the story: "One red-faced Irish man, with a bulbous nose and extraordinary shock of hair coming down to his eyebrows, concealing a villainously low forehead…." "Among them was a carroty haired individual, with a vacant sort of face and expressionless, blueish-gray eyes, which were temporarily burnished up by the excitement and much whisky." "An excited Irishman, who probably came to this country in rags and managed to remain in them ever since…." Much of the piece was in Irish dialect.

***

When Vallandigham arrived in Chicago, the McClellan people were expecting victory not only in Chicago but against Lincoln. But McClellan man S.L.M. Barlow told his candidate, "Vallandigham's advent will, I fear, give serious trouble." Barlow was McClellan's political mentor and was at the heart of his presidential campaign, all the more so because McClellan himself was nurturing the lie that he wasn't pursuing the job.[7] Barlow—part owner of the New York *World*, a major Democratic voice—saw McClellan as the magical candidate: the only Democrat who was popular with the troops.[8] Meanwhile, McClellan's uniform legitimized Democratic criticism of aspects of the war effort.

The McClellan people made no effort to shape the convention in his ideological image. His advisers feared that the Peace Democrats might break off if treated too harshly, a fear that Vallandigham encouraged. The Copperheads were not to be denied. Said one delegate who supported McClellan, "Ohio is the worst of all. Her peace men are rampant and, for peace men, most bloodthirsty."

Vallandigham didn't get in Chicago a welcome like in Hamilton. He had to compete with a lot of other big names. But once there, he was big. Joseph Waugh, in his book *Reelecting Lincoln: The Battle for the 1864 Presidency*: "The prince of the copperheads … had made a stunning comeback.… He was not only now wandering about unmuzzled, but … the center of attention."[9] "The Great Banished," as *The New York Times* called Vallandigham,[10] spoke all over town. He left his doors at the Sherman House unlocked, and his rooms became the "informal headquarters for the avowed peace men," with people wandering in and out past midnight.[11]

Among the visitors were some potential embarrassments: a group of Confederates who had been in Canada and another group, perhaps 60 strong, who had escaped from Northern prisons. They, along with some Northerners, had plans to spark a Copperhead uprising that would result in freeing more rebel prisoners from Camp Douglas in Chicago. The plan fell apart in chaos.[12] Any embarrassment that might have accrued to Vallandigham also failed to materialize in the rush of convention events.

Vallandigham had a full-blown convention plan, honed over months in angry isolation in Canada. It did not include giving a speech. Indeed, he declined an opportunity.[13] Perhaps he knew that too many Lincolnian eyes would be upon him in such an endeavor, forcing him either to soften his tone from 1863 or risk a fuss over his legal status that could interfere with his plan. Not making a speech must have been a physically painful decision for a man who, no doubt, had imagined himself giving a high-profile speech to a Democratic national convention since he had started shaving.

His first step was getting a spot on the committee that would shape the party's platform, sometimes known as the Resolutions Committee. That turned out to be no problem. The McClellan people just weren't fighting this kind of fight.

Meanwhile, Vallandigham's very presence was shaping events in the main hall. The president of the convention was New York Gov. Horatio Seymour, the person most often named as an alternative to McClellan should the front-runner's campaign stall. He straddled the fence between War and Peace Democrats. He had the opportunity to make a good impression with his welcoming speech. But Republican journalist Noah Brooks reported that, "calm and cool, (it) was not well received by the crowd." He meant the spectators, not delegates. They "wanted something more fiery and traitorous; accordingly, 'Vallandigham!' 'Vallandigham!' was the cry—but Val had the discretion to keep still, though I saw his eyes shine with the light of his triumph over his war friends about him." Seymour was reduced to telling the spectators that they were not an official part of the convention. "No sooner was he done speaking than more yells and calls for Vallandigham broke forth."[14]

The McClellan people knew this was a bad sign. Campaign manager and party Chairman August Belmont wrote, "The Vallandigham spirit is rampant & his being placed on the Comm of Resolutions will give trouble."[15] The McClellan people did put up a fight when Vallandigham sought the chairmanship of the committee. James Guthrie, a former treasury secretary, was their candidate. An old friend of Belmont, Guthrie won the job, but only by 13–11, another sign of trouble.[16] Then Vallandigham emerged naturally and without contention as the leader of the Copperheads on the committee.

The committee bogged down in dispute. When it came time to offer the convention a platform, there was none. The chairman, from the podium, asked the convention for another day, and got it. By this time, a subcommittee had been appointed to draft the words, and Vallandigham was on it, too. Even the new deadline had to be extended a bit, but the committee did finally report. The platform it offered was Vallandigham's baby. Nobody doubted that, though he might have made a compromise or two.

The entire platform was 512 words long.[17] That, in itself, was remarkable given this: The Congress elected in 1860 was historic for reasons that went well beyond the war. It expanded the scope of the bare-bones federal government dramatically. It passed the first Homestead Act, which offered people federal land to farm on, encouraging western migration. It passed the historic Land Grant College Act, giving states free land on which to build colleges that were to become central to American education. It authorized various forms of federal involvement in the effort to get railroad lines extended from the Midwest to the West Coast. It created the Agriculture

Department. All of this happened partly because the Southern states had left, dramatically thinning conservative and Democratic ranks. The 1861–62 Congress was the most momentous until the New Deal.

Still, in 1864 the Resolutions Committee decided there was no issue worth addressing other than the war and war-related policies. The committee offered six resolutions. One embraced union. One complained of the loss of civil liberties. The last one supported the troops. One—to be known as the Second Resolution—waxed on the war as follows:

> Resolved, That this convention does explicitly declare … that after four years of failure to restore the Union by the experiment of war, during which, under the pretense of a military necessity of war-power higher than the Constitution, the Constitution itself has been disregarded in every part, (we) demand that immediate efforts be made for a cessation of hostilities, with a view of an ultimate convention of the States, or other peaceable means, to the end that, at the earliest practicable moment, peace may be restored on the basis of the Federal Union of the States."

In other words, the North's pursuit should not be military victory, because the experimental pursuit of victory had failed. And the plank did not demand reunification, just made it a goal of some sort of negotiations.

Republican partisan Brooks at the convention: "The second resolution … was greeted with most vociferous applause, outsiders and delegates cheering, roaring, and hallooing, like mad men for the space of five minutes." Congressman Cox—a McClellan man—"looked black and sad, but (Fernando) Wood and Vallandigham rubbed their hands gleefully as though they rejoiced at their work, as well they might."[18] They literally rubbed their hands? Maybe not.

The Resolutions were not even debated on the floor, but simply adopted in full.

The crucial plank didn't go as far as Vallandigham's call in 1863 for an immediate armistice with Northern withdrawal. Perhaps he gave that up in negotiations. But it demanded nothing from the South before negotiations began. It ignored the notion—embraced by War Democrats—that the war was a necessary response to secession. It had the Democrats implying that the reason for the war was that the North wouldn't negotiate. The plank was simply the Copperheads claiming to have been right all along.

A battle over that plank on the floor of the convention might have been one of the great convention battles ever. But the McClellan people didn't want the fight. The previous Democratic National Convention had torn the party apart over policy. In a plea for unity at Chicago, Belmont played to the widespread sense that Democratic disunity had elected Lincoln (a dubious notion). He believed that unity must be the top priority, after nominating McClellan. Belmont might have believed that Copperhead passions were heightened by the nomination of McClellan, a view buttressed by the eventual nomination of Cincinnati's George Pendleton for vice president, a move that appalled the McClellan team. Brooks wrote that "it (is) well understood that McClellan will go on any platform which is put up for him."[19]

Just before the convention, Lincoln had told Brooks, "They must nominate a Peace Democrat on a war platform, or a War Democrat on a peace platform." In

MARVELOUS EQUESTRIAN PERFORMANCE ON TWO ANIMALS.
By the celebrated Artist, Professor GEORGE B. MAC, assisted by the noted Bare-back Rider, GEORGE H. PENDLETON, on his Wonderful Disunion Steed, PEACEATANYPRICE.
N. B. *The beautiful creature*, PEACEATANYPRICE, *recently imported from Europe, was sired by* JOHN BULL, *and dam'd by* AMERICA.

© 2001 HARPWEEK®

When George McClellan—officially a "War Democrat"—won the Democratic presidential nomination with a "Peace Democrat" running mate and with Vallandigham much in the picture, this cartoon—and many similar ones—resulted. This is from *Harper's Weekly*.

other words, whichever side expected to lose the nomination must be placated by the platform.[20]

***

There was more to the second resolution than the failure clause. The term "Federal Union of the States" at the end was about state rights. Republicans used the simpler term "Union." In a speech in Dayton days after the convention, Vallandigham laid that out. He said the platform had "one great object: the reconstruction of the … old federal union, … delegating certain powers to the common agent and withholding from it those not delegated."[21] In his mind, the word "federal" was in italics.

He was not just saying, "Let's observe state rights from now on." He knew that no words along those lines would convince the South to rejoin. He was, as with his proposal for a four-section country, trying to go beyond words. He clearly had in mind—again—new constitutional constraints on Washington's power that would assuage the South. Not only would they assuage the South, though. They would create the kind of weak confederacy he always would have preferred anyway. So he would be turning this war he called "the root of all evil" (in that same Dayton speech) to his long-term ideological purposes. Again, he was making no small plans.

His "federal union" phrase didn't get much attention in Chicago. In Dayton, Vallandigham was trying to get it some attention. But that effort was swamped by events.

***

In Chicago after the McClellan nomination, Vallandigham had taken to the podium to move that the nomination be made unanimous. That gesture was something the McClellan people passionately wanted.

It was a heady time for Vallandigham. He was seeing himself as President McClellan's link to the Copperheads at a time when Copperhead views seemed to have taken over the mainstream of the party. And that party was expected to win the presidency. It was a remarkable comeback for the Copperheads from a time when Tom Lowe concluded that the debacle of the 1863 election in Ohio.

Just then—literally just as the Democrats were leaving the convention in which they declared the war "experiment" had failed—Atlanta was falling to Gen. William Tecumseh Sherman and his men, an event widely seen as the beginning of the end. Even before the convention, Union Admiral David Farragut had taken Mobile Bay in Alabama. That was a major piece of good war news the Democrats had shrugged off. But now there could be no shrugging. Now the Democrats' talk of immediate cessation of hostilities seemed absurd to anybody who was not already a card-carrying Copperhead. Why would you pursue negotiations if you were about to win? Sherman had taken Vallandigham, too.

McClellan had not accepted the nomination immediately. The country waited to see how he would do that. If the McClellan people had once thought they could accept any platform, some were now thinking, well, not *any*. Even absent the Sherman/Atlanta factor, McClellan would not have liked the Vallandigham platform, the notion that the war he had fought in was a mere experiment and must be abandoned. Now his main supporters bombarded him with the public suggestion that he renounce the platform. Hearing that, Vallandigham wrote him, "For Heaven's sake, hear the words of one who has now nothing so much at heart as your success. Do not listen to any of your Eastern friends who, in an evil hour, may advise you to *insinuate* even a little war"—that is, support for the war—"into your letter of acceptance (lest) two hundred thousand men in the West ... withdraw their support & (perhaps) go further still,"[22] supporting another candidate (perhaps Vallandigham?). Vallandigham was demanding an all-out Peace Democrat statement from the War Democrat.

McClellan agonized through six drafts of an acceptance letter. He rejected Vallandigham's input. Most importantly, he set reunification as "condition of peace," not a goal of negotiations. And he wrote, "I could not look in the face of my gallant comrades of the army and navy who have survived so many bloody battles, and tell them that their labors and the sacrifices of so many of our slain and wounded brethren had been in vain."[23] That was taken—and was meant—as a separation of himself from "failure."

Vallandigham's great victory was undone. He did not deny it. He could not. In his speech in Dayton—after the convention, but before McClellan's letter—he had said that the platform "means now that there shall be no more Civil War in the land." McClellan was definitely not saying that.

The Dayton speech had been mainly a celebration of Vallandigham's role in Chicago. He said that he had originally opposed McClellan "only because (McClellan) was supposed to be" a supporter of the war. He said, "Divested of that, there is not a man in America more fit for the choice." Vallandigham was taking credit for the divestiture, with the passage of the platform. He had converted McClellan! The convention had *not* nominated a War Democrat. Vallandigham said that "no man among the earnest advocates for peace … has … demanded more than the convention has declared." Mission accomplished.

And he said this: "That General McClellan will accept the nomination with the platform, and that these policies shall govern his administration, I have no doubt."

It is difficult to avoid the impression that Vallandigham had thought, once he got a spot on the platform committee, he was going to run the world. What's remarkable is how far he got. He got himself sent to Chicago; he won an assignment to the committee and the subcommittee; he shepherded his inspiration through the committee—hardly scathed—and through the convention, not even debated. He had read the convention correctly, even from Canada, long before the convention.

Perhaps he couldn't imagine the nominee rejecting a platform. It hadn't happened before in American history. Perhaps Vallandigham thought that if any candidate could be manipulated, it would be a military man who was probably more interested in the honor of being president than really vested in any policy cause. Flatter him personally—as Vallandigham did, egregiously—and he'd be manipulable. Get the platform adopted and it would become a force in itself.

Once again—as with his rewrite of the Constitution and more—a plan he had painstakingly, cleverly and creatively worked out on paper hadn't quite worked out in reality. He might have had too much time on his hands in Canada.

When Vallandigham was when stripped of his great vindication, he blew up. He was said to have engaged in some "tall cussing," not a characteristic widely associated with him. So said Rep. Cox. Vallandigham also cancelled his many scheduled campaign speaking engagements for McClellan and threatened to remain mum.[24] That could be a problem for McClellan with Copperhead voters. There followed much fuss. Though some people thought the Democrats would do better without Vallandigham, others made efforts to get him back on the team. Pendleton paid a visit to Dayton and stayed at Vallandigham's home, and all became rosey.[25] Eventually, Vallandigham did get back on the hustings, presumably to save himself a place in the McClellan administration, and to make sure he didn't get blamed for a possible defeat. Meanwhile, though, McClellan was telling friends that "I intend to destroy any and all pretense for any possible association of my name to the Peace Party."[26]

The Republicans were doing everything they could to tie McClellan to Vallandigham. A poster appeared that, at first glance, seemed to be circulated by the Democrats. It listed their candidates for national offices. But it listed Vallandigham for secretary of war. Further down, the poster made clear that it was the work of Republicans. They were out to sell the notion that the Democrats had been "Vallandighamized."

Unmistakably, Vallandigham had set back the Democrat's cause. And he had done so recklessly. Rather than try to work something out with the McClellan forces, he had forged full-speed ahead on his own. He achieved what has been called "one of the most notorious planks in all of U.S. history."[27] He left his party's candidate with no good options. McClellan looked bad for failing to assert a firm hand in the convention, for agonizing afterward, and for coming up with an uninspiring acceptance letter. He appeared as uninspired in politics as Lincoln and the Radical Republicans found him in war. That said, Vallandigham certainly did not cost McClellan the election. The Union army and navy deserve most of the credit for that.

In the 1864 presidential campaign, this poster announced that if the Democrats won, Vallandigham would be secretary of war. It was put out by the Republicans.

The most important charge to be made against Vallandigham is this: If he had had his way—if the scheme he concocted in Canada had worked out, "Federal Union" and all—the result of the Civil War would have been, not to end slavery, but to guarantee its survival under a dramatically different form of government. The plan was grand: The McClellan administration and the Confederacy would negotiate a Vallandigham rewrite of the Constitution. Nothing else would achieve reunification without victory. Perhaps Vallandigham himself would be the negotiator, him being the Southerners' favorite Northerner. He was seeing himself—again—as a new Founder, one who would make sure the job got done right this time.

Delusional or not, it really was a nice try.

***

The outcome of the 1864 presidential election demonstrated—again—the absurdity of the Vallandigham notion that the Republicans were mainly an Eastern phenomenon. Ohio, Illinois, Indiana and Wisconsin all came in for Lincoln a little better than New York, Pennsylvania and Connecticut. Indeed, the biggest margin in any of those states was in Vallandigham's Ohio, at 56.4 percent. And only in the East did Lincoln lose a non-slave state: New Jersey.

Overall, Lincoln won 90 percent of the Electoral College votes with 55 percent of the popular vote. That's an indication that his edge over McClellan was widespread, not concentrated. In other words, however else the electorate may have been divided—along ethnic, economic, urban-rural or other lines—it did NOT divide on regional lines. In truth, Lincoln's showing in the popular vote was not particularly impressive *except* as to its geographic breadth. Vallandigham simply had the East-West thing all wrong.

True, there was one big regional divide among the free states: New England was different from everyplace. Lincoln dominated it, coming in at over 70 percent in Massachusetts and Vermont, over 60 in Rhode Island and 59 in Maine.

Lincoln also utterly dominated in a non-geographic category: the soldier vote. He got 78 percent of those voting in camp, though the camp vote was not decisive in any state.[28] The numbers shocked McClellan's supporters. They thought their candidate's moderation would allow troops who had gone into the military as Democrats to stick with their party. Jonathan W. White, who "wrote the book" on the soldier vote, said the 78-percent figure is misleading if it conjures up an army dominated by gung-ho Lincoln worshippers. He suggested that the troops might have liked McClellan a lot more if not for the Copperhead convention and Vallandigham's support.[29]

18

After the War

On March 4, 1865, Lincoln was inaugurated for the second time. He gave one of his most remembered speeches: "With malice toward none; with charity for all…." It was not universally well received at the time, some finding it murky, excessively religious in attempting to explain the war, lacking in substance and too short. The New York *News* called it "loose and disjointed." The Detroit *Free Press* said, "It contains not a single fact, result or prediction. It is chiefly made up of a short moral lecture on the impropriety of both sides appealing to the Almighty for the justice of their cause…. His speech is more worthy of a puritanical hypocrite, than of an American Executive."[1]

On the same day, of course, Andrew Johnson was inaugurated as vice president. He was drunk. He was not considered *a* drunk, but on this day, perhaps fighting jitters and/or nursing some illness with liquor, and maybe doing both on an empty stomach, he gave an obnoxious speech universally understood to be the product of alcohol. That was a tough act for Lincoln to compete with for attention.

In the wake of the inauguration, the New York *World*—very much involved in the McClellan campaign—ran the following little editorial on it; the reference to "John Brown's Hymn," is to early versions of the "Battle Hymn of the Republic," which also connected God to the war.

> It is with a blush of shame and wounded pride, as American citizens, that we lay before our readers today the inaugural addresses of President Lincoln and Vice President Johnson….
>
> 'The pity of it, the pity of it,' that this dividing, suffering nation should neither be sustained in this crisis of its agony by words of wisdom, nor cheered by words of hope, but mocked in the calamity by a prose parody of 'John Brown's Hymn' from the lips of its chosen Chief Magistrate.
>
> 'The pity of it, the pity of it,' that the life of the Chief Magistrate should be made precious to us by the thought that he at least excludes from the most august station in the land the man who defiled our chief counsel chamber Saturday with the spewings of a drunken boor.

The Dayton *Empire*—for whom the out-of-office Vallandigham was now writing—reprinted that editorial on March 11, with a little editorial note of its own underneath, in the style of the day:

> "We don't see wherein even Andy Johnson makes the life of Lincoln 'precious.' If Mr. Lincoln sees fit to die, we will cheerfully risk the results, whatever they may be. We hope that we have not herein committed treason by 'imagining the death of the King.'"

The paper—so furious about words it interpreted as implicitly calling for violence against it—didn't call explicitly for an assassination; it only welcomed a possible act of God. That was five weeks before the assassination.

***

By the end of 1864, Vallandigham was back at the practice of law in Dayton. The *Empire* ran an ad for his legal services prominently on Page One every day. Such advertising in newspapers was common for lawyers, as was the good placement. Tom Lowe—having returned from Europe—was advertising the same way. Vallandigham presumably got his space for free, and maybe Lowe did, too. Vallandigham set up shop in his home, his ad said, at least for the time being. He declined to replace or repair the front door which Burnside's troops had tried to break through. He clearly wanted the house—and his office—to be a shrine for Copperheads, a reminder of what he had sacrificed. The door was to be a reminder that visitors were entering a historic site. (At the end of 1865, however, he wrote to a friend that he was moving into the "Opera House," which he said was "the only office space left now to us 'copperheads.'" It seems to have been a reference to a new building.[2])

Meanwhile, however, his great interest continued to be politics, not the law. He was writing for the *Empire*. He did not sign his pieces, but his authorship was often obvious because he was a better writer than the brothers Hubbard. Also, he would write about himself—in the third person—with a degree of authority that no other writer could have assumed. He probably did not write the piece that said the paper would welcome Lincoln's death. Not his style. It has a Hubbard quality.

However, when Lincoln was assassinated, Vallandigham went to writerly work. In taking up his pen, he was not going to mention that earlier piece. He plowed ahead as if had never happened. He wrote a striking conventional expression of the national mood. He hadn't been caught up the post–Fort Sumter moment of national unity, but he was caught up in this one, or seemed to be.

The headline: "A Great Public Calamity."[3] "Last night was a night of horror in Washington. President Lincoln perished by the hand of an assassin. At any time, this would have been monstrous—inexpressibly horrible. Just now, it is the worst public calamity which could have befallen the country. Great God! Have mercy upon us! This is the beginning of evils. The hearts and hopes of all men—even of those who had opposed his policy earliest and strongest—had begun to turn toward Abraham Lincoln for deliverance at last. And not without reason; for his course for the last three months has been most liberal and conciliatory." Three months. Not five weeks or less, the time since the editorial welcoming his potential death.

With the war over, the great issue was Reconstruction, the task of putting the nation back together. Some people—mainly Radical Republicans, the dominant wing of the dominant party—were focused on assuring basic rights for southern blacks even at some federal expense and trouble, and they were deeply skeptical of southern whites. On the other hand, people who had always sympathized with or identified with southern whites still did. Lincoln was staking out what might be called a moderate position. He was for "malice toward none." The *Empire* might have liked the sound of that, but, of course, it knew about that line when it welcomed his possible death. After all, he was also toying with the possibility of suffrage for some southern blacks, and he was determined about emancipation, which the paper still opposed.

In the *Empire* after the assassination, a piece adjacent to Vallandigham's said "we" were prepared to approve Lincoln's Reconstruction plan, if not "in all its detail."

The piece did acknowledge "we had always opposed him before." It did not acknowledge getting carried away with that.

In truth, though, neither Vallandigham nor anybody else had put softer thoughts about Lincoln in the *Empire* in the months before the assassination. The castigation was relentless to the end. In February, for example, the *Empire* was outraged about the Lincoln-inspired passage through Congress of the Thirteenth Amendment to the Constitution, banning slavery. The paper was holding out for "the Constitution as it was." In a tone of scandal, it printed the names of the congressional Democrats who voted for the amendment: "The Black Record. The treacherous Democrats ... the men who sold themselves to the Abolition enemy for *greenbacks* are as follows." On March 15, eleven days after the inauguration, the *Empire* approvingly repeated a suggestion by another newspaper that Lincoln be impeached.

There was one sense in which the paper cast Lincoln as a relative good guy, but only on the basis of a story it made up and that misrepresented him. As Grant moved toward final victory over Lee, the *Empire* literally couldn't believe it. On the day before the surrender at Appomattox—at a time when many other newspaper were saying victory was immediately in sight—it wrote, "It is evident that General Lee, with the great mass of his army and nearly all his *materiel,* has made good his retreat in the direction of Danville, to take up the new home of defenses long ago marked out and prepared, thus to protract the war indefinitely."[4] Elsewhere on that day it wrote satirically, "Yesterday for the fourth time we captured General Lee and his whole army, thereby crushing the rebellion at one blow." That piece said, "We expect more battles, more victories, more defeats, more taxation, more drafts." That had been the tone through much of the spring. At one stage, the paper was at war with correspondents of the Associated Press who were reporting good military news (in the *Empire*). The paper said the reporters were "without integrity, decency, moderation, sobriety," and they offered a "persistent stream of stupidity, inconsistency and falsehood."[5] In the last month of the war, the *Empire* would sometimes run a snide, parenthetical comment after a news snippet from the wires. If a reporter predicted a battle at a certain spot, the paper would say, "*He* knows just the spot."[6]

Through early 1865, the *Empire* proceeded on the premise that its readers were more interested in stories about how Northern Democrats were being victimized by Republicans than in war news. When a minister in a nearby county lost his job, the *Empire* attributed that to his being a Democrat.[7]

When the end of the war came, the paper insisted that it wasn't a simple military victory. The paper—desperately searching for an explanation of events that would allow it to save some face—was at pains to pretend that the leniency of Lincoln and Grant toward Southern troops was the result of a negotiated settlement.[8] It tried to argue that—finally!—the Lincoln administration and, mainly, the generals had come around to the Copperhead point of view on negotiations.

"Peace negotiations have been going on for some time," the *Empire* lied on the day after Lee's surrender. "If Mr. Lincoln, *casting off the radical, belligerent and blood-thirsty Abolitionists* ... will begin in earnest the work of peace and settlement ... we should see an end to the war during the summer." It said, "let negotiations ... begin" about the negotiations it said were going on. On the same day, it said, "Let secessionism and abolitionism go down together in one grave."[9] In other words, no emancipation.

So, yes, at this stage the paper was saying relatively nice things about "Lincoln." But it wasn't the real Lincoln. And the subject wasn't Reconstruction. Finally, though, in the few days before Lincoln's death, the subject turned to Reconstruction, briefly. On April 13—two days before the assassination—the *Empire* ran a piece from *The Age* newspaper in Philadelphia saying, "The President's reconstruction speech is denounced by the radicals, with great bitterness in Washington." That was it. The *Empire* wrote nothing itself, nothing in praise of the real Lincoln or any position he took.

Vallandigham was engaged in a whole different project. He was spending a lot of time defending old statements and actions. That was when he was called to testify in Cincinnati about alleged Copperhead subversion. Meanwhile, he responded to a thrust of the Dayton *Journal's* Bickham. The editor couldn't resist pointing out that Vallandigham had promised that if Richmond fell, he would recant his position that war couldn't restore the union. He had said, for example, in 1862, "If (the war effort) is successful in maintaining the Constitution and restoring the Union, I will make full, open, explicit confession that I was wrong, utterly, totally wrong, and will retire to private life the residue of my days."[10]

Vallandigham responded to Bickham in the *Empire* (in an unsigned piece discussing "Vallandigham" in the third person).[11] He said he had never said he'd recant if Richmond fell, but only if, he now said, "the Union as our fathers made it" was restored. (He didn't quote himself as using those words earlier.) Now he insisted that such a union could still only be achieved through negotiation. So he had nothing to recant or to repent of.

Anyway, he said, he was now a private citizen, not somebody "before the public." He also said if he was going to recant, he wouldn't do it in response to Bickham, at least without "some private understanding beforehand." What that meant is unclear. Nothing is known to have come of it.

Meanwhile, Vallandigham was still fighting off "failure," his word about the war in the platform. A week after Appomattox, he wrote, "The Chicago platform *did not* pronounce the war a failure—a military failure. This false quotation has been repeated often enough, and no honest man will so state it again. It did say that for four years the war had *'failed to restore the Union.'* And so it had." But, of course, he had embraced failure as the outcome, a reason to abandon the war. Now he was saying is that he hadn't criticized the military. He didn't address the larger issue: what would have happened if the North had accepted failure before Atlanta fell.

***

In 1865, a new political epoch was forming, and Vallandigham was only 45. He had always worried that people thought he was older than he was. In 1862, he wrote to his wife, "My friends who have never seen me think me an elderly man of large frame and stern aspect, and my enemies something less only than a monster. How little they dream how young I am" (and, he added, how sentimental and given to tears).[12]

Contemplating his future in 1865, he wrote to a friend with unbridled self-pity and self-veneration: "The accumulation of obloquy, persecution & and wrong heaped upon me, & the persistence which they are kept up would assuredly crush any man of less nerve and fortitude than myself," he said. "I have never seen & and do not remember to have read of any thing equal to it. But I still bear it all calmly—bravely, I hope, with an unfaltering trust in a Divine Providence working out justice even here on earth.

"One cause of the ceaseless & embittered crusade which pursues me everywhere … is that in all trials…. I have come off victor, compelling even Lincoln, whom they would now deify, to yield," that is, to let him back in the country. "Had I been conquered & broken down, suing for pardon, they might have been content" to stop the bashing, he wrote.

The letter was to James M. Wall, a newspaperman/politician who had spent two weeks in prison in 1861 on political charges before taking a loyalty oath to get released.[13] Vallandigham wrote of the need to tell the story of their times accurately, and "in the day of account, mete out punishment not, indeed, with blind fury of revenge, but in the spirit of justice, thus guarding the future generations of Americans against tyranny & wrong. I am patient, very patient, & and with our unfaltering faith do 'bide my time.'"[14] That did not mean he was going to sit around and wait for the world to come to him.

The Copperheads refused to dry up and blow away after the war. One can imagine that they might have. They were, after all, associated with opposition to a war that quickly became an honored part of American history. They had been the opponents of people who were now heroes. They were the naysayers who had been proven wrong. But they found ways to continue. Perhaps Exhibit A was George Pendleton, five years younger than Vallandigham. He went into the 1868 Democratic National Convention as the leading candidate for president and was a prospect for that office later. In the 1880s, when in Congress, he had the nation's biggest step toward Civil Service—a central issue in that decade—named after him: the Pendleton Act. Then there was Indiana Rep. Daniel Voorhees, a Copperhead who was to spend 20 years in the U.S. Senate, ending in 1897. The list goes on. Having been against the war was a political problem, but there were ways to deal with it. You could still get mileage out of the racism card. You could make transitions to other issues. You could point to the difficulties of Reconstruction as partial vindication.[15]

Could even Vallandigham survive, this man who had not simply opposed the war, but had been found guilty of undermining it? He certainly thought he could. His dream of holding high office never died. His dream for the country died, of course. First there was the war's outcome. Readers who have come this far can judge for themselves what outcome he had wanted in his heart. Surely, he and his followers would be offended by the suggestion that they did not want the North to win. But at least this much can be said: Any other outcome would have been better for Vallandigham's career: a stalemate and prolonged war, an ongoing guerrilla war, a Southern victory, a negotiated settlement. Anything. And any other outcome would have been less devastating to his worldview.

In the postwar years, things just got worse on that score. The 13th, 14th and 15th Amendments were passed in a few years. They went in exactly the opposite direction from the states' rights approach he wanted and from the amendments he would have proposed and dedicated himself to enacting. Basic rights for black Americans became the law of the land, if not the reality. The revolution he had tried desperately to counter had been enacted by the very people he saw as death to his kind of America, the great enemy he had warned against.

But he saw no reason to withdraw. He remained a national figure. He even bid to make history again.

For a while, he kept his hand in newspaper work. The Dayton *Empire* was sold in 1865 and then was replaced in 1867 by another Democratic paper, the Dayton *Daily Ledger*. Vallandigham had a stake in the latter, and was sometimes referred to as the editor.[16] Under any ownership, the Democratic paper in town continued to be known as Vallandigham's voice. But, as earlier in his life, neither journalism nor the law was enough for him, nor any combination of the two.

His liabilities as a candidate were impressive. He hadn't won an election since 1860, an epoch ago. He was indelibly associated with the spectacular loss of 1863, virtually a laughingstock. The events of the 1864 underlined and increased his problems within his own party. His confident and notorious predictions about the war, slavery and democracy were widely known and utterly discredited. And now the Republicans were stronger than ever, with the war won and Lincoln deified.

Even given all that, it would not have been ludicrous for Vallandigham to think about returning to the House. He was a deity, too, at least in local Democratic circles. But he wasn't thinking about the House. His "life-long aspiration" was the Senate, according to his brother.[17] Sure, he thought about the presidency; that would be natural. But he had come of political age in a time when the smartest, most effective and most renowned politicians were in the Senate—Henry Clay, John C. Calhoun, Daniel Webster, Thomas Hart Benton, Charles Sumner. It's often been called the "Golden Age" of the Senate. These men stayed year after year, whereas presidents came and went quickly. Between 1836 and 1868, no president served two terms. They generally had little impact. Moreover, the Senate was associated with oratory, Vallandigham's thing.

After the whirlwind events from 1862 through 1864, everything mitigated in the direction of Vallandigham taking 1865 off from electoral politics. He needed to make some money. He needed to reestablish his domestic life, having a wife who, at best, did not thrive on all the drama. He did chair the party's state convention that year.[18] And he campaigned for Democrats. The Republicans held the state legislature, but he was hoping the Democrats would take it (they didn't) and elect him to John Sherman's Senate seat the next year.[19]

In 1866, Vallandigham made a foray into national postwar politics and got some national attention. Washington was in turmoil, because racist President Johnson was at dramatic odds with the Radical Republicans who controlled Congress. A call went out for moderates of both parties to meet in Philadelphia with an eye toward buttressing Johnson with a new party. All manner of people went, including Vallandigham, who was probably more interested in monitoring and in being seen than in participating. His presence caused a flap. Many at the convention were appalled. They wanted their effort to be associated only with people of unquestioned loyalty to the union. Vallandigham and Fernando Wood withdrew under pressure.[20] So things were definitely not looking up.

Vallandigham next went for Ben Wade's Senate seat, to be up in 1868 after a legislative election in 1867. Vallandigham threw himself into the legislative races, campaigning for individual candidates as a way to create chits. The task of winning the legislature was decidedly uphill because, after several straight good years, the Republicans now controlled it two-to-one.[21] (The U.S. House delegation from Ohio was 16–3.[22] Nationally, the Republicans held 78 percent of U.S. House seats, their highest point ever, before or since.)

But 1867 was a different kind of year. For one major thing, the ballot included a measure to grant blacks the right to vote in Ohio. It had been placed there by the Republican or Unionist legislature. (During the shaping of the measure, that is, during the discussion of who should be allowed to vote, one proposal was to ban from voting anybody who had voted for Vallandigham in 1863.) Why would the Republicans want this ballot measure, given the rampant racism of the time? One reason was, of course, the honest belief that this was the right thing to do, especially given the contribution of black troops to victory. Another was that black suffrage in the South was a major issue in the Reconstruction debate. The Republicans were for it, but that made the absence of black suffrage in Ohio and other Northern states awkward for them. Another: the Republicans were getting cocky, having done so well in recent elections; they thought they could take a political chance. Also, the Republicans assumed that enfranchised blacks would generally vote Republican, though, really, there were few blacks in Ohio, maybe 1 percent of the population.

One case being made for black suffrage is striking: Some Republicans believed that if blacks were given the right to vote, that would eliminate race from American political debate, thus eliminating a Democratic advantage. The editor of the Cincinnati *Gazette* wrote, "Give the negro the right to vote and … the Democratic party will die. It has lived on negro agitation for thirty-five years and it cannot live without it."[23] In the campaign, some Democrats did everything they could to live up to the charge. The Cincinnati *Enquirer*, in publishing its party's ticket every day, in the style of the time, headed the ticket with: "WHITE MEN'S DEMOCRATIC STATE TICKET."[24]

Black suffrage proposals were on the ballot in four states that year and lost in all. In Ohio, the measure did get 46 percent of the vote; it did much worse in the southern part of the state. It did best where the Republicans were at their strongest. That it got almost half the votes may have been more of a testament to partisanship than racial enlightenment. Voters were told repeatedly by Republican spokesmen that suffrage did *not* mean social and legal equality for blacks.[25]

Black suffrage wasn't the only issue working for the Democrats in 1867. The economy had turned into a postwar recession. And people were having great qualms about the costs of Reconstruction and about the commitment of a Republican-dominated Congress to a hard line with southern whites. For many in the North, securing equal treatment for southern blacks was not a high priority, not a task for the federal government. Meanwhile, the Republicans were in disarray, with many having turned against President Johnson.

The Ohio Senate race of 1868 was central to the legislative election of 1867.

That Vallandigham—of all people—wanted to replace Wade—of all people—gave the race special color and made it a national event. Wade was *everything* that Vallandigham hated, and vice versa. It was as if Bugs Bunny wanted to replace Elmer Fudd as sheriff. Moreover, partly because of the possible impeachment of Andrew Johnson, Wade was a bigger national figure than Vallandigham. As president pro-tempore of the Senate, Wade would become president if Johnson were removed, because there was no vice president. The Radical Republicans had put him in that position with that eventuality in mind. Whether he won or lost his re-election bid, Wade would be in the Senate during impeachment, though possibly as a lame-duck. Some people suggest that, as things turned out, Wade was the reason Johnson wasn't removed from office. After Wade's elevation to president pro-tempore, Lincoln's ascendancy to sainthood had continued.

With a combination of views unusually like those of a modern liberal, Ohio U.S. Sen. Benjamin Franklin Wade was convinced Vallandigham was disloyal (Library of Congress, attributed to photographer Julian Vannerson).

Some Republicans came to wonder about the wisdom of elevating a harsh critic of their saint. Said Wade's biographer, "Many Republicans preferred Johnson with all his faults to the man who was slated to succeed him."[26]

In 1867, Wade supported the black suffrage initiative. He had always been for the idea. Said his 1963 biographer, H.L. Trefousse: "Had the Senator played down the racial issue ... he might possibly have had a chance" to elect enough legislators to gain re-election. "But ... he launched an all-out assault on racism.... 'I say to you ... you cannot prevent the right of suffrage to the negro,' he avowed.... '(Y)ou have got to bear it, and you may as well take it with a good grace as any other way.' It was not a very orthodox way of wooing voters. Republican prospects looked less promising every day."[27]

Vallandigham had his best issue ever. He "visited every section of the State and addressed between seventy and eighty meetings," wrote his brother.[28] As a result of his visibility, the Republicans tried to make him an issue, tying the Democratic legislative candidates to him. Didn't work. The Democrats took the legislature by margins of 56–49 and 18–17.[29] Vallandigham declared personal vindication, arguing that the notion of him as political poison was now officially dead.

He spoke at two "jollifications" after the election. For him, these were campaign speeches, with the Senate race still to be decided by the legislative Democrats. A correspondent for the Cincinnati *Commercial*, a Mr. McCulloch, said Vallandigham was the object of "hero worship" at these events and that those present "conducted themselves ... like so many lunatics."[30]

Vallandigham was back. One event was at Mount Vernon, site of the speech that got him arrested. He gave a new speech—call it Mount Vernon II—that could live in the history of campaign oratory. For chutzpah, for breathtaking spin, for self-congratulation, for emotional fervor and for his passionate determination to have *everything* exactly as he wanted it, it is a prize-deserving classic.

It was, for starters, oddly violent. In referring back to his previous visit to Mount Vernon, he got applause by referring to "the spies and hirelings of him whose name I loathe to utter" (Burnside). He said those spies "tainted the air of heaven with their foul presence (and) did a work of infamy without example in military annals. They did it in secrecy.... Had they been known, and their mission understood, the scattered members of their worthless carcasses (applause) ... would have strewed the ground, a prey to lean dogs and hungry vultures, ... if vulture and dog could consent to crunch and mumble and feed upon such flesh as theirs. (Applause.)"

These lines were about army officers who had been following orders and just taking notes about what he said. The words are so bloodthirsty that one might reasonably doubt if he actually said them. But the text comes from his worshipful brother, whose book provides the parenthetical "applause" additions.[31] James Vallandigham took the text from the *Commercial*, where it appeared without eliciting any apparent denial from Clement.

Vallandigham referred to Burnside as "the 'Butcher of Fredericksburg,' writhing and infuriate under defeat (who) had just been deputed to extinguish the last lingering spark of liberty in the Northwest." So, no longer did Vallandigham express the kind of respect for Burnside that reporter Furay said he expressed at Murfreesboro. Still, Vallandigham made clear that he saw the real villain as, not Burnside, but Lincoln. So much for notion that he had mellowed toward Lincoln.

Vallandigham then assigned himself a role in American history. He referred to "this spot, sacred thenceforth and forever to liberty." That spot at Mount Vernon. Because he had spoken there and been arrested for it. Sacred.

But he was still building to his point. "Your assembling"—in 1863, he meant—"was an act of courage unsurpassed in history." This rhetoric is boggling. He's talking about a literal *picnic* that took place roughly during Chancellorsville and a couple of months before Gettysburg.

But, of course, he wasn't really talking about the picnickers. He was the one whose courage was "unsurpassed in history." He said, "Not Grecian, nor Roman, nor Swiss, nor English heroism ever excelled" the courage shown that day in central Ohio. "You demanded that I should speak in your name, and I obeyed, hurling defiance at tyrants." His point was that he was the candidate who had earned the Senate seat, the one who had fought for the party hardest and paid the greatest price. "I declared the war 'cruel and unnecessary' and it was. So had said Abraham Lincoln. (I said it was) 'not waged for the preservation of the union,' and it was not, but for the purpose of crushing out liberty and establishing a despotism ... and who today doubts it?" He seemed to be talking about federal Reconstruction efforts as despotism. "(I called it) 'a war for the freedom of blacks'; so it was, and this is now the boast of the leaders of the Republican party. (I called it) 'a war for the enslavement of the whites,' and today the wailing cry of six millions of white men (in the South), disfranchised, burdened, oppressed, bruised, and crushed under the heel of a military despotism, ... attests the prescient truth" of that.

He was warming up. He quoted himself as having said at Mount Vernon I that he was "resolved to ... defeat the attempts ... to build up a monarchy." And he asked, "Was ever a prophecy so fulfilled?," meaning was ever anybody so successful. "There is no war in the land today," he continued, "no military despots here, no arbitrary arrests, no military trials, no 'orders' of whatsoever number, no provost-marshal, ... no conscriptions, no bastilles, no mobs, no assassinations, no exile, no scaffolds. (Applause.) There are no spies here today to pollute this sacred presence. In peace, ... with joy welling from every heart ... we are assembled to celebrate the grandest political triumph ever achieved. (Applause.)"

That "grandest political triumph ever" was the election of 1867, that is, the election of a Democratic legislature in Ohio. The Democrats had lost the race for governor to Rutherford B. Hayes. No matter; Vallandigham hadn't been involved in that one.

So, incredibly, he wanted credit for predicting the enslavement of the South (though he hadn't specifically done that), preventing the enslavement of the North and winning the "grandest political triumph ever."

He had decided that the way to deal with being discredited was not to minimize or excuse failures, but to pretend they were monumental successes. If he could have made the case that "tyranny" was still a threat or a reality in the North, he would have said, "I told you so." With that issue absent, he said, "You're welcome." There was nothing he couldn't spin.

But it didn't necessarily work. He was not made a senator the next year. The fight was, by some measures, epic. According to James Vallandigham, "Nearly all the Democratic politicians of the state were enlisted" in the lobbying of legislators. Vallandigham's opponent was Judge Allen G. Thurman, who had just lost the governorship race. Wade had said that, between the two Democrats, he preferred "the bold convicted traitor" to the "slimy, miserable tool of traitors." Thurman was the tool.[32] However, Thurman's fellow Democrats felt that he had just run a creditable race. Moreover, he was not Vallandigham.

Thurman won 51–24. Blowout. Vallandigham did not respond well. The whole state became aware that he was furious and sulking. His brother wrote, "It is useless to conceal the fact that Mr. Vallandigham was deeply chagrined.... (H)e felt keenly at the time, and deeply till the day of his death, the disappointment of his defeat. It was the only defeat he ever suffered (and he was not a fortunate politician) that really grieved him, or caused him more than momentary mortification or depression."

Vallandigham declined to attend a reception for Thurman. Wrote Republican journalist Murat Halstead, "He loves and hates with intensity, concentrating his love upon himself and hating all who do not approve or uphold him."[33]

The sulking went on about a month. But even this was not enough to sour him on his political future. He went to the Democratic National Convention in New York in 1868 without being a delegate. Staying away was not going to revive his career.

Pendleton was the choice of the Ohio delegation for president. He had supported Thurman in the Senate race. He was worried about being seen as too close to a man—Vallandigham—whom many eastern Democrats considered a political pariah.[34] The longstanding tension between Vallandigham and Pendleton became a "full-fledged schism." In the run-up to New York, Vallandigham gave lip service to the Pendleton campaign. It would have been bad form for an Ohioan not to. But he did not work for him. On the first ballot, Pendleton led with 105 votes, but he would have needed a little over 200—a two-thirds majority—to win. In second place, with 65 mainly-Southern votes—was President Johnson, returning to his original party. With multiple votes taking place, Pendleton got as high as 156.5. But he faded fast and eventually withdrew. No single issue predominated

At that point, Vallandigham endorsed Salmon P. Chase.

***

Chase!

Chase had first come to public attention as a young anti-slavery activist in Cincinnati. He thought he possessed better anti-slavery credentials than Abraham Lincoln to be the Republican presidential nominee in 1860. In 1864, he had been supported by Radical Republicans in an effort to supplant Lincoln. He had made a trip to Ohio in 1863 to campaign against Vallandigham.[35] He had helped recruit Schenck to run against Vallandigham in 1862, at least according to Schenck, who quoted him as saying, "You are the only one who can beat the traitor Vallandigham."[36]

During the war and before, the idea of a Chase-Vallandigham alliance would have been laughable. But Chase was no one-dimensional ideologue. He was a man of inexhaustible ambition (now seeking the presidency from his perch as chief justice) and the flexibility that accommodates it. He had bounced around among several parties in his time, including the Democrats, to whom he now seemed to be edging back, with, for example, criticism of military rule during Reconstruction.[37] (At the same time, though, he was for universal male suffrage. How to achieve that in the South without federal military enforcement?) And he was associated with criticisms of Lincoln's civil liberties policies.

Partisan as the times were, people didn't see the two parties as immutable or permanent. The parties had been shaped by slavery, the war and the coming of the war; so had political attachments and emotions. But now the issues were starting to change. Who was to say Chase and the Democrats shouldn't try to work something out if Chase found himself shut out of the 1868 Republican nomination by Ulysses Grant's popularity, and if the Democrats could use somebody who was associated with the war effort?

Still, Vallandigham was not that kind of flexible, party-hopping politician. His partisan rigidity had always been matched by his ideological rigidity. So what was up here? Chase?

On June 13, about three weeks before the Democratic convention, the Democratic New York *Herald* printed a paraphrased interview with Vallandigham. Such pieces were not common. This one—appearing even as Pendleton was running—said

Vallandigham said Chase would be a good nominee for the Democrats, better than any War Democrat (if not better than Pendleton). It said Vallandigham followers would suspect a War Democrat of hostility toward them but "would feel safe under Mr. Chase, whom they give credit for more toleration, mercy and justice." Not very compelling. But there was more. Vallandigham described Chase as "broad, deep and sagacious." A broad, deep and sagacious abolitionist? Nothing in his earlier written words suggests that Vallandigham ever entertained the possibility of such a creature.

In that quote, he was distinguishing Chase from Secretary of State William Seward: "shallow and empiric." Never mind that Seward was generally thought of as a conservative Republican and Chase as a radical. Clearly, Vallandigham was just buttering up Chase. He had to know he was utterly transparent.

Two forces were at work: One, Vallandigham was taking a new look at things. He was, in certain moods, trying to find a way past war issues. The *Herald* piece refers to Vallandigham's people as "'positive' democrats—such is the term they now call themselves in pursuance of the policy to obliterate all traces of the war in the new movement." The name—clearly suggested by Vallandigham—didn't have much life. But it indicated some ferment.

As early as 1866, Vallandigham had written to a friend, that "the past must be forgotten … and the great issues of the (current) hour be made the sole test of present fellowship and cooperation."[38] That certainly wasn't the way he talked the next year at Mount Vernon II. But it was a mood. He was floundering for a posture, a purpose, a cause even by 1868. With "positive" Democrats, he seemed to be responding to the charge that the Copperheads were always just griping about whatever was happening. But, really, "positive" Democrats?

He was also floundering for a job. That was the second force at work in the Chase endorsement. Vallandigham was bucking for a cabinet post. After all, Chase would obviously face some skepticism from Democrats. Vallandigham could imagine that Chase could use a staunch Democrat like him to vouch for him. And he could imagine being rewarded for doing so. None of that is recorded anyplace in the record. But the guy wasn't exactly inscrutable.

In the *Herald* interview, Vallandigham didn't say anything bad about anybody who had a shot at the presidential nomination. He showcased—of all things—his flexibility. He wasn't the ideological fire-breather, the zealot, the cause person. He was a team player; he wanted to be on any president's team, given that, after all, he had already tried getting elected to something himself.

Chase's nomination was a real possibility.[39] But when Pendleton's campaign collapsed and Vallandigham went all out for Chase, the Ohio delegation ignored the Buckeye candidate and the Buckeye promoter. The delegation went for New York's Horatio Seymour. That was crucial in his victory. Chase's biographer thought Vallandigham's support was an embarrassment for Chase.[40] But Chase and Vallandigham continued to nurse a relationship.

After the convention, Vallandigham went all out for the nominee. He didn't hide his hopes. He said publicly, "If we are successful this fall in the election of a Democratic administration, I shall hope for something better in politics than a seat in Congress."[41]

Seymour's biographer also thought that Vallandigham's endorsement "may have hurt Seymour rather than helped"[42] in the general election. Neither biographer felt any need to enlarge on their slam of Vallandigham's impact. Their points apparently seemed obvious to them.

But there was still Dayton. Returning from the convention, Vallandigham found himself being recruited to run for Congress again. At first he resisted. That was the context in which he said he was hoping for a presidential appointment. The statement ended with this: "without a Democratic administration, I have no desire to become a member of that body," the House. Vallandigham's brother insisted that Clement thought the congressional nomination should go to Clement's nephew, John McMahon, who said he didn't want it. A party convention in Hamilton held votes without either name in nomination, and nobody got enough votes. Eventually, the convention turned to Vallandigham, and he agreed.[43] This time, the nomination wasn't completely without controversy. A Democratic editor in Warren County resigned because he couldn't endorse Vallandigham.[44] Still, if ever there was a real draft, this was it.

And yet he surely *did* want to return to Congress if he didn't get a cabinet job. He never liked being out of office. And he still hadn't given up on the Senate. He was again eyeing the seat of John Sherman, this time to come up in 1872.[45] He needed to convince the politicians he was a vote getter. Vallandigham threw his heart into the race against old foe Robert Schenck. The campaign attracted national attention, national money and national figures on the Republican side. "Vallandigham fought almost single-handed," wrote his brother.[46] That was a measure of his standing in his party.

Vallandigham tried in the campaign to change the subject from the war. He called for a "New Departure" that would entail focusing on new issues.[47] But the Republicans were still running on the war; nothing else could possibly be a better issue for them.

Vallandigham lost with 49.3 percent of the vote. His brother wrote that Clement believed "up to the night before the battle that his election was assured."[48]

Again, however, Vallandigham found political solace. He won his pre–1862 district again, and with a slightly improved margin. And he ran better than the Democratic national ticket did. He pointed that out as he kept looking toward 1872.

I draw on my years as a journalist for an analogy. Ohio Congressman Sherrod Brown, a Democrat, faced being redistricted out of his seat in 2002 by the Republican legislature and governor. Word spread that if that happened, Brown might run against Republican Gov. Robert Taft for his job. I had occasion to ask Brown if he would really do that. He said, "Yeah. I love this stuff." That, ultimately, was the Vallandigham factor: He loved this stuff—and nothing else nearly as much. (The Republicans left Brown alone, and Taft coasted to re-election against a less known opponent.)

***

In 1870, the Democrats won back Vallandigham's congressional seat, but without him on the ballot. That must have hurt, given that he had lost it twice. But he pitched in. He represented the party in a post-election court case involving a home in Dayton for injured soldiers from far beyond Dayton.[49] The Democrats didn't want the veterans' votes counted, on the premise that vets tended to be Republicans. The Democratic candidate, ironically, was Lewis Campbell, the man whom Vallandigham beat in his own contested election in 1856, when the party didn't want mixed-race people voting. This time, too, the Democrats won.

Campbell belonged at various stages to several different parties. He had now made the long-term transition from Whig to Democrat. He had been ambassador to Mexico after the Civil War. Roughly during Campbell's stay, Austrian Maximilian I—installed by Napoleon III as emperor—had been deposed (and killed). The 3rd District Democrats were happy to welcome Campbell.

Earlier in 1870, the 15th Amendment—black male suffrage—had been ratified. James Vallandigham wrote that after the election, at a Democratic "jubilee," Clement Vallandigham made some relevant remarks about and to "colored voters, of whom quite a number were present." This is nonsense: the idea that many black voters would be at a Democratic celebration. Most likely, Clement Vallandigham addressed these remarks to absent black voters. The approving responses mentioned must have come from whites—or nobody.⁵⁰

Lewis Campbell, Vallandigham opponent then ally, who offered an insightful eulogy (Library of Congress. Engraving by H.B. Hall & Sons, N.Y.).

"And now," Clement Vallandigham said, "allow me a word to our newly made voters of African descent." That indicated some evolution. A few years earlier, you may recall, Vallandigham was offended when Lincoln referred to "Americans of African descent." He called that "unctuous." But now, with an eye on bigger matters than vocabulary, he said,

> I have no apologies to make tonight for anything in opposition to them which I may have said in times past.... My opinions upon the question of negro suffrage and equality remain unchanged. (Loud cheers.) But you have in fact, at least, been made citizens and voters, and I recognize the fact.
> Some of you speak of me as an enemy of your race. This is not correct. Individually, I have been your friend.... At my doors some of you have received that charity ... which was denied you at the hands of your Abolition friends, so-called. (Cries of 'That's so, we know it.') ...
> (I)f you shall prove yourselves worthy of these rights and capable of exercising them as good citizens, I will then, very cheerfully, and in a manlike manner, publicly confess myself mistaken. Your future is in your own hands.
> But remember that you do not hold the balance of power in this country, nor in this district. (Loud cheers.) ... (N)umbering several hundred voters here, you are yet rather a source

of weakness than of strength to the Republican Party; and you owe nothing to that party.... They did not confer (suffrage) upon you for your sakes, but for their own as partisans and demagogues. (Loud cheers.) ... (T)hey freed you, only now to make you, if you submit, political slaves....

And now I ... warn you.... Beware of ... attempting to make all of your own race act and vote as a distinct body [loyal to one party]. "If you do, then be assured that sooner or later the white race will antagonize you as white men; and here we are as twenty to one. In a political struggle we can overwhelm you. In a contest of arms—in a war of races, if you provoke it—we can crush out and exterminated you....

If you would prove yourselves worthy to be and remain citizens, separate, divide politically and otherwise, as other citizens do. Identify yourselves with the community in which you live. Refuse to be made the slaves and tools of demagogues; and when thus you shall have established your fitness for citizenship, no one will ever attempt to deprive you of its rights.... (B)e assured that the time will come when you will say that I counseled you most wisely and well. (Loud cheers.)

To this day, of course, a legitimate argument can be had about the wisdom of any demographic group being entirely committed to one party. Still, this was just ugly. Vallandigham told black Ohioans they were too few to matter politically, but he revealed himself as profoundly worried about how they would vote. He unmistakably tied their commitment to the Republican Party to the possibility of violence against them. He spoke of race war. He addressed a demographic group of voters as "you," and sided with "we," as in "we outnumber you." He gave blacks no reason to support Democrats except that they had better.

As for his view on Republican motives behind black suffrage, it brings to mind a remark later made about Vallandigham by George Pendleton: "Beyond most men whom I have known, he was sensitive to attacks upon the purity of his motives and character. I have seen him wounded to the quick—his heart lacerated."[51]

***

In 1871, Vallandigham went all the way with the philosophical transition he had been thinking about since about 1866.

A phrase had entered the language. In campaigns, the Republicans were always likely to "wave the bloody shirt." That is, they would try to make the war the subject of the campaign, reminding people who was for and who was against the war. They had a good run doing that. That was the problem Vallandigham was confronting. He wanted to change the subject. He publicly embraced the idea of a "New Departure" for the Democrats. They would not only cease complaining about the war; they would cease complaining about the postwar constitutional amendments. Vallandigham said those acts should be seen as the "natural and legitimate results of the war" and its outcome. The war fight was over. But there was much else to fight about. He said, "The Republican Party, having fulfilled its original mission, (is) rapidly falling into decay," a view hardly confined to partisans. That provided an opportunity for the Democrats and should be the starting point.

In an 1871 memo, Vallandigham insisted that his proposal "does not require ... any acknowledgment of error."[52] And he said he still wanted the party to be committed to strict construction of the (amended) Constitution, to limiting the power of

Washington and to state and local rights. What might the Democrats actually propose? In response to the growth of government and to widespread corruption in the Grant years, Vallandigham supported what is today called Civil Service. With the economy becoming more international, he endorsed taxes on imports for purposes of raising revenue, but not for protection of American industry. With government needing new sources of money, he said internal taxation should be based on wealth. With industrialization starting to take hold, he thought labor must be protected against some practices. He opposed any more granting of federal land to "corporations for railroads or other purposes," but supported it for settlers. He did not confront immigration, nor the urbanization and private-sector corruption and monumental wealth that were coming with industrialization.

On Reconstruction, he could still sound like the old partisan agitator. He saw "military despotism" and an effort to "perpetuate the present administration" in all efforts from Washington to enforce racial equality. Still, he didn't want that range of issues to define the party.

Many agreed with him. At a state party convention that happened to be in Dayton, his proposals—which were made originally to his local party—were adopted. As was typical of him, he saw that as a historic event. He predicted a response "from one end of the country to the other, full of joy and rejoicing tomorrow, from the Atlantic to the Pacific, from the lakes to...."[53] You get the idea.

Vallandigham himself was hot. He once again became the talk of the nation, at least in political circles. The meeting of the Montgomery County Democratic Party to consider his proposal had been front-page news in *The New York Times*.[54] Democratic state conventions took up the idea, as did newspapers of both parties. The *Times* rounded up responses from nine Southern newspapers.[55] So widely discussed was the New Departure that the term came to be laughingly applied to anything. The *Times* reported on local "hackmen" (pre-auto taxi drivers) making a "New Departure" in their professional practices.[56] Every day seemed to bring a different kind of New Departure.

Some people saw the New Departure as more than a party's strategy. If the most famously, bitterly, resolutely anti-war politician in the North was over the war issues, wasn't this a good thing, a turning point for the nation, not just a party? Politics had been so ugly for so long, not just through the 1850s and the war, but through the impeachment of Andrew Johnson. Could the mellowing of the Peace Democrats mean peace in the North? Could Vallandigham himself be the instrument, the deliverer of that change?

The answer lay in the response of Democrats to the idea. The white South was definitely not reconciled to the spirit of the constitutional amendments. If the northern Democrats were breaking from their southern allies on race, that was big. Accordingly, northern Democrats were divided. When the Iowa Democrats adopted a New Departure platform, a group broke off and held a second convention.[57]

Still, the Democratic New York *Herald* said the New Departure was "generally recognized as a party necessity."[58] The paper speculated that Vallandigham had come up with the idea as a way of getting Chase nominated for president in 1872. The logic of that guess: One big problem confronting a Chase nomination was that he had always been in the vanguard of the fight for black rights, which were never popular in the party. The New Departure could mute that issue. The paper's speculation had much to be said for it. Chase had profusely praised the New Departure and Vallandigham's role in it.[59]

But the *Herald* acknowledged that the Departure had its downsides. It would mean that "the bond" of northern and southern Democrats "is broken" permanently.[60] The Cincinnati *Enquirer* was against the ND, arguing that it made the Democrats too much like the Republicans. The *Herald* printed that and attributed it Cincinnati's proximity to Kentucky and the influence of conservatives there on the *Enquirer*.[61] Where the Departure was given lip service in the South, that was typically a duplicitous effort to convince northerners the South didn't need to be monitored anymore, according to historian Eric Foner, a pre-eminent leader in Reconstruction studies.[62]

The too-much-like-the-Republicans argument was heard many times in many ways, in both North and South. The New Orleans *Picayune* said that, as a result of the Departure, "With a few concessions from the (Republicans), it might be feasible to construct a platform which would answer for both" parties.[63] The *New York Times* agreed. It said the only issues that divided the two parties sharply were those that related to the war. It said the Departure would make the next presidential election about not "principles" but merely "spoils."[64] That was actually a pretty good prediction about the political nature of the 1870s.[65]

For Vallandigham, being called watery and lacking in principles, of all things, had to smart. Still, he had accomplished a lot. He had reinvented himself nationally with one swoop and had taken the national stage again. He was a party leader, and it looked like he might be on a path to President Chase's cabinet. Finally, after near-misses, huge misses, embarrassments and frustrations—finally!—his Act II was getting started.

Then he accidently killed himself.

19

Wrong Gun in His Pocket

The middle of June 1871 was to be big in Lebanon, Ohio, halfway between Cincinnati and Dayton. A high-profile murder trial was scheduled, with a celebrity defense team including Clement Vallandigham and a former lieutenant governor. The town was, as they say, buzzing. There was a local trial-of-the-century feel. Many out-of-town newspapers were to run trial transcripts.[1]

A shooting had happened in Hamilton, one county to the east, just north of Cincinnati on the Indiana border. Besides being Vallandigham country, Hamilton was the Wild West, or an Ohio facsimile. A local historian insisted, "The citizens of Hamilton were long … intimidated and awed into silence by desperadoes who regarded neither property or life."[2] A "carnival of crime" had resulted in the formation of a citizens committee to take action.

On Christmas Eve of 1870, one Thomas Myers (sometimes Meyers) was shot dead in a gambling room of a local saloon. Suspicion fell upon a Thomas McGehan (sometimes McGehean), a man of local fame. He had been in trouble with the law, but had also been—even after some of that trouble—a lawman: the elected town marshal, serving for one year. He was a man of means, at least when times were good. He gambled for big money. During the war, he had been a Republican, but he didn't like the way the local Republicans treated him. So in 1868 he went to Vallandigham and offered his help in defeating Schenck. Vallandigham accepted, and they became good friends.[3] These facts are taken from McGehan's memoirs which, admittedly, is dangerous, because the book is absurd. McGehan painted himself as a man who had hardly ever done anything wrong but gamble, but who nevertheless kept getting in trouble with the law and had an amazingly long list of enemies, to whose defamation the book is largely devoted, along with the task of clearing his own name. Nevertheless, the part about how he came to know Vallandigham does seem credible. He connects their meeting with the interests of a whisky ring of which he was a part: a group of people highly motivated to minimize taxes on liquor. Vallandigham, as a strong rejecter of the temperance movement—which favored the high taxes—was a natural ally.

McGehan had the money to hire the best lawyers. He went bipartisan, including on his team Andrew McBurney, a Republican who had just served as lieutenant governor (1866–1868).

Because of McGehan's local notoriety, the defense sought and won a change of venue to Lebanon, 24 miles west, due south of Dayton.

The case against McGehan included the fact that he and the dead man, Myers, had a long history of ill will that included the death of Myers' brother with some alleged involvement by McGehan. McGehan's defense in the current case was that he wasn't even in the room when the shooting happened, though he was in the building.

Vallandigham was apparently convinced of McGehan's innocence. He came up with the theory that Myers had accidentally shot himself. The theory didn't figure prominently in the trial. Indeed, the trial was well underway before Vallandigham had quite worked it out. He was somewhat engaged in the trial; when one witness for the prosecution said that he had seen a certain object from across the street one night, Vallandigham used an almanac to demonstrate there was no moon that night (according to McGehan, anyway).[4]

But Vallandigham wasn't exactly consumed by the trial. That fact was demonstrated when he gave an unrelated interview during it. The Cincinnati *Times and Chronicle* wanted to talk about the bigger national news of the day in which Vallandigham was involved: the New Departure. The interview ran on the day Vallandigham was scheduled to deliver his side's closing statement, Saturday, June 17. In the interview, he made national political news.[5] On the way toward that news, he told the paper that, "if the Democratic party refuses to move to the front to accept the new order of things, it will simply pass away, and some other party ... (will come along) and will take possession of the Government."

As for issues to replace the war, he had a different list than earlier. He said that "control of all the out laying fragments of this continent is the destiny of the American people. We shall have San Domingo (the island including Haiti and the Dominican Republic), Cuba, Mexico and all the rest, mark that." His belief in his predictive ability was apparently not subject to disproof.

The news he made: He was asked whether he could function in the Democratic Party, given factional hostility toward him. He said, "What can I do? The Republicans won't move forward.... (But) ... of one thing I am certain: If the Democratic party fails to become the party of progress and advanced ideas, and I ... (decide) to act with any other political party, that other political party will never stop to inquire what my past political record has been." In other words, another party would take him, just as the Democrats had welcomed Lewis Campbell.

The interviewer was apparently worried that people wouldn't believe that Clement Vallandigham had publicly flirted with the idea of leaving the Democrats. It seemed unthinkable. It apparently shocked the reporter. He wrote, "Those who read (this piece) may construe this expression as they please.... The speaker's earnest manner convinced me that he meant all he said," and Vallandigham repeated it "in various forms."

Back at the trial, Vallandigham was planning to unveil his theory about the shooting in his closing statement. On the day before, he had been out in a clearing doing ballistics tests to see what kind of marks a bullet made on cloth it passed through from certain distances. That night, the former lieutenant governor said he had doubts about Vallandigham's theory. Vallandigham said, "I'll show you in half a second."[6] They were the only two in the room at the Lebanon Hotel, now called the Golden Lamb Inn. It's known today for its 19th century history, including visits by dignitaries such as Charles Dickens. Vallandigham and some colleagues were staying there, the daily roundtrip to Dayton being too arduous.

Vallandigham's theory of the shooting was this: Perhaps the victim, Myers, had been sitting at a card table and had pushed away from it suddenly when some threatening people or person entered the room, and his chair had tumbled with him still in it. In getting up, his hand went to his pocket, where there was a gun. As Myers struggled to his feet, perhaps he was looking around frantically, trying to discern whether he was under attack. He was rising awkwardly, with one hand in his pocket. The gun went off. The bullet hit Myers himself in the abdomen, and he died.

To dramatize his theory, Vallandigham got on the floor in the hotel room with a gun in his pocket. He put his hand in his pocket. He talked as he rose toward his feet. It was all very awkward, he was saying, and…. Vallandigham's gun went off. The bullet hit him in the abdomen. And he died. So he had accidently shot himself to death while demonstrating how another guy had accidentally shot himself to death.

He didn't die quickly, but he never left that room. Local big names from Dayton and Cincinnati were there before he died, along with a doctor. So was Vallandigham's 16-year-old son. His wife was out of town—in Maryland at, fatefully enough, the funeral of her middle-aged brother. In Lebanon, one doctor said Vallandigham was the "coolest man under such circumstances he had ever seen."[7] Defendant McGehan came and broke down in tears.[8]

The Cincinnati *Enquirer* reported that at the time of the accident there had been two guns in the hotel room. Vallandigham had used one for his tests outdoors. It still had rounds in it. The other was to be used in the trial. It was unloaded. Vallandigham put them down together, later to put the wrong one in his pocket.

The pro–Vallandigham *Enquirer* reported[9] that after the ballistics tests the day before, a member of the defense team had been walking with Vallandigham:

> "Mr. Millikin, ever cautious and thoughtful said, 'Val, there are three shots in your pistol yet. You had better discharge them.'
> "'What for?' responded Mr. Vallandigham.
> "'To prevent any accident,' replied the cautious attorney. 'You might shoot yourself.'
> "'No danger of that,' replied Mr. Vallandigham. 'I have carried and practised with pistols too long to be afraid to have a loaded one in my pocket.'
> "'You had better be careful, though,' said Mr. Millikin.
> "'Never fear me,' was the reply."

The gun was a Smith & Wesson .32 caliber with five chambers and a four inch barrel, according to the *Enquirer*. An 1860 model, it was designed as a pocket gun. It did not have a safety mechanism, those being more modern. It did not even have a guard around the trigger. It did need to be cocked, but that could happen by accident, or maybe Vallandigham did it.

If the gunshot wound had not

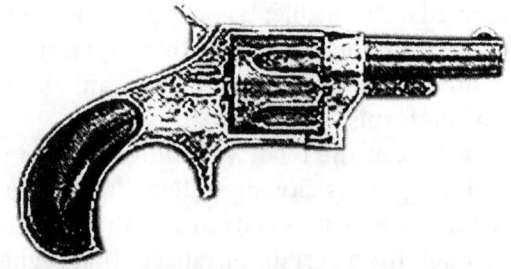

The pocket gun Vallandigham used in Lebanon would have looked much like this. Note the absence of a trigger guard.

been enough to kill Vallandigham, he might have died of embarrassment. He knew exactly what he had done, being of sound mind for hours after the shot. He was quoted as saying it was the most "reckless" act of his life.[10]

The following cliché was used by more than one eulogist: He died as he had lived. He threw himself into the murder case passionately and thought about it hard. He came up with a theory, about which he got excited. He was excited, too, about the verbal combat of the trial. According to the *Enquirer*, he thought the case would establish him as one of the leading defense attorneys in the country and would result in acquittal.[11] And he got carried away, so to speak. This was, indeed, all pure Vallandigham.

As I have told this story in Dayton, I've found that the first thing people want to know is how the trial came out. After Vallandigham's funeral, the trial proceeded. Hung jury. No juror went for murder in the first degree. Four went for acquittal.[12] That resulted in a second trial, this one in Dayton. There McGehan was found guilty of second-degree murder. But the verdict was overturned on the apparently well-documented grounds that one juror had declared himself in favor of the verdict prematurely.[13] A third trial, also in Dayton, found McGehan innocent, and there it ended. Every outcome had happened once—hung, guilty and innocent. The three trials were conducted in well under a year.

McGehan returned to Hamilton. In May of 1872, a citizens committee called him a "monster," and said, "we pledge ourselves to justify, uphold and defend" anyone who might "rid the world of his presence" if he were ever found in the county again.[14] He went to Cincinnati. In 1874, his book came out. It played up the Vallandigham angle of his story, using a picture of Vallandigham as a sort of frontispiece, though the book had no other illustrations.

By 1875, McGehan was back in Hamilton operating a bar and "bowling alley." If he felt the heat had died down, his intelligence was flawed. On a Sunday night in June, somebody came to the window of that establishment and, according to the local historian, "discharged the contents of a double-barrelled shotgun into McGehan's body…. A private reward of $1,000 had been offered to anyone who would kill McGehan. Three or four men from a vigilance committee were seeking their game night and day."[15]

***

Vallandigham's wife Louisa was not at his funeral. On the very day he shot himself, she had left for Cumberland, Maryland, for the funeral of her brother. She was reportedly at the gravesite when she got word via telegram of the accident in Lebanon. Not knowing her husband's condition, she immediately began the difficult journey back home, mainly by train. But when she got home on Sunday, she was sick. The press was quickly reporting, "She is utterly prostrated, and fears are entertained for her life."[16] News stories sometimes described her as "distracted," a euphemism.[17] "When she was taken beside her husband's coffin," said one report, "she gave utterance to shrill unmeaning cries…. She was still unconscious," another euphemism, "up to Wednesday evening…. She does not get any better."[18] In desperation, her family took her back to Cumberland. She died on August 13. Her brother-in-law wrote,

"Sensitive and delicate by nature, her terrible bereavement crushed her to the very earth." She was 48, dead of—apparently—something like a broken heart.[19]

Clement's funeral was widely said to be the biggest ever in Ohio.[20] Dayton filled with people—with Democrats, more precisely, plus the uncategorizable Chase. The cortege of carriages along Main Street was said to be two miles long.[21] Downtown business was suspended for hours. Eulogies—at the funeral, in newspapers, in Washington—abounded.

At the funeral, Lewis Campbell, was insightful. "One of his great traits of character was that of individuality. Most of us are deficient in that respect. We are all too apt to lean upon others for assistance and support in the hour of necessity. But Mr. Vallandigham ... relied upon himself.... (That) was the secret of his success."[22] It might be seen as the secret of his failures. Either way, nowhere is there evidence of him consulting with a broad range of people, of getting advisors together and trying to find a consensus, of bouncing ideas off people he respected, of following somebody else's lead, of searching for insight into public opinion. He simply thought things through for himself and acted. More than one speaker made a point noted in the preface to this book: that Vallandigham "never had a doubt."[23]

Many seized upon the New Departure. Rep. Cox made the following points in a different order: "In our early associations ... especially in Congress during the war, he showed those rigid outlines of character which seemed to many proof of uncharitableness and bitterness.... (A)s he grew older he had a larger humanity.... (I)t seemed that his character became more mellow, graceful and gentle. (That) makes this the most mournful day Ohio ever knew." Cox grabbed the New Departure as a lifeline for a eulogist. Vallandighammers must not have loved that. It made his days as their hero into some sort of adolescence and said all the real good came after his heroic days.

Cox also said that as a debater, Vallandigham "had no peer."[24]

The Dayton Bar offered a resolution that his "brilliant fame marked him at this time as the most conspicuous figure in American politics." "Conspicuous" must have been a highly negotiated word.

The Chicago *Tribune*—which couldn't mention Vallandigham during the war without calling him a traitor[25]—focused now on his good qualities. It found quite a number. He "was a man of ability far ... in advance of any man now prominent in the Democratic Party. He was one of the best public speakers in the country.... Since the death of (Stephen A.) Douglas, he has been more generally acknowledged and looked up to as the leader of the Democratic party than any other man." The paper said his new plan for the party seemed destined to be adopted by his party the next year. And, "In his private life and in all his relations with his fellow men, Mr. Vallandigham was a gentleman—cultivated, kind, warm-hearted and generous." Not that the bygones were all bygones. His pro-slavery position resulted in an "erratic and somewhat unfortunate career." But, "If there can be an honest pro-slavery man, he was."

The New York *Sun*: "His friends were many, even among his lifelong political opponents." There's actually not much evidence of that. Admirers of his ability, yes; friends, no. The paper saw the New Departure as the hope of the Democratic Party and praised Vallandigham for "unsaying his own old ideas."[26] That would have generated a rebuttal from the deceased.

The weekly *Spirit of Democracy* in Woodsfield, Ohio, said, "Like the lamented Douglas, he was stricken down just at the time his political opponents began to learn to do him justice."[27] That, of course, was a reference to Douglas' support for Lincoln after Fort Sumter.

The Cincinnati *Enquirer* repeated the old complaint of his supporters:

> Vallandigham was "ferociously assailed and denounced as no other man of his day and generation had been." Among the paper's fresher observations was that, "He had one of the best and most finely selected libraries in the State of Ohio, and of its treasures his wonderful memory had made him master."
>
> It said Vallandigham had "a career that will never be forgotten. Since the death of President Lincoln, in 1865, no demise of any individual has created so great and universal a sorrow." Universal? The paper also said—referring apparently to the deathbed vigil—"No sentinel perishing at his post, no physician falling a victim to his efforts to save his patients, ever died in a more heroic and worthy manner."[28]

It was left to Vallandigham's brother James, the minister, to remark as Clement would have wanted[29]: "He has gone; but we catch the echo of his words, long ago spoken, though with a different meaning....

> "'Resurgam,' I shall rise again.
> And it will be a glorious resurrection."

Clement Vallandigham had spoken those words during the secession crisis, when war sentiment was rising.[30] He meant the anti-war movement would rise again. Of course, as his brother knew, he expressed the same sentiment about his own after-life again and again.

The resurrection awaits.

20

What Ever Happened To…?

The Daytonians

Though Tom Lowe said the 1863 election outcome demonstrated that the people were for the war—and that was that—he was just expressing a mood. By the next summer he was back in his old ideological groove and his old predictive ways. He was saying the people were tired of the war, and the Democratic nominee for president "will be elected by an overwhelming majority." And he was certain the nominee wouldn't be McClellan.[1]

His determination not to fight in the war remained passionate. But he could not find a substitute, which would have been legal. In 1864—having returned to the country by the end of 1863—he was simply frantic, hammering away in his letters to his brother Will about Will's need to find him a substitute he could pay. He underlined his words and called himself "anxious," then "really anxious."[2] He was certain that if Lincoln were re-elected—his own prediction notwithstanding—the law allowing for substitutes would be revoked, and the war would continue for 20 years.[3] He was rivaling his icon for predictive futility.

Unfortunately, his correspondence with his brother ended—or, at least, the Dayton Metro Library's collection of Tom-to-Will letters ends—before Tom's reaction to the end of the war is recorded.

He never did get drafted. And we do know something about his postwar life. He never moved to Europe. He gradually lost interest in politics, at least as a career. After the war, he was elected to a judgeship, but in middle age he changed his profession to minister, a decision his wife must have loved and seems to have promoted. Ultimately, he and Martha moved to upstate New York, apparently to be with a grown daughter. He participated aggressively—through writing—in internal church debates, holding to a staunchly conservative position on theological matters.[4] His new life wasn't much of a stretch for him. In writing to Will during the war, worrying about the "wicked city" of Nashville, he said he "feared the perils that threaten your soul more than those that have ever threatened your body."[5]

When brother Will is last seen in the library's holdings, he is planning on a military career. And, according to a letter from Tom during the war, he had grown "unduly obese. Your eyes don't 'stick out,' but seem nearly closed in with fat."[6] (Though Will saw much action in the army, there were long periods of inactivity as well, especially during the winter, during which, in some units, officers were fed pretty well.)

Nobody in the family seems to have stayed in Dayton, though unrelated Lowes did.

Imagining Tom Lowe in middle age and later is a little scary, given how passionately opinionated, certain and moralistic he was as a very young man. A reader of his letters has to wonder if they played a bigger role in Tom's life than in Will's. Surviving as the letters did—possibly accessible to Tom—they could have been a reminder to him that he was so wrong about so much. Perhaps they mellowed him. And perhaps they convinced him that politics wasn't his calling after all.

***

Lucien Medlar and Clara Soule—our polarized lovers—did marry, on New Year's Eve, 1863, after a long and tempestuous engagement.

The political aspect of their story, so far as it is known, seems to have ended with Lucien abandoning Vallandigham in favor of Clara. Or, at any rate, his views softened. He didn't acknowledge changing, at least in the diary. It was a process. As early as August 27, 1861, he saw "no way but to fight (the war) out now." He remained against emancipation as far as is recorded. But he apparently voted for the Union ticket, at least sometimes, insisting that the presence of Democrats on the tickets amounted to an admission by the Republicans that their party was ill-conceived and profoundly wrong.[7] At any rate, if he was going to vote for the war, the couple at least came to share a rooting interest.

In 1866, they moved to New York for purposes of her career, an act of gender modernity that must have put them in a small category in their time. She thought her career as a portraitist would flourish more in the big city. And he must have figured that he couldn't do any worse professionally in New York than he was doing in Dayton, as perhaps the most Shakespeare-literate clerk in town. But Lucien never found a more satisfying position. The always-strained relationship did not endure in marriage. It might have suffered from the death of their 14-year-old son Harry in a hunting accident. Two years after that, in 1884, Lucien went back to his family land in Miamisburg, where he died in 1907.[8] A road there is named after the family. Clara stayed in New York.

***

Clement Vallandigham's son Charles was elected to the state legislature from Dayton in the 1880s, then took a full-time job in Columbus,[9] then disappeared from the public eye. He did not leave children behind. Vallandigham's nephew from his wife's family, John McMahon, remained active in local affairs and in the Democratic Party and spent the late 1870s representing Dayton in Congress before being defeated. Later he became president of the Ohio state bar and lost a bid for the U.S. Senate.

The Generals

Ambrose Burnside became a Republican and was elected governor of Rhode Island, then went to the U.S. Senate. He was also the first president of the National Rifle Association.[10] He wasn't a founder. He took the position, he said, because too many northern troops showed up in the army with no experience with rifles, putting them at a disadvantage against southern farm boys, who grew up hunting. He didn't want something like that to happen again. The NRA then did not have the controversial identity of later days.

The Vallandigham episode does not get Burnside mentioned in history nearly as often as his military failures.

***

William Rosecrans, after being replaced after Chickamauga, was reassigned to Missouri, but never again played a high-profile role in the war. Nevertheless, like Burnside, he was sought after by both parties after the war. Though excoriated by many legislative Democrats during the war, he was nominated by the party for governor of Ohio in 1869; but by then he was (briefly) ambassador to Mexico, and he rejected the nomination, causing the party's convention to reconvene. He had political offers in California and Nevada, too. But he rejected them, coming eventually to be called "The Great Decliner." He had business opportunities which he preferred to pursue. But his efforts in mining, railroads and southern California real estate never made him rich. In 1880 he finally did take the politics option; he was elected to Congress from California as a Democrat and was considered a presidential prospect.

In the House, Rosecrans famously and unsuccessfully opposed a bill providing a pension for the broke former President Ulysses Grant. Grant had removed Rosecrans from Mexico. In the pension fight, Rosecrans pointed out that the pension would be a reward for "distinguished" military service, but insisted that, "when true history is written," Grant's service wouldn't look so great.[11] The battle between the two continued in Grant's memoirs. At least three authors consider that hugely-praised book to be unfair to Rosecrans, including one called *General Grant and the Rewriting of History: How the Destruction of General Williams S. Rosecrans Influenced Our Understanding of the Civil War*.[12] One book speculates that Grant was still smarting over the pension dispute when he wrote his book.[13] Another—not the one named here—insists that "The cold, cruel fact is that William S. Rosecrans is forgotten today because of Ulysses S. Grant."[14]

Of course, Grant is the one who rose as a presidential prospect as Rosecrans fell. And that happened when Grant was in Rosecrans' chain of command.

For purposes of this book about politics, the striking thing about Rosecrans is that he didn't let the war make him a Republican. He was horrified and amazed at the Copperheads. During the war, he sounded like a Republican to Democrats and Republicans, alike. Greeley certainly thought he was. Many public figures who served under Rosecrans and considered him important in their lives were Republicans, including three future presidents: James A. Garfield, Rutherford B. Hayes and William McKinley. Then there was thoroughly Republican editor W.D. Bickham, who certainly thought he was being loyal to Rosecrans in picking a party. So what kept Rosecrans from making the natural switch? The biographers mentioned here don't go into that much. Perhaps the explanation has something to do with the postwar Republicans being all about Grant, his nemesis.

The Journalists

After being relieved after Chickamauga, Rosecrans went briefly back to Yellow Springs, near Dayton, where his wife lived during the war. In November, shortly after his arrival, Rosecrans' young daughter died there.[15] When the general was on his way to Yellow Springs, Bickham went to Cincinnati to greet him.[16] That was a measure of their closeness. Bickham used the pages of the Dayton *Journal* to fight Rosecrans' battle for his reputation. He was Rosecrans' favorite newspaper correspondent, his guy.[17] Bickham had represented Rosecrans positively in his book,[18] and the relationship continued.

But Bickham certainly wasn't going to be anti–Grant in his writing, or too critical of the Lincoln administration about the replacement of Rosecrans. So his writing was a bit stilted, and his success in behalf of Rosecrans' reputation—both short-term and long-term—was minimal.

Otherwise, however, Bickham thrived in Dayton. His expressed desire to find a growing community and grow with it was fulfilled. He continued to edit the *Journal* into the 1890s, when he died. The paper had quickly made him rich, and it became an institution both locally and in state political and journalistic circles. In the early 1930s, he was inducted into the Ohio Journalism Hall of Fame. His son delivered the keynote address. He said that when his father came to Dayton, the place was 10-1 Democratic, and that Bickham turned it around, so that the community was supporting the war by the end.[19] Fiction. The ratio was always more like 1-1.

The Dayton *Ledger*—the renamed Democratic paper in town—did not have a long life. Why the Republican paper thrived and sustained while the Democratic papers struggled in Dayton is not clear to this writer. It might have had something to do with Bickham's size and abilities.

***

Sam Medary died the day before Lincoln was re-elected.[20] He was 63 and had been declining. If he was mentally alert at the end, he pretty much knew Lincoln would win, because Ohio and some other states had already had elections and the trend was clear.

We need not wonder how he would have reacted to disappointing events. He would have attributed Lincoln's defeat to some sort of fraud and to the illusion that the war was nearing an end and to McClellan's failure to embrace the Vallandigham platform and to anything other excuse he could gin up. As for the war, he would have insisted first that peace had been achieved through negotiation, then that it wasn't a real peace, then that the South was being repressed, then that peace and reunion could have been achieved so much faster if only his advice had been followed.

More worth wondering about is how he would have reacted to his brother Vallandigham's talk of leaving the Democrats. Military-monitored Reconstruction was still in place. Black people were voting. Southern Democrats were looking for help from their northern party brethren. The Republicans were looking as corrupt as the Democrats had always said they were. And Vallandigham—Vallandigham! the

In the late 19th century, Allen & Ginter cigarettes offered a trading card series featuring newspaper editors. Dayton *Journal* editor W.D. Bickham was featured on one (Heritage Image Partnership Ltd./Alamy Stock Photo).

staunch, the uncowed, the great articulator of the party's proud history—was talking about moving on. Could have been interesting.

The Politicians

Robert Schenck may have missed his shot. True, after defeating Vallandigham for Congress in 1862, he was a national political figure for a decade. Immediately upon his election, the Dayton *Journal* had said, "There is but little doubt that he will be the next speaker."[21] Others were talking that way, too. Here was the wounded general, the former congressman and diplomat, the man who had defeated the loathed Vallandigham. He wasn't made speaker, but he immediately became chairman of the military committee. During the war, that was, of course, a center of action, though the Joint (House-Senate) Committee on the Conduct of the War, under Chairman Ben Wade of Ohio, got more attention. Schenck's approach to his job seems to have been basically to have Lincoln's back, with regard to how to run the draft and other very hot issues.

Schenck was present for Lincoln's address at Gettysburg, and he was on the funeral train.[22] His emotional attachment was strong. After the war, he became a Radical Republican. That is, he was bent on a hard line in treatment of Confederates and on rights for blacks. Schenck's academic biographer speculates that Schenck was radicalized by the assassination. That would be ironic, given that Lincoln was not a Radical, but it does have an emotional logic.

In 1866, Schenck wanted John Sherman's seat in the U.S. Senate. He came at Sherman from the left, so to speak, and he worked hard. But he didn't come close to convincing the Republicans in the Ohio legislature that a change was needed.[23] He was probably over-estimating the political strength his war record and ties to Lincoln gave him in internal party affairs.

However, when the Republicans had an actual opening for a major statewide race, they came to Schenck. The race was for governor in 1867. His political appeal was obvious. But he didn't want the job. His mentor Tom Corwin had been governor and didn't like it.[24] And Schenck still had his eyes set on the Senate. By this time, the impeachment of President Andrew Johnson was looming. That could mean the elevation of Wade to the presidency, opening his seat.

So the governor slot went to Rutherford B. Hayes, another general/politician, who had been wounded four times in the war. Hayes, of course, became president in 1876 and was succeeded in that job by another Ohio Republican general, James A. Garfield.

The question arises: Did Schenck blow his shot at the presidency? He must have wondered. Hayes and Garfield won their presidential nominations in multi-ballot conventions which neither entered as the leader. Clearly, as the conventions looked for compromise, being a governor or other major figure in a major swing state and a former general was useful.

When Schenck was defeated for re-election to the House in 1870—at a time when he was losing interest, anyway, and looking for financial opportunities—he was appointed ambassador to Great Britain by President Grant. Several others had turned the appointment down.[25] Grant had fired his previous ambassador, seeing him as more loyal to Sen. Charles Sumner, the chairman of the foreign relations committee, than to Grant.

Fairly important Civil War issues were at play in the U.S.–Britain relationship. The Confederates had received British help, even as Britain had claimed neutrality and had been treated as a neutral. Most specifically, the South had acquired the consequential blockade runner *Alabama* from the British. Many Americans were furious about that, including Sumner. In payment, Sumner wanted Canada! Actually, Grant had toyed with that idea, too, but gave up on it. Mainly Grant, who had a soft spot in his heart for Britain, just wanted some settlement. Schenck became involved in that effort, though Secretary of State Hamilton Fish was the main American player. Ultimately, the British admitted that they should have made sure the *Alabama* wasn't armed for combat, and they paid a financial penalty determined by international arbitration at Geneva.[26]

That all happened early in Schenck's five-year stay. Later on, Schenck—always struggling financially—got involved in a scandal. Or rather, he had lent his name to a silver mining operation in the West that was caught up in scandal. He didn't look good. He hadn't done anything major wrong, but, in the context of an administration that had all manner of other scandals, this wasn't welcome. He was investigated by Congress and officially criticized for behavior inappropriate to his role as a diplomat. He offered his resignation and came back to Washington.[27]

In his last years in Britain there was another event that some found scandalous. Schenck introduced the Court of St. James—that is, British royalty and such—to poker. He was always a gambler and always looking for a game. That word got around, followed by talk that Queen Victoria herself had asked him how the game was played. That supposedly caused him to go off and write six pages of rules.[28] That word got around, too, and Schenck became known in Britain for his educational endeavors. There were headlines about "Poker Schenck" and "Poker at Court" during times that were, well, Victorian. Then somebody published his rules, which was apparently the first time poker rules had been published.[29] Then *that* word got around back home, and, when Schenck got back home, he put out the booklet in America, too. The title page said, "Put not your trust in Kings and Princes: Three of a kind will take them both."[30]

It turned out that the Queen Victoria story wasn't true. Schenck wrote in the booklet that a Lady W. in Somerset asked him to do the write-up. He noted in the American edition that not everybody in the U.S. approved of this behavior in a man of his position. Little did Lady W. "and her family and guests (know) that they have thus ... brought down on me the wrath and reprehension of so many good people in America." But he didn't attempt to make the case that publishing the booklet was a public service. He just did it, perhaps for the money.

A family history says the reason Schenck had money problems was that he was too generous with his money.[31] Another possibility—though this is *entirely* speculative, supported by nothing in the way of facts—is that he played too much poker. Or perhaps the real problem was simply that he never really made any money outside of government, but put three children through private schools. At any rate, when he returned to the states in 1875—during which year he would turn 66—he still needed to make a living. That may account for his choice of Washington as a place to live, where his background and connections would be an asset as he set up as a lawyer. He lived there until his death in 1890.

When Vallandigham had burned candles in honor of Washington's Birthday, it was because he shared Schenck's veneration of the man. Before the war, they also shared a distrust of abolitionists, fearing they would combine with Southern fire-eaters to bring war. Yet in war-time, there they were: two neighbors, two lawyers in the same small place, two members of the same club of play readers, co-worshippers at the altar of the same political revolution, now seeing each other as forces of, respectively, sedition and despotism.

***

Congressman Samuel (Sunset) Cox, who got his middle name for allegedly getting carried away in a print description of a sunset, went on to have a career in

Washington, eventually becoming ambassador to the Ottoman Empire. In the years when I was working on this book, I was once engaged in a tourist's stroll around the East Village in Manhattan when I happened upon a statue of Cox. It was a disconcerting experience. A statue here of a not-famous historical Ohio congressman? I wondered if I was so immersed in my book that I was "seeing things" connected with it. But the statue was real. Turned out that, after being defeated for re-election in Ohio in 1864, Cox moved to New York and practiced law there and was elected to Congress. The statue—at an entrance to Tompkins Square Park—was funded by an organization that appreciated his work in securing a 40-hour-week and better pay for postal workers.

***

As noted earlier, Robert Schenck said that Salmon P. Chase called Vallandigham a traitor in 1863. On May 20, 1871, Chase publicly wrote to the old traitor, "You have rendered a great service to your country and the party.... Nothing can be truer than your declaration that the movement contemplated by the (New Departure) is the restoration of the Democratic party to its ancient platform of progress and reform." He said, "May God bless you for" the effort.[32]

Schenck as seen by *Vanity Fair* around the time of his return from the Court of St. James in 1875.

By the next year, however, Chase would not have referred to the Democratic Party as "the party." By then he was engaged in the creation of a new party. This one was the Liberal Republican Party. The word "Liberal" was used in reference to classical, Adam Smith, small-government liberalism. Mainly, the party members were tiring of federal efforts at Reconstruction, and they ran against the corruption and cronyism of the Grant years.

In 1872, Chase was trembling with age and did not generate wide support for president, getting two and half votes at the new party's convention.[33] That party picked Horace Greeley. So—incredibly—did the Democrats. They had been backed into a corner. The Liberal Republicans made their pick first and adopted a platform that pre-empted the Democrats' on big issues. All along, the Democrats had been fretting about the difficulty of defeating Grant; now they saw the anti–Grant effort potentially subdividing fatally. So they nominated a man who had been a favorite whipping boy of Democrats for many years, given his Republican, anti-slavery identity. Party differences were becoming murky. Greeley lost the election and then died in the same month.

Chase died the next May. In 1871 and 1872, everything that might have happened to thwart the Chase-Vallandigham partnership happened: Vallandigham died, Chase approached death, and the Democrats did a good imitation of death. One might get the impression fate was determined to make absolutely certain.

Chapter Notes

Preface

1. Steven K. Rogstad in Frank J. Klement, *The Limits of Dissent* by (New York: Fordham University Press, 1998), XXI.
2. James Vallandigham, *A Life of Clement Vallandigham* (Baltimore: Turnbull Brothers, 1872), 552.

Introduction

1. Wilfred E. Binkley, *American Political Parties: Their Natural History* (New York: Alfred A. Knopf, 1944), 264; Eugene H. Roseboom, "Southern Ohio and the Union in 1863," *The Mississippi Valley Historical Review*, Vol. 39, No. 1 (June 1952); 33; Waugh, *Reelecting Lincoln*, 280; and J.G. Randall, *Lincoln the President: Midstream* (New York: Dodd, Mead & Company, 1953), 212.
2. James G. Smart, ed., *A Radical View: The "Agate" Dispatches of Whitelaw Reid: 1861-1865* (Memphis: Memphis State University Press, 1976), Vol. 2, 129.
3. Richard Carwardine, *Lincoln's Sense of Humor* (Carbondale: Southern Illinois University Press, 2017), 74.
4. John C. Waugh, *Reelecting Lincoln: The Battle for the 1864 Presidency* (New York: Crown Publishers, 1997), 267.
5. Amity Shales, *Coolidge* (New York: HarperCollins, 2013).

Chapter 1

1. Clement Vallandigham, *The Record of C.L. Vallandigham on Abolition, the Union and the Civil War* (Cincinnati: J. Walter & Co., 1863), 191.
2. *Ibid.*, 189-190.
3. Klement, *The Limits of Dissent*, 1970, 29.
4. Bertram W. Korn, *American Jewry and the Civil War* (Cleveland: The World Publishing Company, 1961), 57.
5. Clement Vallandigham, *Speeches, Arguments, Addresses, and Letters of Clement L. Vallandigham* (New York: J. Walter & Co., 1864), 524.
6. James Vallandigham, 37.
7. *Ibid.*, 499.
8. Klement, *The Limits of Dissent*, 1970, 8.
9. James Vallandigham, 500-502.
10. Clement Vallandigham, *The Record....*, 194.
11. James Vallandigham, 1.
12. George Knepper, *Ohio and Its People* (Kent, Ohio: The Kent State University Press, Bicentennial Edition 2003), 110.
13. Columbiana County's website.
14. Knepper, 167.
15. James Vallandigham, 566.
16. *Ibid.*, 12.
17. *Ibid.*, 24.
18. Klement, *The Limits of Dissent*, 1970, 26-27, 313 and elsewhere.
19. James Vallandigham, 454, 457 and 491.
20. Jesse Norman, *Edmund Burke: The First Conservative* (New York: Basic Books, 2013) 284, 280, and 97.
21. Clement Vallandigham, *Speeches...*, 355 and 414.
22. Norman, 233-235.
23. New York: Encounter Books.
24. Clement Vallandigham, *The Record...*, 8.
25. *Congressional Globe*, February 2, 1859.
26. James Vallandigham, 219 and 239.
27. Clement Vallandigham, *Speeches...*, 556.
28. U.S. National Archives web page *Lincoln's Spot Resolutions*.
29. Clement Vallandigham, *Speeches...*, 545.
30. Jeremy Duda, *If This Be Treason: The American Rogues and Rebels Who Walked the Line Between Dissent and Betrayal* (Guilford, Conn: Lyons Press, 2017), 130.
31. Michael F. Holt, *The Rise and Fall of the American Whig Party: Jacksonian Politics and the Onset of the Civil War* (Oxford: Oxford University Press, 1999), 249.
32. George Henry Porter, *Ohio Politics During the Civil War Period* (Columbia University dissertation, 1911), 179.
33. Clement Vallandigham, *The Record...*, 125.
34. Article in unidentified publication, Vallandigham folder, New York Historical Society.
35. C.S. Speaker, C.C. Connell and George T. Farrell, *An Historical Sketch of the Old Village of New Lisbon, Ohio* (Lisbon: Centennial Celebration Committee, 1903).
36. Edward Widmer, *Lincoln on the Verge* (New York: Simon & Schuster, 2020), 153-159.
37. Klement, *The Limits of Dissent*, 1970, 10.

38. Harold Holzer, *Lincoln and the Power of the Press: The War for Public Opinion* (New York: Simon & Schuster, 2014), XX–XXII.
39. Daniel Lucien Medlar, *The Gentleman and the Artist: A Journal of D.L. Medlar, September 1, 1859-April 30, 1862* (Dayton: Dayton Metro Library, 2007), 149.
40. Holzer, 188.
41. Dayton *Daily Journal*, May 31, 1862.
42. Knepper, *Ohio and Its People*, 101.
43. James Vallandigham, 477.
44. Joanne B. Freeman, *The Field of Blood: Violence in Congress and the Road to Civil War* (New York: Farrar, Straus and Giroux, 2018) 193–197.
45. Robert J. Zalimas, Jr., "'Contest MY seat sir!': Lewis D. Campbell, Clement L. Vallandigham, and the Election of 1856," *Ohio History*, Vol. 106, Winter-Spring 1997, 7.
46. *Yearbook of Immigration Statistics: 2010*, U.S. Department of Homeland Security.
47. William E. Van Horne, "Lewis D. Campbell and the Know-Nothing Party in Ohio," *Ohio History*, Vol. 76, Autumn 1967, No. 4, 203.
48. Zalimas, 10.
49. Klement, *The Limits of Dissent*, 1970, 15–16. *Dayton Daily Empire*, Oct. 18, 1856.
50. Zalinas, 30 and 27.
51. Clement Vallandigham, *Speeches…*," 180–186.
52. Ibid., 189 and 236.
53. Clement Vallandigham, *The Record…*, 247–248.
54. Ibid., 185.
55. James Vallandigham, 101–102.
56. Ibid., 60.
57. Clement Vallandigham, *The Record…*, 36.
58. Ibid., 27.
59. Ibid., 188–189.
60. Ibid., 148.
61. Ibid., 175.
62. H.W. Brands, *Heirs of the Founders* (New York: Doubleday, 2018), 257.
63. Ibid., 240–241.
64. Ibid., 249–250.
65. Klement, *The Limits of Dissent*, 1970, 18–19.
66. Clement Vallandigham, *The Record…*, 50.
67. Ibid., 5–39.
68. Ibid., 188.
69. Ibid., 45.
70. James McPherson, *Battle Cry of Freedom* (New York: Oxford University Press, 1988) 78 *et seq.*
71. Ibid., 214.
72. James Brewer Stewart, *Joshua R. Giddings and the Tactics of Radical Politics* (Cleveland: The Press of Case Western Reserve University, 1970) 63–67.
73. Clement Vallandigham, *The Record…*, 191.

Chapter 2

1. August 19, 1870, reprinted in The Eaton *Weekly Democrat*, August 25, 1870.
2. Thomas S. Mach, *"Gentleman George" Hunt Pendleton: Party Politics and Ideological Identity in Nineteenth-Century America* (Kent, Ohio: The Kent State University Press, 2007) 62.
3. Charles Wilson, *Cincinnati a Southern Outpost in 1860–1861?*, The Mississippi Valley Historical Review, Vol. 24, No. 4 (Mar., 1938), 475 and 476.
4. Roseboom, *Southern Ohio and the Union in 1863*, 38, in a footnote in which the author does some reporting and some extrapolating.
5. Ibid., 42.
6. George Knepper, *Ohio Politics: A Historical Perspective*, in Ohio Politics, Alexander P. Lamis, ed. (Kent, Ohio: The Kent State University Press, 1994), 4.
7. blackdemographics.com
8. Porter, 14.
9. Frederick Luebke, ed., *Ethnic Voters and the Election of 1860* (Lincoln: University of Nebraska Press, 1971)
10. James Vallandigham, 570, reprinting a eulogy by former U.S. James Wall of New Jersey.
11. J. Staudenraus, ed., *Mr. Lincoln's Washington: The Civil War Dispatches of Noah Brooks, Civil War Correspondent* (South Brunswick: Thomas Yoseloff, 1967), 105–106.

Chapter 3

1. Brian McGinty, *John Brown's Trial* (Cambridge: Harvard University Press, 2009) 58–62; David S. Reynolds, *John Brown, Abolitionist: The Man Who Killed Slavery, Sparked the Civil War, and Seeded Civil Rights* (New York: Alfred A. Knopf, 2005), 330.
2. History.com page on Brown.
3. James Vallandigham, 121.
4. Klement, *Limits of Dissent*, 1970, 7; James Vallandigham, 113–119; McGinty, 58–62.
5. David W. Blight, *Frederick Douglass: Prophet of Freedom* (New York: Simon & Schuster, 2018), 296–298.
6. James Vallandigham, 119–120.
7. James Vallandigham, 120–124.
8. abrahamlincolnonline.org/ under speeches and Cooper Union.
9. Thomas Fleming, *A Disease in the Public Mind: A New Understanding of Why We Fought the Civil War* (New York: Da Capo Press, 2013), 244.

Chapter 4

1. Clement Vallandigham, *The Record…*, 39–58.
2. Widmer, 178.
3. Frank L. Klement, *The Copperheads of the Middle West* (Chicago: University of Chicago Press, 1960), 12.
4. Frank Van Der Linden, *The Dark Intrigue: The True Story of a Civil War Conspiracy* (Golden, Colorado: Fulcrum Publishing, 2007).
5. Stephen E. Towne, *Spies in the Civil War: Exposing Confederate Conspiracies in America's Heartland* (Athens, Ohio: Ohio University Press, 2015).

Chapter 5

1. Clement Vallandigham, *The Record...*, 63.
2. *Ibid.*, 88–91.
3. Roy P. Basler, ed., *The Collected Works of Abraham Lincoln* (New Brunswick: Rutgers University Press, 1953), Vol. V, 537.
4. James Vallandigham, 156–7.
5. McPherson, *Battle Cry of Freedom*, 251–2.
6. *Ibid.*, 274.
7. Roy Morris, Jr., *The Long Pursuit: Abraham Lincoln's Thirty-Year Struggle with Stephen Douglas for the Heart and Soul of America* (New York: HarperCollins, 2008), 214 and 215.
8. Clement Vallandigham, *The Record...*, 92.
9. *Ibid.*, 93–110.
10. e.g., Jon Meacham, *American Lion: Andrew Jackson in the White House* (New York: Random House, 2008), 246.
11. McPherson, *Battle Cry of Freedom*, 269.
12. Basler, Vol. IV, 429.
13. Fleming, 82.
14. Clement Vallandigham, *The Record...*, 18.
15. James Vallandigham, 555–556.
16. *Ibid.*, 569.
17. Tom Lowe to "Johnnie," Aug. 24, 1861, Lowe Papers, Dayton Metro Library. These Lowes are not related to Hollywood personalities Rob and Chad Lowe, who lived in the Dayton area as children. Their father was the first in his family to come to Dayton, he told me in a phone conversation. In the nineteenth century, Lowe was a common name in the Dayton area and was sometimes pronounced lau. Another Lowe family was prominent, active and Republican during the war. To this day an old downtown Dayton building has the Lowe name on it. That is also not the family of Tom.

Chapter 6

1. *Daily Ohio Statesman*, Columbus, July 25, 1861, e.g.
2. James Vallandigham, 216.
3. Clement Vallandigham, *The Record...*, 127.
4. *Congressional Globe*, Feb. 19, 1862.
5. Margaret E. Wagner, *The Library of Congress Illustrated Timeline of the Civil War* (New York: Little, Brown and Company, 2011), 50–51.
6. William C. Davis, *Breckenridge: Statesman, Soldier, Symbol* (Lexington: The University Press of Kentucky, 2010), 296 on last point.
7. Klement, 1970, *The Limits of Dissent*, 50.
8. August 8, 1861.
9. James Vallandigham, 192.
10. Clement Vallandigham, *The Record...*, 120.
11. H.L. Trefousse, *Benjamin Franklin Wade: Radical Republican from Ohio* (New York: Twayne Publishers, 1963), 26.
12. *Ibid.*, 121.
13. James Vallandigham, 200

Chapter 7

1. Dayton *Journal*, July 28. 1863.
2. *Ibid.*, Sept. 7, 1863.
3. Medlar, 120.
4. Feb. 4, 1863.
5. Dayton *Empire*, April, 1865.
6. Medlar, 183–186.
7. Dayton *Journal*, Oct. 10, 1862.
8. McPherson, *Battle Cry of Freedom*, 816–819.
9. The natures of the stores are provided in Charlotte Reeve Conover, *Dayton, Ohio—An Intimate History* (Dayton: Lewis Historical Publishing Co., 1932), 102. The dry goods store was at Second and Jefferson Streets.
10. Dec. 8, 1862.
11. Robert J. Wimberg, *Cincinnati and the Civil War: Under Attack* (Cincinnati: Ohio Book Store, 1999), 185.
12. Clement Vallandigham, *The Record...*, 28.
13. June 6, 1862.
14. August 9, 1862.
15. Clement Vallandigham, *The Record...*, 163.
16. *Ibid.*, 44.
17. Porter, 325.
18. *Ibid.*
19. Dayton *Journal*, July 15, 1862.
20. The hardware store was on the east side of Main Street, between Second and Third Streets.
21. Medlar, IX.
22. *Ibid.*, 120.
23. *Ibid.*, 151.
24. *Ibid.*, 148.
25. *Ibid.*, 151.
26. *Ibid.*, 153.
27. *Ibid.*, 154.
28. *Ibid.*, 145.
29. Carl M. Becker, "The Death of J.F. Bollmeyer: Murder Most Foul?" *Cincinnati Historical Society Bulletin*, Vol. 24, No. 3, July 1966, 249.
30. Medlar, 154.
31. *Ibid.*, 121.
32. *Ibid.*, 161–162.

Chapter 8

1. Charlotte Reeve Conover, *The Story of Dayton* (Dayton: The Greater Dayton Assn., 1917), 148; Robert W. Steele and Mary Davies Steele, *Early Dayton* (Dayton: U.B. Publishing House, 1896), 180.
2. *Williams Dayton City Directory, 1862-63, Vol. 4*, 177. Earlier volumes of the city directory have Vallandigham at the northwest corner of Ludlow and First.
3. James R. Therry, *The Life of General Robert Cumming Schenck* (Georgetown University dissertation, 1968), 163.
4. *Ibid.*, 1–2 of the abstract.
5. Lloyd Ostendorf, *Mr. Lincoln Came to Dayton* (Dayton: The Otterbein Press, 1959), 33–34.
6. Therry, 109.
7. *Ibid.*, 498.

8. *Ibid.*, 129.
9. Epiphanie C. Kokkinou, *The Political Career of Robert Cumming Schenck.*, master's thesis, Miami University, 1955, 116.
10. *Ibid.*, 146 *et seq.*
11. Ostendorf, 11–12.
12. Therry, 171–172.
13. *Ibid.*, 153–155.
14. *Ibid.*, 140 and 155–156.
15. Ostendorf, 13–14 and 25.
16. Schenck's biographer has Schenck speaking in Cincinnati with Lincoln; but when he would have left Dayton is not clear; Therry, 172–173.
17. Ostendorf, 33.
18. Steele and Steele, 187.
19. Therry, 179–181.
20. Basler, Vol. IV, 136.
21. Therry, 184–189.
22. Ostendorf, 38.
23. Therry, 196–198.
24. Ostendorf, 42; Murat Halstead of the Cincinnati *Commercial*.
25. July 23, 1861.
26. Therry, 259–260.
27. Ostendorf, 39.
28. May 19, 1862.
29. 70.
30. Candice Mallard, *Destiny of the Republic: A Tale of Madness, Medicine and the Murder of a President* (New York: Anchor Books, 2011), 30.
31. McPherson, *Battle Cry of Freedom*, 591.
32. Oct. 7, 1862.
33. Therry, 304.
34. *Ibid.*, 224.
35. 78ohio.org/1860-presidential election.
36. Klement's book on Vallandigham is incorrect when it states that Warren County was substituted for Preble. *The Limits of Dissent*, 1970, 102.
37. *The Crisis*, Oct. 14, 1863.
38. Thomas Smith, "Crawford County: A Study in Midwestern Copperheadism," *Ohio History Journal*, Vol. 76, Winter and Spring, 1967, 45.
39. Edward Conrad Smith, *The Borderland in the Civil War* (New York: The MacMillan Company, 1927), 332.
40. Medlar, 182.
41. Porter, 107.
42. Jonathan W. White, *Abraham Lincoln and Treason in the Civil War: The Trials of John Merryman* (Baton Rouge: Louisiana State University Press, 2011), 44–45.
43. Mark E. Neely, Jr., *The Fate of Liberty: Abraham Lincoln and Civil Liberties* (New York: Oxford University Press, 1991), 64 and elsewhere.
44. William Blair, *With Malice Toward Some: Treason and Loyalty in the Civil War Era* (Chapel Hill: The University of North Carolina Press, 2014), 56–57, citing Thomas P. and Beverly A. Lowry, indexing project for courts-martial records held at the National Archives, Washington, D.C.
45. Julie Roy Jeffrey, "'They Cannot Expect... That a Loyal People Will Tolerate the Utterance of Such Sentiments': The Campaign against Treasonous Speech During the Civil War." *Civil War History*, Vol. 65, No. 1 (March 2019), 7, 17, 24 and throughout.
46. James G. Randall, *Constitutional Problems Under Lincoln* (New York: D. Appleton and Company, 1926), 150.
47. John A. Marshall, *American Bastille: A History of the Illegal Arrests and Imprisonment of American Citizens During the Late Civil War* (Philadelphia: Thomas W. Hartley and Co., 1883).
48. Neely, 67.
49. Holzer, *Lincoln and the Power of the Press*, 335–337.
50. Medlar; the *Post* article appears in the diary, but the date of publication is not clear.
51. Porter, 243.
52. July 2, 1862.
53. Porter, 243.
54. William Whiting, *War Powers Under the Constitution of the United States: Military Arrests, Reconstruction and Military Government*" (Boston: Lee and Shepard Publishing, 1871), 221.
55. Klement, *Copperheads of the Middle West*, 15.
56. July 2, 1864.
57. Harper, 234.
58. *Journal of the (Ohio) House of Representatives*, Vol. 59, 101.
59. Harper, 227.
60. Richard Abbott, "Ohio's Civil War Governors" (Columbus: Ohio State University Press for the Ohio Historical Society, 1962), 21–23; Eugene Roseboom, *The History of the State of Ohio, Vol. IV, The Civil War Era, 1850–1873*, Carl Wittke, ed. (Columbus: Ohio State Archaeological and Historical Society, 1944), 391–392.
61. Roseboom, "Southern Ohio and the Union in 1863," 37.
62. Marshall, 598.
63. Robert F. Miller, *States at War, Vol. 5: A Reference Guide for Ohio in the Civil War* (Lebanon, N.H.: University Press of New England, 2015), 169.
64. Holzer, *Lincoln and the Power of the Press*, 338.
65. Marshall, 397–413; the author of *American Bastille* apparently talked to Olds' son and nobody else involved in the story.
66. Jennifer Weber, *Copperheads: The Rise and Fall of Lincoln's Opponents in the North* (New York: Oxford University Press, 2006), 81 and 148.
67. Clement Vallandigham, *The Record...*, 126.
68. Weber, 129 and Robert S. Harper, "The Ohio Press in the Civil War," *Civil War History*, Vol. 3, Issue 3 (1957), 221.
69. Clement Vallandigham, *The Record...*, 143.
70. *Ibid.*, 135.
71. *Ibid.*
72. McNeely, 194.
73. Mary Boykin Chestnut, *Mary Chesnut's Dairy* (New York: Penguin Books, 2011), 335.
74. Clement Vallandigham, *The Record...*, 143.
75. *Ibid.*, 122–134.
76. Aug. 30, 1862.
77. April 14; June 3, 5, 11,12,18; Aug. 13, 16, 30; Sept. 1, 12, 15, 16 e.g.

78. July 8, 1862.
79. July 5, 1862.
80. Wimberg, 77.
81. McPherson, *Battle Cry of Freedom*, 284.
82. *Ibid.*, 516.
83. Dayton *Journal*, July 19 and 24.
84. Wimberg, 53.
85. *Ibid.*, 52.
86. McPherson, *Battle Cry of Freedom*, 857.
87. Earl J. Hess, *Braxton Bragg: The Most Hated Man of the Confederacy* (Chapel Hill: The University of North Carolina Press, 2016).
88. Richard E. Beringer, Herman Hattaway, Archer Jones and William N. Still, Jr., *Why the South Lost the Civil War* (Athens, George: University of Georgia Press, 1986), 174.
89. Wimberg, 66.
90. McPherson, *Battle Cry of Freedom*, 517.
91. Beringer, etc., 274.
92. McPherson, *Battle Cry of Freedom*, 517.
93. Wimberg, 84–85.
94. Dayton *Journal*, Aug. 4, 1862.
95. Tom Lowe to Will Lowe, Sept. 6, 1862.
96. Wimberg, 164.
97. Dayton *Journal*, Sept. 9, 1862.
98. Klement, *The Limits of Dissent*, 1970, 45.
99. James Vallandigham, 141.
100. Clement Vallandigham, *The Record....*, 147.
101. *Ibid.*, 146.
102. Winberg, 80.
103. *Ibid.*, 98.
104. *Ibid.*, 165–166.
105. *Ibid.*, 168.
106. *Ibid.*, 129.
107. McPherson, *Battle Cry of Freedom*, 520.
108. *Ibid.*, 517.
109. Sept. 17, 1862.
110. Dayton *Journal*, Sept. 18, 1862.
111. *Ibid.*, Oct. 9, 1862.
112. *Ibid.*
113. *Ibid.*, Oct. 7, 1862.
114. *Ibid.*, Oct. 10, 1862.
115. Quoted in *The Crisis*, October 22.
116. Klement, *The Limits of Dissent*, 1970, 111.
117. Roseboom, *The History...*, 402.
118. Jonathan White, *Emancipation, the Union Army and the Reelection of Abraham Lincoln* (Baton Rouge: Louisiana State University Press, 2014), 15 *et seq.*
119. *Ibid.*, 18.
120. Dayton *Journal*, May 3, 1862.
121. Reprinted in *The Crisis*, Oct. 10, 1862.
122. Clement Vallandigham, *The Record...*, 161.
123. Porter, 144.
124. *Ibid.*, 167.
125. *Ibid.*, 162–163.
126. Jeffrey, 9.
127. Stewart, 273.
128. James McPherson, *Embattled Rebel: Jefferson Davis as Commander in Chief* (New York: The Penguin Press, 2014), 72–73.
129. Clement Vallandigham, *The Record...*, 159–160.
130. Porter, 144.

Chapter 9

1. Carl M. Becker, "The Genesis of a Copperhead," *Bulletin of the Historical and Philosophical Society of Ohio*, October, 1961, Vol. 19, No. 4, 237.
2. *Ibid.*, 238.
3. Whitelaw Reid, *Ohio in the War: Her Statesmen, Her Generals, and Soldiers, Volume 1* (Cincinnati: Moore, Wilstach & Baldwin, 1868), 1009.
4. *Ibid.*, 1010.
5. *Ibid.*
6. Becker, *Genesis...*, 241.
7. *Ibid.*, 243.
8. Carl M. Becker, *Tom Lowe: A Lesser Angel*, master's thesis, Miami (Ohio) University, 1958.
9. *Ibid.*
10. Tom Lowe to his father, Aug. 3, 1856.
11. Tom Lowe to Will Lowe, Aug. 9, 1862.
12. Becker, *Tom Lowe...*.
13. Becker, *Genesis...*, 247.
14. Becker, *Tom Lowe...*, 26.
15. *Ibid.*, 27.
16. *Ibid.*, 29.
17. Will Lowe to Tom Lowe, April 12, 1862.
18. Lowe Papers, throughout.
19. Tom Lowe to Will Lowe, various dates.
20. Becker, *Tom Lowe...*, 32.
21. *Ibid.*
22. Tom Lowe to the Presbyterian Church, October 7, 1861.
23. Becker, *Tom Lowe...*, 32.
24. *Ibid.*, 39.
25. Martha Lowe to Tom Lowe, 1863.
26. Becker, *The Death...*.
27. Klement, *The Limits of Dissent*, 1970, 142.

Chapter 10

1. Clement Vallandigham, *The Record...*, 173–204.
2. *Congressional Globe*, Jan. 14, 1863.
3. Dayton *Empire*, Jan. 27, 1863.
4. *Ibid.*, March 3, 1863.
5. *Ibid.*, Jan. 14, 1863.
6. Clement Vallandigham, *The Record...*, 172.
7. Dayton *Empire*, March 17, 1863.
8. *Ibid.*, Feb. 2, 1863.
9. Clement Vallandigham, *The Record...*, 169–170.
10. Dayton *Journal*, Feb. 18, 1863.

Chapter 11

1. Dayton *Empire*, Feb. 18 and March 10, 1863.
2. *Ibid.*, Jan. 6, 1863, reprinting a piece from the Allen County *Democrat*.
3. Porter, 167.

4. *Ibid.*
5. Roseboom, *The History...*, 414.
6. William Marvel, *Burnside* (Chapel Hill: The University of North Carolina Press, 1991), 13–14.
7. *Ibid.*, Chapter 2.
8. *Ibid.*, 77 and 93–94.
9. Dayton *Journal*, Aug. 26, 1862.
10. Marvel, *Burnside*, 99–100.
11. *Ibid.*, 159–160.
12. Bruce Catton, *The Civil War* (Boston: Houghton Mifflin Company, 2004 edition), 117.
13. *Ibid.*, 115.
14. Bruce Catton, *The Army of the Potomac, Vol. 3: A Stillness at Appomattox* (Garden City, N.Y.: Doubleday & Company, Inc., 1953), 29.
15. Bruce Catton, *Mr. Lincoln's Army* (New York: Pocketbook, Inc., 1964), 268.
16. Marvel, *Burnside*, XII.
17. *Ibid.*, 425.
18. Shelby Foote, *The Civil War: A Narrative—Fredericksburg to Meridian* (New York: Vintage Books, 1986 edition), 44.
19. Marvel, *Burnside*, 220.
20. Dayton *Journal*, Feb. 24, 1863.
21. *Ibid.*, Feb. 23, 1863.
22. Therry, 264.
23. *Ibid.*, 271–272.
24. *Ibid.*, 304.
25. *Ibid.*, 290.
26. *Ibid.*, 284–287.
27. Eric Foner, *Reconstruction: America's Unfinished Revolution, 1863–1877*, Updated Edition (New York: HarperCollins, 2014), 10.
28. Dayton *Journal*, Feb. 4, 1863.
29. *New York Times*, Feb. 15, 1863.
30. Dayton *Journal*, March 3, 1863.
31. *Ibid.*, March 6, 1863.
32. *Ibid.*, March 7, 1863.
33. *Ibid.*, March 10, 1863.
34. Tom Lowe to Will Lowe, March 7, 1863.
35. March 10, 1863.
36. Marvel, *Burnside*, 222.
37. *Ibid.*, 3.
38. *Ibid.*, 12.
39. *Ibid.*, 223–224.
40. *Ibid.*, 227–228.
41. *The Trial of Hon. Clement L. Vallandigham, by a Military Commission; and the Proceedings Under His Application for a Writ of Habeas Corpus in the Circuit Court of the United States for the Southern District of Ohio* (Cincinnati: Rickey and Carroll, 1863), 7.
42. Blair, Chapter 2.
43. Marvel, *Burnside*, 231.
44. Marvel, *Burnside*, 232–233.
45. Doris Kearns Goodwin, *Team of Rivals: The Political Genius of Abraham Lincoln* (New York: Simon & Schuster Paperbacks, 2005), 520.
46. *The Trial...*, 20, 24 and 25,
47. Randall, *Constitutional Problems...*, 477–478n.
48. *The Trial...*, 37–38.
49. Marvel, *Burnside*, 235.
50. Tom Lowe to Will Lowe, May 11, 1863.
51. Dayton *Empire*, March 6, 1863.
52. Jeffrey, 13.
53. Towne, 82 and 103 on 344; and John Farris Edgar, *Pioneer Life in Dayton and Vicinity, 1796–1840* (Dayton: U.B. Publishing House, 1896), 201.
54. Marvel, *Burnside*, 236.
55. Blair, 56.
56. *The Crisis*, July 22, 1863 and Klement, *The Limits of Dissent*, 1970, 165.
57. *New York Herald*; Cleveland *Morning Leader*, Ebensburg, Pa., *Democrat and Sentinel*, Cadiz, Ohio *Democrat Sentinel*, Millersburg, Ohio *Holmes Co. Farmer* and Woodsfield, Ohio *Spirit of Democracy*, for example.
58. *The Trial...*, 11–12.
59. *Ibid.*, 17.
60. *Ibid.*
61. *Ibid.*, 12–29.
62. Dayton *Journal*, March 3, 1863.
63. *The Trial...*, 25–29.
64. *Ibid.*, 31–33.
65. Minoa Uffelman, "Tennessee's Fighting Parson," *New York Times*, Nov. 20, 2011.
66. Jeffrey, 28.
67. William Marvel, *Lincoln's Autocrat: The Life of Edwin Stanton* (Chapel Hill: The University of North Carolina Press, 2015), 284.
68. Basler, Vol. VI, 216–217.
69. *The Trial...*, 40–44.
70. Vallandigham to Manton Marble, editor and proprietor of the Democratic New York *World*, May 12, 1863; Marble collection at the Library of Congress.
71. *The Trial...*, 263.
72. Lyman Horace Weeks, ed., *Prominent Families of New York* (New York: The Historical Company, 1897), 358.
73. *The Trial...*, 270–271.
74. *Ibid.*, 259–272.
75. Marvel, *Lincoln's Autocrat*, 285.
76. *Lincoln the President*, 212.
77. *Harper's Weekly*, May 30, 1863, Vallandigham folder, New York Historical Society.
78. Marvel, *Burnside*, 210 e.g.
79. Goodwin, 522–523, e.g.
80. Basler, Vol. VI, 269.
81. *Ibid.*, 390.
82. Walter Stahr, *Stanton: Lincoln's War Secretary* (New York: Simon & Schuster, 2017), 276.
83. John Nicolay and John Hay, *Abraham Lincoln: A History*, Vol. VII (New York: The Century Co., 1909), 340–341.
84. Goodwin, 523.
85. Marvel, *Lincoln's Autocrat*, 284 and Stahr, 277.
86. Randall, *Constitutional Problems...*, 179n.
87. Gideon Welles, *Diary of Gideon Welles, Secretary of the Navy under Lincoln and Johnson*, Vol. 1 (Boston: Houghton Mifflin Company, 1911), 306.
88. May 25, 1863.
89. Nicolay and Hay, Vol. 7, 338.
90. Klement, *The Limits of Dissent*, 1970, 177–178.

91. Dayton *Journal*, May 22, 1863.
92. Nicolay and Hay, Vol. 7, 339–340.
93. *Harper's Weekly*, May 30, 1863, Vallandigham folder, New York Historical Society.
94. Vallandigham to Marble, May 12, 1863.
95. Vallandigham to Marble, May 15, 1863.
96. Klement, *The Limits of Dissent*, 1970, 192 *et seq.*
97. Lowe Papers.
98. William Lamers, *The Edge of Glory: A Biography of General William S. Rosecrans, USA* (Baton Rouge: Louisiana State University Press, 1999 paperback edition), 260–61.
99. *Ibid.*
100. *Ibid.*, 6.
101. Feb. 13, 1863.
102. Cleveland *Morning Leader*, April 10, 1863.
103. Lamers, 259.
104. Richmond *Dispatch*, May 30 and Richmond *Enquirer*, in a semi-weekly edition on June 2, e.g.
105. Klement, *The Limits of Dissent*, 1970, 194–195.
106. 267.
107. Cincinnati *Gazette*, May 29, 1863. The article is inexplicably signed "Y.S." But it was Furay's.
108. Dayton *Journal*, June 3, 1863.
109. C.R. Graham, ed., *Under Both Flags: A Panorama of the Great Civil War as Represented in Story, Anecdote, Adventure, and the Romance of Reality* (Veteran Publishing Co., 1896), 310–311.
110. Klement, *The Limits of Dissent*, 1970, 200.
111. Chattanooga *Rebel*, May 29, 1863.
112. Hess, 207.
113. Klement, *The Limits of Dissent*, 1970, 204.
114. Clifford Dowdey and Louis H. Manarin, eds., *The Wartime Papers of R.E. Lee* (New York: DeCapo Press, 1987), 507–509.
115. Louis W. Koenig, "'The Most Unpopular Man in the North,'" *American Heritage*, February, 1964, 12.
116. Elizabeth R. Varon, *Armies of Deliverance: A New History of the Civil War*. (New York: Oxford University Press, 2019), 244.
117. Robert Cowley, ed., *With My Face to the Enemy: Perspectives on the Civil War* (New York: Berkley Books, 2001), 177, comment by the editor, who said it was "perhaps a bit unfair" to Bragg.
118. Hess and Samuel J. Martin, *General Braxton Bragg, CSA* (Jefferson, N.C.: McFarland and Company, Inc., 2011).
119. Hess, 139.
120. *The War of the Rebellion: A Compilation of the Official Records of the Union and Confederate Armies Official Records*, Vol 5, Ser. 2, 958.
121. *Ibid.*, 863.
122. Arthur J.L. Fremantle, *Three Months in the Southern States: April-June, 1863* (New York: John Bradburn, 1864, reprinted Lincoln: University of Nebraska Press, 1991), 5.
123. *Ibid.*, Introduction by Gary W. Gallagher.
124. *Ibid.*, 137–138.
125. Reprinted in the Chattanooga *Rebel*, June 3, 1863.
126. Foote, 19.
127. Klement, *The Limits of Dissent*, 1970, 208.
128. John Beauchamp Jones, *A Rebel War Clerk's Diary at the Confederate States Capital* (Philadelphia: J.B. Lippincott & Co., 1866), Chapter 1.
129. McPherson, *Battle Cry of Freedom*, 648; actually the editorial appeared after the battle; bad news traveled slowly.
130. McPherson, *Embattled Rebel*, 130 and 140.
131. *The Trial…*, 17.

Chapter 12

1. Thomas Smith, "Crawford County…," 46.
2. Porter, 169–170.
3. Roseboom, *The History…*, 414–415.
4. James Vallandigham, 303–304.
5. Stephen Sears, *George B. McClellan: The Young Napoleon* (New York: Ticknor & Fields, 1988), 355.
6. Staunton *Spectator*, June 6, 1863.
7. Klement, *The Limits of Dissent*, 1970, 211.
8. Fremantle, 202–203.
9. *Ibid.*, 203–204.
10. *Ibid.*
11. Page on the Wilmington paper at the Library of Congress newspaper archive at chroniclingamerica.loc.gov.
12. Wilmington *Journal*, July 2, 1863.
13. James Vallandigham, 314.
14. Klement, *The Limits of Dissent*, 1970, 211–212.
15. James Vallandigham, 290–293.
16. Holzer, 430.
17. Dayton *Journal*, Sept. 18, 1863.
18. Samuel Sullivan Cox, *Eight Years in Congress* (New York: D. Appleton and Company, 1865), 327–334.
19. Basler, Vol. VI, 260–269.
20. Holzer, 430.
21. Daniel J. Ryan, *Lincoln and Ohio* (Columbus: Ohio Historical Society, 1923; 2008 edition, Old Hundredth Press, Dover, Ohio), 159.
22. Robert M. Sandow, *Deserter Country: Civil War Opposition in the Pennsylvania Appalachians* (New York: Fordham University Press, 2009), 100.
23. Basler, Vol. VI, 300.
24. Ryan, 152–159.
25. Basler, Vol. VI, 300–306.
26. Goodwin, 121–123.
27. Ryan, 164–170.
28. 448.

Chapter 13

1. J.M.S. Careless, *Brown of the Globe, Vol. 2, Statesman of Confederation, 1860–1880* (Toronto: The Macmillan Company of Canada, 1963). My summary owes much to this book.
2. Klement, *The Limits of Dissent*, 1970, 213.
3. *The Crisis*, July 22, 1863.
4. July 11, 1863.
5. *Official Records*. See subsequent note.

6. *The Crisis*, July 29, 1863.
7. David Hochfelder, *The Telegraph in America, 1832-1920* (Baltimore: Johns Hopkins University Press, 2012), 6-31.
8. Dayton *Journal*, July 29, 1863, e.g.
9. *Ibid.*, August 21, 1863.
10. James Vallandigham, 318-321.
11. August 20, 1863.
12. David L. Mowery, *Morgan's Great Raid: The Remarkable Expedition from Kentucky to Ohio* (Charleston, S.C.: The History Press, 2013), 24.
13. *Ibid.*, 25.
14. *Ibid.*, 77.
15. Marvel, *Burnside*, 255.
16. *The Crisis*, July 22, 1863.
17. Mowery, 83.
18. *Ibid.*, 12.
19. Weber, 114.
20. Klement, *The Copperheads in the Middle West*, 125.
21. Thomas H. Hines, "The Northwestern Conspiracy," *Southern Bivouac*, Vol. II, December 1886, 442.
22. Margaret White Taylor to Thomas T. Taylor, July 16, 1863, Thomas T. Taylor Papers, Ohio Historical Society, Columbus.
23. Weber, 113.
24. July 28, 1863.
25. Vallandigham to Marble, August 2, 1863.
26. John Strausbaugh, *City of Sedition: The History of New York City During the Civil War* (New York: Hachetter Book Group, 2016).
27. Klement, *The Limits of Dissent*, 217.
28. Dayton *Journal*, August 8, 1863.
29. Vallandigham to Marble, August 2, 1863.
30. Marvel, *Burnside*, 279-280.
31. *Official Records*, Series 1, Vol. XXX, Part III, 522 and Series 2, Vol. 6, 231-232 and 276.
32. Porter, 177.
33. *Ibid.*, 180. The Halstead note is in a footnote citing Chase's papers.
34. August 1, 1863.
35. *The Crisis*, Sept. 10, 1862.
36. Porter, 113-120.
37. Roseboom, *The History...*, 418-419.
38. Dayton *Journal*, Sept. 24, 1863.
39. *The Crisis*, August 5, 1863.
40. Excerpted in George Winston Smith and Charles Judah, *Life in the North During the Civil War: A Source History* (Albuquerque: The University of New Mexico Press, 1966), 112-113.
41. *The Crisis*, August 5, 1863.
42. Widmer, throughout.
43. *The Crisis*, Sept. 16, 1863.
44. Porter, 317-318, in footnote citing *The Crisis* of August 5, 1863.
45. August 18, 1863.
46. Dayton *Journal*, August 26 and Sept. 3, 1863.
47. *Ibid.*, August 25, 1863.
48. *Ibid.*, August 28, 1863, for example.
49. *Ibid.*, September 9, 1863.
50. *Ibid.*, August 19, 1863.
51. *The Crisis*, September 2, 1863.
52. Eugene H. Roseboom, "The Mobbing of the Crisis," *Ohio State Archaeological and Historical Quarterly*, 59 (April 1950) and Harper, 230.
53. Dayton *Journal*, Sept. 9, 1863.
54. *Ibid.*, July 30, 1863.
55. *Ibid.*, Sept. 8, 1863.
56. *Ibid.*, Sept. 5, 1863.
57. Harvey W. Crew, publisher, multiple authors, *History of Dayton, Ohio* (Dayton: United Brethren Publishing House, 1889), Chapter XXII, at Dayton History Books Online.
58. Harper, 238.
59. Donald W. Curl, *Murat Halstead and the Cincinnati Commercial* (Boca Raton: University Presses of Florida, 1980), 18.
60. Cincinnati: Moore, Wilstach, Keys, & Co. 1863.
61. Bickham Papers, Dayton Metro Library.
62. Dayton *Journal*, August 26, 1863.
63. David W. Bulla, *Lincoln's Censor: Milo Hascall and Freedom of the Press in Civil War Indiana* (West Lafayette: Purdue University Press, 2009), 157.
64. Sept. 8, 1863.
65. Sept. 23, 1863.
66. Dayton *Journal*, July 17, 1863.
67. *Ibid.*, August 27, 1863.
68. *Ibid.*, August 20, 1863.
69. Delaware (Ohio) *Gazette*, Sept. 18, 1863 and Ashland (Ohio) *Union*, Sept. 30, 1863, e.g.
70. *Ibid.*, Oct. 12, 1863.
71. *Ibid.*, June 19, 1863.
72. *Ibid.*, June 20, 1863.
73. *Ibid.*, June 26, 1863, e.g.
74. *Ibid.*, Sept. 3, 1863.
75. Brett Barker, "Limiting Dissent in the Midwest: Ohio Republicans' Attacks on the Democratic Press," *Union Heartland: The Midwestern Home Front During the Civil War*, Ginette Aley and J.L. Anderson, eds. (Carbondale: Southern Illinois University Press, 2013), 178.
76. Dayton *Journal*, June 3, 1863.
77. *Ibid.*, June 3, 1863.
78. March 7, 1864.
79. Harper, 230.
80. *The Crisis*, August 8, 1863.
81. *Ibid.*, Sept. 30, 1863.
82. *Ibid.*, Oct. 27, 1863.
83. *Ibid.*, Oct. 7, 1863.
84. Tom Lowe to Will Lowe, May 22, 1863.
85. Tom Lowe to Will Lowe, May 30, 1863.
86. Marsha Lowe to Tom Lowe, Sept. 8, 1863, Lowe Papers, Dayton Metro Library.
87. *The Crisis*, Sept. 16, 1863.
88. *Ibid.*, July 29, 1863.
89. *Ibid.*, July 29, 1863.
90. *Ibid.*, August 12, 1863.
91. *Ibid.*, July 29, 1863.
92. Widely reported, including *The Crisis*, Sept. 16, 1863.
93. *Ibid.*
94. Dayton *Journal*, Sept. 21, 1863.
95. *Ibid.*

96. Vallandigham to Marble, August 13, 1863, and *The Crisis*, August 12, 1863.
97. *The Crisis*, July 29, 1863.
98. *Ibid.*, Sept. 16, 1863.
99. Dayton *Journal*, August 3, 1863.
100. *The Crisis*, Sept. 2, 1863.
101. *Ibid.*, August 26, Sept. 9 and Sept. 23.
102. August 1, 1863.
103. *The Crisis*, Sept. 16, 1863.
104. *The Crisis*, Sept. 16, 1863.
105. Dayton *Journal*, May 18, 1863.
106. Dayton *Journal*, June 4, 1863.
107. August 27, 1863.
108. August 28, 1863.
109. Porter, 220.
110. *The Crisis*, Sept. 30, 1863.
111. Duda, 135.
112. James Vallandigham, 348–349.
113. John Sherman, *Recollections of 40 Years in the House, Senate and Cabinet: An Autobiography* (Chicago: The Werner Company, 1896), 271.
114. Dayton *Journal*, Sept. 3, 1863; the British paper is unidentified.
115. Richmond *Dispatch*, August 31, 1863.
116. *Enquirer*, Sept. 22, 1863 quoted in Dayton *Journal*, Sept. 25, 1863 by the *Journal's* man in Washington.
117. Dayton *Journal*, Oct. 3, 1863.
118. *The Crisis*, August 19, 1863.
119. Dayton *Journal*, Oct. 7 and elsewhere.
120. Porter, 184.
121. *Ibid.*em, note.
122. Article 5, Section 1, 1851 constitution.
123. Dayton *Journal*, Sept. 12, 1863.
124. Vallandigham to Marble, Oct. 4, 1863.
125. David G. Moore, *William S. Rosecrans and the Union Victory: A Civil War Biography* (Jefferson, N.C.: McFarland & Co.), 161.
126. Stahr, 326.
127. Dayton *Journal*, Oct. 3 and 9, 1863.
128. *Ibid.*, Sept. 25, 1863.
129. Wagner, 148–161.
130. *The Vallandigham Song Book: Songs for Our Times* (Columbus: J. Walter & Co., 1863)
131. Dayton *Journal*, Sept. 21, 1863.
132. Porter, 181.
133. Sept. 9, 1863.
134. *The Crisis*, Sept. 12, 1863.
135. *Ibid.*, Sept. 19, 1863.
136. *Ibid.*, Sept. 30, 1863.
137. *Ibid.*, Oct. 7 and 8, 1863.
138. *The Crisis*, Oct. 14, 1863.
139. Dayton *Journal*, Oct. 10, 1863.
140. Oct. 12, 1863.
141. Oct. 13, 1863.
142. Dayton *Journal*, Oct. 12, 1863.
143. Dayton *Empire*, Oct. 13, 1863.
144. *Ibid.*, Oct. 12, 1863.
145. Dayton, Journal, Oct. 12, 1863.

Chapter 14

1. Goodwin, 575.
2. Ryan, 172.
3. Klement, *The Limits of Dissent*, 1970, 252.
4. John Niven, *Salmon P. Chase: A Biography* (New York: Oxford University Press, 1995), 336.
5. Goodwin, 575.
6. *Ibid.*
7. Ryan, 172.
8. Klement, *The Limits of Dissent*, 1970, 252.
9. Ryan, 231.
10. Welles, Vol.1. 470.
11. U.S. Census figures for 1850, 1860 and 1870 indicate Ohio grew by an average of 36,000 per year in the 1850s and 33,000 in the 1860s. Growth was presumably slower in the war years than in the late '60s; so the 2.8-percent figure might be too high.
12. *The American Presidency Project*, UC Santa Barbara, https://www.presidency.ucsb.edu/statistics/data/voter-turnout-in-presidential-elections.
13. Computed from 1860 U.S. Census and vote totals.
14. *The Crisis*, Oct. 21, 1863.
15. Clement Vallandigham, *Speeches…*, 520.
16. *The Crisis*, Oct. 21, 1863.
17. Oct. 28, 1863.
18. *Ibid.*em and other editions.
19. Stahr, 324.
20. Niven, 336.
21. Arnold Shankman, "Soldier Votes and Clement L. Vallandigham in the 1863 Ohio Gubernatorial Election," *Ohio History*, Vol. 82, Numbers 1 and 2 (Winter-Spring, 1973), 99.
22. *Ibid.*, 100.
23. *Ibid.*
24. *Ibid.*, 101.
25. Eugene Roseboom, "Southern Ohio and the Union in 1863," 34 and 34n.
26. White, *Emancipation…*, 20.
27. Shankman, 102.
28. White, *Emancipation…*, 6.
29. Shankman, 102.
30. Tom Lowe to Will Lowe, Oct. 26, 1863.

Chapter 15

1. Amy A. Kass, Leon R. Kass and Diana Schaub, eds., *What So Proudly We Hail: The American Soul in Story Speech and Song* (Wilmington, Del.: Intercollegiate Studies Institute, 2011).
2. Edward Everett Hall, Introduction to "The Man Without a Country," *Outlook* magazine, Vol. LIX (May 5, 1898), 116–117.
3. *Ibid.*
4. Jean Holloway, Edward *Everett Hale: A Biography* (Austin: University of Texas Press, 1956), 134–135.
5. *Ibid.*, 133.

Chapter 16

1. David Ross Locke, *The Struggles of Petroleum V. Nasby*, Joseph Jones, ed. (Boston: Beacon Press, 1963), 46–48.
2. Carwardine, 78–85.
3. Vallandigham to S.S. Cox, Oct. 28, 1863, Marble collection.
4. Vallandigham to Marble, Oct. 4, 1863.
5. .Klement, *Lanterns...*, 100–108
6. Elizabeth D. Leonard, *Lincoln's Forgotten Ally: Judge Advocate General Joseph Holt of Kentucky* (Chapel Hill: The University of North Carolina Press, 2011), 182–188.
7. Towne, 5.
8. Weber, 25–26.
9. *The Copperheads of the Middle West* and *Dark Lanterns*.
10. Towne, 113.
11. *Court-Martial Case File #MM-2185*, The Cincinnati Military Commission of 1865, U.S. National Archives.
12. David C. Keehn, *Knights of the Golden Circle: Secret Empire, Southern Secession, Civil War* (Baton Rouge: Louisiana State University Press, 2013).
13. Benn Pitman, ed., *The Trials for Treason at Indianapolis* (Cincinnati: Moor, Wilstach & Baldwin, 1865), 24.
14. Klement, *Dark Lanterns*, 179.
15. Pitman, 31, 42 and 334.
16. *Ibid.*, 28 and 35.
17. Klement, *Lanterns...*, 180.
18. McPherson, *Embattled Rebel*, 176.
19. *Ibid.*, 109 and 110, including note on 110.
20. David E. Long, *The Jewel of Liberty: Abraham Lincoln's Re-election and the End of Slavery* (Mechanicsburg, Pa: Stackpole Books, 1994), 103–105.
21. Klement, *Lanterns...*, 164.
22. *The Crisis*, Sept. 12, 1863.
23. Julie A. Mujic, "'Ours Is the Harder Lot': Student Patriotism at the University of Michigan During the Civil War," *Union Heartland: The Midwestern Home Front During the Civil War*, Ginette Aley and J.L. Anderson, eds. (Carbondale: Southern Illinois University Press, 2013), 43.
24. James Vallandigham, 335.
25. Clement Vallandigham, *Speeches...*, 521–527.
26. Klement, *The Limits of Dissent*, 1970, 240.
27. Wheeling *Daily Register*, March 4, 1864.
28. Harper, 244.
29. March 4 and 5, 1864.
30. March 23 and April 1, 1864, e.g.
31. March 3, 1864.
32. June 17, 1864.
33. March 14, 1864.
34. March 22, 1864.
35. March 9, 1864.
36. March 8, 1864.
37. March 17, 1864.
38. March 14, 1864.
39. Porter, 192.

Chapter 17

1. Klement, *The Limits of Dissent*, 1970, 271–271.
2. Staudenraus, 364–365.
3. June 16, 1864.
4. Reprinted in Wheeling *Daily Register*, June 18, 1863.
5. Dayton *Empire*, June 16, 1864.
6. Chicago *Tribune*, June 19, 1864.
7. Waugh, 280 and elsewhere.
8. *Ibid.*, 277.
9. Waugh, 280–281.
10. *Ibid.*, 322.
11. *Ibid.*, 281.
12. *Ibid.*
13. Brooks in Staudenraus, 367.
14. Brooks in Staudenraus, 370–371.
15. Waugh, 286.
16. Irving Katz, *August Belmont: A Political Biography* (New York: Columbia University Press, 1968), 130.
17. Available at teachingamericanhistory.org.
18. Brooks in Staudenraus, 372.
19. Staudenraus, 372.
20. Waugh, 276.
21. Dayton *Empire*, Sept. 9, 1863.
22. Klement, *The Limits of Dissent*, 1970, 287.
23. Waugh 300–301.
24. Klement, *The Limits of Dissent*, 1970, 288.
25. *Ibid.*, 289.
26. Waugh, 322.
27. White, *Emancipation...*, 100.
28. Waugh, 354.
29. White, *Emancipation...*, 103–117.

Chapter 18

1. Reprinted in Dayton *Empire*, March 17, 1865.
2. Vallandigham to James W. Wall, Nov. 26, 1865, Vallandigham folder, New York Historical Society.
3. Dayton *Empire*, April 15, 1865.
4. April 8, 1865.
5. Dayton *Empire*, March 24, 1865.
6. April 7, 1865.
7. April 10, 1865.
8. April 11, 1865.
9. April 10, 1865.
10. Clement Vallandigham, *The Record...*, 146.
11. Dayton *Empire*, April 17, 1865.
12. James Vallandigham, 483.
13. *New York Times*, Sept. 11 and Sept. 25, 1861.
14. Vallandigham to James W. Wall, Nov. 26, 1865, Vallandigham folder, New York Historical Society.
15. Charles Coleman: *The Election of 1868: The Democratic Effort to Regain Control* (New York: Octagon Books, 1971), 239–242; also Stewart Mitchell, *Horatio Seymour of New York* (New York: Da Capo Press, 1970).
16. New York *Herald*, June 13, 1867 and James Vallandigham, 435.
17. James Vallandigham, 442.

18. Porter, 214.
19. Klement, *The Limits of Dissent*, 1970, 298.
20. Robert D. Sawrey, *Dubious Victory: The Reconstruction Debate in Ohio* (Lexington: The University Press of Kentucky, 1992), 113–115.
21. Roseboom, *The History...*, 452.
22. Ibid., 89.
23. Sawrey, 112.
24. Ibid., photo section.
25. Ibid., 113.
26. Trefousse, 305.
27. Ibid., 289.
28. James Vallandigham, 412.
29. Sawrey, 114.
30. James Vallandigham, 413.
31. Ibid., 414.
32. Trefousse, 289.
33. Klement, *The Limits of Dissent*, 1970, 306.
34. Mach, 127 and 136.
35. Niven, 335–338.
36. Lloyd Ostendorf, *Mr. Lincoln Came to Dayton* (Dayton: The Otterbein Press, 1959), 39, citing Schenck's papers.
37. Niven, 428.
38. Klement, *The Limits of Dissent*, 1970, 304.
39. Coleman, Chapter IX, e.g.
40. Nivens, 429.
41. James Vallandigham, 425.
42. Mitchell, 457.
43. James Vallandigham, 426.
44. Wyandot *Pioneer*, Sept. 10, 1868, reprinting a piece from the Cleveland *Herald*.
45. Klement, *The Limits of Dissent*, 1970, 298.
46. James Vallandigham, 429.
47. Klement, *The Limits of Dissent*, 1970, 307.
48. James Vallandigham, 430.
49. James Vallandigham, 432–433.
50. Ibid., 433–435.
51. James Vallandigham, 564.
52. James Vallandigham, 436–444.
53. Ibid., 450.
54. May 19, 1871.
55. June 13, 1871.
56. June 29, July 1 and July 2, 1871.
57. *New York Times*, June 30, 1871.
58. June 27, 1871.
59. Ibid.
60. August 9, 1871.
61. July 19, 1871.
62. Foner, 412–421 and elsewhere.
63. Quoted in *New York Times*, June 13, 1871.
64. Reprinted in Philadelphia *Evening Telegraph*, May 25, 1871.
65. Carl Wittke, in editor's introduction to Roseboom, *The History...*, XII.

Chapter 19

1. Klement, *The Limits of Dissent*, 1970, 309.
2. Stephen Decatur Cone, *A Concise History of Hamilton, Ohio* (Middletown: Press of George Mitchell, 1901), Vol. 2, 140.
3. Thomas McGehean, *A History of the Life and Trials of Thomas McGehean Who Was Charged with the Shooting and Killing of Thomas S. Myers in the city of Hamilton, Butler County, Ohio, on the Evening of the 24th of December, 1870* (Cincinnati: The Notorious Whisky Ring, of Southern Ohio, 1874) Ch. VI).
4. Ibid., 123.
5. Reprinted in the Wheeling *Intelligencer*, June, 19, 1871.
6. Wheeling *Daily Register*, June 19, 1971, taken from Cincinnati papers.
7. Chicago *Tribune*, June 19, 1871.
8. Widely reported, including Cincinnati *Enquirer*, June 17, 1863
9. June 17, 1871, quoted in James Vallandigham, 524.
10. Chicago *Tribune*, June 19, 1871.
11. James Vallandigham, 522–523.
12. Vinton County *Democrat*, June 28, 1871, taken from Cincinnati papers.
13. Cone, Vol. II, 142.
14. Ibid., 143.
15. Cone, Vol. II, 144–145.
16. Wheeling *Daily Register*, June 19, 1871.
17. Ibid.
18. Vinton County *Enquirer*, June 28, 1871.
19. James Vallandigham, 543.
20. Vinton County *Enquirer*, June 28, 1871, for example.
21. Memphis *Daily Appeal*, June 21, 1871.
22. James Vallandigham, 554.
23. Ibid., 552.
24. Ibid., 449–450.
25. July 17, 1861, August 17, 1861, April 2, 1862 and May 6, 1863, e.g.
26. James Vallandigham, 560.
27. June 27, 1871.
28. James Vallandigham, 561–562.
29. Ibid., 542.
30. Ibid., 149.

Chapter 20

1. Tom Lowe to Will Lowe, August 4, 1864.
2. Ibid., Oct 16 and 29 and Nov. 17, 1864.
3. Ibid., Oct. 16, 1864.
4. Various Lowe letters.
5. Tom Lowe to Will Lowe, Nov. 17, 1864, though the month is difficult to read.
6. Ibid., Oct. 5, 1862.
7. Medlar, 179, 181 and 182.
8. Ibid., 224, Appendix A.
9. Klement, *The Limits of Dissent*, 1970, 311n.
10. Marvel, *Burnside*, 392–413; James Robertson, *After the Civil War: The Heroes, Villains, Soldiers, and Civilians Who Changed America* (Washington: National Geographic Society, 2015), 268.
11. Lamers, 440–448.
12. Frank P. Varney (El Dorado Hills, California: Savas Beatie, 2013); also Lamers, and David G. Moore, *William S. Rosecrans and the Union Victory:*

A Civil War Biography (Jefferson, N.C.: McFarland and Company, Inc., 2014)
 13. Lamers, 446.
 14. Moore, 185–186.
 15. Dayton *Journal*, Nov. 13, 1863.
 16. *Ibid.*, Oct. 27, 1863.
 17. Lamers, 261.
 18. Bickham.
 19. Bickham Papers.
 20. Reed W. Smith, *Samuel Medary and the Crisis* (Columbus: Ohio State University Press, 1995), 144.
 21. Sept. 4, 1863.
 22. Therry, 356.
 23. *Ibid.*, 365–366.
 24. *Ibid.*, 391.
 25. Ron Chernow, *Grant* (New York: Penguin Press, 2017), 698.
 26. *Ibid.*, 721–727, and Therry, 487–488.
 27. Therry, 466–472 and elsewhere.
 28. *Ibid.*, 498.
 29. *Ibid.*, 499.
 30. Robert C. Schenck, *Draw. Rules for Playing Poker* (Brooklyn: privately printed, 1880.
 31. Schenck Papers, Wright State University and elsewhere.
 32. New York *Herald*, June 27, 1871.
 33. Wheeling *Daily Register*, Sept. 6, 1871, reprinting a letter to the editor of the Cincinnati *Commercial* from then well-known Ohioan Roeliff Brinkerhoff.

Bibliography

Abbott, Richard. *Ohio's Civil War Governors*. Columbus: Ohio State University Press for the Ohio Historical Society, 1962.

abrahamlincolnonline.org

The American Presidency Project. University of California at Santa Barbara (online).

Barker, Brett. "Limiting Dissent in the Midwest: Ohio Republicans' Attacks on the Democratic Press." *Union Heartland: The Midwestern Home Front During the Civil War*. Carbondale: Southern Illinois University Press, 2013. 169–187.

Basler, Roy P. *The Collected Works of Abraham Lincoln*. New Brunswick: Rutgers University Press, 1953.

Becker, Carl M. "The Death of J.F. Bollmeyer: Murder Most Foul?" *Cincinnati Historical Society Bulletin*, Vol. 24, No. 3, July 1966.

_____. "The Genesis of a Copperhead." *Bulletin of the Historical and Philosophical Society of Ohio*, October, 1961, Vol. 19, No. 4.

_____. *Tom Lowe: A Lesser Angel*. Master's thesis, Miami (Ohio) University, 1958.

Beringer, Richard E., Herman Hattaway, Archer Jones, and William N Still, Jr. *Why the South Lost the Civil War*. Athens: University of Georgia Press, 1986.

Bickham, W.D. *Rosecrans' Campaign with the Fourteenth Army Corp or the Army of the Cumberland, a Narrative of Personal Observations, with an Appendix consisting of the Official Records of the Battle of Stone River!* Cincinnati: Moore, Wilstach, Keys & Co., 1863.

Bickham Papers, Dayton Metro Library.

Binkley, Wilfred E. *American Political Parties: Their Natural History*. New York: Alfred A. Knopf, 1944.

Blair, William A. *With Malice Toward Some: Treason and Loyalty in the Civil War*. Chapel Hill: The University of North Carolina Press, 2014.

Blight, David W. *Frederick Douglass: Prophet of Freedom*. New York: Simon & Schuster, 2018.

Brands, H.W. *Heirs of the Founders*. New York: Doubleday, 2018.

Bulla, David W. *Lincoln's Censor: Milo Hascall and Freedom of the Press in Civil War Indiana*. West Lafayette: Purdue University Press, 2009.

Careless, J.M.S. *Brown of the Globe, Vol. 2, Statesman of Confederation*. Toronto: Macmillan, 1963.

Carwardine, Richard. *Lincoln's Sense of Humor*. Carbondale: Southern Illinois University Press, 2017.

Catton, Bruce. *The Army of the Potomac, Vol 3: A Stillness at Appomattox*. Garden City, NY: Doubleday, 1953.

Catton, Bruce. *The Civil War*. Boston: Houghton Mifflin, 2004 edition.

Catton, Bruce. *Mr. Lincoln's Army*. New York: Pocketbook, 1964.

Chernow, Ron. *Grant*. New York: Penguin, 2017.

Chesnut, Mary Boykin. *Mary Chesnut's Diary*. New York: Penguin Books, 2011 edition.

Coleman, Charles. *The Election of 1868: The Democratic Effort to Regain Control*. New York: Octagon Books, 1971.

Cone, Stephen Decatur. *A Concise History of Hamilton, Ohio*. Middletown, OH: Press of George Mitchell, 1901.

Congressional Globe.

Conover, Charlotte Reeve. *Dayton, Ohio—An Intimate History*. Dayton: Lewis Historical Publishing Company, 1932.

_____. *The Story of Dayton*. Dayton: The Greater Dayton Assn., 1917.

Cowley, Robert, ed. *With My Face to the Enemy: Perspectives on the Civil War*. New York: Berkley Books, 2001.

Cox, Samuel Sullivan. *Eight Years in Congress*. New York: D. Appleton and Company, 1865.

Crew, Harvey W., et al. *History of Dayton, Ohio*. Dayton: United Brethren Publishing House, 1889. At Dayton History Books Online.

The Crisis (newspaper, Columbus, Ohio).

Curl, Donald W. *Murat Halstead and the Cincinnati Commercial*. Boca Raton: University Presses of Florida, 1980.

Davis, William C. *Breckenridge: Statesman, Soldier, Symbol*. Lexington: The University Press of Kentucky, 2010.

Dayton Daily Journal (also *Daily Dayton Journal* and *Dayton Weekly Journal*).

Dayton Empire (also *Western Empire*, *Daily Empire*, *Evening Empire* and *Weekly Empire*).

Dowdey, Clifford, and Louis H. Manarin, eds. *The Wartime Papers of R.E. Lee*. New York: DeCapo Press, 1987.

Duda, Jeremy. *If this be Treason: The American Rogues and Rebels Who Walked the Line Between*

Dissent and Betrayal. Guilford, CT: Lyons Press, 2017.

Edgar, John Fariss. *Pioneer Life in Dayton and Vicinity, 1796–1840.* Dayton: U.B. Publishing House, 1896.

Emma Goldman, PBS documentary, 2004.

Fleming, Thomas. *A Disease of the Public Mind: A New Understanding of Why We Fought the Civil War.* New York: Da Capo Press, 2013.

Foner, Eric. *Reconstruction: America's Unfinished Revolution, 1863–1877.* Updated edition. New York: HarperCollins, 2014.

Foote, Shelby. *The Civil War: A Narrative—Fredericksburg to Meridian.* New York: Vintage Books, 1986 edition.

Freeman, Joanne B. Freeman. *The Field of Blood: Violence in Congress and the Road to Civil War.* New York: Farrar, Straus and Giroux, 2018.

Fremantle, Arthur J.L. *Three Months in the Southern States: April-June, 1863.* New York: John Bradburn, 1864, reprinted Lincoln: University of Nebraska Press, 1991.

Goodwin, Doris Kearns. *Team of Rivals: The Political Genius of Abraham Lincoln.* New York: Simon & Schuster, 2005.

Graham, C. R., ed. *Under Both Flags: A Panorama of the Great Civil War as Represented in Story, Anecdote, Adventure, and the Romance of Reality.* N.p.: Veteran Publishing Co., 1896.

Grant, Ulysses S. *Personal Memoirs of U.S. Grant.* New York: C. L. Webster, 1885.

Hale, Edward Everett. *The Man Without a Country.* New York: The Heritage Press, 1936 edition.

_____. Introduction to "The Man Without a Country." *Outlook* magazine, Vol. LIX (May 5, 1898).

Harper, Robert S. "The Ohio Press in the Civil War." *Civil War History,* Vol. 3, Issue 3 (1957) 221–252.

Hess, Earl J. *Braxton Bragg: The Most Hated Man of the Confederacy.* Chapel Hill: The University of North Carolina Press, 2016.

Hochfelder, David. *The Telegraph in America, 1832–1920.* Baltimore: Johns Hopkins University Press, 2012.

Holloway, Jean. *Edward Everett Hale: A Biography.* Austin: University of Texas Press, 1956.

Holt, Michael F. *The Rise and Fall of the American Whig Party: Jackson Politics and the Onset of the Civil War.* Oxford: Oxford University Press, 1999.

Holzer, Harold. *Lincoln and the Power of the Press: The War for Public Opinion.* New York: Simon & Schuster, 2014.

Jeffrey, Julie Roy. "'They Cannot Expect… That a Loyal People Will Tolerate the Utterance of Such Sentiments': The Campaign against Treasonous Speech during the Civil War." *Civil War History.* Vol. 65, No. 1 (March 2019) 7–42.

Jones, John Beauchamp. *A Rebel War Clerk's Diary at the Confederate States Capital.* Philadelphia: J.P. Lippincott & Co., 1866.

Journal of the (Ohio) House of Representatives.

Kass, Amy A., Leon R. Kass, and Diana Schaub. *What So Proudly We Hail: The American Soul in Story Speech and Song.* Wilmington, DE: Intercollegiate Studies Institute, 2011.

Katz, Irving. *August Belmont: A Political Biography.* (New York: Columbia University Press, 1968.

Keehn, David C. *Knights of the Golden Circle: Secret Empire, Southern Secession, Civil War.* Baton Rouge: Louisiana State University Press, 2013.

Klement, Frank L. *The Copperheads of the Middle West.* Chicago: University of Chicago Press, 1960.

_____. *Dark Lanterns: Secret Political Societies, Conspiracies, and Treason Trials in the Civil War.* Baton Rouge: Louisiana State University Press, 1984.

_____. *The Limits of Dissent.* Lexington: The University of Kentucky Press, 1970 and New York: Fordham University Press, 1998.

Knepper, George. *Ohio and Its People.* Kent, Ohio: The Kent State University Press, Bicentennial Edition 2003.

_____. "Ohio Politics: A Historical Perspective", in *Ohio Politics,* Alexander P. Lamis, ed. Kent, Ohio: The Kent State University Press, 1994.

Koenig, Louis W. "'The Most Unpopular Man in the North.'" *American Heritage,* February, 1964.

Kokkinou, Epiphanie C. "The Political Career of Robert Schenck Cumming." Master's Thesis, Miami University, Oxford, Ohio, 1955.

Korn, Bertram W. *American Jewry and the Civil War.* Cleveland: The World Publishing Company, 1961.

Lamers, William. *The Edge of Glory: A Biography of General William S. Rosecrans, USA.* Baton Rouge: Louisiana State University Press, 1999 paperback edition.

Leonard, Elizabeth D. *Lincoln's Forgotten Ally: Judge Advocate General Joseph Holt of Kentucky.* Chapel Hill: The University of North Carolina Press, 2011.

Locke, David Ross. *The Struggles of Petroleum V. Nasby.* Joseph Jones, ed. Boston: Beacon Press, 1963.

Lowe Papers, Dayton Metro Library.

Luebke, Frederick, ed. *Ethnic Voters and the Election of 1860.* Lincoln: University of Nebraska Press, 1971.

Mach, Thomas S. *"Gentleman George" Hunt Pendleton: Party Politics and Ideological Identity in Nineteenth-Century America.* Kent, OH: The Kent State University Press, 2007.

Mallard, Candace. *Destiny of the Republic: A Tale of Madness, Medicine and the Murder of a President.* New York: Anchor Books, 2011.

Manton Marble collection, Library of Congress.

Marshall, John A. *American Bastille: A History of the Illegal Arrests and Imprisonment of American Citizens in the Northern and Border States on Account of Their Political Opinions during the Late Civil War.* Philadelphia: Thomas W. Hartley and Co., 1833.

Martin, Samuel J. *General Braxton Bragg, CSA.* Jefferson, NC: McFarland, 2011.

Marvel, William. *Burnside.* Chapel Hill: The University of North Carolina Press, 1991.

Marvel, William. *Lincoln's Autocrat: The Life of*

Edwin Stanton. Chapel Hill: The University of North Carolina Press, 2015.

McGehean, Thomas. *A History of the Life and Trials of Thomas McGehean Who Was Charged with the Shooting and Killing of Thomas S. Meyers in the City of Hamilton, Butler County, Ohio, on the Evening of the 24th of December, 1870*. Cincinnati: The Notorious Whisky Ring of Southern Ohio, 1874.

McGinty, Brian. *John Brown's Trial*. Cambridge: Harvard University Press, 2009.

McPherson, James. *Battle Cry of Freedom*. Oxford: Oxford University Press, 1988.

_____. *Embattled Rebel: Jefferson Davis as Commander in Chief*. New York: The Penguin Press, 2014.

Meacham, Jon. *American Lion: Andrew Jackson in the White House*. New York: Random House, 2008.

Medlar, Daniel Lucien. *The Gentleman and the Artist: A Journal of D.L. Medlar, September 1, 1859-April 30, 1862*. Dayton: Dayton Metro Library, 2007.

Miller, Robert F. ed. *States at War, Vol. 5: A Reference Guide for Ohio in the Civil War*. Lebanon, NH: University Press of New England, 2015.

Mitchell, Stewart. *Horatio Seymour of New York*. New York: Da Capo Press, 1970.

Moore, David G. *William S. Rosecrans and the Union Victory: A Civil War Biography*. Jefferson, NC: McFarland, 2014.

Morris, Roy Jr. *The Long Pursuit: Abraham Lincoln's Thirty-Year Struggle with Stephen Douglas for the Heart and Soul of America*. New York: HarperCollins, 2008.

Mowery, David L. *Morgan's Great Raid: The Remarkable Expedition from Kentucky to Ohio*. Charleston, SC: The History Press, 2013.

Mujic, Julie A. "'Ours Is the Harder Lot': Student Patriotism at the University of Michigan During the Civil War." *Union Heartland: The Midwestern Home Front During the Civil War*. Ginette Aley and J.L. Anderson, eds. Carbondale: Southern Illinois University Press, 2013. 33–67.

Murray, Robert K. *Red Scare: A Study of National Hysteria, 1919–1920*. New York: McGraw-Hill Books Company, 1964 paperback edition.

Neely, Mark E. *The Fate of Liberty: Abraham Lincoln and Civil Liberties*. New York: Oxford University Press, 1991.

New-York Historical Society. Vallandigham folder.

Nicolay, John, and John Hay. *Abraham Lincoln: A History*. New York: The Century Co., 1909.

Niven, John. *Salmon P. Chase: A Biography*. New York: Oxford University Press, 1995.

Norman, Jesse. *Edmund Burke: The First Conservative*. New York: Basic Books, 2013.

Pietrusza, David. *1920: The Year of Six Presidents*. New York: Basic Books, 2008.

Pitman, Benn, ed. *The Trials for Treason at Indianapolis*. Cincinnati: Moor, Wilstach & Baldwin, 1865.

Porter, George Henry. "Ohio Politics during the Civil War Period." Columbia University Dissertation, 1911.

Ostendorf, Lloyd. *Mr. Lincoln Came to Dayton*. Dayton: The Otterbein Press, 1959.

Randall, James G. *Constitutional Problems under Lincoln*. New York: D. Appleton and Company, 1926.

Randall, James G. *Lincoln the President: Midstream*. New York: Dodd, Mead & Co., 1953.

Reid, Whitelaw. *Ohio in the War: Her Statesmen, Her Generals, and Soldiers, Vol. 1*. Cincinnati: Moore, Wilstach & Baldwin, 1868.

Reynolds, David S. *John Brown, Abolitionist: The Man Who Killed Slavery, Sparked the Civil War, and Seeded Civil Rights*. New York: Alfred A. Knopf, 2005.

Robertson, James. *After the Civil War: The Heroes, Villains, Soldiers, and Civilians Who Changed America*. Washington: National Geographic Society, 2015.

Roseboom, Eugene. *The History of the State of Ohio, Vol. IV, The Civil War Era*. Carl Wittke, ed. Columbus: Ohio State University Archaeological and Historical Society, 1944.

_____. "The Mobbing of The Crisis." *Ohio State Archaeological and Historical Quarterly*, 59 (April 1950).

_____ "Southern Ohio and the Union in 1863." *The Mississippi Historical Review*, Vol. 39, No. 1 (June 1952).

Ryan, Daniel J. *Lincoln and Ohio*. Columbus: Ohio Historical Society, 1923 (reprint Dover, OH: Old Hundreth Press, 2008)

Sandow, Robert M. *Deserter Country: Civil War Opposition in the Pennsylvania Appalachians*. New York: Fordham University Press, 2009.

Sawrey, Robert D. *Dubious Victory: The Reconstruction Debate in Ohio*. Lexington: The University Press of Kentucky, 1992.

Schenck, Robert C. *Draw. Rules for Playing Poker*. Brooklyn: privately printed, 1880.

Schenck Papers, Wright State University and elsewhere.

Sears, Stephen. *George B. McClellan: The Young Napoleon*. New York: Ticknor & Fields, 1988.

Shales, Amity. *Coolidge*. New York: HarperCollins, 2013.

Shankman, Arnold. "Soldier Votes and Clement L. Vallandigham." *Ohio History*. Vol. 82, Nos. 1 and 2 (Winter-Spring, 1973) 88–104.

Sherman, John. *Recollections of 40 Years in the House, Senate and Cabinet: An Autobiography*. Chicago: The Werner Company, 1896.

Silbey, Joel H. *A Respectable Minority: The Democratic Party in the Civil War Era*. New York: W.W. Norton and Co., 1977.

Smart, James G., ed. *A Radical View: The "Agate" Dispatches of Whitelaw Reid: 1861–1865*. Memphis: Memphis State University Press, 1976.

Smith, Edward Conrad. *The Borderland in the Civil War*. New York: MacMillan, 1927.

Smith, George Winston and Charles Judah. *Life in the North During the Civil War*. Albuquerque: The University of New Mexico Press, 1966.

Smith, Reed W. *Samuel Medary and the Crisis: The Testing of the Limits of Press Freedom*. Columbus: Ohio State University Press, 1995.

Smith, Thomas. "Crawford County: A Study in Midwestern Copperheadism." *Ohio History Journal*, Vol. 76, Winter and Spring, 1967.

Speaker, C.S., C.C. Connell, and George T. Farrell. *An Historical Sketch of the Old Village of New Lisbon, Ohio*. Lisbon: Centennial Celebration Committee, 1903.

Stahr, Walter. *Stanton: Lincoln's War Secretary*. New York: Simon & Schuster, 2017.

Staudenraus, P.J. *Mr. Lincoln's Washington: Selections from the Writings of Noah Brooks, Civil War Correspondent*. New Brunswick: Thomas Yoseloff, 1967.

Steele, Robert W., and Mary Davies Steele. *Early Dayton*. Dayton: U.B. Publishing House, 1896.

Stewart, James Brewer. *Joshua R. Giddings and the Tactics of Radical Politics*. Cleveland: The Press of Case Western Reserve University, 1970.

Strausbaugh, John. *City of Sedition: The History of New York City During the Civil War*. New York: Hachette Book Group, 2016

Therry, James R. *The Life of Robert Cumming Schenck*. Georgetown University dissertation, 1968.

Towne, Stephen E. *Spies in the Civil War: Exposing Confederate Conspiracies in America's Heartland*. Athens: Ohio University Press, 2015

Trefousse, H.L. *Benjamin Franklin Wade: Radical Republican from Ohio*. New York: Twayne Publishers, 1963.

The Trial of Hon. Clement L. Vallandigham, by a Military Commission; and the Proceedings Under his Application for a Writ of Habeas Corpus in the Circuit Court of the United States for the Southern District of Ohio. Cincinnati: Rickey and Carroll, 1863.

Uffelman, Minoa. "Tennessee's Fighting Parson." *New York Times*, Nov. 20, 2011.

United States Census

United States Department of Homeland Security. *Yearbook of Immigration Statistics, 2010*.

United States National Archives. The Cincinnati Military Commission of 1865. *Court-Martial Case File #MM-2185*.

United States War Department. *The War of the Rebellion: A Compilation of the Official Records of the Union and Confederate Armies*. Washington, DC: Government Printing Office, 1880–1901. (Known as *Official Records* or *OR*.)

Vallandigham, Clement Laird. *The Record of the Hon. C. L. Vallandigham on Abolition, the Union and the Civil War*. Cincinnati: J. Walter & Co., 1863.

_____. *Speeches, Arguments, Addresses, and Letters of Clement L. Vallandigham*. New York: J. Walter & Co., 1864.

Vallandigham, James L. *A Life of Clement Vallandigham*. Baltimore: Turnbull Brothers, 1872.

Vallandigham Song Book, The: Songs for the Times. Columbus: J. Walter & Co., 1863.

Van Der Linden, Frank. *The Dark Intrigue: The True Story of a Civil War Conspiracy*. Golden, Colorado: Fulcrum Publishing, 2007.

Van Horne, William E. "Lewis D. Campbell and the Know-Nothing Party in Ohio." *Ohio History*, Vol. 76, Autumn 1976, No. 4, 202–221.

Varney, Frank P. *General Grant and the Rewriting of History: How the Destruction of General William S. Rosecrans Influenced Our Understanding of the Civil War*. El Dorado Hills, CA: Savas Beatie, 2013.

Varon, Elizabeth R. *Armies of Deliverance: A New History of the Civil War*. New York: Oxford University Press, 2019.

Wagner, Margaret E. *The Library of Congress Illustrated Timeline of the Civil War*. New York: Little, Brown and Company, 2011.

Waugh, John C. *Reelecting Lincoln: The Battle for the 1864 Presidency*. New York: Crown Publishers, 1997.

Weber, Jennifer. *Copperheads: The Rise and Fall of Lincoln's Opponents in the North*. New York: Oxford University Press, 2006.

Weeks, Lyman Horace, ed. *Prominent Families of New York*. New York: The Historical Company, 1897.

Weiner, Greg. *Old Whigs: Burke, Lincoln and the Politics of Prudence*. New York: Encounter Books, 2019.

Welles, Gideon. *Diary of Gideon Welles, Secretary of the Navy under Lincoln and Johnson*, Vol. I. Boston: Houghton Mifflin Company, 1911.

White, Jonathan W. *Abraham Lincoln and Treason in the Civil War: The Trials of John Merryman*. Baton Rouge: Louisiana State University Press, 2011.

_____. *Emancipation, the Union Army and the Reelection of Abraham Lincoln*. Baton Rouge: Louisiana State University Press, 2014.

Widmer, Ted. *Lincoln on the Verge*. New York: Simon & Schuster, 2020.

Wilson, Charles. *Cincinnati a Southern Outpost in 1860-1861? The Mississippi Historical Review*. Vol. 24, No. 4 (March, 1938).

Wimberg, Robert J. *Cincinnati and the Civil War: Under Attack*. Cincinnati: Ohio Book Store, 1999.

Zalimas, Robert J., "'Contest MY seat, sir!': Lewis D. Campbell, Clement Vallandigham, and the Election of 1856." *Ohio History*, Vol. 106, Winter-Spring, 1997, 5–30.

Index

Numbers in ***bold italics*** indicate pages with illustrations.
The abbreviation CV indicates Clement Vallandigham

abolitionist movement and anti-slavery sentiments: Burke support for 14–15; connection of churches to 10–11; distrust of 248; growth of 40; Lincoln support for 14–15, 63; opposition to and great problem for the country 21–23, 24–25, 39–40, 90–91, 95–96, 131; as power grab by the North 39; Republican views on 15, 22, 26, 54, 60–61, 68, 89; start of movement 10
Adams, John 48, 116
Adams, John Quincy 16, 33
Alien and Sedition Acts 48–49, 116
American Party (Know-Nothings movement) 19, 28–29, 40, 89
Anderson, Charles 160
Antietam battle 57, 83, 100, 136
Appomattox and Lee surrender 221–22
armistice proposal speech (The Great Civil War in America speech) 94–98, 99, 124, 175
Army, U.S.: anti-army views 90, 104; appropriations to fund 81, 83; black volunteers 82, 178, 179; desertions 99, 111, 113, 143–44, 146, 147, 176, 179–180; fighting with, CV decision against 81; fighting with, Lowe decision against 91; slaves recruited for service in 103; *see also* draft and anti-draft views
Arnold, Benedict 50, 175
arrests, political and arbitrary 71–77, 85–86, 176
Article of Confederation 43
asylum 129

banishment *see* exile
Bermuda 140–42, 147, 149
Bickham, W.D. ***165***, ***246***; blame for violence against *Empire* 207–8; on cheating potential and allegations 187; Dayton *Journal* position of 165–66, 245; hall of fame induction of 245; politics of 244, 245; rally coverage by 163; Richmond statement by CV 222; Rosecrans relationship with 244, 245
blacks/black people: as Americans of African descent 21; competition between Irish-Americans and 29, 155; Emancipation and move to Ohio by 83–84; military service of 82, 178, 179; population in Ohio 28, 178; prohibition from moving into Ohio 15; rights of 15, 20–21, 224, 234–35; voting by 20–21, 177, 220, 225–26, 232–33
Bollmeyer, J.F. 91–93, 104, 111
Bomberger, John Henry Augustus 18
bounty system 73
Bragg, Braxton ***79***; Chickamauga battle 183, 184; Kentucky campaign 79–80, 132; Morgan raid on Ohio 152–53; opinions about 130; Perryville battle 82–83; reputation of 79; Stone River battle 123, 132; travel to headquarters by CV 122–130; Vallandigham relationship with 132–33
Breckenridge, John C. 52, 102
Brooks, Noah 29–30, 209, 212
Brough, John ***160***; election of 190–96; governorship campaign of 159–160, 174; newspaper coverage of 166, 168; rallies for 161, 185–86; Sherman support for 175–77
Brown, Henry M. 92–93
Brown, John 31–36, ***33***, ***35***, 39, 40, 93, 96
Brown, Sherrod 231
Buell, Don Carlos 82, 123
Bull Run battles 66, 67, 79, 100, 120
Burke, Edmund 14–15
Burnside, Ambrose ***101***; appearance of 101–2; arrest and trial of CV 108–16; background and family of 105; as Butcher of Fredericksburg 227; Cincinnati headquarters of 105–6; Department of Ohio assignment 102, 105–6; Knoxville battle 156–57; military career and reputation of 100–102; Morgan raid on Ohio 152–53; newspaper shutdowns by 121, 142, 168; order on disloyalty and treason 106, 114–15; overriding by Lincoln 120–21; political affiliation of 105, 243; political career of 102; postwar life of 243–44
Butternut tree 59–60

Calhoun, John C. 23
Camp Chase 116, 194
Campbell, Lewis 19–21, ***232***, 240
Campbell, William B. 89
Canada: exile in 7, 130, 132, 133, ***156***; exile in and potential CV win 173–74, 193; exit-and-re-entry strategy 205, 208; Niagara, campaigning from 150–52, 155; proposal of exile to 130, 133; reception in 149–150; return to U.S. from 209–10; travel to 139–142, 149; U.S. takeover of 149; Windsor, campaigning from 7, 132, 155–59, ***157***, 180–81; Windsor, life in after campaign 200–205
canals 18–19, 29
Carrington, Henry 21, 105–6
Catholic immigrants 10, 20, 28
Chancellorsville battle 107, 135, 137
Chase, Salmon P.: alliance with CV 229–231; CV trial role of 116, 118; death of 250; election as governor 24; opinion about CV 66, 229, 249; political career of 229, 249–250; presidential nomination of 38, 229–231, 234–35; Rosecrans support by 123
Chattanooga, Tennessee 79, 183–84
Chicago national convention 208, 210, 211–17, 222

267

Chickamauga battle 183–84, 244, 245
Cincinnati: anti-slavery movement in 17; Burnside headquarters in 105–6; development of 17; German immigrants in 28; invasion of Ohio through and siege of 57, 78–83, 132; martial law declaration in 80; meeting to prepare for national convention 209–10; northern southern, and western characteristics of 17; political party affiliations in 27–29; supply depot in 56
civil liberties issues 70–77, 85–86, 143, 145–46, 147–48, 169, 180–81
Civil War: abolition as cause of 22, 23; anti-war, anti-North groups 200–204; anti-war views 90–91, 99, 104, 132; Appomattox and Lee surrender 221–22; armistice proposal to end 94–98, 99, 124, 175; Confederate successes during 65–67, 69–70, 101–2, 107, 205; Copperhead platform on 7, 205; end of 215, 220, 221; events leading to 9; Fort Donelson surrender 51; Fort Sumter attack and start of 44–45, 49, 59, 65; life in Ohio during 55–61, 253*ch7n9*, 253*ch7n20*; negotiation to end 49, 53, 81, 131, 159, 213, 215, 221–22, 245; opposition to 5, 45, 130–32; peaceable separation and end of 49, 59, 61; political generals during 65, 67; responsibility of CV for start of 84; taking the war to the North 79; Union victories 7, 49, 150, 174–75, 215, 221–22; views in southern Ohio on 28; war policy and support for administration 16
Clay, Henry 13, 14, 23, 52, 63
Columbus: Democratic convention in 138–39, 166, 172; development of 17; political tensions and violence in 104; state convention in 208
Commercial (Cincinnati) 82, 92–93, 165, 173, 210–11
Confederates and Confederate government: armistice proposal and recognition of 94–95, 99, 175; armistice proposal reaction by 98; British and French support for 77, 100, 149; British help for 247; Canadian operatives and sabotage plans 202–3; civil liberties issues 86; Fort Sumter attack by 44–45, 49, 59, 65; interviews with CV 133–36; invasion of Maryland and Pennsylvania by 135–37; invasion of Ohio through Cincinnati 57, 78–83, 132; policy on CV 130–37; recognition of independence of 98; success of 65–67, 69–70, 101–2, 107, 205; warning to not invade the North 136–37

Constitution, U.S.: amendment proposal 42–44; change related to slavery 42; *habeas corpus* provision in 145–46, 147–48; postwar amendments to 43, 221, 223–24, 232–34; slavery and 22, 25, 26
Coolidge, Calvin 6
Copperheads/Peace Democrats: affiliation with and geographic distribution in Ohio 27, 28; background of the name 5; Butternut tree relationship to 59–60; Chancellorsville and strength of 137; desertions and blame for draft 179–180; East Coast speaking tour 103–5; Morgan raid and loyalty of 153–54, 166; opposition to war with south 45; peacemaker characterization of 15–17; Pennsylvania invasion to help 136–37; platform during 1864 convention 7, 205, 211–17, 222, 245; political persecution and arrests of 73–77; rallies of 162–64; role of CV 5; Rosecrans feelings about 244; secret societies of 203–4
Corinth, Mississippi 83, 123
Corwin, Thomas "Tom" 16, 38, 52–53, 63, 64, 247
Courier-Journal (Louisville) 130
courtship during the war 57–61
Cox, Samuel S. "Sunset" 107, 114–15, 139, 142–43, 213, 216, 240, 248–49
The Crisis (Columbus): armistice proposal speech reaction in 97; arrest possibilities, report on 74–75; cheating potential and allegations in 192–93; Democratic focus of 74, 167; rally coverage in 162, 164, 182–83; support for CV by 169, 173; violence against 104

Daily Ledger/Ledger (Dayton) 224, 245
Daily Tribune (New York) 44, 45, 46, 48, 143
Davis, Jefferson 79, 83, 86, 103, 115, 133, 136–37, 176
Dayton: advantages in 18–19; attitude toward CV in 6–8; church life and slavery views in 56–57; development of and conditions in 17, 18–19; floods in 2, 107; German immigrants in 28; life in during the war 55–61, 253*ch7n9*, 253*ch7n20*; Lincoln visit to 64–65, 254*n*16; Lowe families in 253*ch5n*17; martial law declaration in 111–12; militia in 16–17; mob violence and fires in 109–12; offer to own newspaper in 17–18; political party affiliations in 27–29, 245; political tensions and violence in 91–93, 104, 138; return to from Canada 210–11
Dayton Metro Library/Dayton Public Library 57–58, 87
dead body story 52–53
Debs, Eugene V. 7
Democratic Party: affiliation of CV with 13–15; affiliation with and geographic distribution in Ohio 27–29; anti-Grant efforts of 250; Chicago national convention 208, 210, 211–17, 222; conservative views of 15; governorship nominations 99–100, 138–140, 144, 151, 166, 172; leaving by CV, talk about 237, 245–46; philosophical spectrum in Ohio 54; platform during 1864 convention 7, 211–17, 222, 245; positive Democrats 230; as real Union party 77; secessionist charges against 59–61; slavery views in 14; tensions between Republican Party and 56–57, 58–61, 91–93, 168–69
disloyalty and treason: accusations against CV 181; arrest and trial of CV 6–7, 108–18, *110*, 120–21, 142–48; arrests for disloyalty in Maryland 47–48, 71, 72, 102–3; Burnside order on 106, 114–15; defense of disloyalty charges 50–54; exile after conviction for disloyalty 7, 120–21; federal court trial 116–18; implied treason 106; military court trials for 71, 112–16, 118, 121, 143, 145; provost marshal and allegations of 111–12, 143–44
Douglas, Stephen A. 40, 44–45, 64, 99, 102, 240, 241
Douglass, Frederick 32
draft and anti-draft views: enforcement by provost marshal 111–12, 143–44; New York anti-draft riots 105, 154–55, 181; pro-South sentiments and 105; recruitment quotas and national draft 73, 83, 167–68, 179–180; resistance and anti-draft views 104–6, 143–47, 210; Schenck role in 247
Dred Scott decision 48
drinking story 12–13

East Coast/the East: Middle District position of Schenck 102–3; population of 17; speaking tour in 103–5; tension between West and 38–39, 122
Emancipation Proclamation 26, 55, 70, 77, 83–84, 102, 148

Emerson, Ralph Waldo 32
Empire (Dayton): cheating potential and allegations in 188; Democratic focus of 167–69, 206; early name of 17–18; Lowe travelogue in 170–73; meetings of Democrats at 58–59, 60; mob violence against office of 109–11, 206–8; offer to buy and become editor of 17–18; one-liners in 169; performance of 169; racial issues in 206; sale of 19, 224; on Schenck 67; shooting of co-editor of 91–93, 104; shutting down of 75; size and composition of 167; threat of violence against 104; violence, piece in to promote 111; war coverage by 78; writing for by CV 219, 220–21
Enquirer (Cincinnati): armistice proposal speech in 97; Democratic focus of 27–28; denial of peaceable separation letter in 49; disloyalty charges against CV in 50; gun accident reports in 238; New Departure, opinion about 235; rally coverage by 163; shutting down of 72; tension between *Commercial* and 92–93; threat of violence against 104
Europe: democratic parties in 15; immigration from 28; Lowe trip to 170–73
Executive Usurpation anti-Lincoln speech 45–49, 52, 53
exile: boat and train trip south 124–25; Bragg–CV relationship during 132–33; in Canada 7, 130, 132, 133, *156*; Confederate official interviews during 133–36; conviction for disloyalty and 7; governor of Ohio campaign from 7, 150–52, 155–59; history of 7, 116; letters written before 122; Lincoln decision for 7, 120–21; newspaper coverage of 121–22; opposition to Lincoln from 7; propositions and conditions to revoke 147, 149, 150, 173, 205; Rosecrans meeting with CV 124–26; travel to Bragg's headquarters 122–130; unusual punishment of 145

Federal Union of the States 214–15
Federalists 48–49
Fish, Hamilton 247
Forrest, Nathan Bedford 78, 79
Fort Donelson 51
Fort Sumter 44–45, 49, 59, 65
Fort Warren prison 116, 157
Fredericksburg 11, 94, 98, 101–2, 107, 112, 120, 123, 139, 227
Fremantle, Arthur J.L. 133, 140
Fugitive Slave Law 89, 99
Furay, R.S. 124–28

Garfield, James A. 67, 244, 247
Gazette (Cincinnati) 56, 78–79, 81, 97, 138–39, 206
Gazette (Hillsboro) 86
German immigrants 19–20, 28
Gettysburg 135, 147, 150, 155, 160, 174, 197, 247
Giddings, Joshua 25–26, 33, 86
Goldman, Emma 7
government: American system 14; power and importance of governors 99; power of presidency 42–43; purpose of 54; *see also* states rights
governor of Ohio campaign: arrest for disloyalty during 6–7, 108–12, *110*, 120–21, 142–48; bets on outcome of 186; Brough election victory 190–96; crossing into Ohio to campaign 181–82; election day and outcome of vote 184, 190–96; election potential for CV 182–83; exile after conviction 7, 120–21; exile location and potential CV win 173–74, 193; margin in 191–95; Mount Vernon speech 107–8, 113–14, 115–16, 117, 137, 144, 176; Niagara, campaigning from 150–52, 155; nominations for 99–100, 138–140, 144, 151, 166, 172; predictions on outcome 158–59; rallies for 160–64, 166; reactions to arrest during 122, 134, 138–39, 140, 142; support for CV campaign 86, 99–100; trial and conviction during 7, 112–18; violence potential related to CV 173–74, 181–82, 193; Windsor, campaigning from 7, 132, 155–59, *157*, 180–81
Grant, Ulysses S.: Appomattox and Lee surrender 221–22; British–U.S. relationships under 247; Chattanooga siege 184; corruption under 234; Fort Donelson surrender to 51; opposition to reelection of 250; pension for 244; recruitment for Mexican War by 87; Rosecrans relationship with 244; Vicksburg battle 133, 135
Great Britain: poker in 248; support of South by 77, 100, 149, 247; U.S.–British relationships under Grant 247
The Great Civil War in America speech (armistice proposal speech) 94–98, 99, 124, 175
Greeley, Horace 44, 45, 46, 123–24, 148, 178, 193, 244, 250
gun accident 237–39, **238**
Gunckel, Lewis B. 67, 165

habeas corpus rights 47–48, 71–77, 85–86, 116, 118, 143, 145–46, 147–48, 180–81
Hale, Edward Everett 197–99

Halleck, Henry 106, 120
Halstead, Murat 82, 88, 158, 165
Harpers Ferry raid 31–36
Harrison, Benjamin 88
Harrison, William Henry 38
Harshman, Jonathan 89
Harshman, Marsha 89–90
Hayes, Rutherford B. 24, 27, 228, 244, 247
Hickman, John 51–54
historians, bias of 6
Hooker, Joe 107, 184
Hough, Sabin 49

immigration: Catholic immigrants 10, 20, 28; German immigrants 19–20, 28; increase in and voting by 19–20; Irish immigrants 19–20, 28, 29, 154–55, 177, 211; views on 10
Indiana: Centreville speech 85–86; political tensions in 73–74; pro-South sentiments in 105–6
Irish immigrants 19–20, 28, 29, 154–55, 177, 211

Jackson, Stonewall 67, 78, 83
Jacksonian Democrats and Andrew Jackson 13–14, 38, 46, 143
Jeffersonians 48
Jeopardy question 7–8
Jewett, Hugh 100, 139
Jewish rights 10
Johnson, Andrew 219, 224–25, 229, 234, 247
jollifications 85, 226–27
Jones, John Beauchamp 135–36
Journal (Dayton): armistice proposal speech reaction in 98; arrests, reports about 72; blame for violence against *Empire* 207–8; cheating potential and allegations in 186–87, 188; coverage of life during the war 55–57; dead body story in 52–53; draft and recruitment quota articles in 179–180; election coverage by 83, 84; Indiana tensions report in 74; martyrdom accusation against CV in 75; mob violence against and burning offices of 109–11, 154, 164–65; Philadelphia *Journal* piece published by 103; poem about CV in 50; rally coverage by 163, 164, 166, 187–88; Republican focus of 92, 164–67, 245; Schenck promotion by 66–67, 246; success of 245; violence, letters and comments in to promote 104; war coverage by 78, 80–82, 83, 154

Kansas-Nebraska Act 19, 24, 25
Kees, John 72–73
Kentucky: Camp Vallandigham in 53; divisions in 78; invasion

Index

of Ohio through 78–83, 132; Lincoln need to support in 78; Ohio politics and proximity to 27–28; Perryville battle in 82–83; play production company from 55; travel to by CV 52

Klement, Frank, J. 2, 3

Knights of the Golden Circle 105, 201

Know-Nothings movement (American Party) 19, 28–29, 40, 89

Knoxville battle 156–57

Lady Davis 141–42

law career: Dayton practice 18; murder trial and gun accident 236–39, **238**; return to 220; study under James 13; success of 19

Leavitt, H.H. 116–18

Ledger/Daily Ledger (Dayton) 224, 245

Lee, Robert E.: Antietam battle 83, 100; Appomattox and surrender of 221–22; Brown-Vallandigham meeting role of 31–32, 34; Chancellorsville battle 107; Fredericksburg battle 101; Maryland move of 79; on negotiating with the North 132; Pennsylvania invasion by 103, 136–37, 153–54; Union generals to fight 100, 101–2

Liberal Republican Party 250

The Limits of Dissent (Klement) 3

Lincoln (movie) 54

Lincoln, Abraham: antislavery views of 14–15, 63; assassination of 55, 219, 220–21, 247; Burkean views of 14–15; Burnside selection by 100–102; Confederate invasion and unity around 136–37; CV as leading antagonist 5–6; election of 9; election returns, waiting for 190–91; exile decision of 7, 120–21; explanation of arrest in public letters 142–48; German-language newspaper ownership by 18; *habeas corpus* rights under 47–48, 116, 143, 145–46, 147–48, 180–81; Harpers Ferry raid speech by 35–36; inauguration of 219; military failures as political disaster for 174–75, 222; Ohio support for 27; opinion about CV 7; opposition to slavery by 9; overriding Burnside by 120–21; patronage jobs 18, 47, 65, 112, 200; political ambitions of 19; political generals appointments by 65, 67; presidential campaign and election of 64–65; presidential campaign and re-election of 5, 205, 217–18; Schenck relationship with 63–65, 66, 247; troop raising by 44–45; tyranny of and public opinions about 84, 85–86

Lincoln, Willie 51

Lisbon (New Lisbon) 8, 11, 17

Locke, David Ross 200

Long, Alexander 27, 82

Louisiana Purchase 48, 76

Lowe, Chad 253*ch*5*n*17

Lowe, John 87–88

Lowe, Martha 111, 153, 170, 171–73, 242

Lowe, Rob 253*ch*5*n*17

Lowe, Tom: anti-army views 90, 104; anti-war position of 90–91; argumentative nature of 88; background and family of 87; campaign speech for CV by 90–91; courtship of Marsha 89–90; Democratic Party officer role of 91; election outcome views of 196; *Empire* article about Bollmeyer shooting 92; European tripe of 170–73; family of 253*ch*5*n*17; law career of 91, 220; letters of 87, 90, 104, 170–72, 242, 243; military service, decision against 91, 170, 242; on mob violence and fires in Dayton 109–11; Nashville move and life 88–89; political affiliation of 89, 90; on political future of CV 49, 87; postwar life of 242–43; religious views of 91; return from Europe 220; return to Dayton 89–90; slavery views of 87, 88–89; support for CV by 90–91; Vallandigham relationship with 91

Lowe, Will: arrest for disloyalty 106–7; letters to 87, 90, 104, 170–72, 242; military career of 90, 242

Lynchburg meeting 134–37, 139–140

Lyon, Matthew 116

"The Man Without a Country" (Hale) 197–99

Marble, Manton 122, 175, 183

Marshall, John A. 71

martial law 80, 103, 111–12, 180–81

Maryland: Antietam battle 57, 83, 100, 136; arrests for disloyalty in 47–48, 71, 72, 102–3; Confederate sympathies in 50–51, 102; invasion by Southern troops 135–37; Schenck position in 102–3; secession ideas of 46, 71

Matthews, Stanley 23–24

McClellan, George **214**; Copperhead platform rejection by 7, 211–17, 245; governorship nomination for 139; military career and reputation of 100–101; presidential nomination and campaign of 7, 205, 211–18, **217**, 242; Richmond battle 69–70, 78

McDowell, Virginia 66–67

McGehan, Thomas 236–39

McKibbin, Joseph C. "Joe" 125, 127–28

McKinley, William 244

McMahon, John (nephew) 111, 231, 243

McMahon, Louisa 18; *see also* Vallandigham, Louisa McMahon (wife)

Medary, Samuel "Sam" **74**; armistice proposal speech reaction by 97; career and political affiliation of 74; on cheating potential and allegations 186–87, 192–93; death of 245; election coverage by 192–93; postwar opinions of 245–46; race, views on and writings about 177–78; rally coverage by 162, 164, 182–83; on secret societies 203–4; support for CV by 169, 175; *see also The Crisis* (Columbus)

Medlar, Caroline 58

Medlar, Daniel Lucien 57–61, 71, 243, 253*ch*7*n*20

Merryman, John 47–48, 72

Mexican War 16–17, 63, 83, 87, 105, 144–45

minorities 10, 20–21

Missouri 49

Moon, Jennie 106–7

Moon, Lottie 106–7

Morgan, John Hunt 78–79, 152–54, 166

Mount Vernon speech 107–8, 113–14, 115–16, 117, 137, 144, 176

Mount Vernon II speech 227–28

Myers, Thomas 236–37

Nasby, Petroleum V. 5, 200

Nashville 242

National Rifle Association (NRA) 243–44

National Road 19

Native Americans/Indians 14

New Departure platform 231, 233–35, 237, 240, 249

New England 17, 48, 218

New Lisbon (Lisbon) 8, 11, 17

New York: anti-draft riots in 105, 154–55, 181; Copperhead strength in 154–55; rally in 122, 134, 138, 142

New York Times 103–5, 121–22, 234

newspapers: armistice proposal speech reaction in 97–98; arrest of editors 72–73; coverage of life during the war 55–57; disloyalty charges against CV in newspaper 50–54; exchange program 58; exile coverage by 121–22; German-language newspapers 18, 28; one-liners

Index

in 169; one-party newspapers 18; political focus of 17, 18, 27–28, 164–69; political tensions and attacks on 57, 109–12, 164–65, 206–8; rally coverage in 160–64, 182–83, 185–86, 187–89; shooting of a co-editor 91–93; shutdowns of 72, 75, 121, 142, 148, 168; speeches printed in newspapers 30; trial coverage by 112–13, 118–120; war coverage by 77–79
northern states/the North: anti-war, anti–North groups 200–204; feelings about CV *131*, 185; line between North and South *126*; military failures as political disaster for 174–75, 222; opinions about secession 44–45, 49, 130–32; reaction to exile in 121–22; South–North and West–North relationships 37–41; troop raising by Lincoln 44–45; victory in Civil War 7, 49, 150; warning to Confederates to not invade 136–37
Northwest Ordinance 9
Nunnelee, S.F. 128–29

ode to Vallandigham 50
Ohio: anti-war views in 90–91, 99, 104; ban on sale of guns and ammunition in 21; Black Codes and rights of blacks in 15, 20–21; congressional district redrawing in 62, 68–69, **69**, 84–85, 254*n*36; development of western Ohio 17; exit-and-re-entry strategy 205, 208; fighting for defense of by CV 81; invasion by Confederates through Cincinnati 57, 78–83, 132; joining South over North 38; life in during the war 55–61, 253*ch7n*9, 253*ch7n*20; Morgan raid on 152–54, 166; political party affiliations in 27–29; political philosophical spectrum in 54; popularity of CV in 86; population of 17, 28, 37, 178, 191, 259*n*11; public letters exchange with Lincoln 144–48; recruitment and volunteering for military service in 57, 73, 78, 80–81, 83, 167–68, 179–180; slavery views in 9, 11; violence in 104, 138; *see also specific cities*
Ohio Journalism Hall of Fame 245
Ohio State Journal (Columbus) 72, 166, 175
Olds, Edson 73, 76, 108, 159, 254*n*65
Order of the American Knights 201
Order of the Sons of Liberty 200–202, 203, 205
Ould, Robert 134–37, 139–140
Our American Cousins 55

Peace Democrats *see* Copperheads/Peace Democrats
peaceable separation letter 49
Pendleton, George 27, 82, 208, 213, 223, 229–230, 233
Pennsylvania: censorship in 103; invasion by Southern troops 103, 135–37, 153–54; martial law declaration in 103
Perryville, Kentucky 82–83
Piatt, Don 16–17
Pickering, Thomas 48
poem about Vallandigham 50
poker 248
political career: anti–Lincoln Executive Usurpation speech 45–49, 52, 53; arbitrary arrests and political persecution speech 73–74, 75–77; arrest of, possibility of 74–77; aspirations to and preparations for 12–15, 204–5; congressional 1862 campaign and election 62, 66–68, 81, 83–85; congressional 1868 campaign 231; congressional election loss 84–85, 100; defense of disloyalty charges 50–54; defense of statements and actions 222; delegate at Chicago convention 208, 210, 211–17, 222; election to Congress 19–21; future of career after post-Sumter speech 49, 87; liabilities of candidacy 224; margins in election and re-election of 19–21, 27, 68, 84–85, 191–95, 231; opinions about CV 7, 29–30, 240–41; oratorical skills for 12, 13, 29–30, 37; postwar career 222–235; postwar speeches 226–28; presidential ambitions and endorsements 99, 208; reputation and legacy 8, 29–30, 240–41; secessionist agenda 39–41, 95; self image during 37, 222–23; speeches and length of speeches 85–86; state legislature election and service 8, 13, 17; unsuccessful elections 19; Western man speech 37–41; wily agitator 143–44; *see also* governor of Ohio campaign
political parties: disbandment of 40; geographic distribution of 27–29; philosophical spectrum in Ohio 54; tensions between during war 56–57, 58–61
Polk, James K. 13, 16, 145
prisoner of war (POW) 129, 132–36
provost marshal 111–12, 143–44
Pugh, George E. 112, 117, 164, 174, 176, 193

Quakers 11, 68, 105

race and racism: conservative views on 15; Democratic views on 177–79; editorials on 188–89; race baiting in congressional campaign 77; racist rant by CV 20–21; Republican views on 177, 206; Sherman views on 177; views on minorities 10, 20–21; voting rights and end of political debate about 225
railroads 38–39, 64
Rebel (Chattanooga) 129–130, 141
Reconstruction 95, 136, 214, 220–22, 225, 227–28, 234, 245, 250
Reid, Whitelaw 5, 87, 88, 97
religion: church life and slavery views in Dayton 56–57; connection between slavery and churches 10–11; moral and religious focus of CV 10–11; religious views of Lowe 91; U.S. as Christian country 10
Republican Party: affiliation with and geographic distribution in Ohio 27–29; Brown support from 32–36; corruption of 245; disbandment of 40; liberal and business views of 54; philosophical spectrum in Ohio 54; Radical Republicans 15, 54; slavery views of 15, 22, 26, 54, 60–61, 68, 89; tensions between Democratic Party and 56–57, 58–61, 91–93, 168–69; Union Party name for 70–71
Richmond, Kentucky 79
Richmond, Virginia, battle 69–70, 78
Rosecrans, William S. **123**, *184*; background and family of 123; Bickham relationship with 244, 245; Chickamauga battle 183–84, 244, 245; Corinth battle 83, 123; Grant relationship with 244; meeting with CV 124–26; political trouble of 124; politics of 244; postwar life of 244–45; presidential candidacy of 123–24; regiments to put down Ohio traitors 104; reputation of 123–24, 245; Stone River battle 123, 165–66

St. Valandygum church 5, 200
Sanders, William L. 57
Schenck, Robert **63**, *249*; ambassadorships of 62, 64, 247–48; anti-slavery views of 63; background and family of 62–63; cabinet position for 65; congressional 1862 campaign and election 62, 66–68, 83–85, 229, 246–47; congressional election win by 84–85; death of 248; financial problems of 248; involvement in scandals by 248; Lincoln relationship with 63–65, 66, 247; Middle District position of 102–3; military career and injury of 62, 65–67,

81–82, 83, 87, 102; political affiliation of 63, 64, 65, 247; political career of 62, 63–64, 246–47; railroad business of 64
secret organizations/societies 200–204
sectionalism 22, 25, 37–41, 42–44, 89, 95, 98, 214–15
Sentinel (Richmond) 130–32
Seward, William 38, 73, 120, 123, 155, 230
Seymour, Horatio 121–22, 141, 212, 230–31
Sherman, John 38, 76, 84, 159, 175–77, 182, 247
Sherman, William Tecumseh 7, 84, 158, 184, 215
Shiloh battle 57, 90
slavery: amendment to ban 221; church life and slavery views in Dayton 56–57; connection of churches to 10–11; Kansas-Nebraska Act and 19, 24, 25; negotiation over and survival of 49; opposition to going to war over 5, 26; phases of thinking about 21–26; prohibition in newly formed states 9, 42; pro-slavery views of CV 9–12, 14–15, 25–26, 95–96, 98; Southern support for 9, 88–89; states rights and 9, 14, 24–26; Union army service by slaves 77; *see also* abolitionist movement and anti-slavery sentiments
Smith, Adam 250
Smith, Kirby 79–80
Sons of Liberty 200–202, 203, 205
Soule, Clara 243
South (Baltimore) 50–51
southern states/the South: bleeding Dixie and sympathies for 51; commitment to war in 151–52; feelings about CV **131**, 185; line between North and South **126**; northern opinions about secession 44–45, 49, 130–32; popularity of CV in 49; reaction to exile in 121–22; secession of 9, 39–40, 42, 59, 89; secession threat and state rights 25; slavery support by 9, 88–89; West-South and North-South relationships 37–41
squirrel hunters 82
Stanton, Edwin 75, 79, 107, 124, 183
states rights: Democratic views on 14; Kansas-Nebraska Act and slavery 19, 24, 25; secession threat and 25; slavery and 9, 14, 24–26
Stephens, Alexander 21
Stone River battle 123, 132, 165–66
story inspired by Vallandigham 7, 197–99
Sumner, Charles 67, 224, 247

Taft, Robert 231
Taney, Roger 47–48, 118
Taylor, Zachary 38, 64
telegraph communications 150–51
temperance movement 24, 28–29
Thompson, Jacob 203
Thoreau, Henry David 32
Thurman, Allen G. 228–29
Tibbals, Seymour B. 57
Times (Chicago) 121, 142, 150, 168, 205
Tod, David 73, 78, 100, 142, 144, 153, 159, 179
trading card series **246**
treason *see* disloyalty and treason
Trent affair 149, 155
Turner, Nat 23

Uncle Tom's Cabin 55
Underground Railroad 27
United States: foreign policy of 184–85; peaceable separation of 49, 59, 61; polarizing issues in 1, 26; reunification of 42, 49, 53, 59, 94–98, 130–32, 136, 137, 140, 152, 245; U.S.–British relationships 247
University of Michigan students, speech to 204–5

Vallandigham, Charles "Charlie" (son) 18, 243
Vallandigham, Clement (CV) **13**, **32**; biographies of 2, 3; birth and background of 8, 11, **12**; character of 2, 12–13, 15; collections of speeches and writings of 2, 3; death and funeral of 6, 7, 235, 238–39, 240, 250; education of 13; fame and prominence of 5–8; funeral and burial of 6; home in Dayton 62, **108**, 220, 253ch8n2; literate and learned display by 10; marriage and family of 18; nickname of 104; story inspired by 7, 197–99; truthfulness of 12–13
Vallandigham, James (brother) : book by 2, 49, 181–82; study of law under 13; on truthfulness of CV 13; words about CV's death 241

Vallandigham, Louisa McMahon (wife) 18, 153, 200, 239–240
Vallandighammers 71
Vicksburg 78, 94, 133, 135, 150, 174, 182, 195
Victoria, Queen 248
Vienna, Virginia 65–66
voting and voting rights: black suffrage 20–21, 177, 220, 225–26, 232–33; cheating potential and allegations 186–87, 188, 192; election day in Ohio 184, 190–96; immigrants, voting by 19–20; intimidation at polls 180–81; Ohio Constitution on 20; soldier vote 85, 183, 193–95, 218; veterans' votes 231–32; white male suffrage 14; women suffrage 54

Wade, Benjamin "Ben" **226**; anti-slavery Radical Republican views of 54; congressional duties of 246; CV opinion about 54; on disloyalty of CV 54; elevation to presidency of 226, 247; race for CV to replace 225–27; Rosecrans support by 123; violence potential related to CV 182
Wallace, Lew 80, 81, 82
Walters, J.A. 181–82
Washington, George, veneration of and burning candles on birthday of 67–68, 248
Watchman (Circleville) 72–73
Watterson, Henry 130
The Western Empire (Dayton) 17–18; *see also Empire* (Dayton)
Western man speech 37–41
western states/the West: desire to move west by CV 17; geographic concept of the West 17, 37; secession of 39–41, 44, 98; South-West and North-West relationships 37–41; tension between East and 38–39, 122
Whig Party 14, 15, 23, 40, 63, 64, 89
Wilberforce 28
Wilmington, North Carolina 133, 134, 137, 139–141
Wilson, Woodrow 7
Winters, Valentine 88, 89
Wood, Fernando 154, 209, 213, 225
Wright, Hendrick Bradley 96–97

Yellow Springs, Ohio 123, 245

www.ingramcontent.com/pod-product-compliance
Lightning Source LLC
Chambersburg PA
CBHW060338010526
44117CB00017B/2872